The Blackwell Philosopher Dictionaries

A Heidegger Dictionary

Michael Inwood

First published 1999

2 4 6 8 10 9 7 5 3 1

Blackwell Publishers Ltd
108 Cowley Road
Oxford OX4 1JF
UK

Blackwell Publishers Inc.
350 Main Street
Malden, Massachusetts 02148
USA

British Library Cataloguing in Publication Data

A CIP catalogue record for this book is available from the British Library.

Library of Congress Cataloging-in-Publication Data
Inwood, M. J., 1944–
 A Heidegger dictionary / Michael Inwood.
  p. cm. – (The Blackwell philosopher dictionaries)
 Includes bibliographical references (p.   ) and index.
 ISBN 0–631–19094–5 (hardcover : alk. paper). – ISBN 0–631–19095–3
(pbk. alk. paper)
 1. Heidegger, Martin, 1889–1976–Dictionaries. I. Title.
B3279.H48Z44 1999
II. Series
193–dc21   99–17512
                                                                CIP

Typeset in 10 on 12 pt Baskerville
by SetSystems Ltd, Saffron Walden, Essex
Printed in Great Britain by MPG Books, Victoria Square, Bodmin, Cornwall

This book is printed on acid-free paper.

A Heidegger Dictionary

B

The Blackwell Philosopher Dictionaries

Written by leading scholars, each volume in the Blackwell Philosopher Dictionaries series presents the life and work of an individual philosopher in a scholarly yet accessible manner. Entries cover key ideas and thoughts, as well as the main themes of the philosopher's work. A comprehensive biographical sketch is also included. The dictionaries are ideal for both research and course use.

A Descartes Dictionary
John Cottingham

A Hegel Dictionary
Michael Inwood

A Heidegger Dictionary
Michael Inwood

A Hobbes Dictionary
A. P. Martinich

A Kant Dictionary
Howard Caygill

A Locke Dictionary
John W. Yolton

A Rousseau Dictionary
N. J. H. Dent

A Wittgenstein Dictionary
Hans-Johann Glock

Contents

Acknowledgements

I wish to acknowledge some debts. William Inwood (1918–1993) persuaded me to study ancient Greek, long before I recognized its importance for the understanding of German philosophy. My colleagues at Trinity College granted me sabbatical leave to complete the book and have given me much help and encouragement. In dedicating this book to my wife, Christiane Sourvinou-Inwood, I express my gratitude for her constant support and advice.

Trinity College, Oxford
May, 1999

System of abbreviations

In references to Heidegger's texts, a slash separates the pagination of the German work from the pagination of the published English translation. In many translations, especially of BT and the volumes of the *Gesamtausgabe*, the German pagination is recorded. Where this is the case, I have given only the German pagination in my references. My translations often differ from those in the published translation.

Volumes of Heidegger's *Gesamtausgabe*, the 'complete edition' published by Klostermann in Frankfurt from 1975 on, I usually cite by roman numerals, as follows:

I   Vol.1:*Frühe Schriften*, ed. F.–W. von Herrmann (1978), containing writings from 1912–16.

XV   Vol.15:*Seminare*, ed. C. Ochwadt (1986), containing seminars from 1951–73/partially translated in M. Heidegger and E. Fink, *Heraclitus Seminar*, tr. C.H. Seibert (Evanston: Northwestern University Press, 1993)

XVII   Vol.17:*Einführung in die phänomenologische Forschung*, ed. F.–W. von Herrmann (1994), lectures of 1923–4

XIX   Vol.19:*Platon: Sophistes*, ed. I.Schüssler (1992), lectures of 1924–5/*Plato's 'Sophist'*, tr. R. Rojcewicz and A. Schuwer (Bloomington: Indiana University Press, 1997)

XX   Vo.20:*Prolegomena zur Geschichte des Zeitbegriffs*, ed. P. Jaeger (1979: 2nd ed. 1988), lectures of 1925/*History of the Concept of Time: Prolegomena*, tr. T. Kisiel (Bloomington: Indiana University Press, 1985)

XXI   Vol.21:*Logik. Die Frage nach der Wahrheit*, ed. W. Biemel (1976), lectures of 1925–6/*Logic: The Question of Truth*, tr. T. Sheehan and R. Lilly (Bloomington: Indiana University Press, forthcoming)

XXII   Vo.22:*Die Grundbegriffe der antiken Philosophie*, ed. F.–K. Blust (1993), lectures of 1926

XXIV   Vol.24:*Die Grundprobleme der Phänomenologie*, ed. F.–W. von
        Herrmann (1975: 2nd ed. 1989), lectures of 1927/*The Basic
        Problems of Phenomenology*, tr. A. Hofstadter (Bloomington: Indi-
        ana University Press, 1982)

XXV   Vol.25:*Phänomenologische Interpretation von Kants Kritik der reinen
        Vernunft*, ed. I. Görland (1977: 2nd ed. 1987), lectures of
        1927–8/*Phenomenological Interpretation of Kant's 'Critique of Pure
        Reason'*, tr. P. Emad and K. Maly (Bloomington: Indiana Univer-
        sity Press, 1997)

XXVI   Vol.26:*Metaphysische Anfangsgründe der Logik im Ausgang von Leib-
        niz*, ed. K. Held (1978: 2nd ed. 1990), lectures of 1928/*The
        Metaphysical Foundations of Logic*, tr. M. Heim (Bloomington:
        Indiana University Press, 1984)

XXVII   Vol.27:*Einleitung in die Philosophie*, ed. O. Saame and I. Saame-
        Speidel (1996), lectures of 1928–9

XXVIII Vol.28:*Der deutsche Idealismus (Fichte, Schelling, Hegel) und die
        philosophische Problemlage der Gegenwart*, ed. C. Strube (1997),
        lectures of 1929

XXIX   Vol.29/30:*Die Grundbegriffe der Metaphysik. Welt–Endlichkeit–Einsa-
        mkeit*, ed. F.–W. von Herrmann (1983), lectures of 1929–30/*The
        Fundamental Concepts of Metaphysics: World–Finitude–solitude*, tr. W.
        McNeill and N. Walker (Bloomington: Indiana University Press,
        1994)

XXXI   Vol.31:*Vom Wesen der menschlichen Freiheit. Einleitung in die Philo-
        sophie*, ed. H. Tietjen (1982), lectures of 1930

XXXII   Vol.32:*Hegels Phänomenologie des Geistes*, ed. I. Görland (1980),
        lectures of 1930–/1*Hegel's 'Phenomenology of Spirit'*, tr. P. Emad
        and K. Maly (Bloomington: Indiana University Press, 1988)

XXXIII Vol.33:*Aristoteles: Metaphysik Θ 1–3: Vom Wesen und Wirklichkeit
        der Kraft*, ed. H. Hüni (1981), lectures of 1931/*Aristotle's Meta-
        physics Θ 1–3: On the Essence and Actuality of Force*, tr. W. Brogan
        and P. Warnek (Bloomington: Indiana University Press, 1996)

XXXIV   Vol.34:*Vom Wesen der Wahrheit. Zu Platons Höhlengleichnis und
        Theätet*, ed. H. Mörchen (1988), lectures of 1931–2

XXXIX   Vol.39:*Hölderlins Hymnen 'Germanien' und 'Der Rhein'*, ed. S. Zie-
        gler (1980: 2nd ed. 1989), lectures of 1934–5

XLV   Vol.45:*Grundfragen der Philosophie. Ausgewählte 'Probleme' der
        'Logik'*, ed. F.–W. von Herrmann (1984: 2nd ed. 1992), lectures
        of 1937–8/*Basic Questions of Philosophy: Selected 'Problems' of 'Logic'*,
        tr. R. Rojcewicz and A. Schuwer (Bloomington: Indiana Univer-
        sity Press, 1994)

XLIX   Vol.49:*Die Metaphysik des deutschen Idealismus (Schelling)*, ed. G. Seubold (1991), lectures of 1941

LI   Vol.51:*Grundbegriffe*, ed. P. Jaeger (1981:2nd ed. 1991), lectures of 1941/*Basic Concepts*, tr. G. E. Aylesworth (Bloomington: Indiana University Press, 1993)

LIV   Vol.54:*Parmenides*, ed. M. S. Frings (1982), lectures of 1942–3/ *Parmenides*, tr. R. Rojcewicz and A. Schuwer (Bloomington: Indiana University Press, 1992)

LV   Vol.55:*Heraklit. Der Anfang der abendländischen Denkens. Logik. Heraklits Lehre vom Logos*, ed. M. S. Frings (1979), lectures of 1943 and 1944

LVI   Vol.56/57:*Zur Bestimmung der Philosophie*, ed. B. Heimbüchel (1987), lectures of 1919

LVIII   Vol.58:*Grundprobleme der Phänomenologie*, ed. H.–H. Gander (1992), lectures of 1919–20

LIX   Vol.59:*Phänomenologie der Anschauung und des Ausdrucks. Theorie der philosophischen Begriffsbildung*, ed. C. Strube (1993), lectures of 1920

LX   Vol.60:*Phänomenologie des religiösen Lebens*, ed. M. Jung, T. Regehly and C. Strube (1995), lectures of 1918–9, 1920–1, 1921

LXI   Vol.61:*Phänomenologische Interpretationen zu Aristoteles. Einführung in die phänomenologische Forschung*, ed. W. and K. Bröcker (1985), lectures of 1921–2

LXIII   Vol.63:*Ontologie (Hermeneutik der Faktizität)*, ed. K. Bröcker (1988), lectures of 1923/*Ontology (Hermeneutics of Facticity)*, tr. J. van Buren (Bloomington: Indiana University Press, 1995)

LXV   Vol.65:*Beiträge zur Philosophie (Vom Ereignis)*, ed. F.–W. von Herrmann (1989), manuscripts of 1936–8

Other works by, and translations of, Heidegger:

Anax   'Der Spruch des Anaximander', in H, 296–343/'The Anaximander Fragment' in M. Heidegger, *Early Greek Thinking*, tr. D.F.Krell and F.A. Capuzzi (New York: Harper & Row, 1984), 13–58 (A lecture of 1946)

AWP   'Die Zeit des Weltbildes' in H, 69–104/'The Age of the World Picture', in qct, 115–154 (A lecture of 1938)

BT   *Sein und Zeit* (15th ed. Tübingen: Niemeyer, 1979)/*Being and Time*, tr. J. Macquarrie and E. Robinson (Oxford: Blackwell, 1962) (Joan Stambaugh's new translation (Albany: State University of New York Press, 1996) appeared too late for me to make use of it.) (First published in 1927)

CT   *Der Begriff der Zeit/The Concept of Time*, tr. W. McNeill (Blackwell, Oxford, 1992). (A bilingual edition of a lecture of 1924)

D   'Das Ding', in VA, 157–179/'The Thing', in plt, 165–186 (A lecture of 1950)

DS   *Die Kategorien- und Bedeutungslehre des Duns Scotus*, in I, *Frühe Schriften*, 189–412 (*Duns Scotus's Doctrines of Categories and Meaning*: Heidegger's habilitation dissertation of 1915)

EB   M. Heidegger, *Existence and Being* (London: Vision Press, 1949) (Four essays by Heidegger with extensive commentary by W. Brock)

ECP   'Vom Wesen und Begriff der *Phusis*. Aristoteles, Physik, B, 1', in W, 237–299. ('On the Essence and Concept of *Phusis*: Aristotle, Physics, B,1': Written in 1939, first published in 1958)

EHP   *Erläuterungen zu Hölderlins Dichtung* (Frankfurt: Klostermann, 1981) (*Elucidations of Hölderlin's Poetry*: a collection of essays, based on lectures from 1936 on)

ep   *The End of Philosophy*, tr. J. Stambaugh (Harper & Row: New York, 1973), containing NII, 399–490, and OM from VA, 71–99

EPTT   'Das Ende der Philosophie und die Aufgabe des Denkens', in M. Heidegger, *Zur Sache des Denkens* (Tübingen: Niemeyer, 1969), 61–80/'the End of Philosophy and the Task of Thinking', in Krell, 431–449

ER   *Vom Wesen des Grundes/The Essence of Reasons*, tr. T. Malick (Evanston: Northwestern University Press, 1969) (A bilingual edition of an essay first published in 1929)

ET   'Vom Wesen der Wahrheit' in W, 175–199/'On the Essence of Truth', in Krell, 115–138 (First published in 1943, on the basis of a lecture of 1930)

G   *Gelassenheit* (Pfullingen: Neske, 1992)/*Discourse on Thinking*, tr. J.M. Anderson and E.H. Freund (New York: Harper & Row, 1966) (G was first published in 1959, on the basis of a lecture of 1955 and a dialogue written in 1944–5)

H   *Holzwege* (5th ed. Frankfurt: Klostermann, 1972) (A collection of 'wood paths', paths for collecting wood from a forest, hence paths that lead nowhere or 'wrong tracks', first published in 1950)

HB   M. Heidegger and E. Blochmann, *Briefwechsel: 1918–1969*, ed. J.W. Storck (Marbach am Neckar: Deutsche Schillergesellschaft, 1990) (Heidegger's correspondence with Elisabeth Blochmann)

HCE 'Hegels Begriff der Erfahrung', in H, 105–192/*Hegel's Concept of Experience*, tr. J. Glenn Gray (New York: Harper & Row, 1970) (Based on lectures of 1942–3)

HEP 'Hölderlin und das Wesen der Dichtung', in EHP, 33–48/ 'Hölderlin and the Essence of Poetry', tr. D. Scott, in EB, 293–315 (A lecture of 1936)

HJ M. Heidegger and K. Jaspers, *Briefwechsel: 1920–1963*, ed. W. Biemel and H. Saner (Frankfurt: Klostermann, 1990) (Heidegger's correspondence with Jaspers)

ID *Identität und Differenz* (Pfullingen: Neske, 1957)/*Identity and Difference*, tr. J. Stambaugh (New York: Harper & Row, 1969) (Based on seminars of 1956–7)

IM *Einführung in die Metaphysik* (5th ed. Tübingen: Niemeyer, 1987)/*An Introduction to Metaphysics*, tr. R. Manheim (New York: Doubleday, 1961) (First published in 1953 on the basis of lectures of 1935)

K *Kant und das Problem der Metaphysik* (5th ed. Frankfurt: Klostermann, 1991)/*Kant and the Problem of Metaphysics*, tr. R. Taft (Bloomington: Indiana University Press, 1990) (First published in 1929. The later editions contain other essays, including the debate with Cassirer)

Krell M. Heidegger, *Basic Writings*, ed. D.F. Krell (2nd ed. London: Routledge, 1993)

KTB 'Kants These über das Sein', in W, 439–473 ('Kant's Thesis about Being': first published in 1962 on the basis of a lecture of 1961)

LH 'Brief über den Humanismus', in W, 311–360/'Letter on Humanism', tr. F.A. Capuzzi, in Krell, 217–265 (First published in 1947)

NI, NII *Nietzsche*, vols.I and II (Pfullingen: Neske, 1961)/translated in ni-niv, and ep

ni *Nietzsche*, vol.I:*The Will to Power as Art*, tr. D.F. Krell (London: Routledge & Kegan Paul, 1981)

nii *Nietzsche*, vol.II:*The Eternal Recurrence of the Same*, tr. D.F. Krell (San Francisco: Harper & Row, 1984)

niii *Nietzsche*, vol.III:*The Will to Power as Knowledge and as Metaphysics*, tr. J. Stambaugh, D.F. Krell, F.A. Capuzzi (San Francisco: Harper & Row, 1987)

niv *Nietsche*, vol.IV:*Nihilism*, tr. F.A. Capuzzi (San Francisco: Harper & Row, 1982)

OM 'Überwindung der Metaphysik', in VA, 67–95/'Overcoming

Metaphysics', ep, 84–110 (First published in 1951 on the basis of notes of 1936–46)

OWA   'Der Ursprung des Kunstwerkes', in H, 7–68/'The Origin of the work of Art', tr. A. Hofstadter, in Krell, 143–212 (First published in H in 1950, on the basis of lectures of 1935 and 1936)

OWL   *Unterwegs zur Sprache* (9th ed. Pfullingen: Neske, 1990)/*On the Way to Language*, tr. P.D. Hertz (New York: Harper & Row, 1982) (First published in 1959 on the basis of lectures of the 1950s)

P   'Platons Lehre von der Wahrheit', in W, 201–236/'Plato's Doctrine of Truth', tr. J. Barlow, in *Philosophy in the Twentieth Century*, vol.3, ed. W. Barrett and H.D. Aiken (New York: Random House, 1962), 251–270 (First published in 1942, on the basis of lectures of lectures of 1931–2)

PIA   'Phänomenologische Interpretationen zu Aristoteles (Anzeige der hermeneutischen Situation)', ed. H.-U. Lessing, in the *Dilthey-Jahrbuch fur Philosophie und Geschichte der Geisteswissenschaften*, vol.6 (1989), 237–269/'Phenomenological Interpretations with Respect to Aristotle (Indication of the Hermeneutical Situation)', tr. M. Baur, in *Man and World* 25 (1992), 355–93

plt   M. Heidegger, *Poetry, Language, Thought*, tr. A. Hofstadter (New York: Harper & Row, 1975) (Translations of essays from various works of Heidegger)

PR   *Der Satz vom Grund* (6th ed. Pfullingen: Neske, 1986)/*The Principle of Reason*, tr. R. Lilly (Bloomington: Indiana University Press, 1991) (First published in 1957 on the basis of lectures of 1955–6)

PT   'Phänomenologie und Theologie", in W, 47–78/'Phenomenology and Theology', in *The Piety of Thinking*, tr. J.G. Hart and J.C. Maraldo (Bloomington: Indiana University Press, 1976), 5–31 (A lecture of 1927, followed by a letter of 1964, both first published in 1969)

QB   *Zur Seinsfrage/The Question of Being*, tr. W. Kluback and J.T. Wilde (London: Vision, 1959) (A bilingual edition of an essay for Jünger's sixtieth birthday, first published in 1955)

qct   M. Heidegger, *The Question Concerning Technology and Other Essays*, tr. W. Lovitt (New York: Harper & Row, 1977)

QT   'Die Frage nach der Technik', in VA, 9–40/'The Question Concerning Technology', in qct, 3–35 (A lecture of 1953, first published in 1954)

S   *Schellings Abhandlung über das Wesen der menschlichen Freiheit (1809)* (Tübingen: Niemeyer, 1971)/*Schelling's Treatise on the*

	Essence of Human Freedom, tr. J. Stambaugh (Athens, Ohio: Ohio University Press, 1985) (First published in 1971, on the basis of lectures of 1936 and seminars of 1941–3)
T	'Die Kechre', in *Die Tehnik und die Kehre* (8th ed. Pfullingen: Neske, 1991), 37–47/'The Turning', in qct, 36–49 (A lecture of 1950, first published in 1962)
VA	*Vorträge und Aufsätze* (6th ed. Pfullingen: Neske, 1990) (A collection of 'lectures and essays', first published in 1954)
W	*Wegmarken* (2nd ed. Frankfurt: Klostermann, 1978) (A collection of 'way markers', lectures and essays from 1919 to 1961. First published in 1967, but expanded in the second edition.) It is now translated as *Pathmarks*, ed. W. McNeill (Cambridge: Cambridge University Press, 1998), but this appeared too late for me to make use of it.
WCT	*Was heisst Denken?* (4th ed.Tübingen: Niemeyer, 1984)/*What is Called Thinking?* tr. F.D. Wieck and J. Glenn Gray (New York: Harper & Row, 1972) (First published in 1954, on the basis of lectures in 1951–2 and 1952)
WM	'Was ist Metaphysik?' in W, 103–121/'What is Metaphysics?' in Krell, 93–110 (Heidegger's Freiburg inaugural lecture of 1929)
WMI	'Einleitung zu: "Was ist Metaphysik?"' in W, 361–377/'The Way Back into the Ground of Metaphysics', in W. Kaufmann, *Existentialism from Dostoevsky to Sartre* (2nd edn. New American Library: New York, 1975), 265–279 (The 'Introduction to: WM', first published in 1949)
WMP	'Nachwort zu: "Was ist Metaphysik?"' in W, 310–10/'Postscript to "What is Metaphysics?",' tr. R.F.C. Hull and A. Crick, in EB, 380–392 (First published in 1943)
WT	*Die Frage nach dem Ding* (3rd ed.Tübingen: Niemeyer, 1987)/*What is a Thing?*, tr. W.B. Barton and V. Deutsch (South Bend, Indiana: Regnery/Gateway, 1967) (First published in 1962, on the basis of lectures of 1935–6)

Works by other authors:

A	I. Kant, *Anthropology from a Pragmatic Point of View*, tr. M.J. Gregor (The Hague: Nijhoff, 1974) (First published in 1798)
AGW	W. Dilthey, *Der Aufbau der geschichtlichen Welt in den Geisteswissenschaften*, ed. M. Riedel (Frankfurt: Suhrkamp, 1981)

	(A collection of writings, from 1906–10, on the 'construction of the historical world in the social sciences')
Boswell	J. Boswell, *A Journal of a Tour to the Hebrides with Samuel Johnson, LL.D.* (London: Dent, 1928)
CK	E. Casssirer, 'Kant and the Problem of Metaphysics: Remarks on Martin Heidegger's Interpretation of Kant', in *Kant: Disputed Questions*, ed. M.S. Gram (Chicago: Quadrangle Books, 1967), 131–157 (Casssirer's review of K, first published in 1929)
CM	E. Husserl, *Cartesian Meditations: An Introduction to Phenomenology*, tr. D. Cairns (The Hague: Nijhoff, 1973 (Written in 1929)
CPR	I. Kant, *Critique of Pure Reason*, tr. N. Kemp Smith (London: Macmillan, 1968) (First edition 1781, second edition 1787)
DGS	R.B. Farrell, Dictionary of German Synonyms (3rd ed. Cambridge: Cambridge University Press, 1977)
DW	O. Spengler, *The Decline of the West*, I: *Form and Actuality*, tr. C.F. Atkinson (New York: Knopf, 1926) (A first version of *The Decline of the West* was published in 1918; the first volume of the enlarged version, translated here, appeared in 1923)
Feick	H. Feick and S. Ziegler, *Index zu Heideggers 'Sein und Zeit'* (4th ed. Tübingen: Niemeyer, 1991)
Friedländer	P. Friedländer, *Plato: An Introduction*, tr. H. Meyerhoff (New York and London: Bollingen/Pantheon, 1958)
Ideas	E. Husserl, *Ideas Pertaining to a Pure Phenomenology and to a Phenomenological Philosophy, First Book: General Introduction to a Pure Phenomenology*, tr. F. Kersten (The Hague: Nijhoff, 1982) (First published in 1913)
Jünger (1932)	E. Jünger, *Der Arbeiter: Herrschaft und Gestalt* (Hamburg: Hanseatische Verlaganstalt, 1932
Jünger (1950)	E. Jünger, *Über die Linie* (Frankfurt: Klostermann, 1950)
Kahn	C.H. Kahn, *Anaximander and the Origins of Greek Cosmology* (2nd ed. Indianapolis: Hackett, 1994)
LU	E. Husserl, *Logical Investigations*, tr. J.N. Findlay (London: Routledge & Kegan Paul, 1973) (First published in 1900–1)
Mannheim	K. Mannheim, *Essays in the Sociology of Knowledge* (London: Routledge & Kegan Paul, 1952)
Namier	L. Namier, *Conflicts: Studies in Contemporary History* (London: Macmillan, 1942)

OT	I. Kant, 'What is Orientation in Thinking?', tr. L.W. Beck, in *Kant's Critique of Practical Reason and Other Writings in Moral Philosophy* (Chicago: University of Chicago Press, 1949) (First published in 1786)
PES	F. Brentano, *Psychology from an Empirical Standpoint*, tr. L.I. McAlister (London: Routledge & Kegan Paul, 1973) (First published in 1874)
PRS	E. Husserl, 'Philosophy as Rigorous Science', in *Phenomenology and the Crisis of Philosophy*, ed. Q. Lauer (New York: Harper & Row, 1965), 71–147 (First published in 1910)
PW	K. Jaspers, *Psychologie der Weltanschauungen* (Munich and Zurich: Piper. 1985) (First published in 1919)
Rose	W. Rose, 'Rilke and the Conception of Death', in *Rainer Maria Rilke: Aspects of his Mind and Poetry*, ed. W. Rose and G.C. Houston (London: Sidgwick & Jackson, 1938), 43–84.
Safranski	R. Safranski, *Martin Heidegger: Between Good and Evil* (Cambridge, MA: Harvard University Press, 1998)
Scheler (1976)	M. Scheler, *Gesammelte Werke*, vol.9:*Späte Schriften*, ed. M. Frings (Bern and Munich: Francke, 1976)
Scheler (1979)	M. Scheler, 'Tod und Fortleben', in *Die Zukunft des Kapitalismus und andere Aufsätze* (Munich: Francke, 1979), 9–71
Seebohm	F. Seebohm, *The Oxford Reformers* (London: Dent, 1914)
Simmel	G. Simmel, *Essays on Religion* (New Haven: Yale University Press, 1997)
Trevelyan	H. Trevelyan, *Goethe and the Greeks* (Cambridge: Cambridge University Press, 1981)
TW	W. Dilthey, *Die Typen der Weltanschauung und ihre Ausbildung in den metaphysischen Systemen*, in *Gesammelte Schriften*, VIII (Leipzig: Teubner, 1931), 75–118
WN	A. Smith, *The Wealth of the Nations*, vol.I (London: Dent, 1910)

Notes on the use of this book

Each article in this book usually discusses more than one German word, together with their English (and often Greek and Latin) equivalents. Some words are grouped together because they fall under a single broad heading (e.g. SPACE AND SPATIALITY), sometimes because two or more similar seeming words are used by Heidegger in different ways and need to be distinguished (e.g. FATE AND DESTINY, or SIGNS AND HINTS). Not surprisingly, in view of Heidegger's belief that every philosophical question raises every other philosophical question, I have often found it difficult to confine the discussion of a topic to a single article. Thus I have often indicated a cross-reference from one article to another by capitalizing a word that appears in the title of another relevant article. The occurrence of 'PRESENT-AT-HAND' means: Consult the article whose title contains the expression 'present-at-hand'. The main discussions of difficult words and concepts are also indicated in the General Index.

Similarly the index of foreign-language terms indicates the main discussions of foreign words. I have generally italicized foreign words, both in using and in mentioning them. But in quotations from Heidegger I have not italicized German or other foreign words, unless he italicized them in his own text. (But I have usually italicized Heidegger's *Greek* words, while transliterating them into the Latin alphabet.) Another feature of my quotations from Heidegger is that my own omissions are indicated by three dots in square brackets. This is to avoid confusion with Heidegger's *own* use of dots. Nouns or verbs with a preposition, or simply a preposition, are often followed by dots indicating a missing object: e.g. 'The phenomena of the towards . . ., to . . ., by . . . [des zu . . ., auf . . ., bei . . .] reveal temporality as the *ekstatikon* [. . .]' (BT, 329). Here the first three sets of dots are Heidegger's own; the second three sets, in '[des zu . . ., auf . . ., bei . . .]', give the German text that contains the first three sets; the last set, '[. . .]', are my own, indicating that I have omitted the end of Heidegger's sentence in my translation. (Round brackets, by contrast, are always Heidegger's own, when they occur within a quotation.)

Heidegger and his language

'A philosopher, for instance, a rearranger of facts and ideas, who is endowed with this spirit, can fascinate his listeners even when they don't understand a word of his lecture. Spellbound, they will hang on to his lips'.[1] Ernst Jünger was thinking of his friend Heidegger; perplexing but spellbinding. Why is he so perplexing? The difficulty of his subject matter is no doubt part of the answer. But it is not the whole answer. Heidegger was constantly 'on the way'. Never, at the end of a lecture, book or essay by Heidegger, do we feel that we now know what he believes. His answers to questions invariably raise deeper questions, questions that propel his thought along. The questions point beyond the confines of any particular work. His works often end with a question, or with a quotation, say, from Hölderlin, the obscurity of which makes it as good as a question. This helps to explain Heidegger's spell, as well as his difficulty. He is not, we feel, presenting us with truths that he has worked out in advance, not leading us across terrain that he has already explored. He is working out problems as he goes along; the terrain is as new and unfamiliar to him as it is to us. He often needs to retrace his steps and cover the same ground in a different way. He does not know our destination any more than we do; he is on the way – but to where?

Questions are easier to handle if we can tackle them piecemeal, asking about *something* without asking about *everything*. This is alright for the sciences, Heidegger believes, but it does not suit philosophy. Philosophy is not a compartmental discipline: it does not deal with one particular range of entities, and it cannot itself be divided into compartments.[2] Every philosophical question raises every other philosophical question. Even the most trivial seeming philosophical question raises ever more fundamental questions, leading us out into deeper and deeper waters. This too helps to account both for Heidegger's allure and for his difficulty.

1

1. New words

Above all, words matter to Heidegger. Words matter as much as meanings. None of the senses of a potent word is ever definitively excluded from Heidegger's use of it, and no other word, whether in the same or a different language, is ever an exact synonym. Words matter for a variety of reasons. He is convinced he is dealing with questions that have been neglected since antiquity. The stale language of traditional philosophy – 'consciousness', 'ego', 'thing', and so on – is ill-suited to this new territory. If we want to consider Being *as* Being and not simply as a being, then we must use a different vocabulary and even on occasion, a different syntax.[3] If we want to explore 'Dasein' in its 'average everydayness' – another area neglected by philosophers from Aquinas to Husserl – we have to avoid the talk of 'thinking things' and 'extended things' that we find in Descartes. But where do we turn to? One solution might be to revert to the language of the marketplace, the down-to-earth vocabulary used by Socrates in Plato's early, and some of his later, dialogues. Heidegger does this in a way: BT is peppered with everyday talk about hammers, wood, gear, and so on. But this cannot be the whole story. The denizens of the marketplace typically do not speak in general, conceptual terms about the marketplace, as the philosopher tries to do. The broad outlines of the everyday world, and many of its details, are inconspicuous to us. We have thus developed no vocabulary adequate for describing it. If called upon to do so, we tend to resort once more to the language of traditional philosophy. So Heidegger has to develop a vocabulary of his own, one that avoids the simplifications of traditional philosophy and retains its connections with the language of the marketplace, yet, unlike this, enables us to speak in general, conceptual terms about the everyday world and eventually, it is to be hoped, about being itself.

Many examples of Heidegger's linguistic innovations will be discussed in this book. But we shall consider some examples here. The word 'care', which corresponds closely, if not exactly, to the German *Sorge*, has a range of senses. We can see this from the adjectives it forms and the words they contrast with: 'careworn' and 'carefree'; 'careful' and 'careless'; 'caring' and 'uncaring'. These oppositions are not the same: one can be, for example, both careworn and careless. In ordinary usage not everyone is careworn, careful and caring all the time. Some of us are carefree, careless or uncaring. Heidegger makes two innovations. First, he uses 'care' in a broad sense which underlies its diversification into the careworn, the careful and the caring. Second, in this sense of 'care', he insists, everyone cares; no one is wholly carefree, careless or uncaring. It is only because everyone is, in this fundamental sense, care-ful, that we can ever be carefree, careless or uncaring in the ordinary, or as he has it, the 'ontical', senses of these words. In the 'ontological' sense of 'care', everyone cares. All human beings, again, are 'ahead of themselves' (*sich vorweg*), roughly 'up to something' or on the look out for what to do. What about those mired in hopeless despair? Even those, Heidegger insists, are 'ahead of themselves': 'Hopelessness does not tear Dasein away from its possibilities; it is only a particular mode of *being toward* these possibilities' (BT, 236). Heidegger uses this device very frequently. It goes back to Aristotle. We ordinarily use 'sighted' in contrast to 'blind': most of us are sighted, some of us are blind. But there is a sense of 'sighted', Aristotle says, in which all human beings are sighted. And that is why some of them can be blind, suffer, that is, the 'privation' of sight. Moles and stones, though they cannot see, are not 'blind' in this sense, for they are not 'sighted' in the appropriate sense.[4] From Aristotle too comes Heidegger's habit of making nouns out of other parts of speech. Aristotle speaks of *to hou heneka*, 'the [to] for the sake of [heneka] which [hou]; or purpose. Heidegger speaks of 'the for the sake of which', 'the for the sake of', 'the in order to', and so on. The device is not wholly alien to us. We are reminded of 'the wherewithal', 'his whereabouts', and 'the whys and the wherefores' – locutions of a similar origin that have congealed into familiar English phrases.

The word 'blind', Aristotle says, cannot be applied to men, moles and stones in precisely the same sense. This is another reason for Heidegger's concern with language and another motive for his innovation. We, whether we are philosophers or not, tend to ignore the differences between things of different types and to apply the same words to them. We say, to take a simple case, that humans 'eat' and that animals 'eat'. German distinguishes what we assimilate, applying *essen* to humans and *fressen* to animals (cf. XXIX, 308). But not even German is always so discriminating. We say, for example, that humans, animals and even chemical substances 'behave' or *sich verhalten* in certain ways. But this, Heidegger says, is a mistake. Humans, animals and substances are so different in kind that they cannot be said to 'behave' in the same sense. To clarify matters then, we should find a different word for each case, and say that while humans *sich verhalten*, animals *sich benehmen* (cf. MOVE-MENT). Animals figure hardly at all in BT. But the same principle of differentiation is in play there. Beings or entities are of three main types: Dasein or the human being; equipped or the 'READY-TO-HAND'; and mere things or the 'PRESENT-AT-HAND'. Philosophers have tended to

3

assimilate all entities – and even non-entities, such as time and space – to the present-at-hand, supposing that the categories and vocabulary appropriate for stones and trees can be applied to human beings and their equipment. But Heidegger believes that we must find, and if necessary coin, a vocabulary that distinguishes between them. The present-at- and ready-to-hand, for example, are 'within the world', not 'in-the-world' in the way that humans are. In general, Heidegger fights against the substance ontology appropriate to the present-at-hand, in favour of movement and of relationships. We must not think of Dasein as a thing or substance that has the property of 'stretching out' into the past and future, and the property of being in the world, or that sends out feelers to remote times and places. The stretching out and the relation to the world are primary, the biological substratum a secondary accompaniment.

Matters become even more complex when we talk not just about different types of entity, but about non-entities such as space, time, the world, and being itself. To these, Heidegger believes, we cannot apply even the word 'is', unless we hedge it round with scare quotes. We can say 'Being "is" mysterious', but not 'Being is mysterious', for that would imply that being is *a* being or entity. Hence he looks for a verb that will enable him to avoid 'is'. Time 'temporalizes' or 'extemporizes' – here he uses *(sich) zeitigen*, a descendant of *Zeit*, 'time', which has lost contact with it and come to mean 'to bring about, produce'. Being, he says, 'essences', reviving a defunct verb *wesen*, 'to be, etc.' The world 'whirls' or 'wells' – from *walten*, which is more accurately, if less euphoniously, translated as 'to prevail'. But here he also coins a verb and says that the world 'worlds'. His most renowned claim in this genre is: 'The Nothing itself noths'.

Heidegger, as we can see, coins words. German lends itself to this even more readily than English. He does not usually ride rough-shod over standard usage. As he says, in ordinary usage 'philosophy is in variably contained, if we have an ear for it, still latent philosophy as it were. How could it be otherwise, when philosophizing belongs to the essence of Dasein [. . .]' (XXVII, 309f.). Often he revives an old meaning of an existing word. *Lichtung* comes from *Licht*, 'light', but has now lost contact with it and means a 'clearing' in a forest. Heidegger revives its connection with *Licht* and reads it as 'lighting'. Sometimes he restores an older sense, or at least a *possible* sense, by analysing a compound word into its constituents. *Existenz* has come to mean 'presence-at-hand', but it once meant 'stepping forth', and we mark this by writing *Ex-sistenz*. He sometimes calls the original sense of a word the *Wortbegriff* or 'word-concept' (S, 129/107). Again, *Ferne* means 'distance', and *Entfernung* is 'distance, removal'. *Ent-* here intensifies the sense of distance. But *ent-* is, in other cases, privative: *decken*, 'to cover', becomes *entdecken*, 'to uncover'. Thus *Entfernung* could mean: 'removing distance'. Heidegger introduces the word in this sense by writing it as *Ent-fernung* (BT, 105f.). What is the point of this? Heidegger himself warns us 'against assuming too much from the analysis of a word and a word-meaning, instead of dealing with the *question* at issue. The brazen tricks of etymology lead to any number of fruitless inquiries, even fateful errors' (XXXIV, 11f.). Such hyphenation may have a point – if, for example, I wish to distinguish 'unionized' as 'not ionized' ('un-ionized') from 'unionized' as 'organized by a trade union' ('union-ized'). But little is gained by analysing, say, 'disappoint' as 'dis-ap-point'. Here, however, Heidegger is entitled to his hyphens. If something is too close, then we cannot deal with it; it is in a way too far. So removing something to an appropriate distance, *Entfernung*, is also bringing it close enough to handle, *Ent-fernung*.

Heidegger's hyphens do not invariably have the force of analysing a word into its constituents. Often they bring distinct words together to form a single thought. He speaks of *In-der-Welt-sein*, 'being-in-the-world'. 'Being-in', *In-Sein*, is a specific sort of being, distinct, say, from *Mitsein*, 'being with' (BT, 53ff.). The *in* has a specific sense: in this sense of *in* one can only be in the world, and only a human being can be in it. There cannot be a world unless someone is in it. So the constituents of *In-der-Welt-sein* are not strictly separable; they form a single, integrated thought.

2.   Old words

So far we have seen that Heidegger coins new words and revives old words and meanings, insofar as they are required for his current purposes. We need see no special merit in antiquity as such, nor any special reason to think that as a general rule an old word or meaning will shed more light on substantial questions than a new word. We must make good use of a decent word from whatever period it comes. He develops a tendency, however, to believe that antiquity implies merit. This is already visible in the BT period. Ancient philosophers, especially Plato and Aristotle, are better and fresher than their medieval followers and (with the striking exception of Kant) than modern philosophers. Every proper philosopher is in a way a beginner, but every philosopher – at least since the Greek beginnings – works within a tradition. The philosopher does not coin a new vocabulary from scratch, but takes over words and concepts from predecessors: 'nature', 'truth', 'consciousness', and so on. The philosopher takes over the word or concept, but does not usually undergo the 'experience' of its originator, the experience in which the word is rooted. Not only this: the word itself becomes jaded as it is passed on from hand to hand. What started life as Plato's idea has degenerated into our modern *Vorstellung*, REPRESENTATION. What began as the Greek *phusis* has ended up as 'nature'. This happens with everyday talk as well. People talk with first-hand experience of what is there in front of them. They tell it to someone else who was not there with them, and the talk gets passed on as 'chatter'. This in itself would not imply that old words are better, since people talk in the presence of what their talk is about in every generation. But they do not coin all their words anew in each generation. They take over most words from previous generations. They *apply* them to their current experiences. But the words do not, for the most part, emerge from the experiences. The experiences are, in part at least, viewed through the inherited words and concepts. We are not unlike scholars who neglect the original text in favour of articles about it. We are at a double disadvantage as compared with the originators of the words. First, we do not have the primordial experiences that first inspired the words. Second, there is the possibility of a mismatch between our words and our experiences, that the words we have inherited are inadequate for dealing with our being-in-the-world or, as Heidegger later came to believe, with new phenomena such as modern technology.

In BT, as we have seen, Heidegger attempted to devise a new vocabulary. But he also tends to believe, increasingly so after BT, that we cannot properly devise a new vocabulary until we have thoroughly explored the old. Such exploration may free us from the word or it may give it back to us in mint condition. Sometimes we can appropriate an old word, if we revive its old associations and the experience that gave rise to it. In BT Heidegger used the word *Ding*, 'THING', with disapproval, associating it with Descartes's *res*. Later he breathes new life into it and adopts it as his own. Sometimes a word – for example, *Vorstellung*, 'representation' – turns out to have disreputable ancestry, as well as a subsequent history of degeneration, and cannot be revived except for the purpose of analysing the degenerate history that it embodies. But this too interests Heidegger. For he is concerned with the HISTORY OF BEING, and this can best be reconstructed from the history of the words used for 'being'.

Heidegger's interest in words is not an interest in mere words. There are no *mere* words, or at least no mere 'essential words': 'Essential words are not artificially devised signs and marks stuck onto things only to enable us to distinguish them. Essential words are actions, actions that happen in those moments when the lighting flash of a great illumination passes through the world.' Thus when we speak of the Greek language and the words it has bequeathed to us, we speak also of 'the people, the creative force of the people which, in its poets, thinkers, statesmen and artists, performed the greatest assault on the whole of beyng that has ever happened in western history' (S, 31/25). (For this reason no Latin word ever exactly translates a Greek word.) It is the Greeks and their 'first beginning' of western history that mainly interest Heidegger, though the early Germans compete for his favour and often provide a good word such as *Ding*, and, indeed, the words that he needs to translate such good Greek words as Heraclitus's *logos*, 'gathering, assembling'. It is the flash of illumination that he wants to recover or 'repeat'. It helps to put our subsequent history into perspective, and perhaps it will help us to prepare for a new flash of illumination that will halt our spiritual decline: the 'other beginning'.

Heidegger often reminded his contemporaries of Hegel. There are strong similarities – the stress on the whole, on relations, on movement, the distrust of oppositions such as realism–idealism, objective–subjective, rationalism–irrationalism (cf. IM, 135/149: 'The Greeks were more pessimistic than any pessimist. But there were also more optimistic than any optimist'). Another similarity is the pursuit of concepts to their origins or at least to ancient Greece. But mention of 'spiritual decline' suggests a divergence between Hegel and Heidegger. Art perhaps declines, on Hegel's view, but not much else. In religious matters Hegel attaches little weight to the first-hand experience of those who saw Christ and felt his wounds or to the words of the New Testament. What matters is *Geist*, 'spirit', what we subsequently made of the experiences and of the words.[5] Broadly speaking, it is the same with concepts. Hegel's concepts are not inferior to earlier versions of them, though this is in part because they embody these earlier versions. Nor are philosophers in general inferior to their predecessors. He does not, of course, believe that any and every nineteenth-century philosopher is the equal or superior of Plato. But our nineteenth-century world view is richer and more complex, albeit aesthetically inferior, embracing as it does the later development of spirit as well as Plato. Here Heidegger differs. Philosophy has declined since the Greeks along with more or less everything else. Doesn't this ignore Heidegger himself? How can he hope even to understand the Greeks, if our situation is as bad as he claims? Isn't he too on the way to becoming a 'mechanized animal' engulfed in technology? No – technology leaves a loose end for us pull, its own essence. We can think about technology, the essence of technology, if, and only if, we are not engulfed in technology. And if we do that, we can see the world in its sheer simplicity; we can understand the world of the Greeks by contrast with our

7

own; we can follow the route from the Greeks to ourselves. With any luck, we can prepare for 'another beginning'. Hegel left us in the dark over whether he believed history had come to an end, and, if not, what might be left to happen. Heidegger has more to say about it. History, if it continues, will begin again, with a flash of illumination comparable to the Greek and beyond anything imagined (or at least *conceptualized*) by Hegel.

3. The turn

Heidegger often spoke of 'the turn', *die Kehre*. He used it to refer to the turn, at the end of BT, from 'Being and Time' to 'Time and Being', and later for the turn he hoped for from the 'oblivion of being' to the remembrance of it. Others have used the phrase to denote a 'turn' or change in Heidegger's own thinking, though he himself denied that such a change had occurred. The sharp 'about turn!' that the word *Kehre* suggests is barely discernible in Heidegger's thought or language. But there are changes in his thought and also in his language. The style and vocabulary of early works, such as DS, are in the philosophical tradition, with few, if any, peculiarities. BT starts in a fairly traditional manner, but Heidegger then begins to search for a language to express his novel thoughts. Several BT words decline in frequency or even disappear altogether after BT: 'everydayness', 'significance', 'concern', 'authenticity', 'the They', and so on. Other words – notably *Wesen*, 'essence', and cognate words – become far more common. In his post-war writings especially, Heidegger becomes more fond of Germanic words such as *Ding*, and likes to explore their etymology. A change of vocabulary does not automatically entail a change of thought, since a word or expression may be replaced by another, equivalent word or expression. In BT, for example, he often speaks of the *Sinn von Sein*, the 'sense' or 'meaning of being'. Later he prefers to speak of the 'truth of being', *Wahrheit des Seins*. This involves an expansion of the meaning BT assigned to *Wahrheit*, but not necessarily a substantial change of thought.

An interesting feature Heidegger's terminology is the persistence of the same word through a change of its meaning. *Ding* is one example. Another is *Vorstellung*. It begins life, in BT and earlier, with its standard philosophical sense of 'idea, representation'. With the help of a hyphen (*Vor-stellung*), and some explanation, it later comes to involve the idea of presenting someone or something before a court for judgement. The standard sense has not disappeared: the point is that the doctrine that man 'represents' things implies that they are 'presented' to him for judgement or assessment. Changes of meaning are especially frequent in the case of compound words. The meanings of the constituent words rarely determine uniquely the meaning of the compound. Neither the meanings of the words 'gun', 'fire' and 'fighter', nor the general principles of word formation, tell us that a 'firefighter' is someone who fights *against* fire, while a 'gunfighter' is someone who *uses* a gun to fight. Heidegger's compounds are often intrinsically ambiguous in similar ways. His coinage *Seinkönnen* – common in BT, but rare afterwards – is from *können*, 'can, to be able', and *sein*, 'to be'. But is *sein* to be read as a verbal infinitive, making *Seinkonnen* the 'ability to be'? Or is it a nominalized infinitive, *Sein*, making it the 'capacity for being'? This particular problem is avoided by his other coinages, *Seinsvergessenheit* and *Seinsverlassenheit*. The 's' after *Sein* indicates the genitive case and thus shows *Sein* to be nominal.[6] But here another problem arises. Are the genitives objective or subjective? Does *Seinsvergessenheit*, 'oblivion of being', mean we have forgotten being (objective) or that being has forgotten us (subjective)? Does *Seinsverlassenheit*, 'abandonment of being', mean that we have abandoned being or that being has abandoned us (and other beings)? In BT Heidegger complains that we have forgotten being. But by the time he coins the word *Seinsvergessenheit* being itself has moved nearer the centre of the stage, and seems to operate as an independent force. Thus *Seinsvergessenheit* could as well mean that being has forgotten us as that we have forgotten being; no doubt Heidegger had both senses in mind. *Seinsverlassenheit*, he explains, means being's abandonment of us rather than our abandonment of being. And this helps to draw *Seinsvergessenheit* in the same direction.

Heidegger's most famous compound is *Dasein*. It is a common word for 'existence', so familiar that it is hardly felt as a compound. But Heidegger treats it as a compound, hyphenating it, separating out *das Da*, 'the There', and stretching *Dasein* or *Da-sein* this way and that. When *Dasein* is broken down into its constituents it is no longer clear what its meaning is. Does *da* mean 'here' or 'there' – but not too far away from the speaker – or 'then' or something else among the several senses listed for it in a dictionary? What is the force of *sein* and how does it relate to *da*? In BT *Dasein* seems to mean something like 'being-there'. A human being is *Dasein* because it is 'there', in-the-world – not at some specific place, but there in a sense prior to and presupposed by the differentiation of places. Later it comes to mean: 'there, where being "is"', being's anchorage or dwelling-place – a sense that is usually marked by writing *Da-sein* rather than *Dasein*. Heidegger's vocabulary is, in some cases at least, sufficiently flexible to accommodate, without significant alteration, a shift of emphasis from human beings to being itself.

Sometimes Heidegger associates such changes of sense with what he himself calls a 'turn'. A turn is (among other things) a reversal of the order in which two terms occur. Moving from 'being and time' to 'time and being' is a turn. Or we can reverse 'the essence of truth' to become 'the truth of essence', and again 'the essence of language' to 'the language of essence'. Such turns involve, Heidegger argues, a change in the meaning of the terms. In the phrase 'the essence of truth', 'essence', *Wesen*, is used in its traditional, nominal sense, and 'truth' approximates to 'correctness'. In 'the truth of essence', by contrast, 'truth' cannot mean 'correctness', since an essence cannot be correct or incorrect. So too, Heidegger argues, *Wesen* no longer means 'essence' but takes on a verbal sense, conformable to its descent from the obsolete verb *wesen*, and means something like 'essencing'. Reversals of this type do no doubt alter the meanings of the reversed terms. In the phrase 'the love of art', 'love' has the wide sense of 'fondness' or 'liking', while 'art' has a narrow sense, more or less restricted to the fine arts. If we reverse it to become 'the art of love', then 'art' now has, on the most natural interpretation, the wide sense of 'skill', while 'love' has taken on the narrower sense of sexual passion and interplay. What is the significance of this? It surely has no general significance. We knew all along that the sense of a word depends in part on its context. But Heidegger's general point seems to be this: the change of a word from its faded, degenerate sense to its new, Heideggerian sense – a sense appropriate to the other beginning – cannot occur gradually. It happens suddenly in a 'moment of illumination', by a headlong leap rather than by dogged argument, by an abrupt switch of our view of the world.

Heidegger uses new words and revives old words. He does so to express new ideas, to recapture the original vitality of the 'first beginning', and to explore the 'history of being'. It is the aim of this book to consider how he approaches these tasks and how, in particular, language helps him to tackle them.

Notes

1 E. Jünger, *The Glass Bees* (New York: Noonday Press, 1960), p. 62.
2 This is one reason for his reluctance to write 'an ethics' (LH, 349ff/254ff.).
3 Heidegger's use of language is explored by Erasmus Schöfer in *Die Sprache Heideggers* (Neske: Pfullingen, 1962).

4 Aristotle, *Categories*, 12a32ff; *Topics*, 143b34ff.
5 G.W.F. Hegel, *Lectures on the Philosophy of Religion*, tr. E.B. Speirs and J.B. Sanderson (London: Routledge & Kegan Paul, 1895), vol.I, pp. 27ff; vol.II, pp. 342ff; vol.III, 110ff.
6 The absence of this 's' from *Seinkönnen* does not show definitely that *Sein* is here verbal. The genitival 's' is optional in such cases; whether it is included or not depends on euphony as well as sense.

A

aletheia and truth   *Alētheia* is Greek for 'truth; truthfulness, frankness, sincerity'. *Alēthēs* is 'true; sincere, frank; real, actual'. There is also a verb, *alētheuein,* 'to speak truly, etc' (cf. XIX, 21ff.). The words are related to *lanthanein,* with an older form *lēthein,* 'to escape notice, be unseen, unnoticed', and *lēthē,* 'forgetting, forgetfulness'. An initial *a-* in Greek is often privative, like the Latin *in-* or the Germanic *un-*. (The 'privative alpha' occurs in many Greek-derived words: 'anonymous', 'atheism', etc.) *Alēthēs, alētheia* are generally accepted to be *a-lēthēs, a-lētheia,* that which is 'not hidden or forgotten', or he who 'does not hide or forget'.

We reach the 'essence of truth', the 'openness of the open', from two directions: from 'reflection on the ground of the possibility of correctness (adaequatio)' and from 'recollection of the beginning (alētheia)' (LXV, 338). The first procedure is characteristic of BT and early lectures, the second of later works. But early on Heidegger says that *alētheuein* is 'to take out of hiddenness [Verborgenheit], to uncover [entdecken]' (XXII, 25. Cf.XXI, 131; BT, 33, 219); *alētheia* is 'uncovering' (XXI, 162); and *alēthēs* is 'unhidden [Unverborgen(es)]' (BT, 33, 219). This has three implications: 1. Truth is not confined to explicit assertions and discrete mental, primarily theoretical, attitudes such as judgements, beliefs and representations. The world as a whole, not just entities within it, is unhidden – unhidden as much by moods as by understanding. 2. Truth is primarily a feature of reality – beings, being and world – not of thoughts and utterances. Beings, etc. are, of course, unhidden *to us,* and *we* disclose them. Heidegger later coins *entbergen; Entbergung; Entborgenheit,* 'to unconceal; -ing; -ment', since unlike *unverborgen,* they can have an active sense: 'alēthēs means: 1. unconcealed [entborgen], said of beings, 2. grasping the unconcealed as such, ie. being unconcealing' (XXXI, 91). But beings, etc. are genuinely unconcealed; they do not just agree with an assertion or representation. 3. Truth explicitly presupposes concealment or hiddenness. DASEIN is in 'untruth [Unwahrheit]' as well as truth. In BT (222, 256f.) this means that falling Dasein misinterprets things.

13

'Untruth' is not plain 'falsity', nor is it 'hiddenness': it is 'disguisedness [Verstelltheit]' of the truth (XXXI, 91). Later, 'untruth' is still not 'falsity', but 'hiding, concealing [Verbergung]' (LXV, 362). What conceals is no longer man, but being. There are two types of unconcealing: (a) of the open, the world or beings as a whole; (b) of particular beings within this open space. The first type (a) involves concealment: everything was hidden before the open was established, and concealment persists in that the open reveals only certain aspects of reality, not its whole nature. The second type (b) involves a concealment that we overcome 'partially and case by case' (LXV, 338f.). Plato errs in assimilating truth to light. We lose the idea of hiddenness and thus the privative force of *a-lētheia*: the light is constant – never switched on or off – and reveals everything there is to anyone who looks. We lose the idea of the open, which must persist throughout our unconcealing of beings: a single light cannot account both for the openness of the open and for the unconcealing of particular entities (LXV, 339).

Plato's error was fateful. He – not Aristotle, who did his best to repair the damage (NII, 228/niv, 171) – initiated the decline of *a-lētheia* into 'correctness' and truth as agreement (XXXIV, 21ff; P, 201ff./215ff.). *Alētheia* was originally the basic feature of *phusis* (roughly, 'nature') and thus 'essentially rejects any question about its relation to something else, such as thinking' (LXV, 329). In Plato it 'comes under the yoke of the *idea*' (P, 228). *Idea*, from the Greek *idein*, 'to see', refers, on Heidegger's account, to the visual 'aspect [Aussehen]' of entities. The ascent of the prisoners out of the cave is a progressive 'correction' of their vision of this *idea* and the entity whose *idea* it is. Hence *alētheia* is no longer primarily a characteristic of beings: it is 'yoked' together with the soul, and consists in a *homoiōsis*, a 'likeness', between them. *Homoiōsis* has since become *adaequatio* and then 'agreement', and since Descartes, the relation between soul and beings has become the subject–object relation, mediated by a 'representation', the degenerate descendant of Plato's *idea*. Truth becomes correctness, and its 'elbow-room [Spielraum]', the open, is neglected (LXV, 198, 329ff.).

Heidegger's account was attacked by Friedländer, 221–229: 1. It is not certain that *alēthēs* comes from *a-* and *lanthanein*. 2. Even if it does, it hardly ever means 'unhidden' in Homer, Hesiod and later authors, but has three main senses: the correctness of speech and belief (epistemological); the reality of being (ontological); the genuineness, truthfulness and conscientiousness of an individual or character ('existential'). 3. These three aspects of *alētheia* are united in Plato. The ascent from the cave is an ascent of being, of knowledge and of existence. Heidegger misunder-

14

stands this. He assumes that if Plato regards truth as correctness of apprehension, he has jettisoned its other senses, while if another sense reappears, this is because Plato is indecisive and 'ambiguous'. The three senses are fused together in Plato. 4. Interpreting truth as unhiddenness would not save it from modern subjectivity: unhiddenness must be unhiddenness to *someone.*

On 2 and 3 Friedländer is right. Heidegger accepts 2, and implicitly 3, in EPTT (77f./447). His attempts to find *alētheia* as 'unhiddenness' in Plato invariably fail. When Plato says that the things we 'make' by holding up a mirror are not beings *tēi alētheiai,* and that the things painters make are not *alēthē (Republic,* 596d,e), Heidegger takes him to mean that things in mirrors and in paintings are not 'unhidden'. (He also says that to understand how we can be said to make things by holding up a mirror, we must take 'making' in a special 'Greek sense'.) (NI, 206ff./ni, 177ff.) But things are no more hidden in a mirror than in the flesh. Plato's point is that things in a mirror are not *real,* not *alēthē* in the ontological sense. It is also untrue that *idea,* and its near-synonym *eidos,* 'form', mean 'aspect, appearance'; the assumption that the Greeks, if no-one else, invariably used words in accordance with their etymological roots is groundless (cf.NI, 200/ni, 172).

Heidegger's interpretations of *alētheia* and of Plato are indefensible. It does not follow that Friedländer is right on 4. This neglects Heidegger's distinction between the open and the unconcealing of particular beings, and also his belief that we are made, and revealed as, what we are by the opening of the open, not ready-made waiting for things to be unhidden to us. In the Kantian vocabulary rejected by Heidegger, Friedländer thinks in 'empirical' rather than 'transcendental' terms. Heidegger is far closer to Plato, properly interpreted, than he acknowledges.

angst, fear, boredom German has a variety of words in the area of 'emotion': *Leidenschaft* ('passion'), *Affekt* ('affect, emotion'), *Gefühl* ('feeling') and *Stimmung* ('mood'). Heidegger often distinguishes them. An (occurrent) *Affekt,* such as anger or wrath (*Zorn*), is quite different from a (dispositional) *Leidenschaft,* such as hatred: 'Hatred is clear-sighted, never blind; only wrath is blind. Love is clear-sighted, never blind; only love's ardour is blind, fleeting and spasmodic, an affect, not a passion' (NI, 58f./ni, 48). To call a passion a 'feeling' seems to weaken it, but this is because we have a degenerate concept of *Gefühl.* In fact a 'Gefühl is the way in which we find ourselves in our relation to beings and thus also in our relation to ourselves' (NI, 62/ni, 51). *Gefühl* is here equivalent to

15

Stimmung: 'the feeling is not something that takes place in the "interior"; feeling is that basic mode of our Dasein in virtue of which and in accordance with which we are always already raised way beyond ourselves into beings as a whole as they matter, or do not matter, to us'. The body is intimately involved: 'Every feeling is a bodying [Leiben] tuned in a certain way, a mood that bodies in a certain way' (NI, 119/ni, 100). *Gefühl* is sometimes uneasily equated with *Stimmung* (WM, 110/100; LXV, 256), sometimes distinguished from it as a purely inner feeling detached from any object (WMP, 304/385).

Fear discloses the world in a special way and is close to, yet distinct from, *Angst* ('anxiety, unease, malaise'): 'Fear is Angst that is fallen on the "world", inauthentic and concealed from itself as Angst' (BT, 189). What I fear is an entity within the world, e.g. a dentist's drill. This entity is 'detrimental'. Detrimentality is its 'mode of involvement [Bewandtnisart]'. The detrimentality is of a definite sort, pain in the tooth, and comes from a definite region, the dentist's. The region and what comes out of it are familiar to me as 'scary'. The drill is not yet on my tooth or nerve but is coming closer. It is already nearby. (Next month's appointment does not bother me.) It threatens, but is not certain to arrive. I may need no filling; it may not hurt if I do. The uncertainty persists until the last moment. The uncertainty intensifies my fear.

I do not fear the drill simply because of the pain I expect. Some people do not fear the dentist's drill, some perhaps fear nothing at all. They may expect the same intensity of pain as I do, but they do not view it as fearsome and do not pay it the same attention as I do. (Since I do not fear spiders, I am not fearful as I approach the sink in case one is lurking there nor do I 'expect' to encounter one, though it is not unlikely that I shall). Fear is not just an inner feeling; it opens up a world of potential threats. My slumbering fearfulness, my susceptibility to fear, 'has already disclosed the world as a realm from which such a thing as the fearsome can approach' (BT, 141). What I fear for is myself, DASEIN. Even if I fear for my 'house and home' I fear for myself as 'concernful being-alongside' (BT, 141). If I fear for others, I also 'fear for myself' (*sich fürchten*, usually just an intensified form of *fürchten*, 'to fear'); what one is afraid about is 'one's being-with the other, who could be torn away from one' (BT, 142). (How do I fear for myself, if I buy life-insurance out of fear for my family's future?)

Fear is thus a state one is in: it discloses the world, one's thrownness into it, and the 'involvement' of entities within it. *Angst* too is a state one is in, but differs from fear (BT, 184ff.): What *Angst* is about (its *Wovor*, 'Before-which, In the face of which'), is not an intraworldy entity, but the

16

world, being-in-the-world, Dasein itself, or the Nothing (cf. WM, 111/ 101). It threatens no definite harm, is indefinite, and lacks 'involvement'. Only intraworldly entities have involvement; hence *Angst* strips the world of its involvement-totality, its significance, making the world as such all the more obtrusive. Dasein too loses its usual concerns and is individualized down to its naked self, its bare ability-to-be, its 'freedom of choosing itself' (BT, 188). In *Angst* we find everything 'uncanny' (*unheimlich*, lit. 'unhomely') and feel 'not at home [*Un-zuhause*]' in the world. What *Angst* is *for* (its *Worum*, 'About which') is the same as what it is *about*: Dasein and being-in-the-world. *Angst* is calm and collected, while fear makes us 'lose our heads' (BT, 141, 342; WM, 111/100).

Angst has two contary effects: 1. Constant, implicit *Angst* makes us flee from ourselves and take refuge in, or 'fall into', familiar intraworldly things. 2. Occasional, explicit *Angst* rips us away from the familiar, and discloses bare Dasein and its bare world. Explicit *Angst* serves the philosopher in two ways: (a) In general it reveals Dasein in its unity; (b) the philosopher's *own* Angst detaches him from worldly concerns and prejudices, making philosophy possible.

Angst is not the only 'basic mood' (XLIX, 32; cf.58f.) 'Boredom' (*Langeweile*) also discloses beings as a whole by letting everything sink into indifference, but, unlike *Angst*, it does not let them slither away and thus does not reveal the Nothing (WM, 109ff.99ff.). There are three progressively 'deeper' types of boredom, exemplified respectively by waiting on a deserted platform for a train (which, Heidegger unwarrantedly assumes, needs to be late, XXIX, 159), going to a dinner party, and walking the city streets on Sunday afternoon – a 'deep boredom' akin to *Angst* (XXIX, 117ff., esp. 206ff.). *Langeweile* is literally 'long while' and thus more explicitly temporal than *Angst*.

Later, the dominant 'basic mood' varies historically. The basic mood of the 'first [viz. Greek] beginning' was 'astonishment', while the 'basic mood of thinking in the other beginning vibrates in the moods which can be approximately called': fright (*Erschrecken*), restraint (*Verhaltenheit*) – these together are foreboding (*Ahnung*) – and timidity (*Scheu*). Fright makes us 'shrink back from the fact that beings *are*' and that beyng has abandoned them (LXV, 14). More than one word is needed for the mood: 'Every naming of the basic mood in a single word is misleading. Every word is taken from the tradition. That the basic mood of the other beginning has many names does not conflict with its simplicity but confirms its richness and strangeness' (LXV, 22).

Modernity tends to lay every mood bare (or let it all hang out), to make them public and communal, thus disguising the 'growing void' (LXV,

123). But 'Angst before beyng is as great today as ever. Proof: the gigantic apparatus for shouting down this Angst' (LXV, 139).

art and the work Apart from an attempt to establish the antiquity of the association of man with care from a poem by Hyginus (BT, 196ff.), BT has nothing to say about art (*Kunst*) and uses the term *Werk* for the product of a craft rather than a work of art. Heidegger did not lecture on art until the mid-1930s. The concepts of BT cannot easily accommodate the work of art. It is not present-at-hand like a rock or a tree, nor ready-to-hand like a broom or a car. Yet it has features in common with both. Like a rock and unlike a broom, it has no specific purpose and essentially contains conspicuous natural, 'thingly', materials. Like a broom and unlike a rock, it is made by humans, but the artist's creativity has an affinity to the purposeless creation of nature (OWA, 10ff./146ff.). BT might lead us to expect Heidegger to consider art in terms of the artist's *choices*, a choice of this theme rather than that, of this material, of his pigment, etc. But he does not. The work of art is more like a PROJECT, which sets up a world in which choices can be made. Truth, the revelation of being, is 'set into the work' and 'set to work' (a pun on *ins Werk setzen*, cf. LXV, 69), illuminating the world and the EARTH on which it rests. As DASEIN is thrown in its own project and understands itself in terms of it, so the artist is originated by the work of art. The point is not simply that no one is an artist until he creates a work, but that the artist is not in control of his own creativity, art is a sort of impersonal force that uses the artist for its own purposes. A work is to be understood in terms of being and the world, not of its author (NI, 474/niii, 4). (Heidegger often suggests that philosophers too are in the grip of an impersonal force, such as the 'will to power' or the 'beginning' (NII, 290/niii, 214; LIV, 10f.).) A work also needs an audience, or rather 'preservers' *Bewahrenden*, and 'preservation', *Bewahrung*, which means: 'Standing in the openness of beings that happens in the work' (OWA, 55/192). A rock is what it is apart from any onlookers; the purpose of a broom is immanent in it and in any case a broom, like any equipment in good working order, is essentially inconspicuous even when in use, let alone when stored in the cupboard. But a work needs preservers to bring out its meaning and to receive the light that it sheds on their lives. The similarity of (*be*)*wahren*, 'to protect, keep', to *wahr, Wahrheit*, 'true, truth', is not lost on Heidegger, though the words are etymologically unrelated. He dislikes the word *Ästhetik*, from the Greek *aisthēsis*, 'perception', since it focuses on the audience at the expense of the artist and the work, and on the superficial, perceptible beauty of the

18

work: 'The aesthetic [. . .] turns the work of art from the start into an object for our feelings and ideas. Only when the work has become an object, is it fit for exhibitions and museums' (OWL, 139/43. Cf. NI, 91ff./ ni, 77ff; LXV, 503). The work embodies truth first of all, and sensory beauty only secondarily. The work, or art itself, is primary: it generates artist and preservers as a river fashions its own banks (cf. LXV, 476).

Heidegger worked out his views on art in interaction with Nietzsche, in whose posthumous *Will to Power* he found five propositions about art (NI, 82ff./ni, 69ff; 162ff./ni, 138ff.): 1. Art is the most transparent and familiar form of the will to power. 2a. Art must be understood in terms of the artist. 3. Art is, on an extended concept of the artist, the basic happening of all beings; so far as beings are, they are something self-creating, created. 4. Art is the distinctive counter-movement against nihilism. 5a). Art is the great stimulant of life, and/or 5b). Art is worth more than truth. Heidegger rejects 2: Nietzsche ignores the primacy of the work (NI, 138/ni, 117f.). He initially finds 4 at odds with Nietzsche's physiological account of art (NI, 109ff./ni, 92ff.), but modifies this verdict by interpreting physiology as involving no separation of mind and body, 'as if a bodily state dwelt on the ground floor and a feeling on the floor above' (NI, 118/ni, 98; cf. 148f./ni, 126f.). His main disagreement with Nietzsche turns on 5. Truth, for Nietzsche, is the accurate portrayal of the current state of affairs in terms of rigid categories and concepts. Art 'transfigures life, moves it into higher, as yet unlived possibilities, which do not hover "above" life, but rouse it from itself anew into wakefulness, for "Only through magic does life remain awake" (George, "The New Realm")' (NI, 567f./niii, 81). Although both truth (or knowledge) and art are required for life, Heidegger agrees that art is superior to truth in Nietzsche's sense of truth (NI, 635f./niii, 140). But Nietzsche's notion of truth is overly traditional, and he retains Plato's contrast between art and truth (NI, 179/ni, 153; NI, 250/ni, 217; NII, 12/niii, 165). Strictly, or 'originally', truth is not correspondence with fact, but what Nietzsche says art provides: the disclosure of a realm of new possibilities.

The aesthetic view of art stems from the man-centred metaphysic of modernity, and coheres with the conception of beings as what is 'objectively representable' (LXV, 503). My own states, the way I feel in the presence of something, determines my view of everything I encounter (NI, 99/ni, 83). Hence art is in danger of becoming a device for the provision of 'experience [Erlebnis]' (LXV, 91). This is abetted by the view (of e.g. Hartmann) that a work of art is a thing, a crafted thing, with aesthetic value superimposed on it. Despite the Greek use of *technē* for both 'craft' and 'art' (since *technē* means bringing forth beings, whether

19

by craft or by art, into truth or unhiddenness, OWA, 48/184), a work of art is not a product of craft, let alone a thing, with beauty added. It is where truth is sheltered, the truth that enables beings to appear as beings and craftsmen to produce their artefacts (LXV, 69, 243, etc.). Overcoming aethetics is an integral part of overcoming metaphysics (LXV, 503f.). Hegel was wrong to affirm that art has come to an end. Whether art will decline into an 'instrument of cultural policy' or will set the truth (in)to (the) work once more is a matter for 'decision'; the outcome is uncertain (OWA, 66f./204ff; LXV, 91, 507).

Art is 'the letting-happen of the arrival of the truth of beings as such'. This means that all art is essentially 'POETRY' or rather *Dichtung* (OWA, 59/199).

assertion, the apophantic 'As' and logos *Satz* is used in two ways: 1. It is a 'sentence' in general, and occurs in such compounds as *Wunschsatz*, 'optative sentence/clause, linguistic expression of a wish', *Fragesatz*, 'inter-rogative sentence/clause', *Befehlssatz*, 'imperative, command', *Aussagesatz*, 'statement'. 2. It is a 'proposition' or 'theorem', and occurs in compounds such as *Grundsatz*, 'principle'. This divergence stems from the fact that *Satz* means (a) a 'mode of positing' (*Weise des Setzens*), (b) 'what is posited' (*das Gesetzte*) (XXIX, 437). In 'He is fat' and 'Is he fat?' what is posited is the same, his being fat; but the mode of positing is, in the first case, questioning, in the second, stating. (This is similar to R. M. Hare's distinction between 'neustic' and 'phrastic'.) In sense 1, *Satz* denotes primarily the mode of positing, in sense 2 what is posited. Later, Heidegger exploits the fact that *Satz* also means a 'leap' (PR, 95f., etc.).

Assertion (*Aussage(satz)*), is only one form of sentence or TALK, a form in which the speaker's self-expression is subdued. It is not the primary form (XVII, 25; cf. 21: 'Fire!'). But Heidegger often begins with assertion, since it is the most familiar type of discourse, having 'decisively deter-mined the doctrine of talk in general'. The reason is this: 'The fundamen-tal trait of everyday Dasein is that indiscriminate conduct towards beings as just present-at-hand. The corresponding form of discourse [. . .] is this indifferent normal form of the assertion: a is b' (XXIX, 438). Assertion is associated with 'judgement', *Urteil*: an *Urteil* is what an *Aussage* asserts or 'says [*sagt*] out [*aus*]'. Heidegger is hostile to the distinction between temporal judging and atemporal propositions: 'Judging is empirically real, while the true proposition [*Satz*] judged is valid [*gilt*]; ie. lies beyond becoming and change. (That is even more vacuous and absurd than saying: Elliptical functions lie beyond the Kapp putsch!)' (LIX, 72).

Aristotle called an assertion a *logos apophantikos*, a *logos* that reveals or 'shows [*phainei*] forth [*apo*]' (XVII, 19; XXIX, 441; NII, 76/niv, 40), distinguishing it from *logoi*, such as wishes and commands, which do not show forth. BT avoids the phrase *logos apophantikos* and wavers over the link between *logos*, 'talk, discourse', and *apophansis*, 'showing forth'. *Logos* in general shows forth, but it shows forth what the *logos* is about in such a way that showing forth tends to be restricted to assertion, excluding e.g. the request, which also 'makes manifest, but in a different way' (BT, 32; cf. 154, 218f.) Assertion 1. points out the entity that it is about; 2. predicates or asserts something of it, presents 'something as [als] something' – the 'apophantic As [Als]' in contrast to the more fundamental 'HERMENEUTIC As'; 3. communicates to others (BT, 33, 196f; 158). Since they show forth, assertions have truth and falsity, but not in the sense of 'agreement' and 'disagreement' (BT, 33), and the assertion is 'not the primary "place" of truth', since a more fundamental disclosure is required if assertions are to be true (BT, 226).

Assertion remains throughout Heidegger's thought an inferior mode of discourse. We can assert of beings but not of being. To do so presents beyng as an 'object'. Beyng requires *Sagen*, 'saying', not *Aussage*, 'saying out/of' (LXV, 473, 484, 486). Owing to its simplicity, richness and ubiquity beyng (BT, 3f; LXV, 471), is as difficult to talk about as Aquinas's God. Earlier, Heidegger distinguished a 'worldly assertion about what is present-at-hand', which 'can directly mean what is said' from an 'assertion about Dasein and further every assertion about being, every categorial assertion, which, to be understood, needs a redirection of understanding [. . .] to what is indicated, which is essentially never present-at-hand'. Plato and Aristotle took all assertions to be 'world-assertions'; this caused being to be conceived as *a* being (XXI, 410).

Logos has a richer history than *Aussage*. It begins with Heraclitus, for whom *logos* means 'collection' (*Sammlung*), both as 'collecting' and 'what is collected' (IM, 98/108; LV, 266ff.). *Logos* comes from *legein*, 'to tell, say', but originally 'to gather, choose, etc.' (Heidegger resists the suggestion that Heraclitus used *logos* similarly to John, I, 1: 'In the beginning was the Word [logos], [. . .]', IM, 97/107.) This is related to *logos* in the sense of 'word', since a word gathers what is named together in unity (S, 152/126). In later Greek thought, especially Plato and Aristotle, *logos* loses the intimate connexion with *phusis*, 'NATURE', that it had for Heraclitus, and becomes assertion, saying (predicating) something about (of) something. It is also comes to mean 'reason', a development expedited by the Latin translation, *ratio* (BT, 34). Aristotle defined man as the animal that has *logos*, the power of speech; in Latin, this become *animal rationale*, the rational animal (BT, 25, 48, 165). (Heidegger locates our superiority over (other) animals in our having a WORLD, not in our reasoning capacity.)

The Greek *katēgorein* meant 'to speak against [*kata-*], charge, accuse [someone with/of something]', originally in the 'assembly [*agora*]'; *katēgoria* means 'accusation, charge'. Aristotle used *katēgorein* as 'to predicate, assert [something of something]', and *katēgoria* for 'predicate', especially the most general predicates or categories. (Heidegger struggles to connect these two senses (BT, 44f; NII, 71f./niv, 36f.).) Beings are now seen in terms of predicates, of *logos* as assertion, and more generally of thinking. *Logos*-derived categories are no more adequate for being than assertion is (LXV, 280). Nor do they apply to all beings: we need EXISTENTIALs to interpret DASEIN, not categories, which treat it as merely PRESENT-AT-HAND.

Logos gave rise to *Logik*, or *Aussage-Logik*, the 'logic of assertion' (LXV, 458). Despite his sound training in logic and his early review of logical works, including *Principia Mathematica* (I, 17ff., esp. 42f.), Heidegger mistrusted formal logic, and Hegel's dialectical logic. Logic is not prior to ontology; if anything, logic is based on metaphysics, not (as Russell and Couturat held) metaphysics on logic (XXVI, 36, 132; ER, 12 n. 10). Logic 'has its foundation in an ontology of the present-at-hand, and a crude one at that' (BT, 129; cf. 165). To understand a science we must look not at its 'logical structure', but its 'own concrete logic' and its 'historical situation' (LXI, 115). We can never 'say beyng immediately', since every saying and thus all logic comes from beyng and is thus under its sway. 'The inner essence of "logic" is therefore sigetics [*die Sigetik*, the "art of silence", from the Greek *sigan*, "to keep silent"]' (LXV, 79). In a letter of 11 March 1964, Heidegger dubs Carnap's logic-oriented view of language the 'technological-scientistic [*technisch-szientistische*] conception' in contrast to his own 'speculative-hermeneutic experience of language' (PT, 70/24).

Heidegger invariably felt that his own enterprise – ontology, thinking, etc. – was more fundamental than logic, that he needed to transgress canons of logic and could make little use of the formal logician's concepts of POSSIBILITY, necessity, etc.

authenticity and inauthenticity The adjective *eigen*, 'own, separate, peculiar, strange, etc.', was the perfect participle of a defunct verb meaning 'to have, possess', and thus originally meant 'possessed, taken into possession'. *Eigen* gave rise to *eigentlich* 'real(ly), actual(ly), true(ly), original(ly), etc.' To say that DASEIN is not *eigentlich* might thus mean that it is not real, or not really Dasein. But Heidegger denies this, and connects *eigentlich* closely with *eigen*: Dasein 'is essentially something that can be authentic [eigentliches], that is, something of its own [zueigen]' (BT, 42). Hence *eigentlich*, when used as a technical term, is close to 'authentic', which comes from the Greek *autos*, 'self, etc.' and originally meant 'done by one's own hand', hence 'reliably guaranteed'. Heidegger uses *uneigentlich*, normally 'not literal(ly), figurative(ly)', as the opposite of *eigentlich*. He also uses *Eigentlichkeit*, 'authenticity', and coins *Uneigentlichkeit*, 'inauthenticity'. These do not coincide with 'genuine [echt]' and 'false [unecht]': 'There is a false authenticity, i.e. a false case of Dasein's being-at-home-with-itself [Beisichselbstein], and a genuine inauthenticity, i.e. a genuine loss of itself that arises from the concrete Dasein in question' (XXI, 226f; cf. BT, 146). Primarily it is Dasein that is (in)authentic. Everything else that is (in)authentic – temporality, the future, etc. – is so in relation to Dasein's (in)authenticity.

Dasein's possibility of being authentic or inauthentic is rooted in the fact that Dasein is 'always mine [*je meines*]', it must always be addressed by a personal pronoun, 'I', or 'you' (XXI, 229; cf. BT, 42). Since it is mine, I can lose it or grasp it, for the fact that it is mine does not entail that it is properly 'one's own [zu eigen]'; 'it is always mine, so far as it has always already been decided in what way it is mine – not in the sense that it has necessarily taken the decision itself, but that a decision was already made about Dasein. Dasein is always mine, that means factically that it is its own [zu eigen] in this way or that, it has itself so much or so little as its own, has understood and grasped itself so much or so little as its own [als eigenes], or, alternatively, deficiently: it has not yet grasped itself, or has lost itself. Primarily and mostly Dasein has not yet won itself at all as its own, it has not yet found its way to itself, e.g. in the time of youth, or again it has lost itself, perhaps just at the liveliest period of its life. It can only have lost itself, it can only have failed to find itself, in so far as it is, in its very being, mine, i.e. possibly authentic' (XXI, 229; cf. BT, 42f.).

Dasein does not lose itself as it might lose an umbrella (cf. QB, 90). It does so by 'falling concern' (XXI, 231f.). It falls into and is absorbed in the 'world', so that it forgets itself as an autonomous entity and interprets itself in terms of its current preoccupations: 'One is what one does [...] One is a shoemaker, a tailor, a teacher, a banker' (XX, 336). In extreme cases it understands itself as a PRESENT-AT-HAND thing, which one can only deal with by way of its preoccupations. Despite all this, Dasein is still concerned about itself. If it ceased to matter to itself at all, it would cease to be 'care' (*Sorge*) and then it would lose all 'concern' (*Besorgen*) for anything. Inauthenticity is only a 'modification', not the extinction, of

23

care. Dasein is thus never irretrievably lost in inauthenticity. If it were, it would not be 'inauthentic', since it would no longer be Dasein. Inauthentic Dasein continues to speak of itself as 'I', but this refers to the THEY-self or to the self interpreted in terms of the world. If we want to know about authentic selfhood, the 'constant' self that stands on its own two feet, we must look at 'authentic ability-to-be-oneself [Selbstseinkonnen], in. in the authenticity of Dasein's being as care' (BT, 322).

Inauthenticity is often associated with the They. To be authentic is to do one's own thing, not what *they* prescibe. But inauthenticity is often discussed independently of the They (e.g. XXI, 228ff.). The connection between absorption in one's current business and subjection to the They is that insofar as one is attending to one's affairs, one must see things as *they* interpret them, not in one's *own* way. Heidegger sometimes suggests that in 'average everydayness' Dasein is neither authentic nor inauthentic but in a state of *Indifferenz* (XXI, 229f; BT, 43, 53). He may mean that everyday Dasein is not necessarily subject to the They, beyond agreeing with *them* that shoes are for walking and hammers for hammering. But although everydayness begins as a neutral condition, it turns out to be a state of fallenness and inauthenticity.

Inauthenticity is not a moral or a theological notion (XXI, 232; LXV, 302). One reason for this is that the distinction between authenticity and inauthenticity is not imposed on Dasein by Heidegger himself. Every Dasein has an inner voice calling it to authenticity, to self-fulfilment: 'hearing constitutes the primary and authentic openness of Dasein for its very own ability-to-be: hearing the voice of the friend that every Dasein carries with it' (BT, 163).

Later, the distinction becomes less important (but cf. NI, 275f./nii, 24f., etc.). When man as such is no longer *Da-sein*, 'there-being', there is no place for a distinction between authentic and inauthentic *Da-sein*. Two similar notions occur. *Weg-sein*, 'being away' (but as *Wegsein*, 'being out cold, spaced out, out of it, bowled over, etc.') is contrasted with *Da-sein* (XXIX, 95; LXV, 252, 301f., 323f.). It is close to *Uneigentlichkeit*, but in so far as we succumb to *Weg-sein*, we are out of *Da-sein*. *Eigentum* comes from *eigen*, and Heidegger insists that it be read as *Eigen-tum*, by analogy with *Fürstentum*, 'princedom' (LXV, 320): hence 'owndom, ownership'. But he continues to use it in its normal sense of 'property, possessions': the 'appropriating event [Er-eignung] destines man for the Eigentum of beyng' (LXV, 263). Often it is close to BT's *Eigentlichkeit*: 'Selfhood is the unfolding of the ownership [Eigentumschaft] of the essence. That man has his essence as Eigentum means: he stands in constant danger of loss' (LXV, 489; cf. 500). But authenticity now has more to do with one's relation to being than to oneself: 'Dasein is authentic if it belongs to the truth of being in such a way that priority over beings is granted to being' (XLIX, 66). Since we are now more concerned about history and being than about individual Dasein, not everyone needs authenticity, only those laying the ground for the question about beyng (LXV, 285). For the most part: *Der Mensch ist das Weg,* 'Man is the (A)way' (LXV, 323).

B

being: an introduction In its usage, grammatical structure and etymological roots, the German *sein* corresponds closely, though not exactly, to the English 'to be'. Like all German (and English) verbs, *sein* has two simple or synthetic tenses, the present (*ich bin*/'I am', etc.) and the preterite (*ich war*/'I was', etc.). Other tenses are formed analytically, by combining an auxiliary verb (which may be *sein* itself, *haben* 'to have', or *werden*, 'to become') with one of the two infinitives, present (*sein*) and perfect (*gewesen sein*, 'to have been'), or with its perfect participle, *gewesen* '(having) been' (which also supplies the German for 'ESSENCE' and Heidegger's word for the living PAST). 'I shall be', for example is *ich werde sein*. *Sein* has a present participle, *seiend*, 'being', (Heidegger explores the 'grammar and etymology of the word "sein" in IM, ch. II.)

The uses of *sein* may be broadly classified as the predicative ('I am, was, hungry'), the existential ('I think, therefore I am', 'He is no more'), and the auxiliary (*er ist gereist*, 'he has travelled'). There is also an impersonal use, important in Heidegger's account of MOODS: *mir ist schlecht*, 'I feel bad' (lit. 'It is bad to me'), *mir ist unheimlich*, 'It is uncanny, it gives me the creeps'. Heidegger often calls being in the predicative sense 'What-being' (*Was-sein*), since it says *what* something is, and being in the existential sense 'That-being' (*Dass-sein*), since it says *that* something is; occasionally he distinguishes the What-being of something, its essential features (the materiality of a chalk), from its So-being (*Sosein*), its contingent features (its whiteness) (XXXI, 75).

The present infinitive, with or without the neuter definite article, *das*, occurs as a noun: (*das*) *Sein*, 'being'. 'Being' may be the being of something in particular, and then it may be its 'existence' (That-being), or its 'essence' (its What-being or fundamental nature). Or 'being' may be being in the abstract, again either in the sense of 'That-being' or of 'What-being'. Heidegger uses (*das*) *Sein* both for the being of e.g. DASEIN, and for being in general. In neither case is 'being' to be specified as 'What-' or 'That-being', it is simply being; the distinction between existence and essence is something to be explored rather than just accepted. A noun is also formed from the participle *seiend*: (*das*) *Seiende*, 'that which is'. This occurs only in the singular; it no more admits a plural than does the English expression 'the beautiful'. But it is often translated as 'beings' or 'entities'. Heidegger calls the crucial distinction between being (*das Sein*) and beings (*das Seiende*) the 'ontological DIFFERENCE'.

Being, Heidegger argues, is usually regarded as the thinnest of abstractions, the most general feature of everything that is. A distinction may be drawn between That-being and What-being. But then That-being is a homogeneous feature shared by everything that exists: everything is or exists in the same way. What-being too is homogeneous: men are mortal in just the same way as numbers are divisible; the differences between the two cases depend solely on the differences between men and numbers, between mortality and divisibility. Heidegger, by contrast, stresses the rich diversity of *sein*. 1. The verb *ist*, 'is', allows various paraphrases: ' "God is", i.e. actually present. "The earth is", i.e. we experience and think of it as constantly at hand; "The talk is in the lecture room", i.e. it takes place, "The man is of Swabian stock", i.e. he descends from it. "The cup is of silver", i.e. it consists of [. . .]' (IM, 68/75; cf. LI, 30; NII, 247ff./niv, 189). 2. We can ask not only what something is and whether it is, we can also ask how (*wie*) it is, what is its How-being (*Wie-sein*), its type, manner or mode of being (*Seinsart, Seinsweise, Weise zu sein*). Numbers not only have different properties from men; they *are* in a different way, they are beings of a different sort. Men, in turn, differ in their mode of being from tools, and these again from rivers or mountains. An entity's mode of being affects the questions we can appropriately ask about it. We can ask 'What is jade?' or 'What is a hammer?' But we should not ask not 'What is man?' but 'Who is man?', 'Who is Dasein?' and 'Who am I?' Such questions, moreover, call for a decision by way of answer, rather than a list of properties. Heidegger does not always distinguish between How-being and That-being, regarding both as a being's mode of being, in contrast to its What-being or 'constitution' (e.g. XXIV, 291; NI, 425/nii, 163; LXV, 302). One reason for this is his tendency to regard POSSIBILITY, actuality and necessity as modes of being (NI 461/nii, 195f.): if an entity is said to be possible, rather than actual, we are told about its That-being and its How-being in the same breath. The sentence 'Centaurs are an invention of the poets' tells us, in Heidegger's view, not so much about the (actual) non-existence of centaurs as about their mode of being (XXIV, 290: *Modus des Seins*). He is less interested in non-existent 'entities' than the Frege–Russell tradition; he is also less inclined to view them as lacking in being. 3. The verb *sein* can be followed by various prepositions: I am *in* the

27

world, *bei* ('(present) at, alongside, in, by', etc.) things and events, *mit* ('with') other people, *zu* ('towards') entities, death, others, etc. One might say that being is nevertheless homogeneous and abstract; the variety is conferred by the preposition and the following noun. But Heidegger is unwilling to detach being from its context. Being in the world is, he insists, a different sort of being from being at or by things within it, and from being with other people. Hence he often coins *sein*-compounds where German does not already provide them: *Mitsein*, 'being-with'; *Beisein* 'being-at, presence'; *In-sein*, and so on.

These are some of the sources of the diversity of being. Others are provided by philosophers in the course of the HISTORY OF BEING. Heidegger nevertheless insists on being's unity. But being, though unified, is not the thin abstraction that our impoverished understanding takes it to be. It has (like Hegel's 'concept') diversity packed into it, ready to emerge in our everyday dealings with beings, and before the gaze of the philosopher. 'Beyng is the ether in which man breathes; without this ether he is reduced to mere cattle and all his doings to mere cattle-breeding' (S, 118/98).

Being and Time   *Being and Time* was published in February 1927 as volume VIII of Husserl's *Jahrbuch für Philosophie und phänomenologische Forschung [Annual for Philosophy and Phenomenological Rearch]*. It was dedicated to Husserl. This dedication remained in the fourth edition of 1935, but was removed from the fifth edition of 1941 – at the request, Heidegger says, of the publisher Niemeyer, who feared that the book would be banned, if the dedication to Husserl – a Christian convert of Jewish descent and conservative political beliefs – remained (OWL, 269/199). This edition retained Heidegger's expression of gratitude to Husserl (BT, 38 n. 1), though in a letter to Jaspers of 26 December 1926 he says that if BT is 'written "against" anyone, then it is Husserl, who immediately saw that too, but took a positive attitude from the start' (HJ, 39). The dedication was restored in later editions.

BT won Heidegger a full professorship at Marburg: the state government withdrew its objection to the appointment of someone who had so far produced no major work and had published nothing for ten years. He had, however, prepared the ground for BT by lectures on various aspects of it since 1919: time, truth, Aristotle, phenomenology, Descartes, Dilthey, neo-Kantianism, and so on. Apparently marginal themes in BT are often the fruit of intense pedagogical activity in earlier years: sparse references to St Paul and Augustine reflect courses on them in 1920 and 1921 (LX);

the introductory quotation from Plato's *Sophist* stems from his lectures on it in 1924–5 (XIX). BT draws together the threads of ten years of unremitting intellectual labour. It differs in style from his lectures, with their often down-to-earth vocabulary and vivid, concrete examples. It is somewhat scholastic in its language and organization. Heidegger's legendary brilliance as a lecturer does not generally survive the passage to the printed page.

After the quotation from Plato and a brief exposition of it, BT opens with a long Introduction, entitled 'Exposition of the Question about the Sense of Being'. In the first chapter of this, 'Necessity, Structure and Priority of the Question of Being', he explains why it is important to raise this long-forgotten question, why it is prior to other questions, questions about knowledge and questions in the sciences. he also explains that the question of being must be approached by way of an analysis of DASEIN, (the) human being: it is Dasein that asks the question about being (BT, 7). The second chapter is 'The Twofold Task in Working out the Question of Being. The Method of the Investigation and its Outline'. The first of these tasks, intended to occupy the first part of BT, was 'the interpretation of Dasein in terms of temporality, and the explication of temporality as the transcendental horizon of the question about being'. This first part was to fall into three divisions: '1. The preparatory fundamental analysis of Dasein; 2. Dasein and temporality; 3. time and being' (BT, 39). Only the first and second divisions of this part were published. The first division gives an account of Dasein without reference to time and temporality. It covers such themes as the world and being-in-the-world, space and spatiality, being with others, the They, inauthenticity and falling, moods, truth and care. The second division introduces temporality and for much of its course is a 'repetition' of the first division in a temporal key (BT, 17). It opens with a famous first chapter on death, and then proceeds to conscience, guilt and resoluteness. It then 'repeats' the earlier accounts of care and of everydayness, bringing out their temporal significance. History, or rather 'historicity' is Heidegger's next theme, with a coda on the recently published correspondence of Dilthey and Count Paul Yorck of Wartenburg. The final chapter returns to temporality. The penultimate section attacks Hegel's conception of time, and the short concluding section introduces the missing third division, which was intended to explore being in relation to time, independently of the nature of Dasein.

The second task projected in the Introduction was to provide the 'rudiments of a phenomenological destruction [Destruktion] of the history of ontology in terms of the problem-area [Problematik] of temporality [Temporalität, viz. Dasein-independent "temporality", in contrast to

29

Zeitlichkeit, Dasein's "temporality"]'. This second part was also intended to have three divisions, dealing with: '. Kant's doctrine of schematism and of time; 2. Descartes's 'cogito sum' and his debt to medieval ontology; 3. Aristotle's account of time (BT, 39f.). This part never appeared, but its contents are familiar from Heidegger's other writings and lectures. The remainder of the Introduction explains the phenomenological and hermeneutical method of BT.

The intended contents of I, 3 are uncertain. Heidegger says that he wrote it, but decided to omit it: 'The decision to break off was formed in the last days of December 1926 during a stay with Jaspers in Heidelberg. From our lively, friendly discussions over the proofs it became clear to me that this most important division (I, 3), as I had worked it out so far, must remain unintelligible' (XLIX, 39f.). (Heidegger misremembers: letters to Jaspers and Blochmann show that he visited Jaspers on 1 January 1927 (HJ, 72; HB, 19). He regrets his inability to complete BT, but feels that other publications 'lead to the real question by detours' (XLIX, 40; cf. HB, 54). I, 3 was to involve a TURN, veer or swerve: fundamental ontology 'is: 1. analytic of Dasein [viz. BT, I, 1 and 2], and 2. analytic of the temporality [Temporalität] of being [viz. BT, I, 3]. But this temporal [temporale] analytic is also the *turn* [die *Kehre*], in which ontology itself explicitly runs back into the metaphysical ontics [Ontik] in which it always implicitly remains. We need, by the motion of radicalizing and universalizing, to bring ontology to the swerve [Umschlag] latent in it. Here the turning [das Kehren] occurs, and we veer round [Umschlag] into meta-ontology [Metontologie]' (XXVI, 201; cf. 196). Meta-ontology, ontology 'about' or 'beyond' ontology, seems to involve reflection on beings as a whole in relation to being, which still depends on Dasein's understanding of it (XXVI, 199).

BT remains the focal point of Heidegger's thought to the end. He often discusses it later (e.g. LXV, 10, etc. LH, 315ff./221ff; OWL, 92ff./7ff; XV, 274, etc.). BT's focus on being, rather than beings, and the linking of being with time, rather than with thinking, represents an important first step towards the preoccupations of his later years (LXV, 183, 431ff.). It does not succumb to the man-centred metaphysic that he later condemned (LXV, 488ff.). It is, however, a work of 'transition', riddled with the vocabulary and presuppositions of the old metaphysics (LXV, 93, 223, 430, XLIX, 28).

BT is often felt, even in its truncated form, to lack unity. The theme of everyday circumspection, characteristic of I, 1 seems ill at ease with the Angst-ridden resoluteness characteristic of I, 2. One unifying thread is Heidegger's urge to reflect not just on the concerns of philosophy, but on philosophy itself. What is the connection between everyday life and philosophy? What motivates us, and enables us, to philosophize? (Cf. LXIII, 17ff.) It seems a requirement of phenomenology that the desire and ability to philosophize be shown to cohere with, and to emerge from, Dasein's other features. Angst, authenticity, resoluteness: these are what the philosopher needs. Once Dasein has, in I, 2, become a philosopher, then it can ascend, in I, 3, to being itself. Husserl, in his earlier writings, neglected the emergence of philosophy from average everydayness; Heidegger (like another great phenomenologist, Hegel) laid it to heart.

being with others and being alongside things Heidegger discriminates between our relations to people and to things by using different prepositions: DASEIN is *mit*, 'with', others, but *bei* things. Originally *bei* meant 'close, near'; it is related to 'by' in 'bystander'. It corresponds to no single English preposition: 'It is *by* the station', 'He's *at* home', 'She went *to* the doctor's', 'He worked *on* the railway'. He uses a compound verbal noun, *(das) Mitsein*, for 'being-with' others. He does not use *Beisein* for 'being alongside' things, but *Sein-bei* (BT, 192) or *Sein bei* (BT, 131), perhaps because *Beisein* already has a meaning too restricted for his purpose, 'presence' ('in his presence'). *Sein bei*, *Mitsein* and *Selbstsein* ('being-one's-self') are three co-ordinate constituents of being-in-the-WORLD, corresponding to the *Umwelt*, the 'world around one', the *Mitwelt*, the 'with-world, people around one' (BT, 118) and the earlier *Selbstwelt* (e.g. LXIII, 102). Heidegger also uses *Mitdasein*, 'Dasein-with', for the being or the Dasein of others, but not usually for others themselves, and *Miteinandersein*, 'being-with-one-another' (BT, 118f.).

Sein bei, *Mitsein* and *Selbstsein* are *gleichursprünglich*, 'equiprimordial, equally original, primitive' (ER, 100). It is a mistake to take *Sein-bei* and/or *Selbstsein* as primary and derive *Mitsein* or others from them. The self must not be separated from *Sein-bei* and *Mitsein*. Descartes and Husserl (and Nietzsche, NI, 578/niii, 90) make this mistake: 'Since the subject is conceived shorn as it were of this Sein-bei . . ., a fragmentary subject, the question about being-with-each-other [Miteinandersein] and its essence also takes a wrong turn. Since both subjects are underdetermined, a more elaborate arrangement must as it were be found than the nature of the case requires. The underdetermination of subjectivity causes an overdetermination of the relation between subjects' (XXVII, 140). If people are self-enclosed subjects, they have to undertake a careful inspection of each other's physical characteristics before they can communicate. Plainly this is not the case. I am 'with' others even when they are not physically present: 'Being missing and "being away" are modes of Dasein-with and possible only because Dasein as being-with lets the Dasein of others come to meet it [begegnen] in its world' (BT, 121).

Mit(einander)sein does not involve focusing on each other: two ramblers gripped by the same view are 'with each other' without attending to each other. But attending to each other presupposes being-with (XXVII, 86f.). *Mitsein* requires *Sein-bei*, in particular our ability to be *bei* one and the same thing. When two or more people see the same piece of chalk they do not see it as exactly similar; they have different views on the same chalk and thus see it in different ways: 'Sameness [Selbigkeit] and exact similarity [Gleichheit] are two different things' (XXVII, 90). If we could not identify an object perceived by me as the same as the object perceived by you, we could not communicate or recognise each other as persons. Even disagreement presupposes agreement about the thing we disagree about: 'Harmony and discord are thus based on establishing something the same and constant. If we were abandoned to a stream of representations and sensations and swept away in it', there would be no 'us', no others, and no identical entity for us to agree or differ about (NI, 578/ niii, 91). Conversely, *Sein-bei* involves *Mitsein*. What we are usually *bei* are READY-TO-HAND entities: the cloth we are cutting, fields, books, boats. We do not first see them as present-at-hand and then infer the existence of others from their physical contours. We see them at once as involving customers, suppliers, owners, users (BT, 117f.). As Heidegger becomes less preoccupied with the ready-to-hand, he introduces other arguments: Dasein can, of course, be *bei* a thing in the absence of anyone else, while it cannot be with someone else without being *bei* something. But what Dasein is *bei*, and its very *Sein-bei*, is in principle common and shareable with others. *Sein-bei* is not a feeler or a tube that Dasein sends out into the world. 'In Sein-bei and as Dasein, it brings with it from the very first such a thing as a sphere of visibility' (XXVII, 136). Thus 'if a Dasein approaches another Dasein it enters the space of visibility of the other, more precisely their Sein-bei moves in the same sphere of visibility' (XXVII, 134). Even from a distance we recognize a man entering the door of his house; we transport ourselves into his *Sein-bei*, his perspective on the situation (XXVII, 131f.). Again, language is essential for fixing stable objects, 'the one and the same', and language requires, as well as making possible, being with others (HEP, 39/301). *Selbstsein* too both requires and is required by *Mitsein* and *Sein-bei*: I cannot have 'being towards [Sein zu]' myself as myself unless I surmount or TRANSCEND 'myself' (ER, 100). Though *Sein-bei*, *Mitsein* and *Selbstsein* are equiprimordial, they are not separable: each presupposes the others.

'Others' are not to be conceived as alien beings from whom one distinguishes onself: 'the others are rather those from whom one mostly does not distinguish oneself, among whom one is too' (BT, 118). Nor are others undifferentiated 'specimens of the natural scientist's genus homo sapiens'; the *Mitwelt* is 'other people in an entirely definite characterization as student, teacher, relative, superior, etc.' (LX, 11). *Mitsein*, a case of Dasein's 'dispersion [Zerstreuung]', is not based on biological features such as our bodily structure and sexual differentiation; sexual attraction presupposes *Mitsein* rather than explains it, but sex influences the forms that *Mitsein* takes (XXXVI, 174). We can on the basis of *Mitsein* 'put ourselves in another's shoes' (*Sichversetzen*) or emphathize (*Einfühlung*) with them. Whether we can do this with world-impoverished animals, even pets, is a difficult question; we do so in what is, compared with our 'going with [Mitgehen]' other humans, a 'deficient mode' (XXIX, 301f; 307ff.).

between 'Between' is the preposition *zwischen*, related to *zwei*, 'two' and originally 'in between two things'. Heidegger often turns it into a noun, *das Zwischen*, 'the between, what is between, betweenness'. He uses it for the spatial distance between a chair and the wall (BT, 55) and between DASEIN and another entity (BT, 108). More significantly, in considering the view that being-in-the-world is the 'present-at-hand commerce *between* a present-at-hand subject and a present-at-hand object', he suggests that it would be phenomenologically more accurate to say that 'Dasein is the being of this "between"' (BT, 132). This echoes earlier lectures: Dasein is not the world and not a subject; the 'being of Dasein is precisely the "*between*" subject and world. This "between", which does not of course arise from a subject's coming together with a world, is Dasein itself, but again not as a property of a subject! For this reason it is not strictly correct to conceive Dasein as "between", since talk of a "between" subject and world always already presupposes that two entities are given and between them a relation is to obtain' (XX, 346; cf. 379). The 'between' also applies to Dasein's career between birth and death. Dasein does not simply live in each present moment; its 'stretching out' between its beginning and its end colours its whole life: 'The "between" in relation to birth and death already lies in Dasein's very being. [. . .] Factical Dasein exists as born [gebürtig], and as born it is already dying in the sense of being towards death. Both "ends" and their "between" *are*, as long as Dasein factically exists, and they *are* in the only way possible on the basis of Dasein's being as *care*. [. . .] As care Dasein *is* the "between"' (BT, 374).

Heidegger makes ample use of the between later. Sometimes being is the between: 'Beyng, the hearth-fire in the centre of the dwelling of the gods, the dwelling that is also the estrangement of man (the between in which he remains a (the) stranger, precisely when he becomes at home with beings)' (LXV, 487). Beyng is 'the between in whose self-lighting essencing, gods and man re-cognize [er-kennen] each other, i.e. decide about their belonging. As this between beyng "is" no supplement to beings, but that essencer [Wesende] in whose truth (beings) [das (Seiende)] can first reach the safekeeping of a being [eines Seienden]. But this priority of the between must not be misinterpreted idealistically as the "apriori"' (LXV, 428). If 'beyng is conceived as the between into which the gods are coerced, so that it is a need for man, then gods and man cannot be assumed as "given", "present-at-hand". [. . .] Beyng essences as the between for god and man, but in such a way that this space between first grants to god and man their essential possibility, a between that surges over its banks and first lets them arise as banks from this surge, always belonging to the river of the event [Er-eignisses], always hidden in the wealth of its possibilities, always the to and fro of inexhaustible reserves, in whose lighting worlds come together and sink away, earths open up and suffer destruction' (LXV, 476). Sometimes the between is Dasein: 'Da-sein, that between, which, first grounding itself, brings god and man apart and together and fits them to each other' (LXV, 28f.). Da-sein is not identical to man. Man 'stands like a bridge in the between', with one foot in beyng, one foot out (LXV, 488).

In reading Kant's attempt to show how we can know beings that we have not made, we must not focus on the object, or on our experience of it, but realize: '1. that we must always move in the between, between man and thing; 2. that this between only is, when we move in it; 3. that this between does not stretch like a rope from the thing to man, but that this between is an anticipation or fore-conception [Vorgriff], reaching beyond the thing and similarly back behind ourselves' (WT, 188f.).

beyng   *see* DIFFERENCE, ONTOLOGICAL

C

---

care, concern, solicitude Heidegger uses three cognate words: 1. *Sorge*, 'care', is 'properly the anxiety, worry arising out of apprehensions concerning the future and refers as much to the external cause as the inner state' (DGS, 56). The verb *sorgen* is 'to care' in two senses: (a) *sich sorgen um* is 'to worry, be worried about' something; (b) *sorgen für* is 'to take care of, see to, provide (for)' someone or something. 2. *besorgen* has three main senses: (a) 'to get, acquire, provide' something for oneself or someone else; (b) 'to attend to, see to, take care of' something; (c) especially with the perfect participle, *besorgt*, 'to be concerned, troubled, worried' about something. The nominalized infinitive is *das Besorgen*, 'concern' in the sense of 'concerning onself with or about' something. 3. *Fürsorge*, 'solicitude', is 'actively caring for someone who needs help', thus: (a) 'welfare' organized by the state or charitable bodies (cf. BT, 121); (b) 'care, solicitude'.

These three concepts enable Heidegger to distinguish his own view from the view that our attitude towards the world is primarily cognitive and theoretical. Descartes's and Husserl's 'concern for known knowledge' (*Sorge um erkannte Erkenntnis*) is only one type of concern, and not the primary, or a self-evidently appealing, type (XVII, 62; LXIII, 106). But *Sorge* is not specifically practical: it lies deeper than the customary contrast between theory and practice (BT, 193). The concepts are distinct in that *Sorge* pertains to Dasein itself, *Besorgen* to its activities in the world, and *Fürsorge* to its being with others: 'Dasein's basic mode of being is that in its being its very being is at issue. This basic mode of being is conceived as care [Sorge], and this care as Dasein's basic mode of being is just as originally concern [Besorgen], if Dasein is essentially being-in-the-world, and in the same way this basic mode of Dasein's being is solicitude [Fürsorge], so far as Dasein is being-with-one-another' (XXI, 225). Care is the dominant member of the triad but inseparable from the others: 'Concern and solicitude are constitutive of care, so that when we use for short the term 'care' we always strictly mean it, and in our concrete explications understand it, as concerned-solicitous care [besorgend-fürsorgende Sorge], where by care we then mean, in an emphatic sense, that in this concern and solicitude qua care the caring being [das sorgende Sein] itself is at issue' (XXI, 225f.).

The concepts are 'structural concepts', presenting existentials of DASEIN, and must thus be understood in a wide sense. Often Dasein is slipshod and unconcerned, neglectful of others, and uncaring, carefree and careless. But even then Dasein has *Besorgen*, *Fürsorge* and *Sorge*, albeit in a 'deficient mode' (BT, 57): 'If I neglect something, I do not do nothing; I do something, only in the mode of the Not. [. . .] Only where there is care is there neglect' (XXI, 225). (This is a common move in philosophy, not only in Heidegger: usually we regard *some* things as entirely unrelated, but for the logician *any* two things are related in some way or other; even unrelatedness is a sort of relation.)

In BT *Besorgen* is introduced as a general term for Dasein's multifarious dealings with things in the world: 'having to do with something, producing something, [. . .] All these ways of being have concern as their kind of being' (BT, 56f.). In its dealings, concern is guided not by knowledge or explicit rules, but by its informal know-how, by *Umsicht*, 'circumspection', the sort of *Sicht*, 'sight', that is involved in *umsehen*, 'looking around': 'the circumspection of concern is understanding as common sense' (BT, 147). What we mainly deal with in concern is equipment, the READY-TO-HAND, and circumspection is just what we need for this (BT, 69, 121). *Besorgen* begins as a neutral term for Dasein in its 'average everydayness', used to 'highlight Dasein's being as care' (BT, 57). But it ends as an essential feature of the fallen Dasein to which conscience calls: 'The call reaches Dasein in this everyday-averagely concernful [besorgenden] always-already-understanding-itself' (BT, 272; cf. 458ff.). *Besorgen* thus contrasts with care: unlike care, *Besorgen* focuses on the present and on being alongside things within the world (BT, 193).

Fürsorge is for other people, not equipment. There are two types of *Fürsorge*. Inauthentic, 'dominating' *Fürsorge* 'immediately relieves the other of care and in its concern puts itself in the other's place, leaps in for him', while authentic, 'releasing' *Fürsorge* 'attentively leaps ahead of the other, in order from there to give him back care, i.e. himself, his very own Dasein, not take it away' (XXI, 223; cf. BT, 122). Authenticity favours helping others to stand on their own two feet over reducing them to dependency.

Standing on one's own two feet is *Sorge*: 'The expression "care for self" ["Selbstsorge"] by analogy with concern [for equipment, etc.] and solicitude [for others] would be a tautology' (BT, 193; cf. 318). But this, like the claim that Dasein is 'for the sake of itself', means not that Dasein does, or should, act selfishly, but that it does what *it* wills to do, which may well include helping others – even to the extent of reducing them to dependency. Care, rather than the persistence and self-awareness of an I or ego, or the continuity and coherence of experiences, makes Dasein a unified, autonomous self (BT, 318ff.). In care Dasein pulls itself together: 'As care Dasein is the "Between" [birth and death]' (BT, 374). Ontically, I save for a pension because the old man who draws it will be the same person as I am now ('me'); ontologically, he will be the same person as I am now because I am saving for his pension. But *Sorge* also includes *Besorgen* and *Fürsorge*. Thus I might save for someone else's pension, as long as I do not do so much for him that he loses his own care and becomes an appendage of myself.

Care thus unifies Dasein's three central features: existentiality or 'being-ahead-of-itself', facticity or 'being-already-in-a-world', and falling or 'being-alongside' entities within the world (BT, 193, 249). Thus: 'Temporality reveals itself to be the sense of authentic care': existentiality, facticity and falling correspond respectively to the future, past and present (BT, 326).

In BT *Sorge* seems to pertain to Dasein's direction of its own life or 'being'. Later, Heidegger insists that it is 'solely "for the sake of beyng", not the beyng of man, but the beyng of beings as a whole' (LXV, 16; cf. XLIX, 54f.). He speaks in oracular terms of the threefold task of man on the basis of 'Da-sein – care'; '1. the seeker of beyng (event) 2. the true preserver of the truth of being 3. the guardian of the quiet of the passing of the last god' (LXV, 294; cf. 240). Being has moved to the centre and Heidegger's thought is more historical: man must 1. found a culture or a 'world'; 2. preserve it; 3. supervise its decline with dignity.

conscience and guilt   *Conscientia*, 'knowledge [*scientia*] with [*con-*]', is, says Aquinas, the application of knowledge to a particular action. It has three functions: 1. Witnessing: I judge that I have (not) done something morally relevant, e.g. cursed others. 2. Binding and inciting, i.e. prohibiting and commanding: I judge that I ought (not) to do something. 3. Excusing or accusing, tormenting, rebuking: I judge that what I did was (not) done well. (*Summa Theologiae*, 1a, 69, 13). Conscience is not, for Aquinas, a 'voice' or a 'call' (of God), nor does it involve a bifurcation of the self. Conscience is simply practical reasoning about moral matters, and thus as fallible as any other reasoning.

The German *Gewissen* is not directly related to *gewiss*, 'certain', but was a translation of *conscientia*, using *wissen*, 'knowledge', and *ge-*, 'together, with'. Like *conscientia*, it referred initially to function 1 above, the knowledge of what one has or has not done. But Heidegger insists that conscience is not the certainty that one has not done something and is thus not guilty (an 'easy conscience'); he dissociates *Gewissen* from *gewiss* (BT, 291f.). The 'existential interpretation [of conscience] needs to be confirmed by a critique of the way in which conscience is ordinarily interpreted' (BT, 69). The 'ordinary interpretation' differs from Heidegger's in four respects: 1. Conscience has a critical function. 2. It always tells us about a definite deed that has been performed or willed. 3. The 'voice' of conscience has no such radical bearing on DASEIN's being as Heidegger supposes. 4. The basic form of conscience, neglected by Heidegger, is the 'bad' and the 'good' conscience, that which reproves and that which warns (BT, 290). Heidegger strips 'conscience' and 'guilt' of their ethical content in favour of a more fundamental EXISTENTIAL sense: 'Original guilt cannot be defined by morality, since morality already presupposes it for itself' (BT, 286).

Heidegger differs from Aquinas, though not from the 'ordinary interpretation', in supposing conscience to involve a bifurcation of Dasein into a caller and a called. Dasein is two-tiered: I. It is involved in significant worldly affairs under the sway of the THEY. II. It is THROWN naked into a bare, insignificant world in which it is not at home, but feels uncanny. II. explains I: Dasein II's subdued ANGST leads it to 'flee' from itself into level I. II also extricates Dasein from I: naked, homeless Dasein II calls to Dasein I. It calls it to nothing definite: naked Dasein II has nothing definite to say. Thus it does not prescribe a definite course of action, nor does it recommend a permanent state of homeless Angst. It calls on Dasein I to consider its own possibilities, rather than the menu offered by the They, and to choose for itself what to do.

Dasein is essentially guilty (BT, 280ff.), in a sense distinct from, though presupposed by, the theological concept of sin (PT, 64/18f; BT, 306 n.). Dasein is guilty, but Dasein I overlooks, flees, this guilt. Dasein II summons Dasein I to explicit, authentic guilt. *Schuldigsein* and its cognates have four ordinary senses: (a) owing something, having debts; (b) being responsible, to blame, for something; (c) making onself responsible, punishable for, being guilty of (breaking a law); (d) wronging, coming to owe something to, others. Heidegger prefers sense (d), which amounts to: 'Being the ground of a lack in the Dasein of an other, in such a way that this very being a ground determines itself as "lacking" on the basis of that for which it is the ground' (BT, 282). (If I break someone's nose, the broken nose is a lack, and I too am lacking or deficient in view of the lack that I bring about.) We must interpret this not in the usual way, which involves the lack of something present-at- or READY-TO-HAND, but in terms of Dasein's existence, its own existence, not primarily that of others. Existential guilt is thus 'being the ground of a being [Sein] determined by a Not [Nicht, the existential counterpart of a lack of the present-at-hand], i.e. being the ground of a nullity [Nichtigkeit, "Notness"]' (BT, 283). We then look to see if, in what we have so far seen Dasein to be, we can find anything corresponding to this abstract definition.

Heidegger finds such guilt in the tripartite structure of Dasein's CARE: A. thrownness, B. existence and C. FALLING. A involves Notness: Dasein is not in charge of its own entry into the world or the situation in which it finds itself; it does not decide where to start from or whether to start at all. Thrown Dasein is the ground of B and C. B also involves Notness: Dasein has to exist, to make its thrownness the ground of a PROJECTION of its possibilities; but it has no intrinsic nature, rules, or tracks to guide it; Dasein is sheer possibility, intrinsically naked and homeless, so its project is 'null'. Moreover, existence involves rejecting some possibilities in favour of others. A, that is Dasein II, grounds C, the fall from itself into Dasein I: if Dasein were not at bottom guilty and otherwise distressed, it could not fall from this condition nor have any reason to flee from it. In C Dasein takes refuge in the They and forgets about its essential guilt and its various nullities.

Later, Heidegger still speaks of the call, especially the silent call (*Ruf, Zuruf*, etc.): the call of beyng (LXV, 384.), the call of men, gods, earth and world to each other (EHP, 177), the call to us of poetry (OWL, 21ff./ plt, 198f.) and the call involved in naming things (EHP, 188; WCT, 151ff./ 123ff.). But conscience and guilt play little part in Heidegger's work after BT.

Contributions to Philosophy (Of the Event) *Beiträge zur Philosophie (Vom Ereignis)* (LXV) was written between 1936 and 1938. It was first published in 1989 as volume 65 of Heidegger's collected works. It was composed while he was lecturing on Nietzsche and is not unlike Nietzsche's posthumous notebooks, *The Will to Power*, in style and structure. But it is Hölderlin rather than Nietzsche who dominates the work. At times philosophy itself is seen as a preparation for Hölderlin: 'The historical destiny of philosophy culminates in knowledge of the necessity of giving a hearing to Hölderlin's word' (LXV, 422). Hölderlin attains an almost Christ-like stature: 'On what support [. . .] does the conjecture rest, that the impulse of beyng may have already cast a first tremor into our history? Again on a unique fact: that Hölderlin had to become the sayer [Sagende] that he is' (LXV, 485). Many of the central ideas in LXV – earth, gods, etc. – stem from Hölderlin.

LXV has eight parts, each containing sections numbered continuously through the work. Part I is *Vorblick*, 'Preview'. It opens with a complaint that all 'basic words' have become threadbare, so that we have to make do with a bland 'public' title such as 'Contributions to Philosophy'. The real title is 'Of the Event': we are to be 'handed over [übereignet] to the event [Er-eignis], which amounts to an essential change of man from the "rational animal" [. . .] into Da-sein' (LXV, 3). However, the public title expresses the fact that LXV is not a definitive work, but the best that can be expected' in the age of transition from metaphysics to the thinking of the history of beyng [seynsgeschichtliche Denken]' 'an attempt to think from the more original starting-point in the question about the truth of beyng' (LXV, 3). Heidegger conceives LXV as a transition from the 'fundamental ontology' of BT to the HISTORY OF BEING characteristic of his later works.

The Preview explains the structure of LXV outlining six parts, besides the Preview itself: Part II, *Der Anklang*, 'The Echo', refers to the echo of beyng in our present condition of 'abandonment of being'. Part III, *Das Zuspiel*, 'The Pass', invokes the idea of 'playing [Spiel]' or 'passing' a ball 'to [zu]' another player. We study the 'first beginning' instated by the Greeks in order to prepare for the 'other beginning' at some indeterminate future time. Conversely, our preparation for the other beginning enables us to understand the Greeks. Thus the first and the other beginning are like players co-operating by passing a ball to each other. Part IV, *Der Sprung*, is 'The Leap' into beyng. Part V, *Die Gründung*, is 'The Grounding' of the truth of beyng. Part VI, *Die Zu-künftigen*, 'The Future Ones [Zukünftigen]' or 'The Ones to Come [Zu-künftigen]', are those who will bring about the other beginning, thinkers, but not only thinkers; 'thinking is only *one* way in which Few leap forth the leap into beyng' (LXV, 395). Part VII is *Der letzte Gott*, 'The Last God', who is 'quite different from former gods, especially the Christian god' (LXV, 403). This god is not the last god of the first beginning, but the god appropriate to the other beginning: 'The last god is not the end, but the other beginning of immeasurable possibilities of our history' (LXV, 411). LXV concludes with Part VIII, *Das Seyn*, 'Beyng'; it was Part II in Heidegger's original arrangement, but since he indicated that this was the wrong place for it, in LXV it is moved to the end.

Heidegger says that though LXV is not a SYSTEM, Parts II–VII are 'joinings of the joint [Fügungen der Fuge]', coherently connected with each other. It is difficult to discern a firm plan in LXV, especially since the sections within a Part often have no clear connection with the title of the Part. It is tempting to regard LXV as blocks of stone in a quarry, whose relationships are not apparent (cf. LXV, 421, 436). Certain themes run through the book. It reveals religious yearning, and growing hostility to Nazism, which, though not mentioned by name, is unmistakably included in his denunciations of gigantomania (e.g. LXV, 441ff.) and of racism (e.g. LXV, 18f.). In LXV Heidegger worked out ideas that reappear in later writings, such as LH. The difficulties it presents are in turn often eased by other writings and lectures, such as XLV.

D

dasein Mark Twain complained that some German words seem to mean everything. One such word is *da*. It means 'there' ('There they go') and 'here' ('Here they come'), as well as 'then', 'since', etc. Prefixed to *sein*, 'to be' it forms *dasein*, 'to be there, present, available, to exist'. In the seventeenth century the infinitive was nominalized as (*das*) *Dasein*, originally in the sense of 'presence'. In the eighteenth century *Dasein* came to be used by philosophers as an alternative to the latinate *Existenz* ('the existence of God'), and poets used it in the sense of 'life'. Darwin's 'struggle for survival' became in German *der Kampf ums Dasein*. Colloquially it is used for the being or life of persons. (*Dasein* in Heidegger is quite distinct from *Dass-sein*, 'that-being' (XXVI, 183, 228f.).)

In early lectures Heidegger often uses *Leben*, 'life', in speaking of human beings and their being, but *Dasein* occurs in the BT sense in 1923 (LXIII, 7; XVII, 3, but here he still speaks of the *Dasein* of the world, 42). In BT he uses (*das*) *Dasein* for 1. the being of humans, and 2. the entity or person who has this being. In lectures he often speaks of *das menschliche Dasein*, 'human Dasein', and this too can mean either the being of humans or the human being (e.g. XXIV, 21). As a nominalized infinitive, *Dasein* has no plural. It refers to any and every human being, in much the way that *das Seiende*, lit. 'that which is', refers to any and every BEING. When more than one person is in play Heidegger speaks of (the) other(s) or Dasein-with (*Mitdasein*). He revives the original sense, 'being there', often writing *Da-sein* to stress this. *Dasein* is essentially in the WORLD, and lights up itself and the world. The 'There [das Da]' is the space it opens up and illuminates: 'The "There [Das 'Da']" is not a place [...] in contrast to an "over there" ['dort']; Da-sein means not being here instead of over there, nor here and over there, but is the possibility, the condition of oriented being here and being over there' (XXVII, 136). Later, *Da-sein* sometimes means not 'being there', but 'there where being dwells', when it arrives: 'This Where as the There of the abode belongs to being itself, "is" being itself and is thus called Da-sein' (NII, 358/niv, 218).

In BT every man, however inauthentic, is Dasein. 'Man' (*Mensch*) includes women: *Dasein*, though neuter, is sexually differentiated in virtue of the body; sexual relations depend on its original BEING-WITH; we can only understand sex if we first understand Dasein in its neutrality (XXVI, 173ff; XXVII, 146f.). Children and early man are to be understood 'in a privative way', by noting how they fall short of fully fledged Dasein (XXVII, 123ff.). Heidegger often uses *Mensch* in lectures, but avoids it in BT: it presents us as one biological species among others, the 'rational animal', and neglects our peculiar understanding of being. For this reason, he invariably distinguishes his own 'analytic of Dasein' from 'philosophical anthropology', which 'is no longer a fashion but an epidemic' (XXXI, 122; cf. BT, 45ff; K, 205ff./140ff.). *Dasein* unifies man, avoiding the traditional tripartition into body, soul (*Seele*, the life principle) and spirit (*Geist*, the intellectual principle) (BT, 48). It does not locate man's essence in some specific faculty such as reason: one of Dasein's central features, along with THROWNNESS and FALLING, is EXISTENCE, and this means that it has to decide how to be, and is not essentially and inevitably rational. Since *Dasein* exists and is not PRESENT-AT-HAND, it is inappropriate to ask 'what' it is; we should ask 'who' it is, and the answer will depend on, even consist in *Dasein*'s decision: it may be 'I myself' or it may be 'the Nobody to whom every Dasein has already surrendered itself in being among one another' (BT, 128; cf. BT, 45; XXXIX, 57f: 'Whatever one constantly takes part in, practises [e.g. teaching], determines *what* he is [e.g. a teacher]. But if we know *what* we are, do we thereby know *who* we are? No.').

Dasein is 'in each case mine. [. . .] one must always use a personal pronoun when addressing it: "I am", "you are"' (BT, 42). Every man is 'for the sake of himself, [. . .] his own end, as Kant says. This "For the sake of himself" constitutes the self as such' (XXVII, 324; cf. BT, 84, 147). The significance of the world is underpinned by *Dasein*'s needs and purposes. Is *Dasein* an isolated, egotistical individual? ONTOLOGICALLY yes, ONTICALLY no: *Dasein*'s neutrality 'means a peculiar isolation of man, but not in the factual, existentiell sense, as if the philosopher were the centre of the world; it is the *metaphysical isolation* of man' (XXVI, 172). Only because *Dasein* is 'in its metaphysical essence determined by selfhood, can it as a concrete entity expressly choose itself as self' or 'forgo this choice' (XXVI, 244). 'This selfhood is its freedom, and freedom is the egoity [Egoität] which first enables Dasein to be either egoistic or altruistic' (XXVI, 24). It does not help to introduce the I-Thou relation. This would only replace an individual solipsism by a 'solipsism of a couple' (XXVII, 146; cf. XXVI, 241f.). Dasein's egoity lies deeper than this contrast; *Dasein* functions both as I and as you. Because *Dasein* is always 'mine', it is not an instance of a genus in the way that a present-at-hand entity is (BT, 42; cf. LX, 11).

Later, man is distinguished more sharply from *Dasein*. *Da-sein* is not man, but a relationship to being that man acquires and may lose. Man may be simply a SUBJECT or a rational animal (LXV, 62; XLIX, 36). Moreover *Da-sein* is 'between' man and the gods rather than coincident with man himself (LXV, 28f., 31). 'Da-sein exists for the sake of itself', but this now means that it exists for the sake of being, since it is essentially 'guardianship' of being (LXV, 302). It is now man, rather than *Da-sein*, that should not be viewed as an instance of a genus (LXV, 61); we ask 'who' we are or who man is (LXV, 438ff.), not who *Da-sein* is. *Da-sein* has become too impersonal to allow such questions (but cf. LXV, 303). Heidegger assigns the two senses of *Dasein*, the traditional and his own, respectively to the 'first' and the 'other' beginning (LXV, 295ff.).

The later divergence from BT should not be exaggerated. In BT *Dasein* transcends to world: 'But if it is the world, in surmounting to which selfhood first ripens, then the world proves to be that for the sake of which Dasein exists' (ER, 84). *Dasein* may stand in the centre of things, but it is itself 'ecstatic, i.e. eccentric' (ER 98 n.59; XXVII, 11). BT is no more *anthropo*centric than Heidegger's later work.

death and dying   'Death' is *Tod*, 'to die' is *sterben*. *Sterben* is distinct from *ableben, (das) Ableben*, '(to) demise', biological death or dying which '*as an event that occurs is "only" empirically certain*' (BT, 257). Scheler, who anticipated several Heideggerian ideas (such as our tendency, intensified by modern capitalism, to conceal death), argued that one's non-empirical certainty of one's own death stems from the observation that the range of possibilities open to one narrows as one's life advances and seems to converge on the limit of a single possibility, if not to vanish altogether (Scheler (1979), 18ff.). The progressive contraction of my range of options is inferred (it might be objected) from empirical observation, and it depends on my mortality. If eternal youth were granted to me, I could become a general or an actor – options which are now denied to me by the ageing and mortality known to me in other ways. Heidegger presents no such arguments for the non-empirical certainty of death. He assumes that an endless life would be unmanageable and care-less, with no way of deciding what to do or when to do it. He focuses almost exclusively on one's *own* death; even time ends with one's own death (BT, 330f.), a claim hard to reconcile with our essential being-with others – who are unlikely all to die at the same time as oneself. It is, he says, certain that I shall die. It is uncertain when I shall die. I may die at any moment. I cannot do anything after my death. No-one else can die for me. I shall die alone. This is not to deny the soldierly comradeship induced by imminent death: 'The very death, which each individual man must die for himself, which reduces each individual to his own uttermost individuality, this very death and readiness for the sacrifice it demands creates first of all the preliminary communal space from which comradeship springs'. Comradeship springs from Angst, from 'the metaphysical nearness to the unconditioned granted only to the highest self-reliance and readiness' (XXXIX, 73). This is a case of authentic 'being towards death', *Sein zum Tode*, an expression formed by analogy with *Wille zum Tode*, 'will to death', but covering any attitude one might have to one's own death, inauthentic (e.g. denying, forgetting, fearing, dwelling on it, suicide, etc.) as well as authentic.

'But death *is*, as pertaining to Dasein, only in an existentiell *being towards death*' (BT, 234). Heidegger calls this 'dying': 'Let Sterben be the term for the *mode of being [Seinsweise]* in which Dasein *is towards* its death [. . .] Dasein does not first die, or does not really die at all, with and in the experience of factical demise' (BT, 247). What matters is not physical demise, but one's attitude to one's death during life. The 'authentic' attitude is 'running ahead [Vorlaufen]': this '*reveals to Dasein its lostness in the They-self [Man-selbst] and confronts it with the possibility – not primarily supported by concernful solicitude – of being itself, but itself in impassioned freedom towards death [Freiheit zum Tode], released from the illusions of the They, factical, certain of itself and anxious [sich ängstenden]*' (BT, 266). *Freiheit zum Tode* is freedom to die one's *own* death, uninfluenced by what others say, do or think. The idea appears in Rilke: 'O Lord, give to each his own death, / The dying that comes from the life, / In which he had love, sense and want./ For we are just the husk and the leaf./ The great death that each has in himself, / That is the fruit, around which all revolves' (quoted by Rose, 56). *Vorlaufen* frees one not only for death, but also for possibilities before death, my own possibilities, not everyday trivia or the menu offered to me by the They (BT, 264). It makes one a complete, self-contained person.

Heidegger's preoccupation with death does not survive the BT period (cf. XX, 403ff; XXI, 361f. and K, 93/63f. on the interpretation of a death-mask). He corrects misinterpretations of BT's account of death and tries to show its continuing relevance. BT did not advocate obsession with death (XXIX, 425ff.). It treats death not 'anthropologically' or in terms of a 'world-view', but 'fundamental-ontologically'. It does not affirm nihilism or the senselessness of being. Running ahead to death opens us up to being: 'death is the highest and uttermost testimony of beyng' (LXV, 284). BT tried 'to draw death into Dasein, in order to master Dasein in its fathomless range and so to fully measure the ground of the possibility of the truth of beyng'. But 'not everyone need perform this beyng towards death and assume the Self of Dasein in this authenticity; this performance is necessary only in connection with the task of laying the ground for the question about beyng, a task which is of course not confined to philosophy. The performance of being towards death is a duty only for the thinkers of the other beginning, but every essential man among the future creators can know of it' (LXV, 285). In BT running ahead to death primarily secures the integrity and self-constancy of individual Dasein, pertaining only indirectly to the question about being. Later, it reveals being, but only philosophers and others involved in the preparation of a 'new beginning' need bother about it. Both in BT and later, it is clear that philosophers need the detachment from 'everydayness' and the They induced by *Vorlaufen*. It is less clear how it reveals being. Heidegger suggests a 'correspondence' between death and being: 'To the extraordinariness of beyng there corresponds, in the realm in which its truth is grounded, i.e. in Da-sein, the uniqueness of death. [. . .] Only man "has" the distinction of standing before death, since man is insistent [inständig] in beyng' (LXV, 230). Many things besides death are, however, peculiar to man. But 'being towards death [. . .] harbours two basic features of the fissuring [of beyng into earth, world, etc.] and is its mostly unrecognized reflection in the There': 1. negation, 'the Not [Nicht] essentially belongs to being as such'; 2. the 'unfathomable full-bodied "necessity"' of death mirrors the necessity of the fissuring of being (LXV, 282; cf. 324). Death has lost its close link with time: Heidegger is now more interested in long historical time-spans than in the time of the individual (cf. LXV, 324f.). In a later seminar he and Fink gave thought to the significance of death in Heraclitus (XV, 92f./64f, etc.).

difference, ontological The expression *die ontologische Differenz* was first introduced in 1927, to mark the distinction between (BEING *(das) Sein*) and beings or entities *(das Seiende)* (XXIV, 22). The distinction, though not this title for it, is central to BT: 'Being and the structure of being lie beyond every entity and every feature of an entity that there can possibly be. Being is the *transcendens* pure and simple' (BT, 38). The word *Differenz*, from the Latin *differre* (lit. 'to carry apart'), implies that 'beings and being are somehow carried apart from each other, separated and yet related to each other, – and of their own accord, not just on the basis of an "act" of "distinguishing" ['Unterscheidung']" (NII, 209/niv, 155). However, Heidegger often speaks too of the *Unterscheidung* of being and beings. In its literal sense, *differre* is close to the German *austragen*, 'to carry out, deliver, deal with, settle'. *Austrag* is 'settlement, resolution [e.g. of a dispute]'. Hence the *Differenz* of being and beings is also an *Austrag* of them, bringing them together as well as keeping them apart (cf. ID, 63ff./65ff.).

If we knew only of beings, having no understanding of being, we could not relate to or 'comport ourselves' to beings as such. We would, like animals, be affected by beings (XXIX, 273ff.), but we would not be aware of them as beings. To take an analogy: I am presented with things of various colours. Some are of the same colour, 'alike' (*gleich*). I can see red things, green things, and so on. If I see two things of the same colour I may be affected by and respond to them in a distinctive way. But I cannot see them *as alike* in colour unless I have an apriori understanding of *likeness (Gleichheit)* (NII, 214ff./niv, 159ff.).

Is 'being', then, on a par with any other universal or general term? If I cannot see things as alike without an understanding of likeness, or trees as trees without a prior understanding of 'treeness', why is the ontological difference of more significance than the distinction between any general concept and its instances? Being is more fundamental and pervasive than likeness, treeness or redness. Everything, apart from being itself, is a being; anything that is red, a tree or like something else must already *be*. Moreover, beings (unlike trees, red things or similar things) form a whole or a WORLD. Our ability to regard anything as anything, and locate it or ourselves in the world, depends on our understanding of being: 'In every silent comportment to beings too the "is" speaks' (NII, 247/niv, 188f).

The difference between being and beings seems obvious, yet philosophers have tended to obliterate it. They have done so in at least four ways, each involving the elimination or demotion of being in favour of beings:

1. They have represented being as itself a being or entity, usually the supreme being, God. This refers to medieval theologians, above all Aquinas, who regarded God as identical to his own being (*esse*), as something like pure being.
2. They regard being as an empty universal, derived by our abstraction from beings themselves.
3. They regard being as a definite property, alongside other properties of a thing – properties which are in being (*seiend*) as much as the things to which they belong (WMP, 304/384). Being has been equated, for example, with materiality and with perceptibility. But this overrides, firstly, the diversity of being and of our uses of the verb 'to

be' (both at any given time and over history): it is analogous to the 'naturalistic fallacy', to attempts to reduce our similarly diverse and pervasive concept of goodness to a single, simple feature, such as (production of) pleasure. Secondly, it ignores the fact that beings form a whole or world, which can never be constructed from the properties of each being taken separately.

4. They have taken some one entity or type of entity, most commonly man himself, as the paradigm or standard for being in general (LXV, 235, 271, 286, 477; NI, 462/nii, 196f.). 'Being' Heidegger insists, 'is no entity, no thing and no thingly property, nothing PRESENT-AT-HAND' (XXIX, 470; cf. LXV, 286). Being is often contrasted not with beings, but with becoming (Plato, Nietzsche), appearance, thinking and values or the 'ought'. The contrasts tend to restrict the range of being to what is constantly PRESENT, in contrast to the fleeting, illusory or unrealised (IM, 154/169). This is no accident; it is an essential feature of being itself that it lends itself to precisely these contrasts. But they are not to be accepted. For being extends to whatever is supposed to contrast with it. Becoming, appearance, thinking and value – all of these *are*.

Where does the boundary lie between being and beings? Understanding of being, however tacit and deficient, is involved in all our everyday dealings with beings. We never encounter, with no understanding of being, sheer beings, the beings that affect animals or that existed before the emergence of conscience life. Nevertheless there are three questions that we can ask about being:

1. The 'basic question' (*Grundfrage*. XXXI, 203; NI, 13/ni, 4): 'What is (the sense, essence or truth of) being?' This question has been 'forgotten' (BT, 2). (AT XXXI, 73, the *Grundfrage* concerns the connection between being and time.)

2. The 'guiding question' (*Leitfrage*. NI, 13/ni, 4. Cf. XXXI, 73, 203): 'What are beings (as such)?' Philosophers have asked this question. Nietzsche held, in Heidegger's account, that the essence or What-being of beings is 'will to power', while their existence or That-being is 'eternal recurrence of the same' (e.g. NII, 259/niii, 189). In more recent and degenerate times many philosophers have ceased to ask even question 2, confining themselves to 'theory of knowledge', the foundations of knowledge and science.

3. The 'transitional question' (*Übergangsfrage*. LXV, 509): 'Why are there

beings at all rather than nothing?' This was asked by Leibniz and Schelling.

Any answer to 2 must involve some view about the being of beings. For example, 'All beings are material' implies that *being* is materiality. But Heidegger will not allow this to undermine the distinction between questions 1 and 2. He reformulates question 2 as 'What is the being of beings?' or 'What is the beingness (*Seiendheit*) of beings?' (XXXI, 47; NI, 634/niii, 139). This is quite distinct from question 1, now reformulated as 'What is the truth (or essence) of being?' In later works, he often writes '*Seyn*', instead of '*Sein*', an archaic form ('beyng') intended to differentiate Heidegger's being or beyng ever more sharply from the beings and being discussed by other philosophers. He speaks of 'beyng [das Seyn] as the prevailing distinction of being and beings' (ET, 198/137). The ontological difference is now regarded as a subordinate, 'transitional' distinction between being and beings, which is somehow generated by the simple, unique and incomparable beyng (LXV, 471).

The distinction between being and beingness perhaps echoes Aquinas's distinction between *esse* as the *actus essendi* 'act of being', and *esse* as the 'mental uniting of predicate to subject in a proposition' (*Summa Theologiae*, Ia, 3, 4).

49

E

earth, world, gods, man   In BT the poles of Heidegger's universe are man (DASEIN) and world. Earth, *Erde*, and god(s) are absent. Earlier, earth made a brief appearance as the support of our dwellings, but 'earth as nature' is within the world, not counterposed to it (XX, 269f.). In the mid-1930s, under the influence of Hölderlin and of technology, Heidegger revived the concept of earth, but now as the counterpart to world. World and earth are in conflict. A world of human products and activities is established by taming and utilizing the earth on which it rests. The earth fights back, overgrowing, destroying and reclaiming our works if we do not tend and protect them. Earth and world need each other. The world rests on earth and uses earthy raw materials. Earth is revealed as earth by the world. A temple reveals the rock on which it rests, the storm that buffets it, and the stone of which it is made (OWA, 30ff./167ff.). This quasi-Hegelian conflict constitutes and sustains the combatants. Heidegger appeals not to Hegel, but to Heraclitus: 'War is father of all, yet king of all, and it showed some as gods, others as men, made some slaves, others free' (quote XXXIX, 125; OWA, 32/169; IM, 47/51, with Heideggers's own free translations). He also speaks of a *Riss*, 'rift, cleft', between earth and world. *Riss* is chosen because its compounds *Umriss, Aufriss* and *Grundriss* mean 'contour(s), outline', 'elevation, outline' and 'sketch, outline, ground plan'. The rift between earth and world defines their contours and establishes a ground plan of human life: the rift 'is a ground plan. It is an out-line [*Auf-riss* = 1. 'breaking open', 2. as *Aufriss*, 'elevation, outline'], which draws the basic features [*Grundzüge*] of the rise of the lighting of beings. This rift does not let the opponents break apart; it brings what opposes measure and limit into the unitary outline [*Umriss*]' (OWA, 51/189).

Gods hardly appear in OWA; man is the sole beneficiary of the earth–world conflict. But in the same period, again under Hölderlin's influence, Heidegger introduces the contrasting dyad, men and gods (cf. XXXIX, 47f., 93ff.). They are related not by *Streit*, 'conflict', but by *Ent-gegnung*

(LXV, 477ff.). This comes from *gegen*, 'against, towards' and a verb *gegenen*, 'to come towards, approach, meet', which survives only in compounds. One of these is *entgegnen*, once 'to come towards, stand opposite, confront', but now 'to reply, retort'. Heidegger hyphenates *Entgegnung*, 'reply, retort', thus reviving the idea of opposition and encounter – not in an exclusively hostile sense – while retaining the idea of gods and men answering each other's call. He speaks of 'gods' owing to his love of ancient Greece and of nature – once the abode of the gods, but now being destroyed by technology (LXV, 277). But he disavows any definite view on the number of gods (LXV, 411, 437). Gods are intimately connected with man's conception of himself. When man regards himself as an 'extant "specimen" of the genus "human being"' he has no 'claim to a coming of the god, not even a claim to the experience of the flight of the gods. This very experience presupposes that the historical human being is aware of himself as transported into the open centre of beings which are abandoned by the truth of their being' (LXV, 61). Man has no need of gods if he sees himself as just one animal species among others, only if he is conscious of his peculiar finitude as a being aware of beings as a whole. Man and gods arise together from beyng, like the banks formed by the surge of the river between them (LXV, 476).

There are then four items that emerge from the EVENT: world, earth, gods, men (LXV, 310). Heidegger often speaks of the event as a *Zerklüftung* or *Erklüftung*, a 'fissuring (forth)' of beyng, or as a *Sprengung*, an 'explosion, eruption' – a big bang that sends fragments off in four directions, with beyng as their 'Between' (LXV, 311, 400, 485). He also speaks of the truth of beyng as a fire that needs god and man to keep it alight. We cannot know how often the fire has burnt out before. 'If we knew this it would not be necessary to think beyng in the uniqueness of its essence' (LXV, 488).

The *Geviert*, the 'fourfold, square', outlasts Heidegger's interest in speculative history. Later, the four items are: earth, sky, divinities and mortals (D, 165f./173). The 'world' is now 'the eventful mirror-play [ereignende Spiegel-Spiel] of the simplicity' of all four items (D, 172/179). A *Ding*, 'thing', such as a jug, a bridge or a cricket-bat, lies at the intersection of the fourfold. The bat is planted on the earth beneath a sky that sheds light and warmth; the weather is a godsend; the success of the stroke is in the lap of the gods. 'The simplicity in which all essencing has gathered must be found again in each being, no – each being must be found in the simplicity. But we attain that simplicity only if we keep the being, each thing, in the free play [Spielraum] of its mystery and do not think to seize beyng by analysis of our already firm acquaintance with its

51

properties' (LXV, 278f.). When Heidegger writes *das S̶e̶i̶n̶*, 'b̶e̶i̶n̶g̶', to indicate that being is not an object for man nor the whole subject-object relation, the crossing out also 'points to the four regions [Gegenden] of the fourfold and their gathering at the place of the intersection' (QB, 83).

The fourfold is a riposte to Hegel's triangle and triads. It is also harks back to the spatial regions of BT.

essence *Wesen* is the 'essence, inner nature or principle' of a thing. 'Used alone it means "the quintessence of a thing", "its basic nature", "its essential nature", "inner being" [...] But it can also mean the way this essence manifests itself outwardly' (DGS, 394). It is the nominalization of the defunct verb *wesen*, 'to be, stay, last, happen', and originally meant 'dwelling, stay, life, way of being, etc.' It generated *wesentlich* and the less usual *wesenhaft*, 'essential'. The verb *wesen* also supplies the perfect participle, *gewesen*, of *sein*, 'to be', and survives in compounds: *anwesend* ('present') and *abwesend* ('absent'). *Verwesen; Verwesung*, 'to decay, rot; decay', are only remotely related to *wesen*, though Heidegger exploits their similarity to it (LXV, 115, 348). (*Verweser*, 'manager, administrator, one who stands in for [*ver-*] someone else', is closer to *wesen*.) *Unwesen*, lit. 'unessence', means 'bad state of affairs, problem' of e.g. drug addiction. The phrase *sein Unwesen treiben*, lit. 'to drive its unessence' means 'to walk abroad, make a nuisance of itself, etc.', and is almost synonymous with *sein Wesen treiben*, lit. 'to drive its essence', hence 'to be abroad, up to its tricks, etc.' By contrast, *unwesentlich* means 'inessential, irrelevant'.

The Greek *ousia* can mean 'essence', but Heidegger associates *Wesen* with Aristotle's expression *to ti ēn einai*, 'essence, lit. the what [it] was to be', which, like *Wesen*, has to do with the past. He explains it as meaning what a thing was, or has been, before it is actualized, and also what we understand 'earlier', already or apriori about something (XXIV, 120, Cf. BT, 441, marginal note b to 85). The Latin *essentia* invariably contrasts with *existentia*; they refer respectively to the What-being and the How-being of something (XXIV, 124).

(*Das*) *Wesen* is rare in BT, and usually equivalent to the Latinate *Essenz* (BT, 117). BT speaks of the *Wesensverfassung*, 'essential constitution' (BT, 8) and *Wesensbestimmung*, 'essential determination' (BT, 12) of DASEIN. *Wesen* is applied twice to Dasein: 'The "essence" ['Wesen'] of this being lies in its To-be [Zu-sein]. [...] The "essence" of Dasein lies in its existence' (BT, 42). But it is not applied to *Sein*, 'being': 'There is no "essence of being", since being-an-essence [Wesen-sein] is itself a mode of being' (Scheler (1976), 285). The verb *wesen* occurs in the past tense in the coinages *gewesend(e)*, 'in the course of having been', and *Gewesenheit*, 'having-beenness' (BT, 326).

In other works *Wesen* is often used in the non-verbal sense of 'essence'. In 'clarifying the essence' (*Wesenserhellung*) of e.g. freedom we determine three things: 1. its What-being, what freedom is; 2. the inner possibility of the What-being, how it is intrinsically possible; 3. the ground of this inner possibility (XXXI, 12, 179). This is more than an analysis of the concept of freedom or of the meaning of the word 'freedom': it involves our transcendence to a world. The essence of truth changes over history, though there is a persistent core that preserves the identity of the essence (NI, 173f./ni, 147f.). And 'not only the essence of truth, but the essence of everything essential has a wealth of its own, from which each historical age can only ever draw a little as its share' (LIV, 15). A significant statement of the essence of e.g. poetry is a persuasive definition of an essentially contested concept: it 'forces us to a decision, whether and how we take poetry seriously in future' (HEP, 34/294). The new definition should be in tune with the age: 'The essence of poetry that Hölderlin establishes is historical to the highest degree, since it anticipates a historical time. But being a historical essence it is the uniquely essential essence' (HEP, 47/313f.).

Owing in part to the historicality of essences, Heidegger also uses *Wesen* in a verbal sense, linking it directly to the verb *wesen* and coining the explicitly verbal *Wesung*, 'essencing'. Another reason for this innovation is the unsuitability of the non-verbal *Wesen* for the question about being. 'If we ask about the "essence" in the usual sense of the question, the question is about what "makes" a being what it is, thus about what makes up its What-being, about the beingness of beings. Essence is here just another word for being (in the sense of beingness). And accordingly *Wesung* means the event, so far as it happens [sich . . . ereignet] in what belongs to it, truth. Happening [Geschehnis] of the truth of beyng, that is *Wesung*' (LXV, 288, Cf. NII, 344ff./niv, 206ff.). *Wesung*, an original unity of What- and How-being, belongs only to being and to truth (LXV, 289). '*Wesung* means the way in which beyng itself is, namely beyng' (LXV, 484). Beyng neither has nor is a non-verbal essence. Like Plato's idea of the good or Aquinas's God, it confers essences on beings by the light it sheds on them. It *is* not; it 'essences [west]' (LXV, 286).

'Even our words Hauswesen, Staatswesen', Heidegger says later, 'mean not the universal of a genus, but the way in which house and state work [walten], are managed, develop and decline. It is the way in which they wesen. [. . .] "Wesen", in the verbal sense, is the same as "lasting" [währen]

(QT, 34/30). Often it is hard to tell whether *Wesen* is used verbally or not, even in titles (ET, ER). Sometimes it is used in both ways in close proximity. 'The essence of language: the language of essence [des Wesens]': here, Heidegger explains, *Wesen* is non-verbal in its first occurrence, verbal in its second (OWL, 200f.94f.).

Heidegger often uses *Unwesen* and *Un-wesen*. They have, he explains, two senses: 1. the 'pre-essencing essence [vor-wesende Wesen]' before it lapses into the non-verbal essence, the universal; 2. the disfigurement of the already degenerate essence into something even worse. In both senses *Unwesen* is essential to the *Wesen*, not *unwesentlich* (ET, 191/130f.). Sense 2 of *Unwesen*, Heidegger's usual sense, has two applications, corresponding to two ways in which a *Wesen* can degenerate: (a) The *Unwesen* of truth is untruth in the sense both of 'concealing' (or the 'illusion of showmanship', LXV, 347f. and of 'errancy' or going astray (ET, 191/130, 193/132). (b) The *Unwesen* of truth is a degenerate concept of truth: 'correctness' (LXV, 228) or 'reason' and the rational (LXV, 343). The two degenerations are connected: the degeneration of the concept of truth is itself a crucial 'errancy'.

When Heidegger speaks of the *Unwesen* of a *Wesen*, he usually has in mind an application of type (b). To think of being as a 'value' is to think of it 'in its Unwesen' (NII, 55/niv, 23). The 'inauthenticity of nihilism lies in its essence. [. . .] The Unwesen belongs to the Wesen' (NII, 362/niv, 220f.). That is, 1. earlier phases of nihilism such as the 'devaluation of the current highest values [. . .] do not exhaust its essence' (NII, 276/niii, 204), but are nevertheless essential to the long historical process by which nihilism 'enters into its own essence' (NII, 282/niii, 208); 2. since we are ourselves entangled in nihilism, it is essential to nihilism that its essential nature elude us (QB, 383f.). Even CARE has its *Unwesen*: it is not 'gloom and apprehension and agonized distress about this and that. All this is just the Unwesen of care' (LXV, 35).

event, happening, occurrence   1. The most general term for an event is *Ereignis*, from *sich ereignen*, 'to happen, occur'. The words come from *Auge*, 'eye', and were until the eighteenth century spelt *Eräugnis, eräugnen*, lit. 'placing/to place before the eye, becoming/to become visible' – as Heidegger knew (OWL, 260/129). Heidegger also uses, *Ereignung (Eräugnung)*, 'event(uating)', which is similar to *Ereignis*, but more verbal. The words became associated with *(sich) eignen*, 'to be suitable, belong', *aneignen*, 'to appropriate', and *eigen*, '(one's) own', since some dialects pronounced *äu* as *ei*. 2. *Begebenheit*, 'event', comes from *begeben*, 'to issue, put [coins, etc.] in circulation' and *sich begeben*, 'to betake oneself; expose oneself [to danger]; to come to pass'. It is 'often, but not necessarily, something out of the ordinary' (DGS, 110). 3. *Vorgang*, from *vorgehen*, 'to proceed, go on, happen', is 'something changing, evolving, a process. The plural is used of a vague, undefined series of happenings. It thus contrasts with the specific term *Ereignis*' (DGS, 111). 4. *Geschehnis*, 'event, incident, happening', is from *geschehen*, originally 'to hurry, rush on, run', but now 'to happen'. It is 'the most abstract term for "happening". Its use is confined to the written word' (DGS, 111). The nominalized infinitive is also used for 'happening(s), event(s)'. 5. *Vorkommnis(se)*, 'occurrence(s)', from *vorkommen*, 'to come forth, occur, etc.', is a 'happening that concerns a person' (DGS, 111).

Heidegger applies *Vorgang* and *Vorkommnis(se)* to PRESENT-AT-HAND, usually natural events. It is misleading to assimilate different types of event – the warming of a stone, an animal's seeing and grasping – under the heading of *Vorgang* in the sense of a sequence of *Vorkommnisse*. Animals engage in behaviour (*Benehmen*), stones do not (XXIX, 344f.). Early on he distinguishes *Vorgang* from *Ereignis*. An experience is not a *Vorgang*, an occurrence that is an *Objekt* for me, but an *Ereignis*. He writes *Er-eignis* and thus links it with *eigen*, etc: 'Experiences [Erlebnisse] are Er-eignisse, in so far as they live off what is one's own [aus dem Eigenen leben] and life lives only thus' (LVI/LVII, 75; cf. 116). A 'situation' contains 'not static elements, but "Ereignisse". The happening [Geschehen] of the situation is no "Vorgang" – as e.g. an electrical discharge observed in a theoretical attitude in a physics laboratory. Ereignisse "happen to me" ['passieren mir']' (LVI, 205). A situation is not neutral; it provides *Motivation*.

In BT *Ereignis* is still used for an event that happens to me. It can apply to 'a storm, refurbishing one's house or the arrival of a friend, hence to things that are present-at-hand, ready-to-hand or there-with-us' (BT, 250). *Vorkommnis* and *vorkommen* are usually reserved for the *vorhanden*, the 'present-at-hand' (cf. BT, 119). Words beginning with *vor-* are often associated with the present-at-hand and the theoretical, objectifying attitude, as when 'coming across oneself [Sich-vorfinden] perceptually' is contrasted with 'finding oneself in a mood [gestimmtes Sichbefinden]' (BT, 135). But this does not apply when *vor-* has a temporal force, whether of anticipation, e.g. *vorweg*, 'ahead', or of antecedence, e.g. *vorgängig*, 'previous(ly)'. The most potent word for 'happening' in BT is (*das*) Geschehen, which Heidegger associates with its relative *Geschichte*, 'history'. *Geschehen* is understood verbally as 'happening', not as an individual 'event'. It is thus quite distinct from *Geschehnis*, which occurs only twice in BT, to distinguish the 'processes [Vorgänge] of nature and the events

55

[Geschehnisse] of history' (18) and to refer to not fully theoretical 'assertions about events in the world around us' (158). A burst pipe or car crash are *Geschehnisse*, but not *Geschehen*: only DASEIN 'happens'. Dasein's happening is the 'specific movement in which Dasein is *stretched along and stretches itself along*' between its birth and its death (BT, 375). Exploration of this shows us how Dasein 'pulls itself together' into a unified self and thereby gives rise to history: 'Or does the personality of the person, the humanity of man, have its own temporality and correspondingly a "steadfastness" of its own, in virtue of which too the Geschehen-character of man's Dasein, i.e. the essence of history in the authentic sense, determines itself in a radically different way from the Vorgang-character of present-at-hand nature?' (XXXI, 173, Cf. BT, 390f.). Dasein is a happening, not a substance in and to which various things happen. In pulling itself together it 'repeats' or retrieves the historical past.

After BT *Ereignis* becomes important again and jostles with *Geschehen* for Heidegger's favour. Both are contrasted with *Vorgang* and *Vorkommnis*. Sometimes they amount to *Begebenheit*, as a historical event (XXXI, 196, 231). But later they are distinguished from it: *Begebenheiten* are visible, dramatic, but superficial public events, while *Geschehen* and *Ereignis* may be inconspicuous, but are profoundly important (LXV, 28). Nihilism is not just one historical *Begebenheit* among others, but a long, drawn-out *Ereignis* in which the truth about beings as a whole slowly changes and advances towards an end determined by nihilism (NII, 33/niv, 4f.). '[O]nly the greatest Geschehen, the profoundest Ereignis, can still save us from lostness in the bustle of mere Begebenheiten and machinations. Something must happen [sich ereignen] to open up being for us and put us back in it . . .' (LXV, 57, Cf. 97, 256). *Geschehen* is often interchangeable with *Ereignis*. But *Geschehen* is verbal and, having no plural, cannot refer to distinct events. 'Metaphysics is the basic happening [Grundgeschehen] in Dasein', but it is not a distinct event in Dasein's career: 'It is Dasein itself' (WM, 120/109). 'What happens [geschieht] is the history of being' (NII, 388/niv, 243), but the 'history of beyng knows rare Ereignisse at long intervals which are for it only moments', events such as 'the assignment of truth to beyng, the collapse of truth, the consolidation of its unessence (correctness)', etc. (LXV, 227f.). Another such event is the 'commencement [Beginn] of metaphysics' and the distinction between What- and That-being (NII, 401f./ep, 2f.). But *das Ereignis* often refers to the supreme event that constitutes the *Anfang*, 'beginning', the essencing of beyng, the initial revelation of being that first enables us to identify beings. Here Heidegger exploits to the full its supposed kinship with *eigen*, etc: 'it is no longer a matter of dealing "with" something and displaying it as an object, but of being handed over [übereignet] to the Er-eignis, which amounts to a change of man's essence from "rational animal" [. . .] to Da-sein' (LXV, 3). Being appropriates man and makes him *Da-sein*, the site of being's revelation: 'Beyng as Er-eignis. The Er-eignung makes man the property [Eigentum, lit. 'owndom'] of beyng. [. . .] property is belong-ingness to the Er-eignung and this is beyng' (LXV, 263; cf. 254, 311). Beyng as *Ereignis* is not 'becoming', 'life', or 'movement' in Nietzsche's sense. To view beyng in these terms – which depend on being as beingness – makes it an object. We must not make assertions about it, but 'say it in a saying that belongs to what the saying brings forth and rejects all objectification and falsification into a state (or a "flux") [. . .]' (LXV, 472).

ever the while   The adverb *je* means 'ever'. It combined with *mehr*, 'more', to form *immer*, 'always, ever more'. Once, *je* applied to the past, *immer* to the future. This is no longer so. They differ as 'Has he ever [je] lived in London?' differs from 'Has he always lived in London?' In BT, *je schon*, 'ever already', means much the same as *immer schon*, 'always already', formed by analogy with the common expression *immer noch*, 'still', as in 'He still lives in London'. *Je* also has distributive force, as in 'He gave them each [je] an apple', 'To each according to [je nach] his needs!', 'To each according as [je nachdem] he works!' Thus: 'We ourselves are each of us [wir je selbst] the entity to be analyzed [viz. DASEIN]. The being of this entity is in each *case mine [je meines]*' (BT, 41). Heidegger then coins *Jemeinigkeit*, 'in each case mineness': 'In speak-ing to Dasein one must, in accordance with this entity's character of *Jemeinigkeit*, always add the personal pronoun: "I am", "you are"' (BT, 42). He exploits the facility of *je* for entering compounds: *je* also contrib-utes to *irgend*, 'some, any'; *jede(r)*, 'each, every'; *jegliche(r)*, 'any, each'; and *jemand*, 'someone'. It also appears in expressions of the type: 'the [je] bigger, the [je] better'.

Je combines with members of the *Weile*-family. *Weile* was originally a 'rest, repose, pause', but came to mean a 'while, (period of) time'. The conjunction *weil*, once 'while, during', but now 'because', was originally the accusative singular of *Weile*. *Weile* generates *weilen*, 'to stay, tarry, be (somewhere)', and *verweilen*, 'to stay, dwell, linger, while away (the) time'. Later, Heidegger plays on these words and on their similar-sounding, but etymologically remote spatial counterparts, *weit* 'wide', and *Weite*, 'width, expanse' (G, 39ff./66ff; LI, 118ff.). He also exploits the etymology of *Langeweile*, 'boredom, "long while"' (XXIX, 118ff.).

Je and *Weile* come together in the adverb *jeweils*. This can have a temporal force, as in 'jeweils on the last day of the month', i.e. 'on the last day of each month'. But it can be non-temporal: 'the jeweils people concerned', i.e. 'each of the people concerned'. It generates the adjective *jeweilig*, 'respective, prevailing [conditions, etc.]', often with temporal force: 'the jeweilige government', i.e. 'the government of the day', but often not: 'The jeweilige [specific, particular] colouring of an entity is always seen' in the light (XVII, 7). Heidegger coins *Jeweiligkeit*: *'Facticity* is the term for the character of "our" "own" *Dasein's* being. More exactly the expression means: *in each case [jeweilig]* this Dasein (phenomenon of "Jeweiligkeit"; cf. dwelling [Verweilen], not running away [Nichtweglaufen], being-*there*-alongside [*Da*-bei-], Da-sein), in so far as in its very being it has the character of being *"there"* ' (LXIII, 7). He associates *Jeweiligkeit* with temporality and with dwelling as our attitude towards the world: 'Jeweiligkeit means a circumscribed situation in which everydayness finds itself, circumscribed by a specific At first [ein jeweiliges Zunächst], which is there in a dwelling on it. [. . .] Such a dwelling is at first and mostly not merely contemplative, but is occupied with something. Waiting on the street can of course be idly standing around, but even that is quite different from the occurrence of a thing, namely man, between other things, namely houses and terraces. But dwelling in the sense of idle standing around is itself only intelligible against the background of our normal dwelling, which is being on the way to something, [. . .]' (LXIII, 87). Elsewhere *Jeweiligkeit* is distributive rather than temporal: 'this entity, which we call Dasein, [. . .] is jeweils what I myself am. To this being [Sein] – Dasein – belongs the *particularity* [die *Jeweiligkeit*] *of an I*, which is this being [Sein]' (XX, 325. Cf. CT, 6, 8). That is, although *Dasein* is an abstract, not a concrete term (since the human being has no definite nature, but is constituted by its relationship to being and to its own being), *Dasein* is always the *Dasein* of someone in particular. In BT *Jemeinigkeit* supplants *Jeweiligkeit*. But *jeweils* and *jeweilig* occur often, both with and without temporal force.

Later, Heidegger's attention shifts from individual human beings to peoples, owing to his growing interest in large-scale history. In lectures in the summer of 1934, to be published as volume 38 of his works under the title *Über Logik als Frage nach der Sprache. On Logic as the Question about Language,* he is said to have reflected on the passage from *Je-meinigkeit,* 'in each case mineness' to *Je-unsrigkeit,* 'in each case ourness', arguing (like Hegel) that the authentic self is be found not in the I, but in the We, that is, the nation or people (Safranski, 266).

everydayness Heidegger's interpretation of DASEIN purports to show it 'as it is *firstly and mostly* [*zunächst und zumeist*] in its average *everydayness* [*Alltäglichkeit*]' (BT, 16). *Tag*, 'day', and *all*, 'all, every', furnish: *Alltag*, 'weekday; everyday life'; *alltäglich*, 'daily; everyday, ordinary'; and *Alltäglichkeit*, 'everydayness, ordinariness'. In contrast to a 'distinctive, definite way of existing', everydayness is Dasein's 'indifferent Firstly and Mostly [Zunächst und Zumeist]'. Since it is so close to us, it is usually overlooked: 'What is ontically closest and most familiar is what is ontologically furthest, unknown and constantly overlooked in its ontological meaning' (BT, 43). *Alltäglichkeit* 'clearly means that mode of existing which Dasein observes "every day" ['alle Tage'].' But everydayness is not a quantitative concept: ' "every day" does not mean the sum of the "days" allotted to Dasein in its "lifetime".' It means 'a definite *How* [*Wie*] of existence that pervades Dasein "for life".' That is 'the How in which Dasein "lives from day to day", whether in all its conduct or only in certain conduct prescribed by being-with-one-another' (BT, 370). Everydayness contents itself with the habitual, even when this is burdensome. It is uniform, but it finds variety in whatever the day brings. Everydayness is inescapable: 'it determines Dasein even when it has not chosen the THEY as its "hero". [. . .] Existence can, indeed, master the everyday [den Alltag] in the moment of vision, and of course often only "for the moment", but it can never extinguish it' (BT, 371).

Zunächst, 'firstly', Heidegger explains, means 'the way in which Dasein is "manifest" in the with-one-another of publicness [im Miteinander der Öffentlichkeit], even if "at bottom" it has in fact "overcome" everydayness'. *Zumeist* means: 'the way in which Dasein shows itself for Everyman, not always, but "as a rule" ' (BT, 380, Cf. XIX, 98). *Zunächst* has two ordinary uses as an adverb: 'first of all' (as in 'first we do this, then that') and 'for the time being, for the moment'. It is used occasionally as a preposition, 'next to', since it comes from *nah*, 'near, close', and *nächst*, 'nearest, closest'. *Zumeist* means 'mostly, for the most part'. Neither word, in ordinary usage, suggests 'publiceness' or being 'with-one-another'. Nor does Heidegger invariably use them in this way. Here he links them, and thus everydayness, with what one does publicly and with doing what people mostly do, doing what is expected of one. Hence everydayness is subject to the They and inauthentic. It contrasts with resoluteness and the 'moment of vision', which escape publicity.

Everydayness contrasts with science. To the scientist, 'everyday things show yet another face' (WT, 9/12): the sun has gone down before the shepherd sees it set, and the everyday table is accompanied by Eddington's *Doppelgänger*. It also contrasts with philosophy: 'the philosophical concept is an *assault* on man, on man in general – hunted out of everydayness and driven back into the ground of things' (XXIX, 31). By the standards of 'everyday representation' philosophy is 'always something deranged' (WT, 1/1f.). Everydayness tends to homogenize beings and our relationships to them (XXIX, 400). Its errors are more elusive and seductive than traditional theories (XXIV, 82). But philosophy needs the 'immediacy of everyday Dasein [. . .], the *composure [Gelassenheit] of the free everyday glance* – free of psychological and other theories about consciousness, experiences and the like' (XXIX, 137).

existence *Existieren*, 'to exist' was a seventeenth-century translation of the Latin *exsistere*, lit. 'to step forth, out', hence 'to appear, be in existence'. The late Latin *ex(s)istentia* became *Existenz*. *Existenz* traditionally means the existence of an entity, in contrast to its essence. Heidegger uses it in a narrow sense, and applies it only to DASEIN: Dasein has no essence or nature in the way that other entities do: 'The "essence" of Dasein lies in its existence' (BT, 42). Owing to his confusion of two types of BEING, That-being and How-being, Heidegger occasionally suggests that Dasein's only characteristic is to be, i.e. to exist in the traditional sense (XX, 152, 207, 209). But *Existenz* is Dasein's *mode* of being, not the fact *that* it is: Dasein is in charge of its How-being, not (except for the possibility of suicide, which Heidegger rarely mentions) its That-being (XXVI, 216f; XLIX, 34f.). Dasein 'steps forth' into the world and makes something of itself; it is 'ecstatic, ie. eccentric' (ER, 98 n. 59.). *Existenz* involves no contrast with 'essence', unlike Sartre's claim that existence precedes essence (LH, 322/229). Heidegger often writes *Ex-sistenz* or *Ek-sistenz* to stress 'stepping forth' (ET, 186f./126; LH, 321/228; XLIX, 53).

Heidegger gives a brief history of the concept (NII, 473ff./ep, 68ff.). He makes various attempts to find a Greek prototype for *existentia*: Aristotle's talk of being 'outside' the mind (NII, 417/ep, 16), of an actuality (*energeia*) emerging from a potentiality (*dunamis*), and *huparchein*, 'to begin, arise, exist', which Heidegger fancifully translates as 'predominate', i.e. 'to presence [anwesen] by itself', because the root-word *archē* meant both 'rule, dominion' and 'beginning' (NII, 473f./ep, 68f. Cf. XXIV, 108ff.). (Classical Greeks had no readily available words for the medieval distinction between *existentia* and *essentia*. *Ekstasis* is literally 'stepping forth', but means, 'ecstacy, derangement', not 'existence'. Later Greek contrasts *huparxis*, 'existence', with *ousia*, 'essence'.) Medieval philosophers transformed Aristotle's *energeia* into *actualitas*, which like its German counterpart, *Wirklichkeit*, suggests 'making, effecting' (*agere, wir-*

ken); Suarez takes *existentia* to mean 'emergence from its causes', so that to exist is to be causally produced (NII, 418/ep, 17). Descartes conceives existence primarily as the existence of the ego or subject, and whatever else exists exists because it is represented in it. For Leibniz, REPRESEN-TATION in the form of perception and appetition is the actuality of every substance; existence is what the essence strives towards. Existence becomes the Kant 'objectivity of experience'. Schelling, who studied Leibniz (S, 102/84f.), revives the original meaning of *Existenz* – 'Ex-sistenz, what steps forth from itself and manifests itself in stepping forth' (S, 129/107). He contrasts it with GROUND, which forms the base from which *Existenz* (i.e. the existing entity) steps forth. This notion of existence is taken over by Kierkegaard, who restricts it to man, the only being ensnared in the 'contradiction of temporality and eternity' (NII, 475/ep, 70). Hegel's system, Kierkegaard argued, propounds 'eternal' truths. But one cannot live in a system; it gives no guidance on the decisions that life, even the philosopher's life, requires. Eternal truths, especially those of Christianity, cannot be reached step by step from historical truths, but only by a leap of faith. Jaspers adopted Kierkegaard's notion of *Existenz*, retaining the stress on 'communication' and its importance for the formation and maintenance of the self, but severing its relation to Christianity. BT used *Existenz* in a different, though equally restricted, sense: 'The "existentiell" concept of existence (Kierkegaard's and Jasper's) means the individual self of man in so far as it is interested in itself as this particular entity. The "existential" [Heidegger's] concept of existence means the selfhood of man in so far as it is related not to the individual self but to being and the relationship to being' (XLIX, 39; cf. NII, 475f./ep, 70). *Existenz* now concerns Dasein's relation to being, rather than to beings, and thus prepares an overcoming of metaphysics (NII, 476f./ep, 71). The BT use, however, is only 'temporary' (*zeitweilig(e)*, NII, 476f./71). To avoid confu-sion with Jasper's *Existenzphilosophie* of 1931 it is replaced by other words, especially *Inständigkeit*, 'insistence', both in its root meaning of 'standing in', 'standing in [Innestehen] the ecstatic openness of "time"', and in its current meaning, 'urgency", 'remaining in the unremitting essential relationship to the being of beings' (XLIX, 54; cf. LXV, 302f.).

Aristotle listed 'categories', such as substance, quality, quantity, etc., which apply to all entities. But since Dasein exists in a way that other beings do not, we need to distinguish its fundamental characteristics by calling them *Existenzialien*, 'existentialia, existentials', rather than 'categor-ies', e.g. being-in-the-WORLD, an existential of Dasein, is quite different from being-within-the-world, as stones and tools are (BT, 44).

Existenz supplies an adjective, *existenzial*, 'existential'. Heidegger coins another adjective, with a French-derived ending: *existenziell*, 'existentiell'. *Existenzial* applies to the 'ontological structure of existence', i.e. existenti- alia and their interrelations, and to the philosopher's understanding of it. That e.g. *Existenz* involves being-in-the-world is an existential matter, and so is the philosophical understanding of it. *Existenziell* applies to the range of possibilities open to Dasein, its understanding of them and the choice it makes (or evades) among them. If Dasein does what THEY are doing, or alternatively chooses to choose and decides to become a soldier or a philosopher, these are existentiell matters. The distinction between 'exis- tential' and 'existentiell' is parallel to that between 'ONTOLOGICAL' and 'ontical', though these terms are not restricted to Dasein. Like *Existenz*, its derivatives are not much used by Heidegger after BT (cf. NII, 478ff./ep, 73f. on existence and the existentiell).

experience German has two verbs meaning 'to experience': 1. *erleben*, from *leben*, 'to live', has the flavour of 'live through'. One can experience, *erleben*, e.g. fear by feeling it or by witnessing it. An *Erlebnis* is an experience with an intense effect on one's inner life, but not necessarily externally, as in 'That was quite an experience'. 2. *erfahren* from *fahren*, 'to go, travel, etc.', hence lit. 'go forth', has a more external quality. It can mean 'to learn, find out, hear of', but also 'to receive, undergo', something. An *Erfahrung* is an experience as, or of, an external, objective event, and the lessons one learns from such events. *Erfahrungswissenschaft* is 'empirical science'; by contrast, an *Erlebnisaufsatz* is an essay based on personal experience.

Erlebnisse, lived experiences, are especially important in Dilthey. They are inner states, activities and processes that we are aware of or 'live through', but do not usually make objects of introspection. The connec- tion with life is explicit: 'Starting from "life" itself as a whole, [Dilthey] tried to understand its "lived experiences" in their structural and devel- opmental inter-connexions' (BT, 46).

Despite his early attachment to the concept of life (e.g. LIX, 36ff.), Heidegger is uniformly wary of the notion of *Erlebnis* and *das Erleben* ('experiencing'). He associates it with an 'experiencing I, subject or consciousness' (LIX, 92). In BT he has two main objections: 1. An *Erlebnis* is an isolated, temporary experience. 2. An *Erlebnis* is an inner, psychical event, intrinsically detached both from the body and from the external world. To conceive the self in terms of *Erlebnisse* implies that it is either pierced together from intrinsically distinct, momentary experiences or is an underlying thread that persists unchanged throughout its *Erlebnisse*

(BT, 114). To regard moods (BT, 136, 340, 344; XXIX, 123) or conscience (BT, 169, etc.) as experiences ignores their disclosure of WORLD and DASEIN. Dasein is not aware of itself by focusing on its experiences, but in 'what it does, uses, expects, avoids', in things it is concerned about in the world around it (BT, 119). Affects, passions and feelings are not to be seen as inner experiences: 'what we are concerned with here is not psychology, not even a psychology underpinned by physiology and biology, but [. . .] with the way in which man withstands the "There" [das 'Da'], the openness and hiddenness of the beings among which he stands' (NI, 55/ni, 45). 'Fortunately the Greeks had no experiences, [. . .]' (NI, 95/ni, 80. Cf. AWP, 87/134). Hence they did not believe that the point of art is to provide them.

Later, Heidegger uses *Erlebnis* for the experience, sensation or 'buzz' to be derived from, say, a drug or a rally. Technology's erosion of man and diminution of the world are offset by its ability to give us experiences. All that matters is the quality of the feeling (*Gefühl*) or experience, since they can have no significance for our lives or our world (LXV, 406, 495).

Erfahrung is quite different. Heidegger gives a brief history of the word (LXV, 159ff. Cf. AWP, 73ff./120ff; WT, 69ff./88ff.):

1. Experience is at first passive: we come across something without going in search of it.
2. In active experience, we 'go forth' (*er-fahren*) to look for something.
3. We go to something to see (perhaps with artificial aids such as microscopes) what happens to it under varying conditions, either waiting for the new conditions to arise or intervening to produce them.
4. Experiment: we intervene in something to see what happens, if we do such and such, only now we do so in 'anticipation [Vorgriff, 'fore-conception'] of regularity, e.g. when so much – then so much' (LXV, 161).
5. The modern experiment essentially involves 'exact' measurement. Objects are shorn of their essences and regarded as mere individuals conforming to mathematical regularities. These regularities determine in advance what counts as objective. Scientists do not conduct exact experiments to discover whether nature conforms to mathematical regularities; they do so because they presuppose a PROJECTION of nature as mathematical. Experiment in this sense is quite different from 'experience': 'science becomes rational-mathematical, i.e. in the highest sense *not* experimental' (LXV, 163). 'Experiment' and 'experience' were once contrasted with the medieval practice of examining

authorities and previous opinions. Now they are contrasted with mere observation and description, guided by no mathematical 'anticipation'.

Is Heidegger a rationalist or an empiricist? Neither or both. 'Experience', like all basic words, changes its meaning over history. What counts as experience at a given period depends on a prior interpretation of the world that is not itself derived from or vulnerable to experience. Thus the issue between competing scientific theories cannot always be settled by 'experience': 'One cannot say that Galileo's doctrine of the free fall of bodies is true and that of Aristotle, who holds that light bodies strive upwards, is false; for the Greek conception of the essence of body, of place and of their relationship depends on a different interpretation of beings and therefore engenders a different way of seeing and examining natural processes' (AWP, 70f./117). This is an instance of the general idea that our 'mode of access' (*Zugangsart*) to a type of entity, e.g. atoms or historical figures, varies with our prior conception of their being (e.g. WT, 71/93). 'The truth of a principle can never be proved from its result. For the interpretation of a result as a result is conducted with the help of the principle, presupposed, but not grounded' (S, 166/138).

Heidegger explores Kant's account of our finite *Erfahrung* in several works (e.g. K; XXV; XXXI), and also the less obviously finite experience portrayed in Hegel's *Phenomenology of Spirit* (HCE). Occasionally he speaks of the Greek 'fundamental experience [Grunderfahrung] of the being of beings', which underlay, and gave rise to, both the subject-predicate form of their language and their conception of a thing as a subject with accidents (OWA, 12/149).

F

<hr>

falling 'To fall, drop, etc.' is *fallen*; 'fall' is *Fall*. The prefix *ver-* gives *verfallen* and *Verfall* the flavour of lapsing or deterioration. One falls into (*verfällt in*) bad habits (accusative), or falls prey/victim (*verfällt*) to them (dative). *Verfallen* also means 'to decay, decline, waste away'. In early lectures Heidegger uses *ruinant(e)*, *Ruinanz*, 'falling, fall, into ruin', from the Latin *ruere*, 'to fall down, rush' (LXI, 2, 39, 120, etc.). Two years later *Verfallen* is established as a feature of CARE (XVII, 84). In BT the three coordinate, inseparable constituents of care are: existence, facticity, falling (*Verfallen*) (BT, 231, 328, 350). It also one of four 'structures' that constitute 'disclosedness': understanding, the state one is in (*Befindlichkeit*), falling and talk (BT, 335). Falling is distinct from THROWNNESS, which is associated with facticity and *Befindlichkeit*. But Heidegger suggests that DASEIN falls because it 'remains in the throw' (BT, 179).

Despite its air of deterioration, Heidegger insists that *Verfallen* is not a term of moral disapproval and has nothing to do with the Christian fall from grace (XX, 391; BT, 179f; LH, 329/235f.). 'Dasein has first of all always already fallen away [abgefallen] from itself as authentic ability-to-be-itself and fallen [verfallen] into the "world" [an die "Welt"]' (BT, 175). The fall is an Angst-driven 'flight of Dasein from itself as authentic ability-to-be-itself' (BT, 184). Heidegger gives three accounts of what Dasein has fallen into and, implicitly, of what it has fallen away from (BT, 175):

1. *Verfallen* means: 'Dasein is firstly and mostly alongside [bei] the "world" of its concern' (cf. BT, 250).
2. 'This absorption in . . . [Aufgehen bei . . .] mostly has the character of being lost in the publicness of the They'.
3. 'Fallenness into the "world" means absorption in being-with-one-another, so far as this is guided by idle talk, curiosity and ambiguity'.

Account 1 suggests that in virtue of falling Dasein attends to its present concerns. It is hammering in the workshop, busy at the word-processor, disregarding Dr Johnson's advice: 'Whatever withdraws us from the power of our senses, whatever makes the past, the distant, or the future, predominant over the present, advances us in the dignity of thinking beings' (Boswell, 277f.). *Verfallen* is associated with the present, as existence with the future and facticity with the past. In what sense has Dasein fallen away from its 'authentic ability-to-be-itself'? It does not have in view its whole life from birth to death. It interprets itself in terms of the world into which it falls, 'by its reflected light [reluzent]' (BT, 21; cf. LXI, 106, etc.); it thinks of itself in terms of its current preoccupation. It is not making a momentous decision about the overall direction of its life. It is not suspended in Angst, aware only of its bare self in a bare world.

Account 2 introduces a new element. Dasein's present concern is mostly a publicly recognized and approved activity, even if done in private. It need not be: Dasein might be engrossed in an unheard of or outrageous enterprise, 'public' only in the sense that others would see what he was up to if they were present. Heidegger implies that Dasein is doing what it does only because it is what THEY recommend. This need not be so. I may have at some time made a momentous and independent decision to do what I am presently engrossed in. Even if I am doing it because They recommend it, the details of what I do are likely to be left up to me.

Account 3 goes further. What I do may be tacitly guided by others. It in no way follows that I am 'absorbed' in togetherness and in chatter, curiosity and ambiguity. However widespread chatter, etc. are, they do not seem to be essential features of Dasein in the way that some concern for the present and for the public recognition of its activities are. It is hard to accept Heidegger's assurance that account 3 involves no disapproval of falling. His detailed and vivid analysis of chatter, etc. is motivated by his desire to display falling as a 'movement' (BT, 177ff.), perhaps also to rival Hegel's account of the same topics of his *Phenomenology of Spirit*.

Dasein's falling impairs its ability to do philosophy: as well as falling into its world, Dasein also 'falls prey to its more or less explicitly grasped tradition. This deprives it of its own guidance, its questioning and its choosing. That applies not least to the understanding rooted in Dasein's very own being, to ontological understanding and its capacity to develop it' (BT, 21).

The two types of falling are connected: concern with the present, which is central to falling on all three of the above accounts, obstructs a critical inspection of what is handed down from the past, since that would require an explicit examination of tradition in its foundation and development. This is the sense in which Dasein engrossed in its present concerns is 'lost in the publicness of the They': it mostly continues to act and think in traditional ways. Busy shoemakers make shoes in the same old way; Internet-surfing or conference-hopping philosophers stick to the same old ontology. It does not follow that fallenness is a bad thing. Wholly unfallen Dasein, hard as it is to describe (BT, 176), would at least not make shoes or do philosophy. It would have no tradition to start from, to guide it in unravelling the old tradition and establishing a new one.

Later, *verfallen* plays no significant part in Heidegger's thought. *Verfall* is used, but usually in the sense of a historic 'decline' (e.g. XXXIX, 98ff.) rather than a feature of individual man or Dasein. As being supplants man at the centre of the stage, 'abandonment by being [Seinsverlassenheit]' occupies the position once held by *Verfallen*: 'that beyng abandons beings, leaves them to themselves and so lets them become objects of machination. All this is not simply a "fall" ['Verfall']; it is the first history of beyng itself' (LXV, 111).

fate and destiny Heidegger mainly uses *Schicksal* and *Geschick*. The words denote both the power that determines events and the actual events. Both come from *schicken*, now 'to send', but originally 'to arrange, order, prepare, dispatch' and correlative to *geschehen*, 'to hurry, run, happen': *schicken* something is to make it *geschehen*. They are thus related to *Geschichte* 'history'; i.e. what 'happens', *geschieht*. *Geschick* also means 'skill, skilfulness'.

Heidegger sometimes links *Schicksal* with 'grace' and 'calling', Calvinist concepts that he drew from Weber's *Protestant Ethic and the Spirit of Capitalism* (1904/5) (LVIII, 167, 259f.). A more recent influence was Spengler, who argued that while causality reigns in nature and the natural sciences, history involves *Schicksal*. The concept fluctuates. It is unavoidable fate: 'Real history is heavy with fate but free of laws. One can divine the future [. . .] but one cannot reckon it. The physiognomic flair which enables one to read a whole life in a face or to sum up whole peoples from the picture of an epoch [. . .] is utterly remote from all "cause and effect"' (DW, 118). It is also self-chosen destiny: 'One feels that it is more or less of an incident when Goethe goes to Sesenheim [on holiday as a student], but destiny when he goes to Weimar; one regards the former as an episode and the latter as an epoch. [. . .] Perhaps, then, the discovery of the heliocentric system by Aristarchus was an unmeaning incident for the Classical Culture, but its supposed rediscovery by Copernicus a destiny for the Faustian?' (DW, 139).

BT associates history with *Schicksal* and *Geschick*. *Schicksal* is an individual's self-chosen 'fate': 'Only freedom *for* death gives Dasein an outright goal and thrusts existence into its finitude. Once grasped, the finitude of existence wrenches Dasein back from the endless variety of immediate possibilities presented to it, of contentment and care-free shirking, and brings it into the simplicity of its *fate*. This is what we call Dasein's original happening [Geschehen], the happening that lies in authentic resoluteness and in which Dasein *hands* itself *down* to itself, free for death, in an inherited, yet chosen possibility' (BT, 384). *Geschick* is collective 'destiny' composed of individual fates: 'The power of destiny first becomes free in communication and struggle. Dasein's fateful destiny [schicksalhafte Geschick] in and with its "generation" makes up Dasein's full, authentic happening' (BT, 384f.). 'Resolutness involves running ahead and handing oneself down to the There of the moment of vision. This we call Schicksal. Based on this too is Geschick, by which we mean Dasein's happening in being-with others. In repetition fateful destiny can be explicitly disclosed in its bond with the heritage that has come down to us. It is repetition that first reveals to Dasein its own history' (BT, 386). Mannheim utilized Heidegger's remark about 'generation' – a group of 'coevals', with shared experiences, interests and attitudes – in urging the sociological import-ance of generation (Mannheim, 276ff.).

This distinction between *Schicksal* and *Geschick* does not survive BT. They are often used interchangeably (XXXI, 6); he speaks of the *Schicksal* of the Germans, the *Geschick* of an individual, and 'western Schicksal' (NI, 124, 474). He deplores *Historie*'s exclusion of *Schicksal*: 'One admits "chance" and "fate" as determining factors in history, but this only goes to show the exclusive dominance of causal thinking, since "chance" and "fate" only expose the fact that cause-effect relations are not exactly and unequivocally calculable' (LXV, 147). He explores the notion of fate and destiny in Nietzsche – *amor fati*, 'love of fate', NI, 470f./nii, 207 – and Hölderlin (EHP, 86ff., 104ff., 164ff.).

Later, *Geschick* becomes more important than *Schicksal*, and has to do with being rather than DASEIN. Heidegger derives it directly from *schicken* as 'what is sent', often writing *Ge-Schick*: 'Absurdity is impotent against being itself and thus also against what happens to it in the Ge-Schick: that within metaphysics there is nothing to being as such' (NII, 339/niv, 202). Metaphysics, in the sense of surmounting or transcending beings, is a *Geschick* in that it is 'put, i.e. sent [geschickt] on the path of its prevalence' (QB, 86). What sends? Being. Heidegger associates being's sending with the phrase *es gibt Sein*, 'there is being', but literally 'it gives being' – a convenient way of avoiding saying that being 'is'. What does *es*, 'it', denote? Being itself. Hence being gives, i.e. sends, itself or its own truth or lighting (LH, 332f./238f.). The essence of technology, he explains later, 'put man on the path' of revealing things as 'standing resources'. To put us on the path is *schicken*. Hence this collective 'sending' is '*destiny* [das *Geschick*]'. History, *Geschichte*, 'is not just the object of Historie, nor just the performance of human activity. Activity first becomes historical [geschichtlich] as fateful [geschickliches] activity [...] Enframing [Gestell] is a providential sending [Schickung, = 1. "sending", 2. "act of providence"] of fate [Geschickes] like every mode of revealing' (QT, 28/24). *Geschick* is quite different from *Schicksal*, as in 'Technology is the

: 'the inevitability of an unalter-
at, it is a *Geschick der Entbergung*,
iing sent to us by being itself. It

nvariably refers, more or less
finitude. Finitude haunts our
an end [Ende], at which it just
l time is finite' (BT, 331). The
ndary; Heidegger implies that
de by writing *Un-endlichkeit* ('in-

ition of finitude, which has no
intuitus originarius, an 'original
nd is not received from them.
nking as such is the mark of
nly *intuitus derivativus*, intuition
nt create them. Our Dasein is
y is, handed over to it' (K, 26/
ty and sense-organs to receive
The essence of sensibility con-
nung]' (K, 26/18). Heidegger
must the finite entity that we
is to be open to beings which
e able to show themselves of
ne entity among others know
Heidegger's own terminology,
prior UNDERSTANDING of
le possible by our understand-

ing of being creates the leeway or free space (*Spielraum*) in which an entity can appear as an object: a *Gegenstand*, the entity as an appearance to finite cognition, not the 'thing in itself', the same entity as it is known to infinite cognition (K, 32/21). Finitude is responsible for Dasein's special relationship to being: 'There is [gibt es] and must be such a thing as being only where finitude has become existent. Thus understanding of being reveals itself [...] as the innermost ground of our finitude' (K, 228/156. Cf. 280/175: 'For ONTOLOGY is an index of finitude. God does not have it'). Finitude is akin to THROWNNESS: 'The finitude of human cognition lies in thrownness among and to beings' (XXV, 85). Philosophy is an expression of our finitude, an attempt to make ourselves at home in a world that we did not create and do not fully understand (XXIX, 12), and philosophy itself is finite: 'all philosophising, being a human activity, is incomplete, finite and restricted. Even philosophy as knowledge of the whole must be content and give up the idea of grasping the whole at a stroke' (XXXI, 10). We cannot reach a view that is 'true in itself' by playing off different finite standpoints against each other, in the way that Hegel tried to do; no view we arrive at will ever be the only possible view (K, 236f./161). Our tendency to level off and ignore distinctions, e.g. between different types of being, also stems from our finitude (XXXI, 235f.). Heidegger's view that man is, and is regarded by Kant as, finite was challenged by Cassirer, in CK and in a debate with Heidegger at Davos in 1929. The debate turns on whether our free will and our knowledge of 'eternal truths', such as those of mathematics, are marks of our infinity. Cassirer's view is akin to Hegel's, who also regarded man as infinite and rejected Kant's doctrine of the 'thing in itself' (K, 244/166f).

In the mid-1930s Heidegger affirms not only that man or Dasein is finite, but that being or 'beyng' itself is finite. Beyng 'lights itself up as the most finite [das Endlichste] and the richest, [...] For beyng is never a determination of the god itself, but beyng is That which needs the divine activity [Götterung, = 'godizing'] of the god in order to remain, after all, completely distinct from it' (LXV, 240). Beyng is finite, since it needs something else by which it is bounded, a need that it would not have if it were God or a 'determination' or property of God. Later he casts doubt on the sense of saying that being is 'in-finite' or finite, 'if in-finitude [Un-endlichkeit] and finitude are taken as quantitative concepts'. The ESSENCING of beyng stands above the conflict between these two propositions; to say 'Beyng is finite' is meant only as a transitional rejection of 'idealism' of every type (LXV, 268). He distinguishes two types of in-finitude: 1. endless succession or continuation; 2. the 'closed circle', which is in-finite or 'endless' in the sense that it does not come to an end – an idea similar to, but distinct from, the TURN of the EVENT (LXV, 269). 'In-finity' in sense 2 derives from Schelling and Hegel, and Heidegger discerns an 'infinite relationship' in the reciprocal, conflictual interdependence postulated by their friend Hölderlin between EARTH, world, God and man (EHP, 163).

'In such essencing of the sign [Wink] beyng itself comes to its *ripening*. Ripening is readiness to become a fruit and a bestowal. Herein what is *ultimate* essences [west], the *essential end [Ende]* required by the beginning and not imposed on it. Here the innermost finitude of beyng reveals itself: in the sign of the last god. In ripeness, in the power of fruitfulness and the greatness of bestowal, lies too the *hiddenmost* essence of the *Not* [*Nicht*], as Not-yet and No-longer' (LXV, 410). Beyng is finite not simply in the sense that it needs something else (God, etc.) to reveal itself, but also in the sense that its revelation, in a human civilization, has a beginning, a fruition and an end. Heidegger here endorses Spengler's view that a 'culture' undergoes a growth and decay analogous to those of a living organism, though the culture on which Heidegger focuses, the 'western history' that began with the Greeks, has a longer life than any postulated by Spengler. (For Heidegger's early, qualified admiration for Spengler, see e.g. LXI, 75.) 'The end [Ende] *is* only there, where beings have broken loose from the truth of beyng, have denied any questionability and that means any distinction, so as to conduct themselves in the endless possibilities of what is thus let loose in endless time. The end is the ceaseless And-so-on, from which the *ultimate* [das *Letzte*] as the most primordial [das Anfänglichste] has long ago and from the beginning withdrawn. The end never sees itself but regards itself as the completion [Vollendung] and will thus be entirely unready and unprepared either to expect or to experience the *ultimate*' (LXV, 416). There are two prospects before us: 1. Continual progress in the same direction after the 'truth of beyng', the meaning, has finished. This is really the 'end': 'But progress is futureless, since it only promotes the present "further" along its own road' (LXV, 113) and 'The secret goal towards which all this and more is rushing [. . .] is the state of utter boredom' (LXV, 157). 2. An 'other beginning' of history prepared by a return to the 'first beginning' instituted by the Greeks. What immediately precedes such a beginning is the 'ultimate' rather than the end. A civilization is thus 'infinite' in that it returns in a circular fashion to its beginning, but 'finite' in that it does not last forever, or, if it does, its perpetual continuance is itself its 'end'.

'Being' is finite in three senses: (a) It requires other things (God, etc.) to reveal itself in a civilization. (b) No revelation of being reveals everything there is; there is always more than any civilization discloses. (Hence the finitude of beyng refutes any 'idealism'.) (c) Every civilization has a beginning and a end.

71

forgetfulness and abandonment of being Since the time of Plato and Aristotle the 'question about the sense of being' has 'fallen into oblivion' (BT, 1f.). 'Oblivion' is *Vergessenheit*, 'forgottenness', from *vergessen*, 'to forget'. Being is also hidden, *verborgen* (BT, 35). In BT the hiddenness of being is different from its forgottenness: it consists not in our failure to ask about its 'sense', but in our misconceptions about the being of entities, supposing, e.g. that a hammer is a thing with properties rather than ready-to-hand equipment. Later, Heidegger uses *Seinsvergessenheit*, 'oblivion, forgottenness, of being' to convey that being as such is forgotten (NI, 22/ ni, 194). *Seinsverlassenheit* is similar in structure to *Seinsvergessenheit*, *verlassen* being the perfect participle of *verlassen*, 'to abandon'. But it means not our having abandoned being, but being's having abandoned us and other beings: 'What really happens [in machination] is the Seinsverlassenheit of beings: that being leaves beings to themselves and denies itself to them' (NII, 28/niii, 181. Cf. LXV, 111). It is thus similar to the more common *Gottverlassenheit*, 'God-forsakenness', while *Seinsvergessenheit* resembles *Gottvergessenheit*, 'God-forgottenness', in the sense of our having forgotten God (PT, 53/10). *Seinsverlassenheit* consists in the absence of the 'unconcealing [Entbergung] of being as such' (NI, 654/niii, 155), while *Seinsvergessenheit* 'means: the self-concealing of the provenance of the differentiation of being into What- and That-being, in favour of the being that lightens beings as beings and remains unquestioned *as being*' (NII, 402/ep, 3f.).

In BT beings *are* independently of our experience, etc., but 'being "is" only in the understanding of that entity to whose being belongs such a thing as understanding of being' (BT, 183). If there were no DASEIN, there would be no being, but there would be beings. As it is, there 'is' being, and this is not affected by our failure to ask about its sense. Later, matters become more complicated (e.g. NII, 357f./niv, 217f.). *Seinsvergessenheit* persists, we have forgotten to ask about the 'sense' or 'truth' of being. But this is now a consequence of the general phenomenon of *Seinsverlassenheit*. Our forgetfulness of being is engendered by being itself. Being no longer depends on our understanding of it, and Heidegger does not countenance the possibility that being might at any time – even before the emergence of humans on the earth – wholly fail to exist. (Being has become, in this respect, more like God.) But being can be present or, in varying degrees, absent. He uses several terms for its absence, besides *Seinsverlassenheit: Entzug* ('withdrawal'), *Verweigerung* ('denial, refusal'), *Vorenthalt* ('withholding'), *Ausbleiben* ('failing to appear') etc. (e.g. LXV, 293). The absence or presence of being depends on what men do. But what men do depends on being itself. Being would not be absent if we did not forget it, but we forget it because of its absence. Being does not depend on man, as in BT, but creates man as its abode. Da-sein is where being is when it arrives.

Heidegger shows some confusion about the relation between being, beings, and abandonment by being. In 1943 he wrote: 'Without being, whose abysmal, but still not unfolded essence is conveyed to us in essential Angst by the nothing, all beings would remain in beinglessness [Seinlosig-keit]. Only, even this [beinglessness] as abandonment-by-being [die Seins-verlassenheit] is in turn not a blank [nichtige] nothing, if indeed [wenn anders] it belongs to the essence of being, that being no doubt essences without beings, but that a being never is without being [dass das Sein wohl west ohne das Seiende, dass niemals aber ein Seiendes ist ohne das Sein]' (WMP, 304/385). In 1949 he revised the last two clauses to read: 'that being never essences without beings, that a being never is without being [dass das Sein nie west ohne das Seiende, dass niemals ein Seiendes ist ohne das Sein]'. *Seinlosigkeit* has two senses: 1. the sheer non-existence of being, whether present or absent, 'blank nothing'; 2. the absence of being, *Seinsverlassenheit.* In 1943 and 1949 (but not in BT) Heidegger says that there could be no beings at all if there were *Seinlosigkeit* in sense 1. He tacitly implies that there can be beings if there is *Seinlosigkeit* in sense 2 (cf. LXV, 115). In 1943 he says that even if there were no beings at all, there would not be *Seinlosigkeit* in sense 1, there would still be being in some form or other. In 1949 he says that if there were no beings at all, there would be *Seinlosigkeit* in sense 2, being would not 'essence'. The confusion is thus explicable.

In BT *Seinsvergessenheit* affected philosophy, leaving 'average everyday-ness' more or less unscathed. Later, *Seinsverlassenheit* affects the whole of human life, since philosophy or 'metaphysics' is the dominant, subterra-nean influence on human life. *Seinsverlassenheit* is the ground of nihilism in Nietzsche's sense, the absence of any goal (LXV, 119, 138). It underlies technology and the ills of modernity: 'Seinsverlassenheit, brought closer by a reflection on world-darkening and earth-destruction in the sense of *speed*, of *calculation [Berechnung]*, of the claim of the *mass [Massenhaften]*' (LXV, 119). In the gigantomania characteristic of technology 'the Seins-verlassenheit of beings essences; and no longer only in the form of the absence of the questionability of beings, but in the shape of the engi-neered extrusion of all reflection, on the basis of the unconditional priority of the "deed" (ie. of the calculated, always "large-scale" enterprise) and of the "facts"' (LXV, 442).

The escape from *Seinsverlassenheit* involves awareness of it as *Seinsverlas-senheit.* It 'must be experienced as the basic happening of our history

[. . .] And this requires: 1. that Seinsverlassenheit be recollected in its long and concealed, self-concealing history. [. . .] 2. that Seinsverlassenheit also be experienced as the need [Not] that looms across into the transition and lights it up as the way into the future' (LXV, 112). *Seinsverlassenheit* conceals itself behind our intense concern with beings. Hence we are not usually in 'need(iness)' or 'distress' (*Not*) because of it. This *Notlosigkeit*, 'lack of distress', is itself the greatest distress: 'Seinsverlassenheit is the innermost ground of the distress of lack of distress. [. . .] Is there ever a way out of a distress of the sort that constantly denies itself as distress?' (LXV, 119). But if we become aware of our distress, *Seinsverlassenheit* itself reveals being: it is 'the first dawning of beyng as self-concealing out of the night of metaphysics, through which beings pressed forward into prominence and thus into objectivity, while beyng became the supplement in the form of the apriori [viz. Kantian a priori conditions of objectivity]' (LXV, 293). Escape from *Seinsverlassenheit* is possible once we experience it in its most acute form (cf. LXV, 410ff.).

The three 'veils' of *Seinsverlassenheit* are: 1. *Berechnung*, 'calculation'; 2. 'speed', with its 'blindness to the truly momentary, to what is not fleeting but opens up eternity', its 'dread of boredom'; 3. the 'outbreak of the massive [Massenhaften]' – not the 'masses' in the 'social' sense; 'they only matter so much because what counts is number and the calculable, i.e. accessible to everyone in the same way' (LXV, 120f.)

freedom   Man is essentially free: 'Freedom is not a property [Eigenschaft, 'quality'] of man; man is the property [Eigentum, 'possession'] of freedom' (S, 11/9). Heidegger distinguishes seven varieties of freedom: 1. the ability to initiate changes on one's own; 2. unboundness, freedom from . . .; 3. binding oneself to, freedom to . . .; 4. dominance over sensuality (inauthentic freedom); 5. self-determination from the law of one's own essence (authentic freedom); 6. the capacity for good and evil; 7. liberty of indifference (S, 106/88, 117/97, 123/102). Only 2, 3 and 5 are of much importance for him. Freedom is negative – freedom from . . . (compulsion, etc.), and positive – freedom to . . . If I am free *to* worship God, I must be free *from* God, free to turn away from God, not determined or compelled by God to worship him (XXXI, 6f.). Conversely, negative freedom is pointless, unless I am also free *to* or *for* various things. Not random things: freedom involves the 'obligatory' (*das Verbindliche*) or 'binding' (*Bindung*) (XXVI, 247). The obligatory is not imposed on me externally. There are no values or laws independent of ourselves: practical freedom is self-legislation (XXXI, 294, 296). But there must be things that

I have to do, if am to be motivated to do anything at all – even if it is ultimately by my own choice that I have to do them.

Freedom and obligation do not concern only the practical. In assessing the beauty of paintings, I am not *compelled* to think, or to say, that a given painting is beautiful; I am not, like an animal, 'dazed' (*benommen*) by it. I have leeway or elbowroom (*Spielraum*, lit. 'playroom, room for (free) play', XXVI, 248; XXIX, 384, 493ff.) in which to collect my thoughts and consider my judgement. My judgement is free, though responsive to the obligatoriness of the object. Leeway, independence of any particular entity, is secured by my TRANSCENDENCE of beings to the WORLD or beings as a whole. I call on standards of assessment and on memories of other paintings; I am not transfixed by the painting before me. Similarly I am free, albeit obligated, with regard to any of the possibilities confronting me: 'Only because [Dasein] surmounts beings as a whole can it conduct itself by choice to this or that being within the realm of beings; the range of alternatives here is in the main already decided with the factical existence of every Dasein. Within this sphere that is decided there is then of course a leeway of freedom' (XXVII, 306f.).

Has my judgement (or other action) no causal determinants? Or is freedom, as Kant supposed, a special sort of intelligible causation? Freedom is not a species of causation, nor does it compete with natural or psychological causation. This for two reasons:

1. To view beings in terms of cause and effect is to view them as 'PRESENT-AT-HAND' (XXXI, 163, etc.) or as 'actual' (NI, 401/nii, 138, etc.). This is a wrong way of viewing a man, a person or DASEIN. It assimilates him to a natural entity. Neither 'What shall I do?' nor 'Why did I/he do it?' is appropriately answered in terms of causality. Possibilities are more significant here than actuality. Kant's view that the intelligible causality of freedom runs parallel to but independently of, natural causation raises the additional problem of explaining how man can unite both types of causality (XXXI, 301).

2. We only ask *why* something happened, what is its GROUND or cause, if we think it could possibly have been otherwise. Whether something could have been otherwise depends not on itself alone, but on events within the wider world to which it belongs. So we ask 'Why?' because we transcend to the world (XXIX, 528). We transcend to the world in freedom. Hence: 'Causality is grounded in freedom' (XXXI, 303). Are there two freedoms here, one enabling me to transcend, the other secured by my transcending? There are not two *successive* freedoms: Dasein transcends at no particular time, it has

'always already' (*immer schon*) transcended. Nor are there two contemporaneous freedoms, but one freedom circling on itself: the
thrower of the PROJECT is THROWN in his own throw. How can we
account for this freedom? We cannot. It is simply a 'fact' (XXXI,
295f.), not caused or grounded but the condition of all grounding
and causation.

In the 1920s freedom plays a central role in forming the world. In the
mid-1930s it loses this role, since it is being itself (or rather 'beyng'), not
man or Dasein, that initiates a world (S, 232/192). But being still needs
man to keep beings in their TRUTH or unconcealment. Hence: 'The
essence of truth is freedom', a freedom that consists in 'letting beings be'
(ET, 185ff./124ff.). If I let beings be, they let me be, allowing me leeway.
It is an inner force, thought, that drives us, not our *Milieu*; we choose our
milieu and its interpretation: 'The milieu on its own explains nothing;
there is no milieu in itself' (NI, 273/nii, 23).

'Freedom' is one of those 'basic words' (*Grundworte*) whose meaning
varies over history (NI, 168f./ni, 143f.). But only within limits. The
connection of freedom with leeway, obligatoriness and responsibility
(XXXI, 262) remains constant. But the content of freedom, what is
required of one if one is to be free, varies. What was required in
medieval times was free acceptance of the Christian faith in the interests
of one's eternal salvation. Descartes and his generation liberated us from
this obligation, and located freedom in the 'free self-unfolding of all
man's creative capacities' (NII, 133/niv, 89). But 'every genuine liberation is not only an escape from fetters and a shedding of bonds, it is
above all a new conception of freedom' (NII, 143/niv, 97). Liberation
from the old freedom is liberation to a new freedom, setting up new
necessities and obligations. But now the obligation is explicitly conceived
as set up by man himself: in Kant's terminology, 'man legislates for
himself and chooses the obligatory and binds himself to it' (NII, 143/
niv, 97f.). Heidegger does not, like Hegel, regard this change as an
enlargement of freedom. It is simply the replacement of one sort of
freedom by another.

Will such changes go on forever? Heidegger considers the possibility
that technology, rooted in the modern man-centred view of freedom and
unable to let beings be, will subvert freedom by reducing man to the
'mechanised [technisierte] animal' (LXV, 98, 275), that no more transcends to world, and is no more free, than other animals. But it is also
possible that technology can be accommodated into a radical new
'grounding of Da-sein' and thus of freedom (LXV, 275).

future German, and Heidegger, have only one word for the future: *Zukunft.* It derives from the verb *kommen,* 'to come', via its related noun, *Kunft,* 'coming, arrival'. *Kunft* is now defunct and survives only in compounds such as *Ankunft,* 'arrival', and in the adjective *künftig,* 'about to come', hence 'future'. The preposition *zu* means, among other things, 'to(wards)', and *zukommen (auf)* is 'to come to(wards)'. Hence *Zukunft* is literally 'coming towards', a sense which Heidegger often stresses by writing *Zu-kunft;* the adjective is *zukünftig,* 'future, futural, coming towards (us)'. For Heidegger, *Zukunft* is not something else coming towards DASEIN, but Dasein's coming towards itself: ' "Future" [Zukunft] does not mean here a Now that has not yet become "actual" but will be sometime, but the coming [Kunft] in which Dasein comes towards [zukommt] itself in its very own ability-to-be.' Thus Dasein itself is 'futural, coming towards': 'Anticipation [Vorlaufen, lit. running ahead] makes Dasein *authentically* futural [zukünftig], but anticipation itself is only possible because Dasein, simply in virtue of being, always comes towards [zukommt] itself, is, that is, futural in its very being' (BT, 325). Dasein is always 'ahead [vorweg] of itself', 'beyond itself' (BT, 191f.), it has always 'projected itself on definite possibilities of its existence' (BT, 315), and this 'self-projection on the "For the sake of itself" [das 'Umwillen seiner selbst'] is grounded in the future' (BT, 327). (The 'For the sake of itself' is modelled on Aristotle's *to hou heneka,* 'purpose, the for the sake of which'.) Having decided, however, tacitly, what it wants to achieve, Dasein 'comes back to itself' in the present to take steps to achieve it. Only AUTHENTIC Dasein, not every Dasein, anticipates, 'runs ahead' to its own death (BT, 262), but its ability to do so depends on Dasein's constantly being ahead of itself. Dasein's futurity is prior to the futurity of anything else: 'it is not because I have an idea of the future that my being is transported [entrückt] into the future; I can only represent what is future because my being as Da-sein has the basic feature of letting what is coming [Kommendes] come towards it, of being transported into the coming [in das Kommen]' (XLIX, 50).

'The primary phenomenon of original and authentic temporality is the future'. Not only in authentic temporality: 'The priority of the future', albeit in a modified form, 'will still come to light even in derivative "time" ' (BT, 329). Kant held that 'for the complete comprehension of what is given in appearance, we need the grounds, but not the consequences' (CPR, A411, B438). This, Heidegger demurs, applies to natural occurrences but not to history: 'a historical event is essentially understood from its consequences' – if we can call them 'consequences' in view of their intrinsic involvement in the event. The 'historical past [Vergangenheit] is not determined by its position in what has been [im Gewesenen]', nor by any and every event that happens to result from it, but by 'possibilities of its future [Zukunft] [. . .] what is future [Künftiges] as possible. Therefore history of the present is an absurdity', since we do not yet know the possible, let alone the actual, consequences of present events (XXXI, 213). The priority of the future in the case of history is grounded in the structure of Dasein. The present of our awareness and action is never a durationless instant, but a stretch of time of indeterminate length. One cannot assign boundaries to the present, say what someone is doing 'now', or decide what to do 'now', without taking account of the agent's future-oriented purpose. The agent's purpose also determines what segment or aspect of the past – the living PAST (*Gewesenheit*), not the dead past (*Vergangenheit*) – bears on the present, whether, say, a writer is trying to fulfil a contract signed five years ago or to change the course of philosophy by revitalizing the ideas of Aristotle. Authentic or RESOLUTE Dasein runs further ahead into the future than everyday Dasein and recoils correspondingly further back into the past, before it comes to rest in the present and does what it has to do now. Time is finite, ending with Dasein's own death. So Dasein must come back, it cannot run ahead indefinitely: I cannot decide what to do now in view of the consequences and significance of my action in 3000 A.D. Since it is finite, the future (unlike the past) is always living, always somewhere I can run ahead to, if I so choose.

Various words express our relation to the future. Besides *vorlaufen*, which pertains to the authentic future, and the neutral *vorweg*, there are 1. *gewärtigen; gewärtig*, 'await, be prepared (for); awaiting, prepared (for), etc.,'; 2. *warten*, 'to wait (for)'; 3. *erwarten*, 'to expect'. *Gewärtigen* is to the future as *behalten*, 'to retain' is to the past and *gegenwärtigen*, 'to make present', to the PRESENT. It enables us to indicate a future occasion as 'then' (*dann*), while *Behalten* refers to a past 'then' (*damals*) and *Gegenwärtigen* to 'now' (*jetzt*) (XXVI, 262). *Gewärtigen* 'characterizes the inauthentic future'; 'Dasein comes toward itself not primarily in its very own, autonomous [unbezüglichen] ability-to-be; it awaits itself [or perhaps 'awaits its ability-to-be': seiner gewärtig] concernfully from what is yielded or denied by what concerns it [das Besorgte]. Dasein comes towards itself from what concerns it'. I do not *first* decide who I am and *then* decide what to do; I wait to find out who I am from what I do, from the world around me. *Gewärtigen* is constant and subdued, unlike expecting and waiting for. But it makes these possible by having 'opened up the horizon and field from which something can be expected.' Expecting is the inauthentic counterpart of anticipating, e.g. death. (BT, 337). The root verb, *warten*, also appears in *Gegenwart,* 'present, lit. waiting towards', and *gegenwärtigen.* Thus *gewärtigen* is closely associated with *gegenwärtigen,* often hyphenated with it. In curiosity, *Gegenwärtigen* 'arises [entspringt, lit. leaps away]' from *Gewärtigen*: when I 'await' something, I cannot wait to 'make it present', find out about it, but once I have done so my attention turns to something new, awaiting 'leaps after' [*nachspringt*] making-present (BT, 347).

Later, as Heidegger's interest in death diminished, he became more interested in the future of the 'West'. 'Progress has no future: it simply promotes the present "further" along its own road' (LXV, 113). Hence he looks forward to the 'other beginning', for which we must prepare by an 'engagement [Auseinandersetzung]' with the 'first beginning' of the Greeks. 'Our hour is the age of decline [Untergang, 'going down, downfall']'. But we are going down to the 'silent preparation of the future [des Künftigen]' (LXV, 397), of the 'future ones [die Zukünftigen]' (LXV, 395). We are 'on the way back' out of abandonment by being, 'quite different from mere reacters, whose "action" is absorbed in blind attachment to the short-term present. They have never beheld what has been [das Gewesene] in its intrusion into the future [ins Künftige], nor the future in its call to what lives on as having been [das Gewesende]' (LXV, 411).

'Our technologized time, technologized even in spiritual life, has corresponding forms of expectation: one needs only move the lever, then the points switch and the train leaps onto the other track' (LVIII, 22).

G

God and theology 'Just as an erotic person is always erotic in nature, whether or not he has created – or ever will create – an object of love, so too is a religious person always religious, whether or not he believes in a God' (Simmel, 5). Heidegger was a religious man, but not a religious philosopher. Philosophy is distinct from theology. Theology as a 'positive science' studies a range of beings already revealed and accessible in our prescientific dealings with them, and illuminated by a preconceptual understanding of being. What theology (lit. the 'study [logos] of god [theos]') studies is not God, but Christian faith or the beings disclosed by it, faith not simply as belief or knowledge but in the Lutheran sense of a rebirth affecting one's whole life, as 'faithfully understanding existence [gläubig verstehendes Existieren] in the history revealed, ie. happening, with the crucified' (PT, 54/10). We might call theology the 'self-conscious-ness of Christianity in its world-historical appearance' if it were not for the fact that as a science theology belongs to everyone, not specifically to Christians (PT, 51f./9). The beings disclosed by faith, including faith itself, are the subject of theology, the science of faith. Theology is a historical discipline. It does not confer or confirm faith. Faith, *Glaube*, comes of its own accord. Faith is itself non-conceptual, but theology gives a conceptual interpretation of it. Philosophy is needed since the basic concepts of a science cannot be explicated fully in isolation from our overall understanding of being. Faith involves rebirth, so that DASEIN's irreligious, pre-Christian existence is 'existentielly-ontically' overcome. But what is thus overcome by faith is still involved in it 'existentially-ontologi-cally'. For example, the theological concept of sin involves the non-theological concept of guilt, an 'original ontological determination of Dasein's existence' (PT, 64/19). In explicating such concepts as guilt, 'philosophy is the formally indicating ontological corrective of the ontical, and indeed pre-Christian content of the basic theological concepts' (PT, 65/20. Cf. LX, 62ff.). It supplies a 'formal indication [formale Anzeige]' of the 'ontological region' in which the concept of sin lies. It helps theology to conceptualize sin, and marks out boundaries that it cannot transgress. But theology and philosophy remain distinct. 'There is no such thing as a Christian philosophy, that is absolutely "wooden iron". But there is also no neo-Kantian, value-philosophical, phenomenological theology, any more than there is a phenomenological mathematics' (PT 66/21. Cf. NI, 14/ni, 5; IM, 6/6). 'The more unequivocally theology steers clear of the application of some philosophy and its system, the more *philosophical* it is in its scientific birthright' (PT, 58/14).

Heidegger disavows the Thomism of his youth, which presents Christian faith in Aristotelian terms. Theologians did to Aristotle what Marx did to Hegel (NII, 132/niv, 88). He returns to Paul and Augustine (cf. LX, 67ff.), and cites I. *Cor.* I, 20–23 against the Christian appropriation of Greek metaphysics: 'hath not God made foolish the wisdom of this world? [. . .] For the Jews require a sign, and the Greeks seek after wisdom: But we preach Christ crucified, unto the Jews a stumbling-block, and unto the Greeks foolishness' (WMI, 374/276). He often sounds atheistical: 'man is not the image of God as the absolute petit-bourgeois [Spiessbürgers]; this god is the fake product [Gemächte] of man' (XXXI, 136). But what he objects to is the wrong sort of God, in particular God conceived as the supreme entity: 'What looks, and must look, to the ordinary understanding like "atheism" is at bottom the opposite' (NI, 471/nii, 207f.). The existence of God cannot, without blasphemy, be proved, any more than we can prove causality (NI, 366/nii, 106). But we can try to show how the idea of being as the all-powerful, as holiness – more appropriate than understanding God as an absolute Thou, as *bonum*, as value or as eternity – stems from our TRANSCENDENCE and overall understanding of being. Heidegger's neglect of this gave the impression of atheism, but 'better to swallow the cheap accusation of atheism, which in any case, if intended ontically, is fully justified. But is not the supposed ontical faith in God at bottom godlessness?' (XXVI, 211, n. 3). He disavows atheism: 'The last god has his uniquest uniqueness and stands outside the calculating determination meant by the terms "mono-theism", "pan-theism" and "a-theism". There have been "monotheism" and all kinds of "theism" only since Judaeo-Christian "apologetics", which has "metaphysics" as its intellectual presupposition. With the death of this god all theisms collapse' (LXV, 411). Nietzsche's 'God is dead' is not the 'word of atheism, but the word of the onto-theology of that metaphysic in which authentic nihilism becomes complete' (NII, 348/niv, 210). Nietzsche's view of the world as 'chaos' is a 'negative theology without the christian god' (NI, 353/nii, 95).

Heidegger constantly speaks of 'god(s)', but his/their ontological status

81

is obscure: 'God [Der Gott] is neither "existent" ['seiend;] nor "non-existent" ['unseiend'], nor to be equated with *beyng; beyng* essences [west] temporo-spatially as that "Between" ['Zwischen'] that can never be grounded in God, and not in man either as present-at-hand and living, but in Da-sein' (LXV, 263). God needs beyng, but is not identical to it. Beyng is between gods and beings, like the 'hearth-fire in the centre of the dwelling of the gods' (LXV, 486; cf. 243f; LH, 328/234). Beyng is nevertheless remarkably like Aquinas's god: It is simple and unique. It is not thin and universal, but rich and replete. It does not differ from entities in the way that one entity differs from another. It has many names; none of them captures its full essence, but each thinks it '"as a whole" ['ganz']' (LXV, 471; cf. 486). Aquinas's god is a being (*ens*), but a being of a peculiar sort, identical with its own (act of) being (*actus*) *esse(ndi)* and with its own essence; it is pure undiluted being. It is closer to Heidegger's beyng (or to Hegel's 'concept') than to the god of Moses. Thus Heidegger's view is this: Men need God or gods. The god(s) are as real as anything else we project. But they are not beyng, or Aquinas's 'god'. They are historically variable manifestations of beyng. The gods died with the Greek city-state, though poets and scholars intermittently revive them. The Christian God is now dead or dying, killed off by, and partly responsible for, the metaphysics and technology that threaten humanity's survival. To survive this danger we shall, like every preceding age, need a new god or gods – the number is yet to be decided (LXV, 437) – 'the last god, quite different from the gods of the past, especially the christian god' (LXV, 403, Cf. XXXIX, 93ff.). The last god is the 'truth of beyng', not beyng itself (LXV, 35).

Heidegger's 'theology' is influenced German idealism, especially Hölderlin and Schelling. He was, perhaps, the Catholic Hegel.

ground and abyss *Grund* comes from an archaic verb meaning 'to grind' and was originally 'coarse sand, sandy soil, earth'. It has acquired a variety of senses, and corresponds closely, if not exactly, to 'ground'; 'soil, land; (building) plot; field; bottom, (sea)bed; foundation, depths, basis; reason, cause'. To say that something is *grundlos*, 'groundless', can mean that it provides no support, that it has no cause, or that it has no right, claim or entitlement (XLIX, 76). *Grund* gave rise to (*sich*) *gründen*, 'to ground, found, base, set up, be based, founded on', and thus to *begründen*, 'to ground, establish, justify, give reasons for', and *ergründen*, 'to fathom, get to the bottom of'. It takes prefixes, especially as *Abgrund*, strictly 'earth going down(wards)', i.e. 'unfathomable depths, abyss, underground, etc.';

Ungrund, 'unground', i.e. 'groundless ground'; and *Urgrund,* 'primal ground' (cf. LXV, 379f.). It is itself a prefix, in e.g. *Grundsatz,* 'principle', *Grundstimmung,* 'basic mood'; *Grundlegung, grundlegen,* 'laying, to lay, the foundations'; *Grundbegriffe,* 'basic concepts', but also 'those representations which, in their constitutional interrelation of all knowledge of beings, give the ground' (XXVII, 196). Heidegger associates *Grund* with the Greek *archē,* which means both 'beginning, first principle' and 'rule, dominion' (ER, 4f; S, 220ff./181ff.; XLIX, 77).

Grund had two main roles in pre-Heideggerian philosophy. *Grund, Ab-, Un-,* and *Urgrund* play a significant part in the speculations of such mystics as Eckhart and Böhme about the nature of God and the soul. Schelling followed this path, saying, e.g. that such oppositions as the real and the ideal presuppose an *Urgrund* or *Ungrund,* which is neither of the two opposites but the absolute *Indifferenz.* He contrasted *Grund* with *Existenz:* every entity involves a ground which strives to actualize itself in existence (cf. NII, 476f./ep, 70f. Cf. 446ff./ep, 42ff. on Leibniz's similar view). Secondly, Leibniz formulated the 'principle of sufficient reason', known in German as *der Satz vom zureichenden Grund,* that 'nothing ever happens unless it has a cause or at least a determining reason' (*Theodicy* II, para.44). Heidegger usually prefers Wolff's Latin version: *Nihil est sine ratione (cur potius sit quam non sit),* 'Nothing is without a reason (why it is rather than is not)' (XXVI, 141; ER, 14; PR, 31). A *Grund* or *ratio* need not be a cause: 'every cause [Ursache] is a type of ground. But not every ground produces something in the sense of causing it. Thus e.g. the true universal assertion 'All men are mortal' contains the ground of our seeing that Socrates is mortal. But this universal assertion does not produce, is not the cause of, Socrates's dying' (PR, 191f.). (The general point is correct: see Schopenhauer, *The Fourfold Root of the Principle of Sufficient Reason* (1813). But the argument conflates the truth of a proposition with the assertion of it, and Socrates's mortality/dying with our recognition of it.) 'The relation in which *cause* and *ground* stand to each other is questionable' (XXXI, 137).

In BT DASEIN '*is* in *existing,* the ground of its ability-to-be. [. . .] And how *is* it this thrown ground? Only by projecting itself onto possibilities into which it has been thrown. [. . .] It has been *released* from the ground, *not by* itself but *to* itself, so as to be *as the ground*' (BT, 284. Cf. LXV, 239). Dasein does not lay the ground or basis: it does not choose its entry into the world or the range of possibilities that initially confront it. But it assumes these possibilities as its own and makes them a spring-board for its subsequent trajectory. Its ability to do this depends on its 'ecstatic temporality': 'Even if concern remains restricted to the urgency of everyday needs, Dasein is never a pure making present; it springs from a retention that awaits, and exists in a world on the ground of this retention or as itself this "ground"' (BT, 356, Cf. 436). ER finds three senses of, *gründen* – 1. 'founding', *Stiften*; 2. 'gaining ground', *Bodennehmen*; 3. 'giving reasons', *Begründen* (ER, 104) – involved in Dasein's being-in-the-world: 'The essence of ground is grounding's threefold dispersal, arising tran-scendentally, into [1] world-projection, [2] captivation among beings and [3] ontological rationalization [Begründung] of beings' (ER, 120). Dasein 1. grounds, 'projects' or 'transcends' to, a world, 2. grounds itself in it as one being among others, and is thus enabled to 3. ask for reasons why such-and-such is the case. All this involves freedom, 'the ground of the ground' (ER, 126). No reason or cause can be given for our initial free world-projection. Our awareness of a world, of beings as a whole, discloses alternative possibilities, both for beings in general and for our conduct. We can then ask: Why (do) this rather than that?

BT shows little interest in the idea that being is the ground of beings: 'The sense [Sinn] of being can never be contrasted with beings or with being as supporting "ground" of beings, since "ground' is accessible only as sense, even if it is itself the abyss [Abgrund] of senselessness' (BT, 152). Later, being is the ground of beings: 'Beyng as the ground in which all beings as such first come to their truth (sheltering and arrangement and objectivity); the ground in which beings sink (abyss), the ground in which they also assume *indifference* and *self-evidence* (unground)' (LXV, 77). Yet: 'being offers us no ground and basis, on which we build and in which we dwell -as do the beings to which we turn. Being is the nay-saying [Ab-sage] to the role of such a grounding, denies everything grounding, is a-bysmal [ab-gründig]' (NII, 252/niv, 193). Now that Heidegger's thought is more historical (LXV, 451), he is concerned about the grounding of Da-sein, the truth of beyng, and the event. Since there are various types or senses of *Grund*, grounding is often reciprocal: 'The event grounds Da-sein in itself (I). Da-sein grounds the event (II). Grounding is here reciprocal [kehrig]: I. supporting looming through, II. founding projecting' (LXV, 261). He is constantly vexed by the question why there are any beings at all – a question that opens up beings as a whole and also raises the question why we ask 'Why?': 'Why beings? [. . .] Grounds! Ground and origin of the Why. Always away beyond beings. Where to? Because being essences. Why beyng? From itself. [. . .]' (LXV, 509).

Later still, Heidegger finds two senses of the principle of sufficient reason: 1. It expresses the demand of modern technology that everything render an account (*ratio*) of itself, represent itself, to man. He quotes Goethe: 'Yet enquiry toils and strives, its spirits ever high,/To find the

84

law, the ground, the How and Why.' 2. It answers the question about the sense of being, saying that being is ground and thus 'remains without ground, i.e. now without Why' (PR, 206). 2 is the basis of 1: 'Yet the principle of representation is valid only because the word of being is true. The principle of reason [Grund] as word of being first gives the ground for the principle of representation' (PR, 208). 'Being is experienced as ground. The ground is interpreted as ratio, as account' (PR, 210).

H

hearing   *Hören* goes back to a root-word that meant 'to attend, notice, hear, see', but it now means 'to hear (of, about); to listen (to); to attend, obey'. *Horchen*, 'to listen (to, in), hearken, hark', developed out of *hören*, but has more the flavour of listening to sounds, while *hören* involves *understanding*. Thus one can *horchen* without *hören*: 'Someone who cannot hear in the genuine sense (as when we say of a person, "He cannot hear" – which does not mean he is deaf) may listen [horchen] very well and for that very reason, since mere listening is a definite privative modification of hearing and understanding' (XX, 368). But even listening involves understanding: 'Even listening is phenomenally more original than the mere sensing of tones and the perceiving of sounds. Even listening is hearing with understanding, i.e. "originally and at first" one hears not noises and sound-complexes but the creaking wagon, the electric tram, the motor-cycle, the column on the march, the North wind. It takes a very artificial and complicated attitude to "hear" such a thing as a "pure noise"' (XX, 367, Cf. BT, 163; OWA, 15/151f.).

Hören forms several compounds connected with hearing, such as *überhören*, 'not to hear, ignore', and *hinhören*, 'to listen' (cf. BT, 271). It also gave rise to *gehorsam*, 'obedient', and *hörig*, 'in thrall, in bondage, enslaved'. The most important for Heidegger is *gehören*, which once meant 'to hear, to obey', but then lost contact with hearing and came to mean 'to belong (to), be fitting, etc.' *Gehörig*, 'belonging, fitting', and *zugehörig*, 'accompanying, belonging', developed out of *gehören*. Thus: 'Dasein hears [hört] because it understands. As understanding being-in-the-world with others it is "in thrall" ['hörig'] to Dasein-with and to itself, and in this thraldom [Hörigkeit] it belongs to [zugehörig] them' (BT, 163). And: 'Being-with has the structure of *hearing-obedient-belonging [Zu(ge)hörigkeit]* to others, and only on the basis of this primary belonging [Zugehörigkeit] are there such things as separation, group-formation, development of society, and the like' (XX, 367). Hearing is essential to talk: 'Hearing belongs to talking as being-with belongs to being-in-the-world'. Neverthe-

86

less, we 'hear first of all what is said, what the talk is about, not the saying of it and the talk about it'. Physiology, like acoustics, is secondary: 'That there are for hearing such things as ear-lobes and ear-drums is pure chance' (XX, 368).

Later, Heidegger argues that we hear not only others, but language itself: 'We do not just speak language, we speak *out of* it. We can do this only by having always already listened to language. What do we hear there? We hear the speaking of language [das Sprechen der Sprache]' OWL, 254/124). *Die Sprache spricht*, 'language speaks in that it says, i.e. shows. Its saying [Sagen] wells up from the saying [Sage] that was once spoken and is so far still unspoken, the saying that pervades the structure [Aufriss] of language. Language speaks in that it is the showing that reaches into all regions of presence [Anwesens] and lets whatever comes to presence [Anwesendes] from these regions appear and fade away' (OWL, 254f./124). Language opens up, reveals and orders the world for us. It reveals aspects of the world of which particular speakers are not usually aware. The affinity of *gehören* and *hören*, for example, was 'once spoken' explicitly, but it is long forgotten, 'so far still unspoken'. It is still there in language, waiting for us to hear it.

hermeneutics and circularity Heidegger gives a brief history of *Hermeneutik*, 'hermeneutics', in LXIII, *Ontology: the Hermeneutics of Facticity*. He begins with Plato's *Ion*, where Socrates calls poets the 'interpreters', *hermēnēs*, of the gods (*Ion*, 534e4–5). *Hermēneuein* is Greek for 'to interpret', and *hermēneia* is 'interpretation', *Auslegung*, disclosing the previously hidden (LXIII, 11). *Hermeneutik* is now not interpretation, but the doctrine or study of interpretation. This discipline was systematized by Schleiermacher as '(the doctrine of) the art of understanding [Kunst(lehre) des Verstehens]', primarily of written texts (LXIII, 13). Schleiermacher's biographer, Dilthey, extended hermeneutics to the 'humane sciences [Geisteswissenschaften]', which include philology, but also the study of history, theology, art, social institutions, etc. Hermeneutics is now the methodology, the study of the method, of these sciences. Heidegger uses *Hermeneutik* to mean 'interpretation', interpretation of 'facticity', that is, of our own DASEIN (LXIII, 14). This philosophical task is a development of what every Dasein does. Dasein essentially interprets itself, as, say, a soldier, and such self-interpretation makes Dasein what it is (LXIII, 15). Not that Dasein always interprets itself authentically: 'Dasein speaks of itself, but it is only a mask it holds before itself so as not to terrify itself', it takes over the interpretation of the THEY (LXIII, 32). Being essentially conceals itself beneath tradition. Hence we need a 'dismantling [Abbau] of tradition' (LXIII, 71). 'Hermeneutik ist Destruktion' (LXIII, 105). Interpreting human life is like interpreting a text overlaid by centuries of distorting exegesis. We must make sure that our 'fore-having [Vorhabe]', our preliminary approach to it, is 'original and genuine', not taken over from tradition or the They (LXIII, 80). Elsewhere, the fore-having, for-sight and fore-grasp presupposed by interpretation are called the *hermeneutische Situation* (LXI, 3, 187; XVII, 110, 115; BT, 232).

Heidegger argues that hermeneutics in his sense embraces other senses of the term: 1. It is, primarily, interpretation, 'uncovering the meaning [Sinn] of being and the basic structures of Dasein'. 2. Since hermeneutics in sense 1 'displays the horizon for every other ontological study of entities that are not Dasein-like, it is also hermeneutics in something like Schleiermacher's sense': it elaborates the 'conditions of the possibility of every ontological investigation'. 3. Dasein's ontological priority over other entities depends on its possibility of EXISTENCE. Thus in interpreting Dasein's being, hermeneutics in sense 1 must analyse the 'existentiality of existence'. This sense of 'hermeneutics' is 'philosophically primary': philosophy sets out from the 'hermeneutics of Dasein', since all philosophical questioning arises from existence and returns to it (BT, 38, 436). 4. The 'hermeneutics of Dasein' 'ontologically works out the historicality [Geschichtlichkeit] of Dasein as the ontical condition of the possibility of history [Historie]. So the 'methodology of the historical sciences' is rooted in hermeneutics in sense 3. This is a derivative sense of 'hermeneutics', viz. Dilthey's sense (BT, 37f.).

Heidegger refers to 'hermeneutics' rarely after BT. He returns to the subject in OWL (95ff./9ff.). His interest in it arose from his concern about the relation between the 'word' of the Bible and speculative theology, which is, he now realizes, a veiled form of the relation between language and being (96/9f.). In view of its association with Hermes, the messenger of the gods, hermeneutics first means 'not interpreting, but before that the bringing of tidings and a message' (122/29). It no longer concerns Dasein and its existence, but being, or rather 'presence of the presencing [Anwesen des Anwesenden], ie. the twofold of the two in their oneness. [. . .] Man thus essences as man by responding to the call of the twofold and revealing its message. [. . .] Thus what prevails and sustains man's relation to the twofold is language. Language determines the hermeneutical relation' (122/30). Language assumes greater importance now that Heidegger's interest in worldly significance has diminished (cf. 137f./41f.).

As Schleiermacher and Dilthey recognized, hermeneutics involves a circle: we cannot understand a part without some understanding of the whole, yet we cannot understand the whole without understanding its parts. BT discusses three such circles: 1. To learn what being is we need to examine Dasein's being. How can we do that unless we already know what being is? (7f.) 2. All understanding and interpretation, of Dasein, of a text, etc., requires presuppositions, a 'fore-structure [Vor-struktur]'. So it moves in a circle from presuppositions to interpretation. (152f) 3. To understand the distinction between existence and reality, we need to understand being in general as the 'horizon' of the distinction. We can only get the idea of being from Dasein's understanding of being and we can only work this out by understanding Dasein. But to do this we need the idea of existence (314f.). None of these, Heidegger argues, is a strict circle. The preliminary understanding required is in each case rough and implicit. 1 goes from an implicit grasp of being to an explicit concept of it. 2 goes from implicit understanding to explicit interpretation. 3 goes from an imperfectly elaborated idea of existence, a type of being, to an idea of being in general that enables us to elaborate it fully. To the objection that our unsupported presuppositions determine the outcome of our inquiry, Heidegger replies that they can be modified in the course of the inquiry. We must start with Dasein's present understanding of being, etc. but we can 'destroy' the traditional logic and ontology that mould this understanding (XVII, 113). Heidegger suggests that the circle in understanding stems from Dasein's inherent circularity, that while it is being-in-the-world, its being is at issue (BT, 153). But he denies that mathematics and natural science – themselves products of Dasein – are circular in the way that history and philology are. This is unfair. Our overall understanding of mathematics and physics is as circular as any-thing else. Explicit mathematical or scientific arguments are not circular. But nor are explicit arguments in 'humane' disciplines.

Later, Heidegger finds other circles: OWA, 8/144: How can I learn what art is except by studying works of art? How can I recognize a work of art unless I know what art is? My implicit prior knowledge of art enables me to recognize clear cases of works of art. OWL, 149f./50f: We learn about language not by speaking *about* it and thus distortingly making it an object, but by conversing in language. How can we know that it is a conversation 'from the essence of language' unless we already know what language is? Or: How does the messenger get to hear the message unless he already knows about it? But Heidegger now declines to speak of a hermeneutical circle: 'talk of a circle always remains superficial' (151/51).

Heidegger avowedly uses 'force [Gewalt]' in interpreting other thinkers

(LXV, 253). His justifications are that great thinkers leave much of their thought 'unsaid' (NI, 158/ni, 134), that all 'discussion [Auseinandersetzung] operates on the basis of an interpretation that is already decided and removed from any debate' (NII, 110/niv, 70), and that he is not trying to produce a 'historiologically [historisch]' correct interpretation but 'historically [geschichtlich]' to prepare the 'future thinking' (LXV, 253).

historiology German has two words for 'history', *Geschichte* and *Historie*. Both refer ambiguously to history as events or happenings and to history as the study of events. Heidegger disambiguates them, assigning *Geschichte* to events, 'history', and *Historie* to the study of events, 'historiology, the historian'. His choice is not arbitrary: *Geschichte* comes from *geschehen*, 'to happen', while *Historie* comes from the Greek *historein*, 'to enquire, etc.' Philosophy of history is customarily divided into two types: 1. 'speculative' philosophy of history, concerned with history as events, primarily in order to find a large-scale pattern or plan in events which eludes ordinary historians; 2. 'critical' philosophy of history, concerned with the historian's study of events, its categories, presuppositions, the nature of historical explanation, and the objectivity of historical claims. Spengler was a speculative philosopher of history. Simmel, who undertook an '"epistemological" [. . .] clarification of the historian's [historischen] approach' and Rickert, who explored the 'logic of concept-formation in the historian's account' (BT, 375) are critical philosophers of history. In BT Heidegger falls into neither camp. He accepts, more or less, the standard objections to speculative history raised by philosophers and historians, while displaying considerable sympathy for the enterprise and the questions it raises (LXII, 38ff.). He believes, however, that history is too important to be left to historians: to consider history (*Geschichte*) only as the 'object of a science' is on a par with viewing the world around us only through the eyes of the natural and social sciences. He raises the quasi-Kantian question: How is *Historie* possible? What is it about human beings that enables them, or some of them, to study their own history? The answer lies in the historicity, *Geschichtlichkeit*, of all DASEIN, even of those who do not study it: 'How history [Geschichte] can become a possible *object* of the historian [Historie] may be gathered only from the mode of being of the historical [Geschichtlichen], from historicity and its roots in temporality' (BT, 375. Cf. 392). *Historie*, like every science, is 'primarily constituted by thematizing' (BT, 393). A science PROJECTs 'entities that we somehow always already encounter': it articulates our understanding of being, demarcates a field of inquiry, outlines appropriate concepts for it, and treats these entities as 'objects': 'thematizing' (BT, 363). Dasein is historical, that is, 'open in its having-beenness [Gewesenheit] on the basis of ecstatic-horizonal temporality', and this clears the way for *Historie* to 'thematize' the PAST, *Vergangenheit*. Heidegger derives or 'projects' the 'idea [Idee]' of *Historie* from Dasein's historicity, rather than gleaning it from the work of actual historians. Since only Dasein is historical *Historie* studies past Dasein, 'Dasein that has been there [dagewesenem Dasein]', in a world that has been there. (BT, 393). It does so with the help of remnants and documents surviving in the present world, but these alone do not account for *Historie*. They 'presuppose *historical being towards* Dasein that has been there, that is, the historicity of the existence of the historian'. *Historie* is authentic if the historian approaches the theme in accordance with 'authentic historicity and the corresponding disclosure of what has been there, repetition'. REPETITION 'understands Dasein that has been there in its authentic possibility which has been' (BT, 394). The 'history that has been there' is then disclosed in such a way that 'the "force" of the possible intrudes into the factical existence' of the historian. It thus concerns primarily the historian's future, not the present: 'the *historian's* disclosure grows [zeitigt sich] *out of the future*' (BT, 395). Heidegger's own history of philosophy exemplifies this 'idea' of *Historie*. He asks about 'being'. The question is not primarily historical, nor has he yet answered it: he hopes to answer it in the future. To answer it he needs to see how past philosophers asked and answered this question, or perhaps distorted and suppressed it. He needs to consider what they said not as a sheer fact but as a possibility, in several senses: a possibility that is not available in the philosophical discourse of the present; one possibility selected from a range of possible alternatives open to them; a possibility that they were striving towards but did not succeed in achieving or expressing in their actual words; or a possibility that we may endorse in the present. Heidegger's 'idea' is applicable, albeit less readily, to *Historie* of other types. Editing reliable texts and examining the 'history of the tradition [Überlieferungsgeschichte]' by which 'what has been there' has been transmitted to us, but also overlaid by contestable interpretation, have a more secure place in the authentic historian's repertoire than 'plunging right away into the "world view" of an era' (BT, 395f.). But authentic historicity need not give rise to *Historie*. 'The Greeks were unhistoriological [unhistorisch], *historein* aimed at the present and present-at-hand [Gegenwärtige-Vorhandene], not the past [Vergangene] as such. But the Greeks were historical [geschichtlich], so originally that history itself still remained hidden from them, i.e. did not become the essential ground of the formation of their "Dasein"' (LXV, 508).

After BT Heidegger's thought became more historical: 'The thinking became more and more historical [geschichtlicher], i.e. the distinction between historiological [historischer] and systematic reflection became ever more untenable and inappropriate' (LXV, 451). But he was hostile to *Historie* as practised by others: 'But just as one takes "subjectivism" as something self-evident and then scours history from the Greeks to the present in search of forms of it, so one also pursues historiologically [historisch] the history of freedom, power and truth. Historiological comparison thus bars the way to history' (NII, 144/niv, 98). *Historie* is 'of the same essence as technology' (NII, 27/niii, 180). *Historie* causally explains the past and 'objectifies' it, in terms of the present, not the future. It serves man's will to establish himself in a 'surveyable order', and degenerates into journalism (NII, 385f./niv, 240f. Cf. LXV, 153, 493). The history of being and the preparation of the other BEGINNING elude *Historie*. 'History only *arises* when we directly leap over the historiological' (LXV, 10. Cf. 479). *Historie* thinks causally, making life and experience accessible to causal calculation, and unable to recognize that historical beings have a different mode of being. It regiments its objects for exploitation and 'breeding [Züchtung]' (LXV, 147f.). *Historie* involves comparison, and its 'progress' consists in the replacement of one respect of comparison by another; the respect adopted reflects the present in which the historian stands. The 'discovery of so-called new "material" is always the consequence, not the ground, of the newly selected respect of explanation' and comparison (LXV, 151f.). In the hands of *Historie* history becomes ahistorical: 'Blood and race become the bearers of history' (LXV, 493).

Heidegger himself is a *Geschichtsdenker*, a 'thinker of history', rather than a 'historian' or a 'philosopher of history'. The *Geschichtsdenker* 'always has the centre of his reflection and presentation in a definite realm of creation, of decisions, of the peaks and crashes within history (whether it be poetry, or the plastic arts, or leadership and the founding of states).' He does not explain history historiologically or reckon it up into a 'definite picture' for purposes of edification; he restores 'history itself to the uniqueness of its inexplicability' (LXV, 154).

history and historicity German has two words for 'history', *Geschichte* and *Historie*. Heidegger finds six distinct senses of *Geschichte* (LIX, 43ff. Cf. BT, 378f.):

1. The science or subject of history (*Geschichtswissenschaft*): 'I am studying (or "doing") history'. This is history as a 'coherent theoretical attitude, as the concrete logic of a field' (LIX, 59).
2. The 'actual realizations' of work on e.g. a problem or philosophy: 'Approach the problem through its history'; 'He has little understanding of philosophy, but he is an expert on its history'. This is history as the past (*das Vergangene*), what has happened, in its totality, particularly men's individual and social achievements.
3. To speak of tribes and peoples with no history means not that they do not study history, that they have no real ancestors, or that they are not the product of a preceding reality, but that they have no tradition (*Tradition*), 'they do not "feel" like successors of earlier generations' (LIX, 46). Tradition is history as one's *own* past, which one constantly carries with one, preserves and renews.
4. History is the great teacher of life, e.g. for politics. This is the past, not one's own past, but the past highlighted by Dasein's current, not specifically personal tendencies as it seeks guidance from what is familiar to it.
5. We say: 'This town has a varied history', 'He has a sad history'. This history is one's very *own* past, which one 'has' in the most intimate sense of that ambiguous phrase 'having a history' (LIX, 52ff.).
6. We say: 'It's the same old story [Geschichte]', 'I was involved in a very unpleasant affair [Geschichte, "business"]'. This is history as HAPPENING, in the way that events happen in real life, in the world around us, to oneself and to the people around one.

By the time of BT Heidegger refers to history in sense 1, the systematic study of past events, as *Historie* ('historiology', or in some contexts 'the historian'), and reserves *Geschichte* for the history that happens. Similarly, the adjective *historisch* pertains to the study of past events, while *geschichtlich* and *Geschichtlichkeit* ('historicality') pertain to what happens. Heidegger often uses *Historie* and *historisch* disparagingly: '[. . .] historiology endeavours to alienate Dasein from its authentic historicality. Historicality does not necessarily require historiology. Unhistoriological eras need not for that reason be unhistorical' (BT, 396).

There could, conversely, be no *Historie* if there were no *Geschichte*. But *Geschichte*, or *Weltgeschichte*, 'world-history', in turn depends on *Geschichtlichkeit*. There could be no history in either sense if DASEIN were not historical. Even a member of an 'unhistorical' people in sense 3 above is 'historical' in this more basic sense. Being 'historical' in Heidegger's sense is a condition of being *either* historical *or* unhistorical in the usual sense.

Dasein's historicality depends on its happening or 'historizing', the peculiar way in which it stretches itself along between its birth and its death (BT, 374f.). A mountain or a dog *has* a past which affects its present condition. But Dasein '*is* its past' (BT, 20): it acts as it does in tacit view of its past. I do not keep promises, repent for my sins, or vote for my party in an election because of the causal effect on me of what I have done or undergone in the past or merely to secure certain desirable results. I do so in view of my coherence and integrity as an enduring person with a past as well as a future. But Dasein's 'own past [. . .] always means the past of its "generation"' (BT, 20. Cf. 385). So Dasein is not simply its 'very own' past, but the past of its community, before as well as after its own birth; its happening intermeshes with that of past Dasein. It has 'grown up into and in an inherited interpretation of Dasein', in terms of which it understands itself and its possibilities (BT, 20). A philosopher needs to undertake a DESTRUCTION, a critical inspection, of this tradition. Non-philosophical Dasein performs a REPETITION of the possibilities tradition provides, if it is authentically historical, while if it is not, it remains dispersed in present affairs, its interest in history confined to historical remains and records. Dasein's historicality gives it access to the historical past and thus provides the basis for historiology. The historian's work is initiated and guided not primarily by remains and documents but by a prior conception of history, as well as by the nature of the historian's own historicality (NII, 110/niv, 70, 206/niv, 152).

BT is unhistorical in the sense that it presents Dasein's condition as relatively unchanging. Authentic Dasein makes resolute choices in view of the future, but these need not alter Dasein's general way of life or anything beyond the life of the individual agent. Philosophy has a history: it began with the Greeks and has since developed, perhaps declined. But this again seems to leave everyday Dasein unscathed. In the mid-1930s history acquires additional significance: First, Dasein's everyday life has a history, culminating in the current dominance of technology. This history depends in large measure on the history of metaphysics. Second, Heidegger shows more interest in the 'first BEGINNING', the original founding of 'western' history and philosophy by the Greeks. The end of western history may be followed by 'another beginning' of history, for which we need to prepare by a 'critical engagement' (*Auseinandersetzung*) with the first beginning (NII, 29/niii, 182; LXV, 10, etc.) Finally, history is the history of being itself rather than of man: 'History [Geschichte] is no prerogative of man; it is the essence of beyng itself. History plays alone in the Between of the interchange [Entgegnung] of gods and man, the Between that is the ground of the conflict of world and EARTH; history is nothing but the event [Ereignung] of this Between. Hence history eludes historiology' (LXV, 479). The founding of history, of a world, cannot depend solely on human choices: choices can only be made within an already established world. Thus man is increasingly seen as the instrument of impersonal forces: being, art and philosophy.

history of being   Heidegger assigns the first appearance of the concept of *Seinsgeschichte*, 'history of being', to ET, delivered in 1930 and published in 1943 (QT, 28/24): the 'ek-sistence of historical man begins at the moment when the first thinker takes a questioning stance towards the unhiddenness of beings by asking what beings are. [. . .] History first begins when beings themselves are specifically promoted to unhiddenness and maintained in it, when this maintenance is conceived in terms of questioning about beings as such. The initial unconcealing of beings as a whole, the question about beings as such, and the beginning of western history are the same [. . .] Man ek-sists – this now means: the history of the essential possibilities of a historical mankind is maintained for it in the unconcealing of beings as a whole. The rare and simple decisions of history spring from the way the original essence of truth essences' (ET, 187f./126f.).

BT contains the germ of this idea: since Dasein is 'historical' its questioning about being is also historical. Thus in asking about being we must also explore the history of asking about being. Heidegger assumes – reasonably enough, though it is not obviously entailed by Dasein's 'historicality' – that philosophers from the Greeks to the present have held varying views about being. His explicit reason for examining their views, rather than simply affirming his own view, is that we tend to succumb to tradition. We employ traditional concepts and categories without adequate inspection and without exploring the original 'sources' from which they were drawn. (BT, 20f.) We may, for example, use the notions of 'form' and 'matter' without recalling Aristotle's reflections on a craftsman shaping his material or wondering whether they are so readily applicable to entities other than artefacts (cf. OWA, 16ff./152ff.). To guard against such possibilities, Heidegger undertakes a *Destruktion* of the tradition, not destroying it in the usual sense, but 'loosening it up' so as to discern the 'original experiences' that gave rise to it. This will show the merits, failings and limitations of traditional concepts. It may reveal new possibilities that the tradition obscures. It will loosen the grip that tradition has on us and enable us to take a fresh, unblinkered look at being (BT, 22, Cf. NII, 415/ep, 14f.). BT is not, however, historical in the way that ET is. It does not suggest, as ET does, that Dasein's world is first opened up by philosophical questioning or that crucial changes in it depend on philosophical developments. BT does not consider the question how and when Dasein came to be in a world, nor does it imply that the world undergoes significant change. BT sketches a history of questioning about being, but not of being itself.

In the 1930s, when Heidegger began to use the expression *Geschichte des Seins* (e.g. IM, 70/77), the history of being is not initiated or promoted primarily by men, but by being itself. Metaphysics or philosophy still plays a dominant part in the history of being. But metaphysics springs from the history of being, not from human choices. For example, the 'conversion of man into a subject and of beings as a whole into the "world-picture" can arise only from the history of being itself (here the history of the transformation and levelling of being's ungrounded truth)' (NII, 25/niii, 179). A thinker is 'one of those individuals who have no choice, who must give expression to what beings *are* at any given stage in the history of their being' (NII, 37/niv, 7). *Seinsgeschichte* is thus associated with *Geschick*, 'fate, destiny', but for Heidegger 'a sending, what is sent', owing to its affinity to *schicken*, 'to send'. For example, the medieval distinction between *essentia* and *existentia* reaches us from a *Seinsgeschick*, from 'being's fateful sending'; (LH, 326/232. Cf. 322ff./238ff.). Heidegger distinguishes *Seinsgeschichte* from Hegel's history of 'spirit' (LH, 332/238f.). There is no law by which being progresses, no 'dialectical' change of one category into another (LXV, 135). Thus major turning-points in the history of being are 'providentially sent' and opaque to us, not intelligible consequences of what went before. Nevertheless Heidegger, like Hegel, believes that philosophical thoughts are the mainspring of history and that, since such thoughts form and transform human beings, they must be the product not of ordinary human thought and activity, but of a large impersonal force such as being or spirit. 'History is the history of being' (NII, 28/niii, 182). Does this contradict BT's view that being is 'projected'? Heidegger thinks not (NII, 235/niv, 178; LXV, 231, etc.). The PROJECT is thrown and the projecter is thrown in the project. The projecter is not a definite, historically situated individual, choosing his project as one might choose a dinner-menu. He only becomes an individual capable of choice in virtue of his project. The project may thus be governed by being itself.

The history of being involves various 'epochs', *Epoche(n)*. Heidegger relates the term to the Greek *epochē*, 'restraint'. Throughout the history of metaphysics being 'keeps to itself, restrains itself', and 'from the particular distance of its withdrawal' – a distance which varies over time – determines 'a particular epoch of the history of being' (NII, 383/niv, 238). *Epochē* comes from *epechein*, 'to hold on, stop, etc.'; a historical 'epoch' begins when ordinary time-reckoning 'stops' – at a point that Heidegger calls an *Augenblick*, 'moment (of vision)'. Being has a history because it withdraws from us and provides only partial and occasional glimpses of itself: 'All events in the history of being, which is metaphysics, have their beginning and ground in the fact that metaphysics leaves the essence of being undecided and must do so, since from the start metaphysics remains preoccupied with the salvation of its own essence and indifferent to an appreciation of the question-worthy' (NII, 459/ep, 56. Cf. ID, 64/66). Metaphysics focuses on beings; it does not explore the full abundance of being, or reduce it to a single aspect of itself, extruding everything else from it. So being can unfold its essence through the ages, revealing hidden aspects. Being is like a rich text. If a commentator were to destroy the text, leaving only his interpretation, interpetation of the original text would cease. But if the original remains along with its interpretation, interpretation can continue, successively revealing different aspects of the text.

home(lessness) and the uncanny   *Heim* is 'home, dwelling-place'. It engenders *Heimat*, 'home-(town), homeland' (cf. LH, 335/242). It also generates adjectives: *heimisch* once meant 'belonging to the home', but is now 'indigeneous, native, local, etc.' and also 'familiar, at home' as in being or feeling 'at home' in a place, a language, etc. *Heimlich* too once meant 'belonging to the home, familiar', but acquired the meaning of 'hidden, secret(ly)' and has lost its link with *Heim*. Another *Heim*-derived adjective, *geheim*, suffered the same fate, and now means 'secret', with *Geheimnis*, a 'secret, mystery'. 'The authentic un-ESSENCE of truth is the mystery', not a 'particular mystery about this and that', but the 'concealing of what is concealed as a whole, of beings as such', the overall concealment presupposed by the unconcealing of truth as ALETHEIA (ET, 191/130).

Unheimlich, strictly 'not belonging to the home', does not mean 'unconcealed', but 'eerie, sinister, uncanny'. Thus 'in Angst one feels "unheimlich"', it gives one the creeps. But '"Unheimlichkeit" here also means not-being-at-home' (BT, 188, Cf. XX, 400ff.). *Haus* is 'house, home'. 'To be at home' is *zu Hause sein* or *zuhause sein*. Thus 'not-being-at-home' is *Nicht-zuhause-sein*. In THEY-dominated everydayness DASEIN feels at home. Angst disrupts familiarity and 'being-in enters the existential "mode" of the *not-at-home [Un-zuhause]*'. Homelessness is our primary condition and impels us to seek a home: 'The falling flight *into* the at-home [*in* das Zuhause] of publicness is a flight *from* the not-at-home [*vor dem Unzuhause*], that is, the Unheimlichkeit that lies in Dasein as thrown being-in-the-world, delivered over to itself in its being' (BT, 189). Later, this thought acquires a more historical flavour: 'The unhomeliness [Unheimische] of beings as such brings to light the homelessness [Heimatlosigkeit] of historical man within beings as a whole' (NII, 394f./niv, 248). This homelessness drives man on to 'the conquest of the planet Earth and the venture into cosmic space': 'Homeless man lets himself be driven – by the success of his enterprise and of his organization of ever greater masses of his own kind – into flight from his own essence, in order to represent this flight as his homecoming [Heimkehr] to the true humanity of homo humanus and to take charge of it himself' (NII, 395/niv, 248). But is not only the moderns who are driven on by homelessness. Sophocles too, by Heidegger's (controversial) reading, held that man's achievements are propelled by *Unheimlichkeit* (IM, 111ff./123ff.).

Philosophy too is motivated by homelessness. Heidegger quotes Novalis: 'Philosophy is really homesickness [Heimweh], an urge to be at home [zu Hause] everywhere' (XXXIX, 7). To be at home everywhere, Heidegger explains, is 'to exist among beings *as a whole [im Ganzen]*', and this is 'a peculiar questioning about what this "as a whole" – which we call *world* – means.' This questioning involves man's finitude, which implies 'an ultimate *isolation* of man, in which everyone stands on his own as a solitary individual before the whole.' Such questioning is based on an emotion: 'Every emotion [Ergriffenheit] is rooted in a mood. At bottom what Novalis calls *homesickness* is the *basic mood of philosophizing*', and thus close to boredom (XXIX, 11f., 120). To philosophize properly, we must not feel at home in the world. We must try to restore the *Geheimnis* of man's Dasein, the *Unheimlichkeit,* on which the 'liberation of the Dasein in man' depends (XXIX, 255, 490).

Horizon In Greek a *horos* was a 'boundary, limit, frontier, border; landmark; definition [of a word]'. It gaves rise to *horizein,* 'to divide or separate as a boundary; to mark out boundaries, limit; to appoint, settle, define, etc.' *Ho horizōn (kuklos),* 'the separating (circle)', was 'the horizon', a term used not only in optics and astronomy, but also for the boundary of human knowledge. This boundary is finite at any given time, but it can be extended indefinitely, since we can always conceive of a standpoint enabling us to transcend the current boundary of our knowledge. Husserl speaks of *(der) Horizont* in his account of perception. We do not perceive a solid object all at once, only an aspect of it. The potential perceptions of all the aspects of the object constitute its 'inner horizon'. An object is related to other objects, and these to further objects. This is the object's 'outer horizon', which is indefinitely extendible and embraces the whole world.

In Heidegger, a horizon is dissociated from sense-perception (XXVI, 269). It is usually a vantage point from which one can view certain matters, ask and answer appropriate questions about them. If we want to ask about the distinction between nature and history, or between the natural and the social sciences, we cannot adopt the 'horizon' of the natural sciences or that of the social sciences. We must find a vantage point from which we can view both nature and history, and their respective sciences (XX, 7). If we want to justify morality or belief in the external world, we cannot remain within the horizons of everyday naive realism or morality; we must find a vantage point outside them, disclosing a wider horizon (XVII, 74ff. Cf. XXXI, 89 on the horizon of Plato and Aristotle, and 132ff., 199 on the horizon for the problem of freedom).

BT begins and ends with the suggest that time is the 'horizon of (the understanding of) being' (BT, 1, 437). This is connected with the fact that, since the 'existential-ontological constitution of Dasein's wholeness is grounded in temporality' the 'ecstatical projection of being must be made possible by a way in which ecstatical temporality originally temporalises' (BT, 437). It is also connected with the 'horizonal' nature of temporality itself. The 'ecstases' of past, present and future are each a 'horizon', not definite things and events but an indefinitely expansible field in which things and events are located. This makes possible a world and the entry of beings into it. Leibniz said that monads (i.e. DASEIN) need no windows because they have everything inside them. 'We would say the contrary: They have no windows not because they have everything inside, but because there is neither inside nor outside – because temporalisation ([Leibniz's] drive) intrinsically implies the ecstatic happening of world-entry, insofar as transcendence is already intrinsically the possible leap over possible beings that can enter into a world. [. . .] Time essentially opens up and explodes into a world' (XXVI, 271, Cf. BT, 364ff.). Horizonal time generates the world of beings. Hence it is the horizon for our understanding of being.

Later, Heidegger associates *Horizont* with Nietzsche's *Perspektive* and his idea that the world can be interpreted only through various alternative perspectives. A perspective or a horizon imposes a 'schema' on the underlying chaos of becoming and makes it 'constant'. 'Every perspective has its horizon' (NI, 646/niii, 148). But the 'horizon, the sphere of the constant that surrounds man, is not a wall shutting man off; the horizon is *transparent*, it points beyond to what is not made fast, to what becomes and can become, to the possible' (NI, 574/niii, 87). Heidegger exploits the derivation of *Perspektive* from the Latin *perspicere*, 'to see through': we look through the horizon to what *can* emerge from the chaos next. He ignores the sceptical implications of perspectivism – that there is no neutral, independent criterion for the truth-value of a perspective. He hints that perspectivism prefigures the 'enframing [Gestell]' of technology, getting things into a manageable framework in which they can be calculated and manipulated (NI, 576/niii, 89; 580/niii, 92; NII, 271/niii, 199). *Horizont* and *Perspektive* 'are grounded in an *original essential form* of man's being (in Da-sein), which Nietzsche no more sees or can see than any previous metaphysics' (NI, 574/niii, 87).

Later still, Heidegger associates the *Horizont* with the 'representational' thinking that reduces things to *objects*: 'The horizonal is thus only the side turned towards us of the open space surrounding us. The open is filled with a prospect [Aussicht] onto the aspect [Aussehen] of what appears to our representing as an object' (G, 37/64). Thus *Horizont* is unsatisfactory for 'releasement', which requires the more fundamental concept of the *Gegend* or *Gegnet*, the 'encountering region'. The horizon is 'the side of the Gegnet turned towards our re-presenting [Vor-stellen]' (G, 48/72f.). A horizon is too dependent on our own position and on the entities which it transcends to serve as the target of releasement.

humanism The Latin term *humanista* arose in Italy in the fifteenth century for a 'humanist', a student of the Greek and Latin languages and cultures. Humanism, the revival of ancient culture and a primary concern with human affairs, began earlier with Petrarch, a devotee of Cicero. Humanity and antiquity were connected, in that ancient literature was the only significant secular literature, unencumbered by scholasticism and the authority of the church. But Renaissance humanism was not incompatible with belief in God and the practice of Christianity. Erasmus was both a humanist and a Christian, while Luther was averse to humanism, since his main concern was the salvation of souls and our relationship to God, not the autonomous development of humanity. In Germany ancient culture was revived by Winckelmann and promoted by Lessing, Herder, Goethe, Schiller, W. von Humboldt and Hölderlin (cf. LH, 318/225, where Heidegger insists that Hölderlin was not a humanist, since he 'thinks the destiny of man's essence more primordially than this "humanism" can'). This movement is sometimes called *Neuhumanismus*, 'neohumanism'. The Germans were more directly concerned with, and better informed about,

Greek culture than were the Italian humanists, who viewed the Greeks largely through Roman eyes (cf. LH, 317f./224f.). Neohumanism too was not incompatible with Christianity: Hölderlin strove to reconcile his devotion to Christ and to the Greek gods. In the twentieth century the title 'humanism' has been adopted by those who reject all transcendent religious beliefs, and recommend an exclusive concern with human welfare in thie earthly life, the only life available.

Heidegger refers only occasionally to 'humanism'. It did not, in his view, liberate ancient philosophy from 'Christian theology': 'Ancient philosophy was pressed by Christian dogmatism into a very definite conception, which persisted through the Renaissance, humanism and German idealism and whose untruth we are only today beginning slowly to comprehend. Perhaps the first to realize it was Nietzsche' (XXIX, 64). He associates it with 'anthropology'. The more object-like the world appears, the more prominent the subject becomes: 'No wonder that humanism first arises where the world becomes a picture. But no such thing as a world-picture was possible when Hellenism was at its height, and humanism could make correspondingly little headway. So humanism in the narrower historical [historischen] sense is nothing but a moral-aesthetic anthropology. This name [. . .] denotes the philosophical interpretation of man that makes man the be all and end all of its explanation and assessment of beings as a whole' (AWP, 86/133). In 1946 Heidegger's French admirer Beaufret asked him, among other questions, 'How do we restore a sense to the word "humanism"?' (LH, 313/219). The question refers to Sartre's lecture 'Existentialism is a Humanism' (1946). Sartre argues that 'existence precedes essence', that is, that man has no essential nature, but simply is what he does, how he acts. This, he believes, excludes the existence of God, or at least of a god who created us for a purpose and expects certain things of us. (That it does not exclude the existence of God altogether is suggested by the Renaissance humanist, Pico della Mirandola, who in his *Oration on the Dignity of Man* imagines God telling Adam that he has assigned him no definite nature but left him free to choose what he shall become.) Heidegger replies that the term 'humanism' can be applied very widely, since not only Roman and Renaissance humanists have a view about man's nature, but also Marxism and Christianity, locating man's nature and salvation respectively in society and in redemption by Christ. But all these humanisms agree in basing their view of man on a prior interpretation of beings as a whole, with a man as one being among them, a rational animal. They are concerned with beings, not with being and man's special relationship to it. Heidegger's *Existenz*, or, as he now writes, *Ek-sistenz*, is not to be confused with Sartre's 'existence'. 'Existence' is the scholastic *existentia* and contrasts with 'essence' or *essentia*. Sartre simply reverses the order of these terms. *Eksistenz*, like 'being' itself, is prior to the distinction between 'existence' and 'essence', and means 'standing forth' into the 'truth of being'. In one respect, humanism overrates the role of man, placing him at the centre of the universe and assessing everything from man's point of view. In another respect, it underrates his role. It fails to recognize that man is not only one being among others, but the being that opens up a WORLD, or beings as a whole, in the first place. For humanism, man is the spoilt child who thinks all the toys in the shop are for him. For Heidegger, man is the entrepreneur who founded and sustains the toyshop by resisting the temptation to consume its contents.

I

I and the self   The first person singular pronoun in German, corresponding to *egō* in Greek and *ego* in Latin, is *ich*. It readily becomes a noun and
then takes an initial capital: *das Ich*, 'the I' (BT, 116, 318, etc.). It helps to
form other nouns: e.g. the fourteenth-century *Ichheit*, 'I-hood' (BT, 116,
318, 323), and Heidegger's coinages, *Ichding*, the 'I-thing' (BT, 107, 119),
Ichsubstanz, the 'I-substance' (BT, 322). *Das Ich* is similar to *das Selbst*, 'the
self'. This comes from the demonstrative pronoun *selbst*, '-self' as in 'I hit
him *myself*, he did it *himself*, etc.' This is distinct from the reflexive
pronouns, *mich*, 'myself', *sich*, 'him-, her-, itself', as in 'I hit *myself*, he did
it to *himself*'. But in compound nouns *selbst* often has reflexive force:
Selbstmord is 'suicide, killing oneself', not a killing that one does oneself
without assistance. *Sichkennen*, the minimal 'self-knowing' one has unless
one is e.g. so beside oneself with anger that one no longer knows oneself
(BT, 124), differs from *Selbsterkenntnis*, explicit 'self-knowledge (BT, 146),
but this depends more on the difference between *kennen* and *Erkenntnis*
than between *sich* and *selbst*. *Selbst* was originally the genitive of *selb*, which
survives in *derselbe*, 'the same', and in such fixed phrases as 'on the same
day, at the same time'. *Selb* also survives in *selbständig*, 'standing/constant
[*ständig*] by itself [*selb*], independent, self-subsistent', which allows Heidegger to speak of the 'constancy of the self [die Ständigkeith des Selbst] no
less than its possible "dependency" ['Unselbständigkeit']' (BT, 117), and
to coin *Selbst-ständigkeit* for the 'constancy of the self, steadfastness' and
Unselbst-ständigkeit for the corresponding deficiency (BT, 322). By empha-
sizing the constituents he gives the words new meanings.

   Heidegger is generally hostile to *das Ich*. He associates it with theories
that isolate the I from the world and from other entities, like a snail in its
shell (XX, 223f.), treat the I as an object of theoretical observation, and
regard it as a thing or substance. The I is not the same as the self: 'That
"pure I", that "I-point", is just an empty accompaniment, it does not help
us grasp experiences, it is unsuited to the role of the self' (LVIII, 247). I
do not usually focus on myself explicitly or in isolation from my involve-

ment with things and with others: 'I experience myself, encounter myself in all possible ways, but just as I experience other things: the clock on the desk, the underlinings, the marginal notes on the scholarly investigation. In a social circle: we are all enjoying ourselves or thinking about something, [. . .] I myself melt away in the company [Mitwelt], I need not be there in any other way in the fugitive experience, of such and such a hue' (LVIII, 97). Early on, Heidegger describes such subdued, everyday self-awareness as *das Michselbsthaben*, 'having-myself'. To have myself is not to focus on the I as an object, to infer from my experiences an experiencing I, or to view the I as resulting from the aggregate of all my experiences. It is 'the living process of gaining and losing familiarity with the concrete lived life itself, [. . .] I have myself, means: *the living situation becomes intelligible*' (LVIII, 165f.Cf.W, 29).

Descartes's main error, in expounding his *cogito ergo sum*, 'I think, therefore I am', was to concentrate on the *cogito*, the thinking, and neglect the *sum*, the being (XX, 210), ' "sum" as assertion of the basic constitution of my being: I-am-in-a-world and that is why I can think at all' (XX, 296). (Heidegger usually omits *ergo*, 'therefore': he believes no inference is involved.) Hence Descartes slid easily into regarding the *ego* as a *res cogitans*, a 'thinking thing', a 'world-less' present-at-hand entity, on a par with, but essentially distinct from, *res extensa(e)*, 'extended thing(s)'. Kant accepted the *cogito*, but rejected the inference that I am a *res cogitans*. We cannot infer, from our experience of the 'I think', that the I is a substance, a person, simple and immortal (CPR, A 348ff., B 399). But then Kant too neglects the being of the 'I think' and by regarding the I as a *Subjekt* (which for Heidegger, unlike Kant, is close in meaning, as well as etymology, to *Substanz*) 'slips back again into the *same* inadequate ontology of the substantial' (BT, 319): 'For the ontological concept of the subject characterizes *not the selfhood of the I qua self, but the sameness and constancy [Beständigkeit] of something that is always already present at hand.* [. . .] The being of the I is understood as reality of the res cogitans' (BT, 320).

Heidegger's view of the I and the self differs in three respects: 1. Descartes, Kant and also Scheler, for whom a person is a performer of intentional or mental acts (XX, 175), leave the relation of the I to the body unclear. The self is not, in Heidegger's view, pieced together from a body, soul and spirit; we must consider it as a whole (XX, 177, 422; BT, 47f.). 2. Descartes, etc. regard selfhood as an all or nothing matter: either one is a self or one is not. For Heidegger it is not. Even if one says and thinks 'I', one need not be, properly speaking, one*self*. One may be, and usually is, dispersed in the THEY and thus the They-self, *das Man-selbst*, not the 'authentic, [. . .] specifically apprehended self' (BT, 129): ' "Natural" I-talk is conducted by the They-self' (BT, 322). 3. For Descartes, etc. experiences and activities are the experiences of a single self, of myself, in virtue of the prior existence of an I or self, independently of what it subsequently does and undergoes. For Heidegger my selfhood depends on how I conduct myself. I become an authentic self by pulling myself together, by 'self-constancy' or 'anticipatory resoluteness' (BT, 322). When I relax I revert to the They-self. It may be objected that even in the depths of average everydayness we retain a minimal self-awareness, such that e.g. if I hit my thumb with a hammer I know that it is I who feel the pain, not my assistant. Heidegger might reply that this is because we never relax completely, always retain a modicum of self-constancy, and thus do not fall entirely and irretrievably into the They. A self or an I, at whatever level, is not a thing or substance that acts, but a type of activity with no inert substratum, an activity that ranges out beyond the here and now into the world and into the past and future. This is one reason for Dasein's 'nullity', *Nichtigkeit*: 'Dasein constantly exists along this edge of the Not [Nicht]' (XXVII, 332).

interpretation and the hermeneutical 'As' German has three words for 'interpret, -ation': 1. *deuten, Deutung*, suggest 'intuition or an inspired inference which may be based on no more than a sign' (DGS, 163). They are used informally by Heidegger but have no special significance for him. 2. *auslegen*, with *Auslegung*, comes from *legen*, 'to lay, make lie', and is literally 'to lay out [aus]', hence 'to display, set out, put on show; to lay, cover [e.g. a floor with a carpet]; to lay out, advance, lend [money]; to explain, interpret'. *Auslegen* implies 'an explanation that proceeds from and appeals to reason or commonsense'. While *deuten* tends 'to be used with things that are felt to be weighty, exalted or secret', *auslegen* tends 'to be used with more pedestrian matters' (DGS, 163). 3. *interpretieren, Interpretation*, are used in both ways, and are 'common with works of art' (DGS, 163). Heidegger uses *auslegen* very widely, whenever we interpret or take something 'as [als]' such-and-such or a so-and-so. *Interpretieren* applies to more systematic interpretation: 'Phenomenological interpretation [Interpretation] [. . .] must, as it were, let Dasein interpret [auslegen] itself' (BT, 140).

Dilthey regarded *Auslegung* – the 'systematic understanding of permanently fixed expressions of life' (AGW, 267) – as the distinctive task of the 'humane' sciences, the *Geisteswissenschaften*, while explanation, *Erklärung*, is the task of the natural sciences. Nietzsche by contrast regarded all thinking and knowledge as *Auslegung*. Heidegger sided with Nietzsche.

Our everyday life is pervaded by interpretation, both of ourselves and of other entities. Everyday, 'circumspect' interpretation is prior to the systematic interpretation undertaken by the humane sciences, and prior to the explanations of the natural sciences. A scientist has to find the way to the library or laboratory, and interpret its contents as books or other equipment, before doing any science. According to Heidegger, we interpret all the way down. We do not *first* see uninterpreted black marks on a white background or *first* hear pure sounds, and *then* interpret them as printing or as speech. We perceive them right away as printed or spoken words, even if we cannot understand them: 'What we "first" hear is never noises or complexes of sounds, but the creaking wagon, the motor-cycle. [. . .] It requires a very artificial and complicated frame of mind to "hear" a "pure noise". [. . .] Even where the speech is indistinct or the language unknown, we immediately hear *unintelligible* words, not a multiplicity of tone-data' (BT, 163f. Cf. 150). Heidegger was at this stage influenced less by Nietzsche and far more by Dilthey, who had in his later writings travelled a good way along Heidegger's own path. The ubiquity of interpretation does not, for Heidegger, imply Nietzschean scepticism. The fact that I immediately interpret speech as speech or a tool as a tool does not entail that my interpretation is unreliable or incorrigible or that it creates the meaning of what is interpreted. At most it undermines the view that interpretations are based on, or answerable to, uninterpreted foundations.

Auslegung is not sharply distinct from understanding (*Verstehen*), but a 'development' of it: 'In interpretation understanding appropriates what is understood understandingly. [. . .] Interpretation is existentially grounded in understanding; understanding does not arise from interpretation. [. . .] The ready-to-hand comes *explicitly* into the sight that understands' (BT, 148). Understanding is global, interpretation local. I understand the world around me, the town, the room or the office with its network of 'significance [Bedeutsamkeit]' and 'involvement [Bewandtnis]'. When I focus on some particular entity I see it '*as* a table, a door, a carriage or a bridge' (BT, 149). I see it too as *for* something: for eating at, for entering the room, etc. Interpretation of an entity makes explicit its relations to other items in the environment and to the 'possibilities' in terms of which I understand that environment. Whenever I deal with a piece of equipment I see it *as* such-and-such and for something. I need not *assert* that this is the case. Interpreting something as something involves not the As (*Als*) of assertion, the 'apophantic' As, but the 'hermeneutical' As, the As of interpretation (XXI, 187f; BT, 158). Interpretation is prior to assertion and, in BT, prior to language. Seeing something without seeing it *as* something is difficult and unnatural. It is not basic, but derivative and 'privative': if I look at something in this as-free way I cease to understand it altogether. Interpretation is not based on as-free perception. The 'as' is essential to DASEIN: 'this "as such", being as such, something as something, a as b. This wholly elementary "as" is [. . .] what animals lack' (XXIX, 416).

Auslegung involves presuppositions, a 'fore-structure [Vor-Struktur]' as well as an 'As-structure [Als-Struktur]' (BT, 151). This involves three elements: 1. 'fore-having [Vorhabe]', the general understanding of the entity to be interpreted and of the 'totality of involvement [Bewandtnisganzheit]' in which it lies. 2. *Vorsicht*, in ordinary German 'caution, circumspection', but taken by Heidegger literally as 'fore-sight'; I set my sights on what I want to interpret or on the aspect of it that I want to interpret. 3. *Vorgriff,* usually 'anticipation', but literally 'fore-grip or -grasp' and associated for Heidegger with *Begriff,* 'concept'. I can only interpret things in terms of concepts at my disposal. I can see something as an implement, but not as a violin if I lack the concept of a violin. This fore-structure applies to interpretation at every level of sophistication. A sociologist has a broad understanding of human beings, a fore-having, that he shares with, say, an economist. But he has a different fore-sight from the economist's: he looks at the social behaviour of humans rather than their economic behaviour. He has a certain fore-grasp: concepts such as power, conflict, co-operation. The fore-structure, especially the fore-grasp, may be defective, taken from 'fancies and folk-concepts' rather than worked out 'in terms of the things [aus den Sachen selbst her]' (BT, 153). He may draw a distinction, between 'state' and 'civil society', say, with no application to the society in question. This might be corrected as the research proceeds. A fore-structure can be amended, but only by appeal to further interpretations, not to raw facts: 'Even a *description* is already "interpretation" ['Auslegung'], something as "colour", as "sound", as "size". There is interpretation and interpretation. *Physical interpretation!*' (LXV, 166).

Correlative to understanding and *Auslegung* is *Sinn,* 'sense' or 'meaning'. What is understood has *Sinn,* though what is understood is the entity, not its *Sinn.* Things do not have *Sinn* apart from Dasein's understanding or failure to understand. 'Hence only Dasein can be meaningful or meaningless' (BT, 151).

K

Kant and the Problem of Metaphysics   Heidegger's second important book, *Kant and the Problem of Metaphysics* [K], was published in 1929. It was preceded by lectures in the winter of 1927–8 on the *Phenomenological Interpretation of Kant's Critique of Pure Reason*, where he interpreted Kant in the spirit of Kant's own belief that the 'idea [Idee]' of a philosophy may not be fully expressed, so we should understand a philosopher better than he understood himself (XXV, 2f. Cf. XXIV, 32ff.). (Heidegger adds that this applies to the interpreter too: he too is 'finite' and can be understood better than he understood himself (XXV, 4).) By this time Heidegger believed that Kant was not an epistemologist, but an ontologist and a metaphysician (XXV, 10, 66). Here Heidegger challenged a central belief of the dominant philosophical school of the time, the neo-Kantianism that heavily influenced his early thought: that Kant was an epistemologist, whose aim was to explore the foundations of our knowledge, especially the sciences. The neo-Kantians rejected the development of Kantianism undertaken by the German idealists in the early nineteenth century: they – Fichte, Schelling and Hegel – tended to regard man as infinite, capable of knowing the innermost depths of God, the world and the soul.

K proposes a new interpretation of Kant, differing both from German idealism and from neo-Kantianism. Man is finite. He makes things and makes and remakes himself. But he is never a pure maker, he always fashions what is already available in the world and in himself, and in his specific historical situation. He depends on entities other than himself. Kant is concerned with the nature of man, not with epistemology. He is not a subjective idealist. His problem is not 'How do objects come to be?' but 'How do we get in touch with objects? How do we transcend ourselves and get into the world?' Heidegger ousts reason and logic from the centrality Hegel assigned to them. In the first, 1781, edition of CPR, Kant postulates three faculties: sensibility, understanding and imagination, *Einbildungskraft*, which is the 'root' of the other two. Man is primarily an imaginative, not a rational being. In the second, 1787, edition Kant retreated and restored reason to its traditional position. Kant's main interest is not epistemology, but metaphysics, primarily 'special' metaphysics dealing with God, the world, immortality and freedom. Hume shook his confidence in the viability, not the value, of metaphysics. So he tried to lay the foundations of metaphysics. But this involves laying the foundations of 'general' metaphysics, or ontology, which considers the nature of beings as such. Ontology occupies the first part of CPR, the 'Transcendental Analytic'.

How can Kant's primary concerns be *both* metaphysics *and* man? To say that man is finite, Kant frames the idea of an infinite being, whose knowledge is an 'originary intuition', an intuition that is not received from objects, but brings objects into existence. An infinite being needs no thought, hence no metaphysics. Only those finite beings whose finitude is an issue for them need metaphysics. Unlike an atemporal, omniscient God, we must think in order to transcend and get to grips with objects; we need time and a 'schematism' to connect our temporal intuitions to our concepts. Metaphysics is of two types: 1. 'preontological' metaphysics, which enables us to experience objects, an 'understanding of being' (Heidegger) or a 'transcendental synthesis' (Kant) of which we are rarely explicitly aware; 2. ontological metaphysics, the philosopher's explicit account of being or of transcendental synthesis. Both are distinct from, and make possible, the 'ontical' questions raised in the sciences and everyday life. Heidegger's Kant is no idealist; he does not doubt that these metaphysics reveal the world as it really is. Things in themselves and the appearances accessible to us are the same thing. We are concerned with appearances, because we have no infinite, godlike intuition of things, our knowledge is finite. We need a sense of being to find our way around the world, as we need a sense of direction to find our way around cities. This does not entail that the world or cities are, or may be, very different from their appearance. But Heidegger forgets special metaphysics. Kant reserved the unknowable things in themselves postulated by theoretical reason as a blank space in which faith or practical reason could locate God, freedom and immortality. Heidegger eliminates this otherworldly space. Hence freedom, though not God or immortality, is located in this world as our human existence (cf. XXXI, 139ff.).

In March 1929, Heidegger debated his interpretation of Kant with Cassirer at Davos, Switzerland. Cassirer was a neo-Kantian with an admixture of Hegelianism. Our categories vary over history; he held. 'Symbolic forms' – language, art, myth, religion – are as important as the sciences. Man is in a way infinite, when he ascends to symbolic forms. To Heidegger's stress on finitude, he retorts that Kantian ethics, which applies to all 'rational beings', not just men, reveals man's infinity, as does our knowledge of eternal truths such as mathematics. Heidegger replies that we only need moral law because we are finite, and that mathematics, for Kant, is dependent on our special type of sensibility and thus no more eternal than our understanding of being. Cassirer and Heidegger are often at cross purposes, since their philosophical differences are deep. Cassirer is interested in 'objective spirit' or culture (our maps), Heidegger in existence or DASEIN, our primitive sense of direction. Cassirer deals with the content of morality, Heidegger with what we must be like for morality to get a grip on us. Cassirer (like Pelagius) takes our freedom for granted, Heidegger (like Augustine) regards freedom as arduous and imperfectly realized. Hence while Cassirer purports to describe our freedom and our culture, Heidegger aims to promote our liberation.

Heidegger often returns to K and to Kant (WT, 41ff.). For all his faults – he does not explore Dasein (XXXI, 157) or ask what being is (XXXI, 203), etc. – Kant is unique 'since the Greeks in bringing the interpretation of beingness (*ousia*) into a certain relation to "time", but like the Greeks he gives priority to thinking (LXV, 254). In K 'force was applied to Kant in the interests of a more original conception of the *transcendental* project in its unitariness, *emphasis of the transcendental imagination.* This Kant-interpretation is "*historiologically*" ['historisch'] incorrect, certainly, but it is *historical* [*geschichtlich*], i.e. related to, and only to, the preparation of the thinking of the future, a historical sign-post to something quite different' (LXV, 253).

knowledge and epistemology Soon after the death of Hegel in 1831, German idealism lost its influence in German universities. Its claim to all-embracing knowledge of the world was undermined by the rapid growth of the natural and historical sciences. This presented a problem to philosophers. What could they do, but record the findings of the sciences, perhaps applying some of them, such as psychology, to traditional philosophical problems? In the 1860s, several philosophers found an answer: 'Back to Kant!' Not the Kant of the German idealists, but a more modest Kant who restrains our metaphysical pretensions and examines the foundations of the sciences. If the sciences leave no area of the world for philosophers to explore, they at least leave the possibility of examining their own foundations. Hence the 'neo-Kantians' devoted themselves to *Erkenntnistheorie*, 'theory of knowledge' or 'epistemology', in contrast to ontology or metaphysics. For Riehl, an early neo-Kantian, philosophy is just *Erkenntnistheorie*, concerned more or less exclusively with the foundations of the natural sciences, with the basic concepts, such as 'stuff', 'force', 'cause' and 'motion', by which we transform perception into science. But most neo-Kantians were interested in culture in general: ethics, law, art, religion, as well as science. Each of these fields has its own appropriate method, a method distinct from that of the natural sciences, and its own type of *Geltung*, 'validity', and *Wert*, 'value' (cf. XIX, 26; XXI, 78ff., 82ff; BT, 99f., 166f.). The neo-Kantians are not (as Heidegger occasionally suggests) exclusively concerned with the natural sciences or with scientific cognition. They are concerned with what Hegel and Cassirer, a late neo-Kantian, called 'objective spirit', objective interpersonal norms, values, truths, etc. rather than with DASEIN or *Existenz*, the choices we make in our everyday lives and at moments of crisis. They deal with language and paintings rather than with speakers, painters or whole human beings, with maps rather than our sense of direction. Husserl was primarily influenced by Brentano's Aristotelian realism, though he fell under neo-Kantian influence from 1900 onwards. Like the neo-Kantians he focused on consciousness or the subject, knowledge, natural science, and the relation between philosophy and psychology (LIX, 87ff; XVII, 61ff; XXI, 31ff.).

Heidegger was averse to *Erkenntnistheorie* even before he decided that Kant was a metaphysician rather than an epistemologist (XXII, 272f., 286). *Erkenntnis* is philosophical or scientific 'knowledge', though its parent verb, *erkennen*, often means simply 'to know, recognize, etc.': 'not every knowing [Erkennen] is scientific Erkenntnis' (S, 63/52). *Erkenntnis*, and even *Erkennen*, presuppose a tacit, unspecialized awareness of the world and of one's own life and doings – Dasein or *Existenz* – that they can never fully capture. *Erkenntnis*, and thus *Erkenntnistheorie*, presuppose an account of being: 'The question about the essence of Erkenntnis is [. . .] already a thoughtful *projection* of the essence of man and his position in the midst of beings and a projection of the essence of these beings themselves' (NI, 561f./niii, 75. Cf. XX, 215ff.). For everyday being-in-the-world, Heidegger prefers such words such as *verstehen*, 'to understand', or, before BT, *sich auskennen*, 'to know one's way around': 'Knowledge [Wissen] in the widest sense' includes 'not only theory, but knowing one's way around [Sich-auskennen], e.g. in a trade' (XXII, 265, Cf. LXIII, 99; XXI, 143). *Wissen*, 'to know [how to, that, about, etc.], contrasts with *kennen*, 'to know, be acquainted/familiar [with something or someone]'. *Wissen* was originally a past tense verb, 'to have perceived'. Since it is used for knowing how, that, etc., it is not now closely related to vision. But Heidegger associates it with seeing and having seen (OWA, 47f./184). He regards *das Wissen* as the 'safekeeping of truth', while *Erkennen* is 'a way in which truth is unfolded and acquired' and *Erkenntnis* is 'truth-acquisition' (S, 63/52). He sometimes uses *Wissen* in a wide sense that includes 'theory', *Erkenntnis*, as well as knowing one's way about (XXII, 265). Sometimes he uses it more favourably than *kennen*-words, for philosophical knowledge or knowledge of the whole: 'Ordinary knowledge [Kennen] ends with the non-knowing [Nichtkennen] of what is still knowable [Kennbaren]. Essential knowledge [Wissen] begins with the knowing [Wissen] of something unknowable [Nichtwissbaren]' (NI, 477/niii, 5f., Cf. XXIX, 213). *Erkenntnis* always contrasts with moods and with willing. *Wissen* need not. The *Wissen* conveyed by a great work of art does not 'consist in merely knowing [Kennen] and representing something. Whoever truly knows [weiss] beings, knows what he wills in the midst of beings. [. . .] The Wissen that remains a willing, and the willing that remains a Wissen is the ecstatic involvement of existential man in the unhiddenness of beings', and thus akin to resoluteness in BT (OWA, 55/192). Thus merely 'having information [Kenntnisse], however abundant it may be, is no Wissen' (IM, 16/17). In our technological abandonment by being, *Wissen* tends to degenerate into 'the calculated, rapid, mass-scale dissemination of ununderstood information to the greatest possible number in the shortest possible time' (LXV, 122).

Heidegger discusses various Greek knowledge-words. *Technē*, 'skill, craft, art', is not, he insists, 'a "making" and producing, but the Wissen that sustains and guides every human outbreak in the midst of beings' (NI, 97/ni, 8lf. Cf. OWA, 47f./184). The Greek counterpart (and relative) of *wissen* is *eidenai*, originally 'to have seen', hence 'to know', and the source of *eidos*, 'form', and *idea*, which Heidegger regularly regards as what is seen, an 'aspect' (XXI, 56. Cf. BT, 171). But *eidenai*, like *wissen*, is often used for knowing that, what, etc. To know a person is sometimes *eidenai*, sometimes *gignōskein*, which, with is noun *gnōsis*, often has the flavour of knowledge by acquaintance. *Epistasthai*, 'to know, etc.', is, for Heidegger, 'to be on top of [vorstehen, lit. 'stand before'] something, know one's way around it' – he associates it (controversially) with *histanai, histasthai*, 'to place, set (up)', 'to stand'. The derived noun *epistēmē*, 'knowledge', means 'approaching something, knowing one's way around it, mastering it, penetrating its substantial content' (XXIX, 49). Aristotle gave it the meaning of 'science', but in a sense distinct from modern scientific 'research [Forschung]' and 'experiment' (AWP, 74/121. Cf. XIX, 31ff., 91ff.).

No great philosopher has, in Heidegger's view, been an epistemologist. Cartesianism is an ontology, not epistemology: 'This story of Descartes, who came and doubted and thus became a subjectivist and so founded

KNOWLEDGE AND EPISTEMOLOGY

epistemology, gives the usual picture; but it is at best a bad novel' (WT, 77/99); 'Descartes does not doubt because he is a sceptic; he has to become a doubter because he posits the mathematical as the absolute ground and seeks a corresponding foundation for all Wissen' (WT, 80/103).

L

language and chatter 'To speak' is *sprechen*. A derived noun, *Sprache*, once the process or capacity of 'speaking', now means 'language'. Another noun, *Spruch*, means 'what is said', i.e. a 'saying, verdict, etc.' All three words form compounds, which Heidegger exploits: 'Being-with-one-another is talking as assenting and refusing, inviting, warning, as discussion [Aussprache, lit. 'speaking out'], consultation [Rücksprache, lit. 'speaking back'], recommendation [Fürsprache, 'speaking for'], [...]' (BT, 161). In discussing Nietzsche and nihilism, we 'submit to the claim [Anspruch] of language [Sprache]', viz. to 'the "nihil", the nothing, in the word "nihilism"' (NII, 337/niv, 200). 'J[apanese]: How would you present the hermeneutic relation now? I(nquirer): I would steadfastly avoid both presenting it and speaking *about* language. J: So everything would depend on reaching a corresponding [entsprechendes, from entsprechen, once 'respond, answer'] saying of language. I: Such a saying correspondence could only be a dialogue [Gespräch]' (OWL, 151/51f.).

'There is language, only because there is talk [Rede] (XX, 365). But Heidegger sometimes derives language not directly from TALK, but from *Gerede*, 'chatter', passing on what THEY say – e.g. that Rembrandt is estimable – without any first-hand experience of one's own. Unlike talk in the presence of what the talk is about, chatter must be spoken: 'The hardening of interpretedness [Ausgelegtheit] undergoes a further intensification in that the communicated talk is always spoken out [ausgesprochen] and the spokenness [Gesprochenheit] of the interpretedness (which is just what language is) has its rise and decline'. For 'every language itself has Dasein's mode of being. [...] Every language is – like Dasein itself – *historical* in its being' (XX, 373. Cf. XXI, 152). Language is not a free-floating thing in which we all share. It seems to float freely, since it belongs to no particular DASEIN, it belongs initially to the They. But we do not have to speak only as They speak. One can, by a mastery of words or by a fresh understanding of one's subject-matter, appropriate language in an original way.

114

Since language has 'Dasein's mode of being', a language can be 'dead'. A dead language as 'spokenness' no longer grows, but it can still be 'alive' as talk and interpretedness: 'The "death" of a language does not exclude the "living vitality" of the talk and disclosure belonging to it, just as dead Dasein can historically still come to life in a potent sense, far more genuinely perhaps than in the time when it was genuinely there' (XX, 374). But if Latin texts can come alive for us today, it is still the case that Latin words cannot change their meanings in the way that the words of living languages can. Thus Latin suits the Catholic church: it preserves its dogmas unchanged. A living language, by contrast, continues to change historically. Thus *erleben*, 'to experience', and *Erlebnis*, 'experience', became common before World War I, while afterwards they were supplanted by the 'dubiousness [Fragwürdigkeit] of existence' and 'decision': 'Slogans and catchphrases are indices of chatter, a mode of being of Dasein in the They' (XX, 375). Even good, original words are prone to debasement by chatter, though poetry in particular can protect them against it.

BT derives language directly from talk, not from chatter. Chatter appears as a phase of FALLING, not as a prelude to language (BT, 167ff. CF. XX, 376ff. where *Gerede* appears again, this time as a phase of falling). Heidegger is no longer certain about language's mode of being: 'Is it equipment ready-to-hand within the world, or has it Dasein's mode of being, or neither? What kind of being does language have, if it can be "dead"? [. . .] Is it chance that meanings are firstly and mostly "worldly", prescribed by the significance of the world, indeed often predominantly "spatial", [. . .]?' (BT, 166, Cf. XX, 344)

Later, Heidegger toys with the idea that language has Dasein's or man's mode of being, but eventually rejects it. Language is essentially related to beings and to man. Hence views of language vary with the conception of the 'rational animal' and of the connection of the word with beings. Language is often regarded as a possession, a tool, or a work of man. Since its relation to man is so intimate, language is even taken as a symbol of man: just as man has a body, soul and spirit, so language has a body (the audible word), a soul (the mood, feeling-tone, etc. of a word), and a spirit (the thought or represented content). But this stems from metaphysics, the focus on beings at the expense of being. We must 'discern the origin of language from the essencing of beyng itself' (LXV, 503), that is, from the original revelation of beings as a whole. We do not so much have a language, as a language has us (XXXIX, 23).

To do justice to the question of language's mode of being, Heidegger should have considered: 1. how the fundamentals of one's language are more intimately connected with oneself and one's identity than any equipment, while less familiar parts of one's language are more like tools to be adopted for specific jobs; 2. how the birth, decline and death of a language compares with those of a person and also with the production or invention of a tool and its breakdown or obsolescence.

letting and releasement   *Lassen* is 'to let, allow, stop, etc.' It forms several compounds: *auslassen*, 'to leave out, vent, let out/go etc.', *(sich) einlassen (auf/mit)*, 'to let in, admit; to get involved in/with something/somebody', *verlassen*, 'to abandon', etc. *Lassen* is also used as a modal auxiliary, in such contexts as 'to *have/get* something done', 'to *let* someone know', 'he *can't* be persuaded, the window *can't* be opened', '*let's* go', etc. (cf. NII, 360f./niv, 219f.). The infinitive governed by *lassen* is almost always active whether its sense is active or passive. Thus when Heidegger speaks of 'letting something be seen *as* something', he writes: etwas *als* etwas sehen lassen, literally 'letting see something *as* something' (BT, 33). The explanation of this idiom is that e.g. 'someone' or 'us' is understood: 'letting [us] see something *as* something'. By contrast, when he speaks of letting beings come to meet us (BT, 73: *begegnen lassen*), of letting beings be (BT, 84: *sein lassen*), or letting them go their own way or 'be involved' (BT, 85: *bewenden lassen*), the infinitive governed by *lassen* is active in sense as well as in form.

Bewendenlassen, 'letting be involved', applies to the READY-TO-HAND. In the ontical sense, *Bewendenlassen* involves letting something be, without interference or alteration. In the ontological sense, it covers any dealing with equipment that lets it be the equipment that it is. This may be leaving it alone in the ontical sense, but it can also involve 'working on it, improving it or smashing it to bits' (BT, 85). *Bewendenlassen* is a type of 'Sein'-lassen, 'letting-"be"' (BT, 354; cf. 84f.). But letting-be applies to all beings, not just the ready-to-hand, as Heidegger explains in a later note: 'Das Seyn-lassen ['letting-be' or 'beyng-letting']. Cf.ET, where letting-be [Sein-lassen] applies fundamentally and without restriction to *every* being!' (BT, 441 *ad* 84). Letting things be is required if we are to share in them. If you and I are to perceive the same piece of chalk, I may use the chalk, but I cannot regard it as merely a function of my own perceptions and purposes, nor perhaps can I 'grind it up in a mortar' (XXVII, 102). We have a 'metaphysical indifference to things' grounded in our freedom (XXVII, 103). We differ from insects, which are "aware" of things only insofar as they impinge on them directly and trigger off appropriate behaviour (XXIX, 368, 397ff.). There are specialized modes of letting-be:

the scientist 'steps back' from things, regarding the *zuhanden* as *vorhanden*, a plough as a material body (XXVII, 183f.). *Seinlassen* usually means 'leave alone, drop, stop doing'. But Heidegger's *Sein-lassen* involves *Sicheinlassen*, 'getting into, engaging with, getting involved with' beings (ET, 185/125). We open up a space in which beings can be themselves. We enter that open space and there engage with beings *as beings*, as independent entities that are not simply appendages of ourselves. Freedom enables us to open up the space (truth) and let beings be. There we exercise our freedom in making choices and 'correct' assertions that are guided, but not forced on us, by beings (ET, 185ff./124ff.Cf. XXXI, 303).

The perfect participle of *lassen* is *gelassen*, '(having been) let, left, etc.'. It also means 'calm, cool, composed'; one has 'let' oneself, or 'settled', down. Mystics such as Eckhart and Seuse used it in the sense of 'devout, devoted to God, pious'. *Gelassenheit* was used by mystics for the peace one finds in God by taking one's distance from worldly things. It now means 'calmness, composure, detachment, "releasement"'. It is similar to the *apatheia*, 'impassivity', recommended by the Greek stoics, and to the basic mood of *Verhaltenheit*, 'restraint', recommended by Heidegger (LXV, 8, 395, etc.). *Gelassenheit* is a remedy for technology. Technology 'alienates [entfremdet]' us from our 'native habitat [Heimat]' by reducing the size of the globe, making it all familiar and within our reach: 'Every week films bear them away into realms of imagination – often strange, often quite ordinary; they feign a world which is no world' (G, 15/48). This threatens our *Bodenständigkeit*, our 'root(ednes)s in the soil': 'The loss of Bodenständigkeit comes from the spirit of the age into which we are all born' (G, 16/48f.). This 'entirely new position of man in and towards the world' stems ultimately from philosophy. 'The world now appears as an object on which calculative thinking conducts its assaults, no longer to meet any resistance. Nature becomes one gigantic filling station, the energy source for modern technology and industry' (G, 17f./50). Can a 'new ground and soil be given back' to us, on which 'humanity and all its work might flourish in a new way – even in the atomic age?' (G, 21/53). We cannot resist technology. What we *can* do is this. Use technological objects, but 'keep free of them so that we always let them go [loslassen]'. In using them, we can 'let them rest [auf sich beruhen lassen] as something that does not affect our innermost, authentic selves' (G, 22f./54). 'I would like to give this attitude of a simultaneous Yes and No to the technological world an old name: *releasement to things [die Gelassenheit zu den Dingen]*' (G, 23/54). *Gelassenheit*, together with 'openness for the mystery [Geheimnis]', for the hidden 'sense of the technological world', may, if we cultivate them, supply us with a new *Bodenständigkeit*, even one day 'restore the old, now rapidly disappearing Bodenständigkeit in an altered form' (G, 24/ 55).

In a dialogue Heidegger explores *Gelassenheit* more thoroughly (G, 29ff./58ff.). It involves the disinterested reflection that technology threatens to eliminate (cf. G, 25/56). It abandons willing, but it is not passive and does not let things slide and drift. It is not, as Eckhart supposed, the abandonment of sinful selfishness and of self-will in favour of the divine will. It is thinking, but not thinking in the sense of representation. It is a sort of 'waiting [Warent]' (G, 35/62). Waiting, not expecting, and not waiting for anything in particular, but waiting 'for [auf]' the openness, which Heidegger now calls *(die) Gegnet*, the 'regioning', an old form of *Gegend*, 'region', which means 'free expanse' (G, 39/66, 50/74), and is almost equivalent to 'truth' in Heidegger's sense (G, 63/83f.). *Gelassenheit* is *Gelassenheit*, not now to things, but 'to the regioning [zur Gegnet]' (G, 50/74).

Heidegger's idea is this. Technology cannot let beings be. Everything, including man himself, becomes a disposable object for it. Hence the open, the world, not only becomes smaller; it threatens to disappear altogether, reducing man to a 'mechanized animal', just one thing among others (LXV, 98, 275). *Gelassenheit* is the thinker's attempt to keep the open open, 'letting a world world [Weltenlassen einer Welt]' (LXV, 391). We do this by taking a detached stance towards the technological devices threatening to engulf us, letting *them* be, and by 'releasement' into the open. Thus we preserve the open space of the world and our human integrity by a special effort that was not required in the past.

life and biology *(Das) Leben*, 'life', from *leben* 'to live', was a central concept in Dilthey, Scheler and Nietzsche. It was not, except perhaps in Nietzsche, conceived biologically, but metaphysically and historically. Life is dynamic. It is at odds with materialism, idealism, and objective value and truth. It is a reaction against 'representing', the 'I', and the subject–object relation (LXV, 326). It embraces both our mental states, conscious and unconscious, and the expressive and creative acts that constitute our history. Heidegger's early lectures speak, under Dilthey's influence, of *Leben* in a sense close to the later 'DASEIN' (LVIII, 29ff; LXI, 2, 79ff.). 'Our life is our world – and rarely such that we survey it; we are always, albeit quite inconspicuously, hiddenly, "involved" ['dabei sind']: "captivated", "repelled", "enjoying", "resigned". [. . .] And our life is only *life*, so far as it lives in a world' (LVIII, 33f.). We cannot escape from life and view it from outside: 'Life speaks to itself in its own language' (LVIII, 231;

cf. 42, 250). Life is 'self-sufficient'. Life also 'expresses' itself and possesses 'significance' (LVIII, 137). Philosophy emerges from life: 'Every genuine philosophy is born from the *distress* of the fullness of life, not from an epistemological pseudo-problem or a basic question of ethics' (LVIII, 160; cf. 253f.). Heidegger is at odds with Husserl, who tended to neglect life: I should let myself be carried along by the steam of life, '*joining in* lived experience [*Mitmachen* des Erlebens]' rather than withdrawing from it in the *Epoche*; we must 'understand' life from within – by way of history – rather than focus on intentional experiences of 'things' (LVIII, 254ff.).

By 1923 'factical life [faktisches Leben]' is equated with *Dasein* (LXIII, 81). *Lebensphilosophie*, 'philosophy of life', is 'intrinsically a tautology, for philosophy deals with nothing except Dasein itself. "Philosophy of life" is thus about as clever as "botany of plants"' (XXI, 216. Cf. BT, 46). *Leben* is not biological: we understand plants and animals only in terms of our prior understanding of human life (LXI, 81ff; BT, 49f., 194). But Heidegger prefers *Dasein* to *Leben* (cf. NI, 278/nii, 26f.). Not because *Leben* must be conceived as a series of discrete *Erlebnisse*, 'lived experiences': Dilthey was interested in the overall shape or structure of 'life as a whole' (BT, 46). It is because 'life' is a fuzzy concept, in constant danger of reduction to merely biological life. Moreover, *Dasein* conveys, better than *Leben*, our relationship to *being*, a concept which was not prominent in the early lectures.

In Nietzsche 'the word and concept "Leben" fluctuates', meaning in turn 'beings as a whole', 'living creatures (plant, animal, man)', and 'human life' (NI, 573/niii, 87. Cf. LXV, 365). *Leben* is linked with the 'body'. *Leib*, the human body, in contrast to *Körper*, the merely physical 'body' (XV, 322: 'the limit of the Leib is not that of the Körper'), comes from *leben* and once meant 'life'. A verb derived from it, *leiben*, now survives only in the expression *wie er leibt und lebt*, 'to the life, to a T, "as he loves and lives"'. Heidegger revives *leiben* and its links with both *Leib* and *Leben*, speaking of *leibende Leben*, 'bodying life' and *leibende-lebende Mensch*, 'bodying-living man': *Das Leben lebt, indem es leibt*, 'Life lives, in that it bodies' (NI, 163, 223, 565/ni, 138, 192, niii, 79). The body is not, however, a physical or biological substratum on which higher levels are superimposed: 'We do not "have" a body, we "are" bodily [leiblich]' (NI, 118/ni, 99). Nietzsche often spoke of biology, but Heidegger does his best to acquit him of 'biologism', the view that our basic concepts and beliefs depend on our biological nature. Life in Nietzsche's sense has to do with 'biography' rather than 'biology', both words from the Greek *bios*, 'life' (NI, 517/niii, 39. Cf. XXI, 34, where *bios* is distinguished, as 'human existence', from *zoē*, as 'biological life'.). Heidegger has two main objec-

119

tions to biologism. First, biology as a science cannot ground metaphysics, since it is based on metaphysics. That we select living beings as a realm for study and the way in which we study them depends on our metaphysics. (NI, 524ff./niii, 44ff.) Second, our freedom implies that we are not determined by our biology. Nietzsche suggests that our knowledge and categories are rooted in our biology, that even the law of contradiction is a biological necessity: man must avoid contradiction so as to master the chaos surrounding him; as the jellyfish develops and extends its prehensile organs, so the animal 'man' uses reason and its prehensile organ, the law of contradiction, to find its way around in its environment and survive (NI, 593/niii, 103). This is not so. Man is not biologically specialized, like the lizard that hears a rustle in the grass but not nearby gunfire (NI, 244/ni, 212). Men can and do contradict themselves, overtly as well as implicitly: there is 'no compulsion', but 'a peculiar *freedom*, which is perhaps the ground not only of the *possibility* of self-contradiction, but even the ground of the *necessity* of the principle of contradiction avoidance' (NI, 596/niii, 105f; cf. 614/niii, 121). Knowledge cannot be explained by its usefulness in the 'struggle for survival', since something can be of use to us only if we are already of such a kind as to make use of it and/or we can discern the use only retrospectively from the viewpoint of the knowledge supposedly explained by it: 'But a use and usefulness can never be the ground for the essence of a basic attitude [Verhaltens], since every use and every assignment of a useful purpose is already posited from the perspective and is thus always only the consequence of an essential constitution' (NI, 610/niii, 118).

Heidegger was consistently averse to attempts to explain human conduct and its variations biologically, believing, with Kant, that our human finitude is prior to our biological equipment (XXV, 86f. Cf. K, 229/156) and, with Adam Smith, that the significance of the intrinsically slight and insignificant differences between men depends on what we make of them (cf. WN, 14f.). To the claim that 'Poetry is a biologically necessary function of the people', he replied: 'And so is digestion' (XXXIX, 27). He is also averse to the idea that philosophy should be 'relevant to life', *lebensnah* (XXXI, 35).

M

man and anthropology   German has two words for 'man'. *Mann,* like the
Latin *vir* and the Greek *anēr,* means 'man, male', in contrast to 'woman'.
Mensch, like the Latin *homo* and the Greek *anthrōpos,* means 'man, human
being', including women. Since Heidegger rarely discusses sexual differences, he almost invariably uses *Mensch(en)* in speaking of 'man' or 'men'.
In BT, he purports to avoid the word *Mensch,* along with other traditional
philosophical ways of referring to ourselves. Terms such as 'I' or 'ego',
'subject' and 'consciousness' distort our 'phenomenal reality', implying
that one is always aware of oneself, that one is an underlying thing, or
that one is fully aware of objects. At best, such terms, and others such as
'soul' or 'spirit', pick out one aspect or phase of the human being. Other
terms, such as 'life', 'person' or 'man', are inadequately elucidated and
lull us into a false sense of security (BT, 46). (*Person* differs from *Mensch*
in implying 'self-responsibility', XXXI, 263.) One disadvantage of 'man' is
that in philosophy it is encumbered with traditional definitions of man.
The Greeks defined man as *zōon logon echon,* the 'animal that has logos';
Heidegger translates *logos* as '(the power of) talk' rather than 'reason'
(BT, 25, 165). In Latin this became *animal rationale,* which is unmistakably
a 'rational animal'. But reason, Heidegger objects, may be purely theoretical, leaving man's conduct at the mercy of non-rational drives (XXXI,
263f.). The essence of man depends on his 'relation to being', not on any
sort of rationality (NII, 193f., 357f./niv, 139f., 217f.). Man is not an animal
with something added. Everything about us differs from its apparent
animal counterpart. Animals have *Benehmen,* 'behaviour', not, as we do,
Verhalten, 'conduct, comportment', since they are *benommen,* 'dazed, captivated', by objects around them. They do not perceive 'something as
something'; at bottom they have no perception, only something analogous
in a different key. They cannot relate to beings *as such* or to beings *as a
whole* (XXIX, 376). Men have been, some still are, and all may become,
rational animals, but this is an unsatisfactory condition in which we are
out of touch with being and with Da-sein (LXV, 28, 62, etc.).

Nevertheless, Heidegger often speaks of *Mensch* in BT itself, as well as in lectures and after BT. Traditionally man is seen as involving three constituents: body (*Leib*), soul (*Seele*, the animating principle responsible for our being alive and for our lower, appetitive and emotional life), and spirit (*Geist*, our 'reason', our 'capacity for I-saying', LXV, 53). Philosophers have usually selected one of these constituents as the dominant one and then used it to explain beings as a whole. Mostly they have picked spirit or reason, though Nietzsche, 'in *intention*' preferred the body or the soul (LXV, 313. Cf. BT, 48, 117, 198). Often man is assigned to different sciences: the body to biology, the soul to psychology, and spirit to psychology or logic. Anthropology, the study of man, *anthrōpos*, now attempts to reunify man, but its error is to treat man as a being with an intrinsic nature of its own, bereft of its special relation to being (BT, 45ff; K, 209ff./142ff; XXVIII, 10ff.). This is quite distinct from Kant's anthropology (K, 132ff./91f.). Kant alone made *Einbildung*, 'imagination', central to man, and saw the 'poetizing [dichtenden] character of reason' (NI, 584/niii, 95f. Cf. K, 63/42). *Einbildung* is not just a capacity for forming images of entities, but for opening up a world in which we can encounter entities at all (K, 84/57. Cf. LXV, 312). Kant views man in relation to world and God, as well as the soul; metaphysics is rooted in man's nature (XXXI, 206). He transcended the 'biological liberalism' of the body-soul-spirit view, seeing that the 'person is more than "I"; the person is grounded in self-legislation' (LXV, 53) – which comes close to the view that Dasein's being is an issue for it (BT, 42). Kant and German idealism gave 'I-centred [ichhafte] self-consciousness a quite different form, in which an assignment to the "we" and to the historical and absolute is involved' (LXV, 68).

Insofar as man is not just another animal, he is made what he is not by his intrinsic features but by his relation to being and truth: 'Metaphysics knows, and can know, nothing of the way in which the essence of truth and of being and the relation to them determine the essence of man, so that neither animality nor rationality, neither the body nor the soul, nor the spirit, nor all three together, suffice to comprehend the basic essence of man' (NII, 195/niv, 142). But being and truth do not have a fixed nature readily accessible to us. We give different accounts of them at different times, and what they are at any given time depends in part on our questions and answers about them. Thus what man is at a given time also depends on our questions and answers. We ask 'Who are we?', but there is again no answer independent of *our* answers, even if they are given only in our actions (LXV, 49). Even the term 'we' is problematic: '*whom* do we mean by "we"? [. . .] Ourselves, just those

122

present at hand, those who are here and now? Where does the dividing line run? Or do we mean "man" ['den' Menschen] as such? But only as historical "is" man unhistorical. Do we mean ourselves as our own people? But even then we are not unique, but a people among other peoples. [. . .] It immediately becomes clear that the way in which we state our theme in the question, "we", already involves a decision about the Who' (LXV, 48). Man 'takes himself as a present-at-hand "example" of the genus "human being"' (LXV, 61). But a man's relations to other men are not unchanging like those of animal species. I may think of myself as an individual, as a teacher, as a German, or as a member of the human race. The answer I give to the question who I am will not apply to all men at all times. Whether I am an individual or not itself depends on my relationship to being: 'the self of man is made a particular "I" by *restriction* to the surrounding unhiddenness. [. . .] It is by restriction that man becomes the [Greek] *egō*, not by a removal of constraints of *such* a sort that the self-representing I usurps the role of standard and centre of everything representable' (NII, 138/niv, 93f. Cf. WT, 35/46: 'the I-standpoint is something modern and therefore ungreek. For the Greeks the polis set the standard'.)

'The less of a being man is, the less he insists on the being he finds himself to be, the closer he comes to being. (No Buddhism! the opposite!)' (LXV, 170f.). Heidegger was as fond as Hegel of Sophocles's *Antigone*, especially the 'poetic projection of man' in the first chorus, which begins: 'There is much that is strange, but nothing that surpasses man in strangeness' (ll.332f. at IM, 112/123. Cf. NII, 395/niv, 248: man's uncanny homelessness drives him to conquer the earth).

meaning, sense and significance *Sinn* originally meant 'journey, way' but now corresponds closely, but not exactly, to 'sense'. *Bedeutung* corresponds to 'meaning'. Frege's distinction between *Sinn* as 'sense' and *Bedeutung* as 'reference' is not usual in German, but it exploits the derivation of *Bedeutung* and *bedeuten*, 'to mean, signify, etc.', from *deuten (auf)*, 'to interpret; to point at/to, indicate'. *Bedeutung* also means 'significance, importance'. *Bedeutsam* is 'significant, meaningful; important'. Heidegger also uses *Bedeutsamkeit*, 'significance, meaningfulness'. He owes much to Dilthey, who used these words both for what is signified or expressed by a sign and for the 'meaning' of a complex whole such as a life, a historical process, etc. Dilthey often uses *Sinn* for the meaning of the whole – a life, a sentence – and *Bedeutung* or *Bedeutsamkeit* for the meaning of its parts – events, words (AGW, 171, 245f.). In early Heidegger meanings,

Bedeutungen, are constituents of the sense (DS, 290). (German uses *Sinn* rather than *Bedeutung* for the 'meaning' of (a) life.) *Bedeutsamkeit* was for Dilthey a central 'category of life' in contrast to the natural world.

Husserl distinguished between the 'act of meaning [das Bedeuten als Akt]' and the *Bedeutung* as the 'ideal unity of the diversity of possible acts'. The subjective acts that bestow meaning on expressions are variable, but objective *Bedeutungen* cannot change. Linguistic change is consigned to the sphere of psychology. In DS Heidegger accepted Husserl's separation of meaning and natural language. But later he rejects it as 'banal Platonism' (XVII, 94; cf. XXI, 58ff.). With the concepts of DASEIN, existence, history, etc. he avoids the Scylla of 'psychologism' and the Charybdis of timeless meanings. He sometimes uses *Sinn* and *Bedeutung* interchangeably (e.g. XXI, 357), but *Sinn* tends to refer to the whole rather than its parts. Hence while *Bedeutung* often occurs in the plural, the plural *Sinne* is rare, except when it means the five 'senses' or the 'senses' one has taken leave of. *Sinn* also means the 'sense' of e.g. beauty (cf. BT, 137).

Heidegger uses *Bedeutsamkeit* (always singular) for the network of relationships that knit together Dasein's world. He connects it with *bedeuten*, sometimes writing *be-deuten* to stress the sense 'to point; to interpret': 'We conceive the relational character of these relations of referring [Verweisens] as *signifying* [*be-deuten*]. In its familiarity with these relations Dasein "signifies" ['bedeutet', i.e. interprets] to itself, it primordially gives itself to understand its being and ability-to-be with regard to its being-in-the-world. The For-the-sake-of-which [Das Worumwillen] signifies [bedeutet, i.e. points to] an In-order-to [ein Um-zu]; this in turn signifies a For-this [ein Dazu]; the For-this signifies an In-which [ein Wobei] of letting-be-involved; the In-which signifies a With-which [ein Womit] of involvement. [...] The relational whole of this signifying [Bedeutens] we call Bedeutsamkeit' (BT, 87; cf. 359f., 364). The *Worumwillen* is, say, Dasein's need of shelter; this signifies an *Um-zu*, something *for* making a house; this signifies a tool, a *Dazu*, e.g. hammer. The *Wobei*, etc. signified by the *Dazu* is the various tasks in which a hammer can be involved. The *Womit*, etc. is the purposive connections between these tasks, both the ultimate task of building a shelter – the For-which, *Wozu*, that has no further involvement, since it is a rock-bottom need of Dasein – and various intermediate For-whiches, such as fastening planks, required in order to build a shelter (BT, 84f.). Heidegger's down-to-earth terminology (abandoned after BT) is inspired by such coinages of Aristotle as *to hou heneka*, 'the for the sake of which', and by Aristotle's accounts of practical inference (cf. XIX, 48ff.). While Aristotle sketches the logical

124

form of practical inferences, Heidegger uncovers the background involve-
ment-relationships that make them possible. *Bedeutsamkeit* 'makes up the
"worldliness of the world"' (BT, 86).

Bedeutsamkeit enables Dasein, when it interprets things, to disclose
Bedeutungen, on which 'word and language' are founded (BT, 87). In a
later note Heidegger rejects the implied dependence of language on prior
worldly significance: 'Untrue. Language is not superimposed [aufges-
tockt]; it *is* the original essence of truth as There' (BT, 442). But at the
time of BT meanings, though invariably associated with words, are logically prior to words and rooted in the significance relations of the world:
'From the start our essence is such that it forms intelligibility and
understands. [. . .] [H]ence vocal sounds which we, like animals, produce
can have a meaning. The meaning does not accrue to the sounds; on the
contrary, the vocal expression first develops from already developed and
developing meanings' (XXIX, 444f. Cf. BT, 161; XX, 287).

Heidegger often uses *im Sinne* . . . 'in the sense (of)', to explain the
sense in which he is using a word. But *Sinn* in his technical sense is
correlative to a general understanding not yet articulated in words, an
understanding that stems from a projection and enables us to understand
particular entities: 'Taken strictly Sinn means the Upon-which [das Wora-
ufhin] of the primary projection of the understanding of being. [. . .]
When we say: beings "have Sinn", this means: they have become accessible
in their being, which is what first of all, projected on its Upon-which,
"strictly" "has Sinn"' (BT,324; cf. 151). Heidegger is inclined to say that
'only Dasein "has" Sinn', since it is Dasein's PROJECT that confers *Sinn*
on other things (BT, 151). The Upon-which is not like a screen existing
independently of the project – raw, Dasein-independent beings. It is the
upshot of the projection, what makes being intelligible to us – more like
a film than a screen: 'In BT "Sinn" names the project-realm [Entwurfsber-
eich], [. . .] the lighting of being that opens up and grounds itself in the
projecting' (NII, 20/niii, 174). But since our conception of being is
rooted in time, the Upon-which of its projection is time and the original
or Greek *Sinn* of being is PRESENCE, *Anwesenheit* (BT, 365; XXIV, 437;
XV, 334ff.). Later, 'Sinn of being' is supplanted by 'truth of being' (NII,
20/174; LXV, 43). *Sinn* suggested that the projection of being is a
'structure of subjectivity – as Sartre takes it, since he bases himself on
Descartes (who ignores alētheia as alētheia)', when in fact it was a
'disclosure that opens up [eröffnenden Erschliessung]'. 'Truth' is not
'correctness', but the 'locality [Ortschaft]' of being. Hence Heidegger
now speaks of the 'topology of beyng [Topologie des Seyns]'. (XV, 335).
Being is no longer – as BT strongly suggested – simply something

projected by Dasein. It is more like electricity that finds an outlet in man or Dasein.

metaphysics 'Metaphysics' comes from a Greek expression meaning 'the things after [meta] the physics', assigned by Aristotle's editors to his work on what he called 'first philosophy'. First philosophy was to study 1. the features common to all beings [onta] (such as the fact that no being can both be and not be at the same time), and 2. the nature of the first or highest being, God or the unmoved mover. Among Aristotle's reasons for allocating God to first philosophy are that God does not move or change, and so is not dealt with by physics, and that consideration of the highest being sheds light on all the rest. Heidegger regards 'metaphysics' as equivalent to 'ONTOLOGY' (XXIX, 73; NII, 209/niv, 154f.). But owing to its association with God, which persists beyond Aristotle down to Hegel, he often calls it 'ontotheology' (XXXII, 140ff; NII, 321, 348/niii, 241, niv, 210; WMI, 373f./275f.; ID, 50ff./54ff.).

The 'meta' in 'metaphysics' originally meant 'after', Heidegger argues, but soon came to mean 'across' or 'beyond', so that 'metaphysics' came to mean 'going beyond physical, i.e. natural things, i.e. beings' (XXIX, 59ff.). This is similar to TRANSCENDENCE, except that metaphysics is *primarily* a philosopher's speciality, not something that every DASEIN does. Heidegger initially approved of 'metaphysics'. Like 'ontology', it contrasts with 'epistemology' (*Erkenntnistheorie*), to which he is invariably hostile, and with science, which studies beings, but not BEING (or the NOTHING). It is equivalent to '(good) philosophy', what Heidegger himself does. A metaphysical or philosophical question has two distinguishing features: 1. It concerns the whole (WM, 103/93; XXXI, 14, etc.): we cannot consider e.g. freedom without raising the whole range of metaphysical questions. Unlike science, metaphysics *goes beyond* any particular being or domain of beings to beings as a whole, the WORLD, and being itself. 2. The questioner is embroiled in the question (WM, 103/93f.) or philosophy involves an 'assault' not simply on man in general, but on the questioner as an individual, going to his root (XXXI, 34f., 131). It attacks the questioner because he, like every Dasein, is a being in the midst of beings and *implicitly* transcends to beings as a whole: 'Metaphysics is the basic happening in Dasein' (WM, 120/109).

IM, based on lectures from 1935, is still favourable to metaphysics. But his first lectures on Nietzsche, in the winter of 1936–7, indicate hostility to it: Nietzsche represents the 'end of western metaphysics' and we must pass on to the 'wholly different question of the truth of being' (NI, 19/ni,

10). We must attempt what Nietzsche failed to achieve: the 'overcoming' of metaphysics (NII, 12/niii, 166. Cf. OM). 'Metaphysics' has a new meaning that depends on Heidegger's sharpening of the ontological DIFFERENCE. Metaphysics, i.e. traditional philosophy since Aristotle, askes the 'guiding-question', What are beings as such? but not the 'basic question', What is (the truth of) being? Metaphysics goes 'beyond' beings to beings as a whole (NI, 530/niii, 50), interpreting them variously as spirit, matter and force, becoming and life, representation, will, substance, subject, *energeia* (Aristotle) or eternal recurrence of the same (Nietzsche) (WMI, 361/265). Often its interpretation of beings is anthropomorphic (NI, 356ff., 376ff./nii, 98ff., 115ff.). Often it postulates a transcendent, supersensible world (NI, 628/niii, 133). Metaphysics addresses four main questions: 1. the nature of man; 2. the being of beings; 3. the essence of the truth of beings; 4. how man takes and gives the 'measure [Mass]' for the truth of beings, e.g. whether (as Heidegger supposes Descartes to have held) what is depends solely on what man can be certain of (NII, 137, 190f., 203ff./niv, 92, 136f., 150ff.). But it does not go so far beyond as to ask about being (or 'beyng').

Why should we ask about being? For several reasons: 1. Being is, or sheds, the light which enables metaphysics to see beings as beings (WMI, 362/265; QB, 92). Since metaphysics does not look at the light itself, it does not understand its own essence: to understand metaphysics, we need to go beyond metaphysics (LXV, 174). 2. Heidegger hardly suggests that the question 'What are beings?' exceeds man's capacities. But he often implies that being is too diverse to allow a single answer to the question, and – despite his aversion to 'epistemology' – that a prior question is: How does man, a finite being among beings, transcend beings, so as to ask what beings as a whole are? 3. Basic words such as 'being' change their meaning over history. For all its diversity 'western metaphysics' remains within the confines of the broad meaning of 'being' established by the Greeks: permanence and PRESENCE. To give an answer to 'What are beings?' that is not historically parochial and blinkered, we need to examine the history of 'being'. 4. Metaphysics is not simply a diversion for a leisured elite. It is the 'ground of western history' (NII, 274/niii, 202. Cf. NI, 448ff./nii, 184ff; NII, 343/niv, 205). The central feature of modern history, the TECHNOLOGY that engulfs the earth and threatens world and Dasein, stems ultimately from metaphysics, from Descartes's interpretation of nature as *res extensa* and the central position assigned to the subject and its representations (NII, 165ff./niv, 116ff.).

Metaphysics cannot help our plight; it can only take us further in the same direction. A return to an earlier, more benign phase of metaphysics, such as Thomism, is impractical, and also ineffectual, since any earlier phase of metaphysics has a tendency to malignancy: metaphysics is not in the control of individual thinkers, it is an impersonal force that takes them over (NII, 258/nii, 188), nor is it simply the metaphysic of will (to power) that is the ground of real NIHILISM, but metaphysics as such (NII, 343/niv, 205). So our only hope is to overcome metaphysics. This does not mean eliminating or ignoring metaphysics. We cannot do that: 'As long as man remains the animal rationale, he is the animal metaphys- icum'. We must try to go back into the GROUND of metaphysics. This may effect a 'transformation of the essence of man' and thus a 'transfor- mation of metaphysics' (WMI, 363/267).

Later, Heidegger speaks of 'getting over' (*Verwindung*) metaphysics rather than 'overcoming' (*Überwindung*) (QB, 86ff.).

modes of being: the ready-to-hand and the present-at-hand DASEIN tends to treat all entities – and indeed *non*-entities such as space, time and being itself – as if they were beings in just the same way (XXXI, 44). But there are, and implicitly we recognize that there are, different ways or modes of being (*Seinsweise(n), Seinsart(en)*), that things differ in how (*wie*) they are as well as in what (*was*) they are. One mode of being is *Vorhandenheit* or *Vorhandensein*, 'presence-at-hand'. It comes from a com- mon word, *vorhanden*, lit. 'before the hands, at hand', but now '(to be) there, present, available'; it is used of things, not of people. Heidegger often, especially when discussing the views of others, uses *Vorhandensein, - heit*, in the sense of the 'existence' of something (XXIV, 32). But more often he uses it for a particular mode of being, for things that we find neutrally reposing in themselves. Typically, what is *vorhanden* is a natural entity rather than an artefact. But one can regard artefacts as simply *vorhanden*, especially if they are broken or useless, and natural entities can be other than *vorhanden* if we make use of them.

Vorhandensein, especially since it also means 'existence', has become the 'average concept of being' (XXIV, 30). But not everything is *vorhanden*, and *Vorhandenheit* is not the primary mode of being. Dasein itself is not *vorhanden*, nor are articles of use or 'equipment', *Zeug*. *Zeug* once meant 'means, tools, material, etc.', but since the eighteenth century it has come to mean 'junk, trash'. Its earlier sense survives in compounds: *Schreibzeug*, 'writing equipment', *Schuhzeug*, 'footgear', etc. Heidegger extracts *Zeug* from such compounds and revives its older sense of 'gear, equipment, tool(s)', things that have the character of the *Um-zu*, the 'in-order-to' (BT, 68). *Zeug* is *zuhanden*; its mode of being is *Zuhandensein, -heit*, 'readiness-

128

to-hand'. *Zuhanden,* lit. 'to, towards, the hands', is now, unlike *vorhanden,* not a common word. It is used in such phrases as 'for the attention of [zuhanden] so-and-so'. Again Heidegger breathes new life into the word and applies it to things that serve human purposes in some way: articles of use, raw materials, footpaths, etc. Only non-human things are *zuhanden.* The mode of being of other people is *Mitdasein,* 'Dasein-with'.

Zuhandenheit is prior to *Vorhandensein:* what we first and immediately come across are articles of use rather than neutral things. When we do see a *Zeug,* we do not first see it as merely *vorhanden* and then interpret it as e.g. a book for reading. Even if it is in an unknown language, we see it as a book in an unknown language, not just as paper with black marks on it (cf. BT, 164; NI, 563/niii, 77f.). Even unknown *Zeug* in an unfamiliar work environment (*Zeugganze, Zeugganzheit,* 'equipmental totality') is immediately recognized by any human being as *Zeug* in a *Zeugganze* (XX, 334). We can suggest how the *Zuhandenes* comes to be seen as *vorhanden,* when it is unusable and thus 'conspicuous', goes missing and is thus 'obtrusive', or gets in the way of our purpose and is thus 'obstinate': if e.g. I have my wood and hammer but find that I cannot use them because I have run out of nails, the nails become obtrusive (*aufdringlich*), while the wood and hammer are seen as merely *vorhanden* (BTm 73ff.). Conversely, it is difficult, if not impossible, to show how what is first seen as *vorhanden* could come to be seen as *zuhanden,* apart from the exceptional case of hitting on a use for a hitherto neutral object. Hence *Vorhandenheit* is a 'deficient mode' of *Zuhandenheit* (BT, 73).

Zeug, unlike the merely *Vorhandenes,* hangs together in a coherent way and thus belongs to a world, first the world around us, the *Umwelt,* then the wider *Welt* beyond. Heidegger uses several concepts to characterize this 'coherence' or 'hanging together' (*Zusammenhang*). One is *Verweisung:* 'In the structure of the 'In-order-to' lies a reference [Verweisung] of something to something' (BT, 68). *Verweisung,* from *verweisen,* 'to refer; to expel, relegate', is 'assignment, referral, expulsion'. No tool stands on its own. The hammer passes the buck: it refers to nails, to wood and to the workshop. Consequently, we do not usually notice or focus on the hammer as such. What we are first aware of is the whole workplace; within it, within the 'equipmental totality', particular tools come into focus as they are needed. Owing to *Verweisung* individual entities can remain inconspicuous but still there within the world unified by their references. We do not need to piece the world or the *Umwelt* together from individually discriminated items (BT, 68f.). A similar idea is expressed by *bewenden* and *Bewandtnis.* They come from *wenden,* 'to turn', but are now used only in such expressions as: *es dabei bewenden lassen,* 'to let it wend its own way, i.e. to leave it at that', *das hat seine eigene Bewandtnis*, 'that has its own turning or twist, i.e. that's a long story'. Tools are turned towards or 'involved' with other tools, independently of any given tool user. They go their own way and Dasein can let them do so. It need not focus on each one and piece them together like a jigsaw puzzle. It can thus 'let things be' (XXVII, 102ff.). Hence Dasein can be in a world, a world containing entities other than those that engage its current attention.

Heidegger later complains that BT was misunderstood: 'for Heidegger the world consists only of cooking-pots, pitchforks and lampshades; he has nothing to say about "higher culture" or about "nature"' (XLIX, 44). *Zeug* and the *Umwelt* were brought in, he insists, only to introduce the concept of world (ER, 81 n.55). Nevertheless in lectures he analyses the affinity and differences of *Zeug*, machines, organs and organisms: 'Every machine is a Zeug, but conversely not every Zeug is a machine' (XXIX, 314).

In BT the word *Ding*, 'thing', is used pejoratively: a thing is invariably *vorhanden*. To 'reify' *verdinglichen*, e.g. consciousness (BT, 46, 437), to treat it as a thing when it is not a thing, is a central failing of past philosophers. Later, *Ding* is used more favourably (XXXI, 56ff; D, 157ff./165ff.). To regard something as a *Ding* is to let it be what it is without interference. Heidegger is now more concerned about the ravages of technology than the reification of philosophers. One sort of *Ding* is the work of art, which has some affinity to *Zeug* and some to nature or the *Vorhandenes*, but differs from both (OWA, 10ff./146ff.).

mood and the state one is in   Heidegger uses three expressions

1. *Stimmung* means 'mood', as in 'in a good mood, not in the mood for', including a 'general mood' or 'atmosphere'. It also means 'tuning, pitch'. It comes from *Stimme*, 'voice', hence 'vote'. This gave rise to *stimmen*, originally (a) 'to let one's voice be heard, shout', (b) 'to fix, name', (c) 'to make harmonious, identical'. Sense (a) generated the sense of 'to cast a vote', (b) found its way into *bestimmen*, 'to deter- mine, destine, etc.', a word often used by Heidegger but of no special significance for him, while (c) was originally used of the human mind but is now 'to tune' a musical instrument. There is also an intransitive use of *stimmen* for 'to be fitting, suitable, correct'. The perfect partici- ple *gestimmt* means 'attuned, in a certain mood', the precise mood being usually determined by an adverb. This generates *Gestimmtheit* and *Gestimmtsein*, 'attunement, having a mood, being in a mood'.

2. Moods are not psychical states or feelings, arising in the I or subject, not 'like gloves that one now puts on, now takes off somewhere else. [. . .] Moods are not placed in the subject or in objects; we are, together with beings, *trans-planted* [*ver-setzt*] into moods. Moods are the all-enveloping force that comes over us and things together' (XXXIX, 89). So Heidegger likes to use an impersonal construction similar to 'It is raining': 'The mood reveals "how one is and is getting on" [wie einem ist und wird, lit. 'how it is and becomes for one']' (BT, 134). This locution is commonly used to say e.g. 'I feel ill, cold [mir ist/wird schlecht/kalt]', but it can express moods: *mir ist/es ist mir langweilig* ('boring') / *unheimlich* ('uncanny'). The subject is impersonal, since nothing in particular is boring or uncanny, it just is so for one 'as a whole' (WM, 111/101). Heidegger uses the indefinite *einem*, 'for one', rather than *mir*, 'for me', since in intense boredom or Angst I fade away as a distinct individual, sinking into 'indifference' along with everything else (WM, 111/101).

3. 'What we indicate *ontologically* with the term Befindlichkeit is *ontically* the most familiar and everyday thing: die Stimmung, das Gestimmtsein' (BT, 134). *Finden* is 'to come across/upon something, to find'. The prefix *be-* made *befinden* refer to intellectual finding, 'to experience, get to know, etc.' It also means 'to evaluate' something, 'to find it, e.g. in order'. The reflexive *sich befinden* strictly means 'to notice that one is in a place'. Now it means, like the French *se trouver*, 'to be present, situated, located, etc.' It often occurs where English would use 'to be': 'he *is* on a journey, on the way to recovery, in error, etc.'. It is also used to ask *Wie befinden Sie sich?* 'How are you doing/feeling? How do you feel?'; the reply requires an adverb, e.g. *Ich befinde mich wohl*, 'I feel well'. The adjective *befindlich* once meant 'demonstrable, perceptible', but since the eighteenth century has meant 'to be found, present, being, situated, etc.'. (It is now officialese and *sich befinden* is usually preferred.) Heidegger coins *Befindlichkeit*, which combines the ideas of 'situatedness' and of 'feeling/faring somehow', of *where* and *how* one finds oneself. Unlike *Stimmung*, it is too abstract to have a plural.

Befindlichkeit has three 'essential features' (BT, 137).

1. It 'discloses Dasein in its thrownness, at first and mostly in the mode of evasive turning away' (BT, 136). Certain moods, notably Angst and deep boredom, reveal with peculiar intensity the sheer fact *that* I am in the world, stripping me of my usual distinctive features, occupations

131

and surroundings. They bring home to me the fact that my being is at issue, that I have to make something of myself. My everyday moods – I am always in some mood or other – tend to obscure this fact, indeed they stem from a flight from it, though they are perturbed by occasional glimpses of a 'naked "that it is and has to be"' (BT, 134).

2. Mood 'has always already disclosed being-in-the-world as a whole, making it first possible to direct oneself towards something in particular' (BT, 137). It is by moods that I become aware of the world or beings as a whole, an open realm in which I can encounter other people and things. In deep boredom and Angst, things and others sink into a uniform indifference. But when such intense moods return to their usual subterranean status and are overlaid by more genial moods, I can engage with the familiar inhabitants of the world opened up for me. Even everyday moods disclose the whole to a certain range, since their object is no particular entity. 'World-impoverished' animals have pains, but no moods (XXXIX, 82; XXIX, 261).

3. *Befindlichkeit* attunes DASEIN to being affected by things and affected in certain ways. Unless I am in a mood I will not be 'affected', touched or interested (*betroffen*, the perfect participle of *betreffen*) by anything, nothing will 'matter' (*angehen*) to me (BT, 137). Only in a certain mood can I be affected in certain ways. No amount of 'pure perception, however far it penetrates into the inner core of the being of the present-at-hand, could ever discover such a thing as a threat' (BT, 138). To moodless contemplation nothing appears as ready-to-hand, as a tool to be used; it flattens everything out to a uniform presence-at-hand, though it also makes discoveries inaccessible to everyday moodiness. But even such contemplation has a mood of its own: '*tranquil* dwelling on . . . [Verweilen bei . . .]' (BT, 138).

Mood, unlike the affects and feelings made possible by them, is not a mere accompaniment of our being-in-the-world. It discloses the world, reveals our thrownness into it, and enables us to respond to beings within it. These functions are performed by moods of different types. Deep Angst or boredom reveals our thrownness, but it does not reveal tools for use or threats to be parried. A more humdrum mood is needed to attune us to everyday contingencies, a mood in flight from the more intense mood. Being-in-the-world is constituted (in part) by a hierarchy of moods.

Later, a *Grundstimmung*, 'basic mood', is one that: 1. 'carries us away to the limits of beings and puts us in touch with the gods [. . .]; 2. unites us with 'the earth and our native habitat'; 3. 'opens up beings as a whole [. . .] as the unity of a world'; 4. 'hands our Dasein over to beyng, to

undertake, shape and sustain it' (XXXIX, 223). Like all Dasein, philosophers need their mood: 'All essential thinking requires its thoughts and
propositions to be dug out like ore, each time anew, from the basic mood.
If the mood fails, then everything is a forced clatter of concepts and word-
husks' (LXV, 21). The basic mood – boredom (XXXIX, 121ff.) or Angst
(BT, 182ff; WM, 110ff./100ff.) – plays a part similar to Husserl's *Epoche*,
stripping things of their customary significance.

movement, comportment and behaviour   'To move [something]' is *bewegen*, and 'to move [oneself]' is *sich bewegen*. *Bewegung* is 'motion, movement'. Heidegger also often uses *Bewegtheit*, 'movedness, movement'.
Bewegen's affinity to *Weg*, 'way, path' enables him to read it as *be-wëgen*,
meaning 'to make way, provide [a region] with ways' (OWL, 197f./91f).
Often when he speaks of motion, he has in mind Aristotle's account (cf.
PIA; XXXI, 58ff; ECP, 241ff; XXXIII). Aristotle distinguished different
types of motion or change, *kinēsis*, according to the category in which it
occurred. A substantial change is the coming into being, or passing away,
of a substance, e.g. the birth or death of a person. A qualitative change is
the acquisition of a quality by a substance, e.g. a person's becoming
brown. A quantitative change is increase or decrease in the size of e.g. an
organism. A change in the category of place is locomotion. When something changes, it changes from being potentially (*dunamei*) so-and-so to
being actually (*energeiai*) so-and-so. A block of marble (the matter or
material cause) is potentially a statue and becomes an actual statue (the
final cause) owing to the imposition of a form (the formal cause) by a
sculptor (the efficient cause). A ball that is potentially in the opposing
team's goal (and potentially in indefinitely many other places) is moved
into the goal actually by a kick. The untouched block of marble is
potentially a statue, and the stationary ball is potentially in the goal. When
they are in motion towards the end, *telos*, that they have not yet reached –
the marble in the process of being carved, the ball in flight towards its
destination, their potentiality is actualized *as a potentiality*. This account of
change, primarily of locomotion, serves Aristotle's account of time: it is
the 'number' or 'measure' of motion with respect to the before and after
(BT, 421; XXIV, 330ff.). But Heidegger often speaks of DASEIN's 'movement' in ways that owe little to Aristotle and even contradict him: he
resists Aristotle's view that movement is always the movement of a substance or, in substantial change, of underlying matter. Dasein does not
first exist and then move; it is constituted by its movements: falling and
thrownness (BT, 177ff., 348), happening or historizing (BT, 375, 389).

Heidegger's inquiry into Dasein's historicality is bedevilled by the 'enigma' not only of being, but of movement (BT, 391. Cf. LXI, 93, etc.).

Heidegger regrets that philosophers since Aristotle have neglected movement. He attempts a quasi-Aristotelian classification of 'motion', in Aristotle's generic sense of 'change': 'The type of possible movement and of rest [Bewegtheit bzw. Unbewegtheit] varies with the type of entity in question. The problem of motion [Bewegung] is grounded on the question about the essence of beings as such' (XXXI, 31). Types of motion are: 1. 'mechanical motion, the mere pushing and shoving of material particles'; 2. The 'mere running and unfolding of a process [Vorganges]'; 3. growth and atrophy; 4. 'being a cause, letting ensue [Folgenlassen], beginning, ending'; 5. the 'behaviour' of animals; 6. the 'comportment' of men'; 7. complex forms: e.g. a journey 'is not merely, in fact not at all, mechanical locomotion with a machine (train, ship, plane), nor a mechanical motion plus a comportment of men; it is a specific happening, whose essential character we know as little as we know the essence of the other types of motion mentioned' (XXXI, 30).

Animals 'behave [sich benehmen]', men 'comport themselves [sich verhalten]'. This distinction has little apparent basis in ordinary German. (Das) Benehmen usually refers 'to the behaviour of individuals considered as free human beings in society' (DGS, 40f.). It comes from nehmen, 'to take'; hence sich benehmen is literally 'to betake oneself'. Heidegger reserves it for animals, since its perfect participle, benommen, means 'captivated, dazed, stupefied'. In the BT period, Dasein is said to be benommen: 'by the world of its concern' (BT, 61), by beings (W, 85), and in such moods as Angst (BT, 344; ER, 108). Later, only animals are benommen, 'captivated' by what immediately affects them (XXIX, 344ff.). By the capacity to distinguish being from tangible beings 'man is delivered from mere captivation [Benommenheit] by what besets and occupies him, into the relation [Bezug] to being; he becomes in the literal sense existent, he ex-sists, instead of merely "living"'. But now Heidegger fears that ex-sistence is not easy to maintain and that many humans may be victims of Seinsblindheit, 'blindness to being'. (ECP, 262).

(Das) Verhalten 'can denote conscious or unconscious behaviour [...] in reference to individuals or animals, [...] to substances (i.e. in the sense of "reaction"). It is also the appropriate term when the element stressed in behaviour is the taking of an attitude (e.g. in relation to a country, a government)' (DGS, 41). As a transitive verb verhalten, from halten, 'to hold, keep', means 'to hold back, restrain' (cf. BT, 253). Hence sich verhalten suggests 'restraining oneself': Dasein does not rush headlong at beings it encounters, it restrains itself. The derived noun, Verhältnis, means a 'proportion, relation(ship)'. Hence *sich verhalten* suggests 'relating (oneself)' to something or someone (cf. BT, 124). Heidegger often speaks of our (*Sich*)*verhalten zu Seiendem* (BT, 192, etc; XXIX, 346ff.), 'comportment towards beings'. But it also suggests 'relating oneself to beings'. Animals cannot do this, both because they are captivated by beings all along and because they are not aware of beings *as beings* (XXIX, 361).

N

nature and phusis *Natur* comes the Latin *natura*, 'birth, character, natural order, etc.', and this in turn from *nasci*, 'to be born, grow, be produced', with its perfect participle *natus*. The Greek *phusis* has a similar range of meaning, and comes from *phuein*, 'to grow, bring forth', and, in the passive voice, 'to grow, spring forth, etc.' Heidegger insists that the Latin translation of *phusis*, as with all potent Greek words, destroyed its original force (IM, 10f./11. Cf. LIV, 57ff.). *Phusis* occasionally appears in early lectures. The Greeks regarded being as 'presence and presence-at-hand [Anwesenheit und Vorhandenheit] of phusis in the widest sense' (XXI, 77). 'Phusis is not "nature"; it is [. . .] "what is of its own accord", what subsists in itself' (XXII, 287). But it does not appear in BT, and does not become prominent until later.

In early lectures and BT, *Natur* is often contrasted with 'history', as the realm of the natural sciences in contrast to that of the 'humane' or 'social sciences' (*Geisteswissenschaften*) (XX, 1). It also contrasts with 'grace' or the 'super-natural', with 'art', and with 'spirit' (ECP, 237). That *Natur* contrasts with other fields is one of its defects. It represents not an original, uncontaminated view of being(s), but a specific realm of beings demarcated in view of a prior conception of beings as such, before any such demarcation occurs. It is this original conception of beings that Heidegger wants to uncover, delving beneath subsequent lines of demarcation. There are two important senses of *Natur*: 1. nature as circumspectly disclosed in our everyday dealings with things; 2. nature as known theoretically by the natural sciences (XXI, 314; BT, 65; ER, 81 n.55). These are not identical. A house is not a part of nature in sense 1, though the trees in the garden and the wasps in the loft may be. For the physicist, the house is as much a part of nature as the trees and the wasps, though they are not viewed *as* a house, trees and wasps. Later, nature in sense 1 becomes EARTH.

Phusis, the watchword of Anaximander, Parmenides, and Heraclitus (cf. Kahn, 201ff.), originally embraced the whole of beings: 'phusis as these

136

beings as a whole is not meant in the modern, late sense of nature, perhaps as a concept contrasting with history; it is more original than both these concepts, in an original meaning that before nature and history embraces both and also in a way includes divine beings' (XXIX, 39). *Phusis* is 'what emerges of its own accord (e.g. the emergence of a rose), self-opening unfolding, issuing into appearance in such unfolding, and persisting and remaining in appearance, in short, emerging-lingering prevailing [das aufgehend-verweilende Walten]' (IM, 11/11f. Cf. XXIX, 38ff.). Later, *phusis* came to mean not just beings as a whole, but also their 'nature' or essence (XXIX, 46ff.). *Phusis* also entered into contrasts, primarily with *technē*, 'art, skill, know-how' and its products, and also with *nomos*, 'law, convention'. The Greeks asked: Is justice, the wrongness of certain actions and the rightness of others, natural or conventional? Does virtue come by nature or by teaching? *Phusis* became a 'regional concept [Gebietsbegriff]' (XXIX, 46. Cf. IM, 13/13f.). Originally, *phusis* was not sharply distinct from ALETHEIA, the unhiddenness into which beings emerge, or from *logos*, the 'gathering' or 'collection' of beings in the open. But as the Greeks asked *about* beings, they came to distinguish their questioning from the beings asked about; hence *phusis* is contrasted with *technē* (LXV, 190). Plato identified *phusis* with the 'idea'; this developed from the essential, and static, 'aspect' of beings into a representation intervening between ourselves and beings. *Logos* became an 'assertion' about beings, and *alētheia* became the 'correctness' of an assertion. Man became an 'animal having logos [discourse, reason]'; originally *phusis* was 'logos [gathering, collection] having man' (IM, 134/147). *Phusis* was translated as *natura* towards the end of its decline; so its original meaning eludes the Latin.

'Nature, separated out from beings by natural science – what happens to it in the hands of technology? The growing destruction of "nature", or rather the destruction unfolding to its end. What was it once? The site of the moment of the arrival and sojourn of the gods, when it was still phusis and rested in the essencing of beyng'. In its decline it successively becomes 1. beings of a specific type; 2. the counterpart to 'grace'; 3. the milch cow of 'calculating machination and economy', 4. ' "landscape" and a chance for relaxation, now reckoned up on a gigantic scale and arranged for the masses' (LXV, 277). This need not be the end. One matter up for 'decision' is 'whether nature is debased to a realm for reckoning and arrangement to exploit and to an opportunity for "experience", or it is the self-closing earth and bears the open of a world without a PICTURE' (LXV, 91). Heidegger has no clear idea how this will come about. The organic view blocks us off from nature; it is the culmination of the mechanical view. This is why 'an age of unrestrained "technologism" can find its self-interpretation in an "organic world view"' (LXV, 155). 'Nature' as the object (*Gegenstand*) of natural science and of technological exploitation cannot tell us about beings, even if it is supplemented by 'philosophy', since philosophy is now at home in the 'objectivity of objects'; as epistemology, as ontology, it always involves REPRESENTA-TION. A return to Goethe's 'intuition of nature', 'wallowing in the irrational', a romantic attempt to 'transfigure beings' – all this will leave everything as before, even confirm it (LXV, 496): 'where irrationalism determines the world-picture, rationalism celebrates its triumphs. Dominance of technology and susceptibility to superstition belong together' (NI, 531/niii, 50. Cf. BT, 65). Nothing can be decided as long as 'beings themselves remain unquestioned regarding their beyng and despite their expansion and vitalization disappear unnoticed, leaving behind objectivity as their counterfeit' (LXV, 497).

near and far Apart from their role in SPATIALITY, *Nähe*, 'nearness', from *nah*, 'near', and *Ferne*, 'farness, distance', from *fern*, 'far', are constantly present in Heidegger's thought. 'Near' and 'far' are contraries, but each involves the other. If something is too near, it is far: DASEIN is 'ontically nearest to us, but ontologically the farthest' (XXIV, 220, Cf. BT, 15). TRANSCENDENCE puts a decent distance between ourselves and things: 'Man is a creature of distance [ein Wesen der Ferne]! And only through genuine original distance that in his transcendence he establishes towards all beings does true nearness to things come to arise in him. And only the ability to hear into the distance brings about the awakening of the answer of those men who should be near to him' (XXVI, 285). One can be near to or far from beings, and also being itself, which is 'further [weiter] than all beings, since it is the lighting itself' (LH, 333/240). Descartes's and Husserl's concern for certainty involves *Seinsferne*, 'remoteness from being', remoteness 'both from the *being of the world* and all the more from the *being of Dasein as such*' (XVII, 282). In a different way, when the Germans establish their place among other nations, the 'homeland of this historical dwelling is nearness to being' (LH, 335/242).

Nearness and farness have little to do with measurement along the dimensions or 'parameters' of space and time. Two solitary farmhouses an hour's walk away from each other across the fields can be 'the best of neighbours [benachbart]', while two townhouses opposite or adjacent to each other may 'know no neighbourhood [Nachbarschaft]' (OWL, 210/103). Quantitative measurement considers colourless, uniform *Abstand*, 'distance', and has no place for the 'face-to-face' encounter involved in neighbourliness and nearness (OWL, 211f./103f.). Technology makes the world ever smaller. Great distances are covered in a short time; television brings distant events into our homes. The removal of 'distance [Entfernung]' does not bring everything *near*. It tends rather to abolish the distinction between the near and the far: 'Everything is merged together into uniform distancelessness [das gleichförmig Abstandlose]' (D, 158). There are antidotes. We can focus on original or poetic language (OWL, 214ff./107ff.) and/or on the THING (D, 170ff..177ff.). These reveal the 'fourfold', the four regions of the world that technology threatens to obliterate – earth, sky, gods, mortals – in their nearness to each other and in their receding farness.

The 'uniformity' resulting from technology is not unlike the 'indifference [Gleichgültigkeit]' of everything produced by deep boredom and by Angst (WM, 110f./99ff; XXIX, 207).

Nietzsche In 1961 Heidegger published *Nietzsche* (N) in two volumes. N is for the most part a revised version of his lectures on Nietzsche from the mid-1930s, beginning with 'Nietzsche: the Will to Power as Art', from the winter of 1936–7, and concluding with 'Nietzsche's Metaphysics', advertised for the winter of 1941—2, but not delivered. It omits only the course on 'Nietzsche II: Untimely Meditation', from the winter of 1938–9. N concludes with some pieces that were not intended as lectures, the latest of which, 'The Determination of Nihilism in terms of the History of Being', was written between 1944 and 1946 (NII, 335ff./niv, 199ff.).

Heidegger admired Nietzsche early on. He shares Nietzsche's sense of personal involvement in philosophy (DS, 196). He quotes Nietzsche's dictum, 'Every word is a prejudice', in support of his claim that through 'language itself we live in a quite definite conception of things' (XVII, 36). He respectfully discusses Nietzsche's account of the 'Use and Disadvantage of Historie for Life' (BT, 396f.). But his intensive work on Nietzsche began in the 1930s and continued into the 1950s, with, apart from N itself, two essays, 'Nietzsche's Saying "God is dead"' (H, 193ff./ qct, 53ff.) and 'Who is Nietzsche's Zarathustra' (VA, 97ff./nii, 211ff.), and a lecture course with abundant discussion of Nietzsche (WCT, esp. 19ff./ 48ff.).

N takes as its basic text not one of Nietzsche's own publications, but his posthumously published notebooks, called by his editors *The Will to Power* (1901, enlarged edtion 1906): 'What Nietzsche published in the period of his creativity is always the superficial foreground. [. . .] The real philosophy stays behind as "remains" ['Nachlass']' (NI, 17/ni, 9). Nietzsche could not write a traditional book on the will to power; hence his remains are crucial (NI, 485/niii, 12). Heidegger interprets Nietzsche not, like Bäumler, as a political thinker, nor, like Klages, as a biological thinker, but as a metaphysician, 'the end of western metaphysics', through a 'discussion[Aus-einander-setzung]' of which we can proceed to 'the quite different question about the truth of being' (NI, 19/ni, 10). Heidegger's concept of metaphysics is fluid, however, and his interpretation of Nietzsche fluctuates accordingly. It has several aspects: 1. Nietzsche does not rethink traditional concepts such as truth and being, he simply revalues them. He accepts that truth is propositional 'correctness' or correspondence, and thus rejects truth (NI, 179/ni, 153). He retains the traditional contrast of being and becoming, and prefers becoming to being (NI, 655f./niii, 155f.). 2. Nietzsche asks not about (the truth or essence of) being, but about the nature of beings as such or as a whole. In a thoroughly traditional manner he asks about the What or essence of beings and about their How or existence. Will to power, he answers, is the essence of beings, eternal recurrence is their existence (NII, 38, 260/niv, 8, niii, 189). 3. Nietzsche's central doctrines fit together as a system. Will to power, for example, has no goal, it simply circles around in itself. Hence it can do nothing but reproduce the same thing; eternal recurrence is its inevitable consequence. 4. Metaphysics involves, by Nietzsche's account, anthropomorphism (NI, 356ff., 376ff./nii, 98ff., 115ff.). Nietzsche's interpretation of beings in toto as will to power is 'the anthropomorphism of the "grand style"' (NI, 653/niii, 154). 5. Nietzsche places man at the centre of the universe. Everything has to present itself to man for judgement. In this respect, he develops the man-centred metaphysic of Descartes, and heralds the technological MACHINATION of modernity. This coheres with the will to power and his conversion of the essence of all beings into 'value' (NI, 539/niii, 57). Values are what technocrats calculate with, will to power is what drives their conquest of the earth, an enterprise as senseless and aimless as will to power itself: 'Senselessness now becomes the "sense" of beings as a whole' (NII, 23/niii, 177. Cf. LXV, 98). Nietzsche's 'superman' is the technocrat, 'the unconditional mastery of pure power' (NII, 39/niv, 9), the new man required and dominated by the 'machine economy' (NII, 165/niv, 116). (Later, the superman becomes more like a 'thinker' or a 'shepherd of being', e.g. WCT, 67/69.) 6. It is true that Nietzsche 'inverts' Platonism, in the sense that he rejects any supersensory or ideal world beyond the sensory world (NI, 177ff./ni, 151ff.). But this shows not that Nietzsche is not a metaphysician, but that he is the last metaphysician, that with him the possibilities of metaphysics are exhausted (NII, 16, 201/niii, 170, niv, 148). 7. Heidegger does not invariably interpret Nietzsche's doctrines as overall claims about beings. 'Art as the will to illusion [Schein] is the highest form of the will to power' (NI, 251/ni, 218). Art transcends our static categories of being and sets our thought in flux or becoming, until we once again settle down into a new form of static being. But this will to power, Heidegger adds, is not confined to art, but the 'basic character of beings' (NI, 251/ni, 218). Appealing to *Thus Spoke Zarathustra*, Heidegger interprets eternal recurrence not as a claim about beings in toto as a 'present at hand thing' (NI, 318/nii, 62), but as a thought which we must grasp in the interests of our decision in the 'moment [Augenblick]'; what matters is not the truth or correctness of the doctrine but its effect on its adherents (NI, 310ff./nii, 56ff.). Heidegger later treats this as an EXISTENTIELL, rather than a metaphysical interpretation, though he doubts whether this distinction is applicable to Nietzsche (NI, 334./nii, 78). But it brings out the fact that eternal recurrence has both the central features of a metaphysical thought: not only does it concern beings as a whole, it includes and rebounds on the thinker (NI, 447f./nii, 183f.). The *Rückschlag*, 'rebound', is not simply a consequence of the thinker's being a being and thus included in the scope of a thought that may otherwise leave us unmoved; the thinking of the thought has a vital impact on our life-choices that is not entailed by the mere universality of the thought.

Heidegger's interpretations of Nietzsche are not generally regarded as 'correct'. They are, however, novel and ingenious, and not to be lightly dismissed. Nietzsche's rejection of Platonism was a major influence on Heidegger's critique of 'western philosophy' and on his 'history of being'.

nihilism *Nihilismus* comes from the Latin *nihil*, 'nothing', and is thus literally 'nothingism'. It usually denotes the rejection of tradition, authority, and religious and moral principles rather than the claim that nothing at all exists. Heidegger gives a brief history of the term (NII, 31ff./niv, 3ff.): It was first used philosophically by Jacobi, in his *Letter to Fichte* (1799), calling Fichte's idealism *Nihilismus*. In his *Vorschule der Ästhetik* (*Aesthetics for the Nursery*), Jean Paul called romantic poetry a poetic 'nihilism'. Turgenev popularized the term in *Fathers and Sons* (1862), where Bazarov applies it to his own position: only what is sense-perceptible is real, while tradition and authority are to be rejected – a position often called 'positivism'. Dostoievsky commended Pushkin for his portrayals of rootless Russian nihilists.

Heidegger regards 'nihilism' as one of the five 'key-terms' of Nietzsche's thought (NII, 31ff./niv, 3ff.). The others are: 'will to power', 'eternal recurrence of the same', 'the superman' and 'revaluation of values' (or 'justice', NII, 314ff./niii, 234ff.). For Nietzsche nihilism is more than a doctrine espoused by a few radicals and it is distinct from positivism. It is a 'historical movement' affecting 'Western history' and epitomized as 'God is dead'. The Christian God has lost his power over beings and human destiny; he is like a long-dead star continuing to shine illusorily (NII, 33/niv, 4). The results in a 'devaluation of the highest values', stemming from what Nietzsche calls the 'collapse of cosmological values' (*Will to Power*, nos. 148–151): the universe has no 'sense [Sinn]' or 'purpose'. It has no 'unity' or 'wholeness'; there is no 'whole of beings' to give man his value: 'Nihilism concerns the position of man in the midst of beings as a whole, the way and manner in which man gets into relation with beings as such, forms and affirms this relationship and thus himself' (NII, 62f./niv, 29). There is no 'true world' above this world of becoming, no place for eternal truths and values, hence no 'truth'. The 'cause' of nihilism, and thus the beginning of its long and complex history, is Platonic and Christian morality, 'the positing of supernatural ideals of the true and good and beautiful, which are valid "in themselves"' (NII, 279/niii, 206).

Hume, whose diagnosis of the human condition somewhat resembles Nietzsche's, accepted all this with equanimity. But Nietzsche could not. He strove to 'overcome', *überwinden*, nihilism by positing new values. This too is a sort of nihilism, since it accepts the demise of the old values and the futility of their restoration. But it is 'active' nihilism: it does not passively accept that, since there is no truth 'in itself', there is no truth; it makes its own truth (NII, 95/niv, 55f.). It clears the decks and makes way for new possibilities by a 'revaluation of values [Umwertung der Werte]'. This does not mean simply putting new values in place of the old. The 'place' itself has disappeared: there is no true world for values to occupy. New values cannot come from Heaven, only from beings. So beings must be interpreted so that they can fulfil this role. Nietzsche thus produces a new 'metaphysic', interpreting beings as 'will to power', i.e. simply power, but with the recognition that power essentially strives for its own increase. Power has no external goal: it just increases itself and circles on itself, thus producing an eternal recurrence of the same. 'Revaluation of values' now means not only that power is established as the highest value, but that power posits and sustains values. Now man assumes unconditional power, restrained by no god, values or ideals except man himself. Will to power is the only basic value, and the superman is its highest form (NII, 39/niv, 9). The essence of the superman is to go beyond (*über*) the men of the present, in the way that power always surpasses itself. If the superman seems indeterminate, this is because raw power is indeterminate. If it has any aim it is the 'aimlessness of man's unconditional mastery over the earth. The man of this mastery is the super-man' (NII, 125/niv, 82). Nietzsche speaks 'from the noonday clarity of the mood by which man is made the unconditional centre and the unique measure of beings as a whole' (NII, 126'niv, 83). Thus Nietzsche amplifies the man-centred metaphysic which was pioneered by Descartes and underpins modern technology (NII, 118ff./niv, 129ff.).

Nietzsche, Heidegger concludes, has not succeeded in overcoming nihilism. If anything he intensified it. Real nihilism is the 'withdrawal' and 'failure to appear' of being itself, that is, the neglect of being by metaphysics: 'The essence of nihilism is the history in which there is nothing to being itself' (NII, 338/niv, 210. Cf. LXV, 138). Nihilism can be effectively combatted only by acknowledging being as such, whereas Nietzsche recognizes only beings as such and the being of beings. He makes matters worse by regarding being as a 'value' that we superimpose on the chaotic 'becoming' of beings. Being itself becomes a pawn in the game played by will to power to secure its own subsistence and increase. Nietzsche cannot discern the real nature of nihilism, since he is entangled in it. Indeed, it is essential to nihilism that it conceals its true nature and presents itself in various superficial guises: 'The most pernicious nihilism consists in presenting oneself as a defender of Christianity and even laying claim to the most christianly Christianity on the basis of one's public services. All the danger of this nihilism lies in the fact that it entirely conceals itself, sharply and legitimately contrasting itself with what one might call crude nihilism (e.g. bolshevism). But the essence of nihilism is really so profound (since it reaches down into the truth of beyng and the decision about it) that precisely these wholly contrasting forms can and must belong to it' (LXV, 140). Real nihilism cannot be overcome in the way Nietzsche proposes. To try to do so would mean that 'man from his own resources combats being itself in its failure to appear'. This would 'lift the essence of man off its hinges', for man is essentially the 'abode that being prepares for itself' (NII, 365f./niv, 223f.). Being is not at man's beck and call. We can prepare for its coming, but not force it: 'The preparation of the overcoming of nihilism commences in the fundamental experience that man as the grounder of Da-sein is *used* by the godhood of the other god. But the most essential and difficult thing in this overcoming is the *knowledge* [*Wissen*] of nihilism' (LXV, 140f.). Heidegger speaks of the coming of being as if it were the coming of Christ.

Jünger (1950) considered the nihilism resulting from technology. Heidegger's QB is an open letter to him about it.

nothing and negation The German for 'nothing' is *nichts*. Usually it amounts to 'not . . . anything': 'Nothing is simple' means 'There is not anything that is simple'. But *nichts* has been nominalized as *(das) Nichts* since the sixteenth century, especially to say that God created the world out of *das Nichts*. In Hegel's logic, *das Sein*, 'being', and *das Nichts*, both being wholly indeterminate, pass into each other and thus give rise to becoming and determinacy. *Das Nichts* also has other uses. It can refer to some particular non-being or nonentity, such as the world or the elbowroom that enables us to encounter beings (K, 72/49). Such a nonentity is 'a Nothing', *ein Nichts*, but not necessarily the one and only *Nichts*. *Das Nichts* can also refer to a use or sense of the word *Nichts*, as do some occurrences of *das Nichts* in LXI.

Heidegger was intrigued by the Nothing from his early lectures. In discussing the *Ruinanz* or *Sturz*, 'drop, fall', of 'factical life', he says that the destination of the fall is 'the Nothing of factical life'. But not all Nothings are the same. Formally 'Nothing' stems from 'Not [Nicht]' and 'No [Nein]', but an interpretation of 'nothing' in these terms will not necessarily fit all concrete situations nor must 'no' be taken in a purely theoretical sense: there as many different 'nots' and 'noes' as there are 'nothings'. There is 'the Nothing of historical uneventfulness, the Nothing of unsuccessfulness, the Nothing of pointlessness, the Nothing of despair [. . .]'. The 'Nothing of [not] being present-at-hand and at one's disposal', though it comes readiest to mind, is not obviously the 'original' Nothing (LXI, 145f.). If I say 'There's nothing in the fridge', I most likely mean not that there is strictly nothing at all in the fridge (which is unlikely to be true, since fridges contain nitrogen, etc.), but that there is nothing (much) edible in the fridge. I may mean, reassuringly, that there is nothing untoward in the fridge, no dead rat or severed hand (cf. NII, 50/niv, 18f.). Elsewhere, Heidegger correspondingly distinguishes the Something (*Etwas*) of formal logic from the Something charged with worldly significance, the various ways in which I can say 'There's something in the fridge' (LVI/LVII, 114f; LVIII, 216f., 220). He concludes that the 'Nothing of life' to which life falls is *Vernichtung, Nichtung*, 'annihilation, nihilation – the Nothing of life matured in a definite nihilation, [. . .]', that is, the 'Non-occurrence' or inconspicuousness of life, its absorption into the world around it (LXI, 148).

WM, a work famously attacked by Carnap, begins with a negative use of *nichts*, in which it means 'not ... anything': 'Only beings are to be examined [by the sciences] and besides that – nothing [nichts]' (105/ 95). It proceeds to a positive use, in which *nichts* cannot be replaced by 'not ... anything': 'How is it with this Nothing [dieses Nichts]? [. . .] How is it with the Nothing [das Nichts]?' (105f./95f.). And finally: *Das Nichts selbst nichtet*, 'The Nothing itself noths' (113/103). The indefinite pronoun is nominalized, and a cognate verb applied to it. *Nichten*, 'to noth, nihilate', is coined from *nicht*, 'not'. It is similar to *vernichten*, 'to annihilate', but distinct from it. Owing to this affinity, *nichten* has a transitive flavour, though it never takes an accusative object. *Nichtung*, 'noth-ing, nihilating', is what the Nothing does, just as *die Welt weltet*, 'the world worlds' or light light(en)s. 'The nothing' is used positively: Heidegger is not saying 'There is not anything that noths', but 'Something noths, namely the Nothing'. The Nothing is not to be explicated in terms of negation: it is 'the origin of denial' (116/105).

The Nothing and its nihilating are given in experience – in ANGST, when beings as a whole, including oneself as a distinct individual, seem to be slipping away from us, depriving us of any support (WM, 111/101. Cf. BT, 184ff.). We are anxious only occasionally, but the Nothing noths continually, obscured by our everyday focus on beings (WM, 115/104). The argument is this: To exist as DASEIN I cannot simply be affected by the entities in my immediate vicinity, I must transcend to world or to beings as a whole. Only then can I be aware of beings *as* beings, conduct myself freely in relation to them, notice that something is missing – not there, or not as it should be, regard something as possible or as impossible, or wonder why something is so and look for reasons for it. If, like a 'world-impoverished' insect, I am transfixed by a single entity, I cannot be aware of possible alternatives to it, freely decide how to treat or assess it, notice that it is not as it should be, or ask why it is so rather than otherwise (cf. XXIX, 274ff.). To escape the grip of particular entities, I must transcend them to world, the bare world rather than the entities within it. This happens not (as in stoicism and in Spinoza) by primarily intellectual means, but by a mood, in which the beings that beleaguer us slither away from me, without ceasing to be altogether. The philosopher becomes aware of this in occasional, explicit Angst, but to be in-the-world Dasein must have constant, implicit Angst. Heidegger's view is different from Hegel's: being and the Nothing go together not because they are both indeterminate, but 'because being itself is in essence finite and reveals itself only in the transcendence of Dasein held out into the Nothing' (WM, 119/108).

Heidegger's fascination with the Nothing outlasted his interest in Angst.

145

He insisted on the importance of the question 'Why are there any beings at all rather than Nothing [Nichts]?', not because he can answer it, but because it opens up 'beings as a whole as such' (IM, 3/4; cf. WM, 121/110). The question was asked by Leibniz and Schelling (NII, 446ff./ep, 42ff.). But Heidegger later explains that he meant by it something different: 'Why is it that everywhere only beings have priority, that the Not of beings, "this nothing", i.e. being in regard to its essence, is not rather considered?' (QB, 98; cf. WMI, 377/278f.). Here being is identified with (the) Nothing because it is not a being (cf. LXV, 246). Being is also associated with the Nothing and the Not because it withdraws from beings (LXV, 245f.), and because the revelation of being in world and EARTH involves conflict and tension (LXV, 264).

The Nothing intrinsically has little to do with death or with NIHILISM, but Heidegger's later thought about it intersects his thought about nihilism (NII, 49ff./niv, 18ff.).

O

---

ontology and fundamental ontology The present participle of the Greek *einai*, 'to be', is *ōn*. The neuter singular of this, with a definite article, is *to on*, 'that which is, the being, the entity, being' – Heidegger complains that, in Aristotle's usage, it ambiguously means both 'what is' and the 'being' of what is (IM, 23/25). The plural of *(to) on* is *(ta) onta*, 'beings', which, combined with the Greek *logos*, 'word, saying, reason, etc.', gives *Ontologie*, a word coined in the mid-seventeenth century and used, Heidegger says, by J. Clauberg, a German pupil of Descartes and professor at Herborn (NII, 208/niv, 154). Ontology is the 'study of beings as such', but it can be a 'regional' ontology, concerned with the BEING or nature of e.g. numbers, space, or a work of literature (XXII, 8). In contrast to such ontological, *ontologisch(e)*, inquiry, the inquiry and findings of unphilosophical mathematicians, geometers or philologists are *ontisch(e)*, concerned with beings, not with their being. (*Ontologisch* is often coupled with *existenzial*, and *ontisch* with *existenziell*: the two distinctions are similar, but 'EXISTENCE' applies only to DASEIN.) But 'ontology', like its near-equivalent, 'metaphysics', usually indicates a general study of beings (NII, 209/niv, 155). ('Ontology' and 'metaphysics' lose favour with Heidegger in tandem.)

'The ontical distinction of Dasein lies in the fact that it is ontological' (BT, 12). That is, Dasein, unlike other entities, understands the being of beings. But if 'ontology' is reserved for a theoretical, conceptual inquiry into being, it is better to say that Dasein is 'pre-ontological; (*vorontologisch*), i.e. it has an implicit, pre-conceptual UNDERSTANDING of being. Dasein thus has three tiers: 1. It engages with entities ontically, acquiring ontical knowledge of them. 2. It can only do this because of its pre-ontological understanding of being. 3. As a philosopher it may attain a conceptual understanding of being, based on 2 (XXVII, 201). Regional ontology, including what T. S. Kuhn called 'revolutionary science', which establishes a new 'paradigm' for a (newly conceived and/or demarcated) range of entities, falls between 2 and 3 (cf. BT, 8ff.); 'routine science', by contrast, is similar to 1, related to the paradigm in the way that 1 is related to 2.

BT's enterprise is not merely *Ontologie* but *Fundamentalontologie* (BT, 13; XXVI, 196, 201f.). Fundamental ontology 1. analyses the being of Dasein, as 2. a preparation for the 'fundamental question' about (the sense or meaning of) being. It is fundamental, since regional ontologies and sciences 1. are 'modes of being of Dasein' and presuppose Dasein's pre-ontological access to entities (BT, 13), and 2. not only presuppose an understanding of being, but cannot do their job properly without first 'clarifying the meaning of being' (BT, 11). Since *both* Dasein *and* being are prior or 'fundamental' to other ontologies, *Fundamentalontologie* some-times denotes the ontology or 'analytic' of Dasein (BT, 13), sometimes the investigation of being to which the analytic of Dasein is merely 'preparatory' (BT, 154, 182f., 436f.). Feick, pp. 32f., disparages the latter sense: fundamental ontology, like all ontology, studies the being of beings, *onta*, not being as such. But Feick exploits the traditional sense of 'ontology', while Heidegger prefers 'ontology taken in the widest sense, independent of ontological trends and tendencies' (BT, 11), an ontology that includes the question about being as such (IM, 31/34).

Later, Heidegger criticizes the term *Ontologie*: it invites confusion with a traditional discipline concerned exclusively with beings (IM, 31/34; WMI, 375/276f.). Traditional ontology was upheld by Hartmann, a refugee from neo-Kantian 'epistemology' (Cf. BT, 208n.), who examined the being or nature of things, not just our ways of knowing them, and postulated a hierarchy of levels of entity – inanimate nature, plants, animals, man. Heidegger rejects such stratification. It leaves no place for tools and technology (LXV, 273ff.). It denies the dependence of lower on higher levels, when 'lower' entities (e.g. EARTH) are illuminated and in a way constituted by 'higher' (e.g. world): 'No stone and stream without plant, animal' (LXV, 277). Fundamental ontology was a 'transitional' way of overcoming traditional ontology, by asking about its 'ground and funda-ment' (NII, 209/niv, 155; LXV, 182, 205, 228, 283, 305). It thus moves away from beings to the other side of the ontological DIFFERENCE, being. As traditional ontology PROJECTS beings onto beingness, so we now project 'beingness as beyng onto its truth' (LXV, 450). Fundamental ontology is meta-ontology.

After BT, being is still related to Dasein. BT proceeds from Dasein to being, but the order is now reversed. 'If the question about being seeks not only the being of beings but being itself in its essence, then we need a complete and explicit grounding of Dasein, guided by this question. For this reason alone the grounding assumed the name "fundamental ontology" [. . .]' (IM, 133/146). This grounding is not simply a revamped version of traditional ontology: 'We must fit man's historical Dasein – and that always includes our very own future Dasein, in the whole of the history allotted to us – back into the power of being, which is to be originally opened up' (IM, 32/34). Heidegger's task is now to restore man to his primordial relationship to being, not simply analyse his being. Ontology is supplanted by the HISTORY OF BEING: 'In general: to rethink the whole human essence, as soon as it is grounded in Da-sein, being-historically [seinsgeschichtlich] (but not "ontologically")' (LXV, 103). The change is not merely terminological. Heidegger's thought is now more historical: the answer to the question 'What are beings?' is not independent of what men do, say and think, of the answers they have given and will give to the question. Being is approached directly rather than by way of Dasein. Man's coincidence with Da-sein is not guaranteed.

The contrast between *ontologisch* and *ontisch* persists in Heidegger's later thought. He and Fink argue over whether the word *kosmos* in Heraclitus is to be taken ontically or ontologically (XV, 132/79, 177/109) and about the difference between ontic and ontological proximity (XV, 232ff./ 144ff.).

Ontotheology *Ontologie* is the 'study [logos] of beings [onta]', *Theologie* the 'study of God [theos]'. Heidegger combines these Greek-derived words to form *Onto-Theologie* or *Onto-Theo-Logie*. The idea, but not the words, stem from Aristotle, whose 'first philosophy' considers both beings as such and the highest being (K, 220/150; WMI, 373/275). Thus onto-theology asks two distinct questions: 1. What are beings as such in general? 2. What is the highest being, and what is its nature? (KTB, 443). The questions are easily conflated in German, since Was ist das Seiende?', 'What are beings?', is literally 'What is the being?' or 'What is that which is?', which might be either question 1 or question 2. Sometimes Heidegger gives a different account of the two questions. Question 1 is 'about beings as such [nach dem Seienden als einem solchen]', question 2 is 'about beings as a whole [nach dem Seienden im Ganzen]' (K, 220/150). He imputes this conflation to his earlier self: in WM, 'metaphysics is defined as the question about beings as such *and* as a whole [nach dem Seienden als solchem *und* im Ganzen]. The wholeness of this whole [Die Ganzheit dieses Ganzes] is the unity of beings, the ground that brings them forth and unifies them. To anyone who can read, this means: metaphysics is Onto-Theo-Logie' (ID, 51/54). Elsewhere he locates the confusion in the whole phrase *das Ganze des Seienden als solchen*, 'the whole of beings as

149

such', which might mean: 1. 'the most general features of beings', or 2. 'the highest and thus divine being' (WMI, 373/275). (Aristotle is innocent of *this* confusion: his god is one being among others, not the whole of beings. But in ID Heidegger is dealing with Hegel, whose god is the overall structure of beings, not an individual being.)

Biologie is the 'study' or 'science' of living creatures. But in *Onto-Theologie*, *-logie* plays a grander role. *Logos*, from *legein*, 'to lay out, arrange, gather, say, etc.', means 'ground [Grund], letting (things) lie before (us) [Vorliegenlassen]', and also 'gathering [Versammlung], uniting' (ID, 54f./57; 67/69). Metaphysics does both. It gathers beings together to consider them 'as a whole'. It regards being as the 'ground' of beings: 'Ontology and theology are '-logies' because they get to the bottom [ergründen] of beings as such and ground [begründen] them as a whole [im Ganzen, lit. 'in the whole']' (ID, 56/59). Hence Hegel called metaphysics 'logic'; it is *Onto-Theo-Logik*.

How does God become *a* being, the highest entity, rather than simply *Sein*, 'being'? Being and beings are distinct but inseparable. Being 'grounds [gründet]' beings, and conversely beings 'beground [begründen]' being. But beings can beground being only in the form of a single supreme being, a cause that is *causa sui*, 'cause of itself': 'This is the appropriate name for the god of philosophy. Man cannot pray to this god, nor offer sacrifices to him. Man cannot fall to his knees in awe before the causa sui, nor dance and play music before this god' (ID, 70/72). Heidegger thinks that 'god-less thinking', in rejecting this god of philosophy, is 'perhaps closer to the divine god' (ID, 71/72): 'the onto-theological character of metaphysics has become questionable for thinking, not on the basis of any atheism, but from the experience of a thinking which has seen in onto-theo-logy the still *unthought* unity of the essence of metaphysics' (ID, 51/55). In thinking about this unity, and about the DIFFERENCE that metaphysics discerns only hazily, Heidegger goes beyond metaphysics.

origins and beginnings   Heidegger uses two main word-groups:

1. *Springen*, 'to leap, jump, spring', was originally 'to spring up, burst forth' and applied especially to springs or sources of water. *Sprung*, 'spring, leap, jump', once meant a 'spring, source'. The verb *erspringen*, 'to leap/spring forth [er-]' has now been supplanted by *entspringen*, 'to rise, arise, spring from, etc.', but the corresponding noun, *Ursprung*, survives in the sense of 'origin'. It originally meant the

'leaping/springing forth, source [esp. of water]'. (*Ur-* was originally *er-*, 'forth', but has come to mean 'original, primordial'; hence *Ursprung* can be felt as 'original, primordial leap'.) *Ursprünglich,* 'original, initial, first; natural, unspoilt, "re-sourceful",' was first used by mystics, but became common in the eighteenth century under the influence of the French *original. Ursprünglich(keit)* does not mean 'original(ity)' in the sense of 'novel(ty), eccentric(ity)'. It suggests the 'primitive, primeval, primordial'. *Ursprung* is close to *Herkunft,* 'origin, extraction, descent, lit. where something comes from', but Heidegger distinguishes them (cf. OWA, 7/143, 64f./202).

2. *Fangen* is 'to catch, grasp, seize, capture'. Hence *anfangen* was originally 'to take hold of, grab', but came to mean 'begin, start'. *Anfang* is 'beginning'; *anfänglich,* 'initial(ly)', is close to *ursprünglich. Anfang(en)* is also close to *Beginn* and *beginnen,* but Heidegger differentiates them: an *Anfang* is more radical and fundamental than a *Beginn,* and gets its prophets – Anaximander, Parmenides and Heraclitus – in its 'grasp' (LIV, 2, 9ff.).

Ursprünglich occurs often in BT, in a sense combining ontological, evaluative, and sometimes (implicitly) historical priority. Thinking, interpretation, etc. is *ursprünglich* insofar as it discloses (or asks about) an *ursprünglich* phenomenon, etc. Is our view of DASEIN as care, Heidegger asks, an *ursprüngliche* INTERPRETATION of Dasein? What is our criterion for *Ursprünglichkeit?* What do we mean by it? He replies that an ontological interpretation is *ursprünglich* only if: 1. the 'hermeneutical situation' , viz. our fore-having, fore-sight and fore-grasp, conforms to the phenomena; 2. our fore-having embraces the whole of the entity under consideration; 3. our fore-sight gives not just a 'first-sketch' of the being of the entity, but views it 'with regard to the *unity* of its actual and possible structural features' (BT, 231f.). Heidegger's interpretation of Dasein in its 'average everydayness' fulfils only condition 1. It fails 2, since it encompasses only a brief span of Dasein's career between birth and death. It fails 3, since it considers Dasein only in its inauthenticity or neutrality, without explaining authenticity or even its possibility. The two failures are connected: only authentic Dasein surveys itself as a whole, and the philosopher's (conceptual) interpretation of Dasein is guided by Dasein's own (non-conceptual) self-interpretation. In discerning Dasein's 'authentic ability to be a whole [Ganzseinkönnen]', the philosopher unearths Dasein's 'original being', finding that temporality is the 'original ontological ground of Dasein's existentiality', since only temporality explains the 'articulated structural totality' of care, indeed 'constitutes the original sense of Dasein's being'

151

(BT, 235). *Ursprünglich* is here close to 'fundamental': a 'fundamental' theory or interpretation encompasses the whole of the interpretandum, reveals its 'fundamental' nature, and explains secondary features in terms of it. The 'original', e.g. finite temporality, is sometimes contrasted with the 'derived [abgeleitet(e)]', e.g. infinite temporality (BT, 330f.).

The 'original totality of Dasein's constitution', care, is articulated and grounds a multiplicity of secondary phenomena. Originality does not entail simplicity: 'The ontological Ursprung of Dasein's being is not "slighter" than what springs from it; it exceeds it in power from the start; in the field of ontology all "springing from" ['Entspringen'] is degeneration. Ontological penetration to the "Ursprung" does not arrive at what is ontically obvious for "commonsense"; it shows how questionable everything obvious is' (BT, 334. But cf. XXXI, 103, where Heidegger agrees with Aristotle that 'the simpler, i.e. the more original, is more of a principle'.) But 'if we question more originally [than Nietzsche did about truth], that never guarantees a more certain answer, but on the contrary only a higher questionability of the essence of truth; and we need this questionability; for without it the truth remains indifferent' (LXV, 362).

Different phenomena within CARE, such as concern and solicitude, being by one's tools and being with others, are *gleichursprünglich*, 'equally original, equiprimordial': neither is derivable from or based on the other (XXI, 226; BT, 181). This does not mean that they are in principle separable: we could not deal with things if we were not with others, or be with others if we could not deal with things. If phenomena are *gleichursprünglich*, neither grounds the other unilaterally, but each may imply or entail the other. Thus, tools and products imply customers and suppliers. Conversely, recognisable others imply communication, which in turn implies intersubjectively identifiable things to name and talk about.

Later, Heidegger's thought becomes more historical. *Ursprung* and its near-equivalent *Anfang* usually refer to a historic event (XXXIX, 200ff., 239ff.). An *Ursprung* or *Anfang* is not simple or primitive; it is a massive *Sprung*, 'spring, leap' forth, implicitly anticipating whatever springs from it (OWA, 63ff./201ff; IM, 119/130). Hence it is inexplicable. 'The purity and greatness of historical scholarship lies in understanding the mysterious nature of this beginning. Knowledge of a pre-history [Ur-geschichte] is not unearthing the primitive and collecting bones. It is not natural science in whole or in part; if it is anything at all, it is mythology' (IM, 119/131). This is the 'first', the Greek, beginning, of philosophy and of 'western' history, a 'great and unique moment of creation' (LXV, 196). 'Primordial [anfängliche] thinking *transfers* its questioning about the truth of beyng *far back* into the first beginning as the origin of philosophy. It thereby gets a guarantee that it will come *from afar* in its other beginning [. . .]' (LXV, 59). To prepare for the 'other beginning' of human history, which will be 'no counter-movement', since counter-movements 'get caught in their own victory, [. . .] fall into the clutches of the vanquished', we must take issue with the first, while keeping our distance from it, both to understand it and avoid entrapment in it (LXV, 186). The *Sprung* involved in a beginning is similar to a PROJECT. Da-sein 'grounds itself in the spring. The destination of the spring, opened up by it, is first grounded by the spring' (LXV, 303). The spring opens up the There (*Da*). But now 'only a few come to the spring and these by different paths' (LXV, 236).

Heidegger says virtually nothing about pre-Greek cultures. To the questions: Were they Dasein or human? Did they have a philosophy? his reply is: we can understand them only 'privatively', in terms of our own Greek-derived thought.

P

past and having been The usual words for 'past' and 'the past' are *vergangen* and *(die) Vergangenheit.* These come from the perfect participle, *vergangen,* of *vergehen,* 'to pass, go by, die, lit. go [gehen] away [ver-]'. Thus they have the flavour of 'over and done with'. This did not suit Heidegger: 'The past [Vergangenheit] – experienced as authentic historicality – is anything but the bygone [das Vorbei]. It is something I can return to again and again' (CT, 19). But what is past is sometimes over and done with: saying someone or something 'is history' can mean that it lives on in the present, but it can mean, especially if it is 'ancient history', that it is dead and gone. So Heidegger coins another word, using the perfect participle of *sein* ('to be'), *gewesen,* '(having) been': *(die) Gewesenheit,* '(having) beenness, living past' (XXI, 413; BT, 326). The perfect tense of most German verbs is formed from the perfect participle and the present tense of *haben,* 'to have', as an auxiliary: *ich habe gerufen,* 'I have called'. Some verbs form their perfect using *sein* as an auxiliary: *ich bin gereist,* 'I have [lit. am] travelled'. The verb *sein* uses *sein* as an auxiliary: *ich bin krank gewesen,* 'I have [lit. am] been ill'. Heidegger exploits this in explaining the sense of *Gewesenheit:* ' "As long as" Dasein factically exists, it is never past [vergangen], but it has [ist, lit. 'is'] always already *been* [gewesen] in the sense of "I *am*-having-been" ["ich *bin*-gewesen"]' (BT, 328). The phrase 'always already' (*immer schon*) or 'ever already' (*je schon*) is formed by analogy with *immer noch,* lit. 'always still', an emphatic form of 'still' – 'He's *still* not working!' (NII, 319/niii, 238). Heidegger connects it with DASEIN's THROWNNESS: 'the "already" [das 'Schon'] means the existential temporal sense of the being of that entity which, in so far as it *is,* is ever already [je schon] thrown' (BT, 328). It is also applied to other aspects of Dasein's being: 'we always already operate in an understanding of being' (BT, 5). It expresses two ideas: 1. Every Dasein is cast into the world, has acquired an understanding of being, and carries its past along with it. 2. *I* cannot manage, or observe, my *own* entry into the world or my acquisition of features essential to my Dasein-hood; from my *own* perspective I have *always* been in the world, etc. *Gewesenheit* has more to do with what I 'always already am' than with chronology.

Gewesenheit, together with *Zukunft*, 'future', and *Gegenwart*, 'present', is one of the three 'ecstases' of TEMPORALITY. *Ekstase(n)* comes from the Greek *existanai*, 'to displace, derange, etc.' via *ekstasis*, 'distraction, derangement, astonishment, trance, etc.' Heidegger restores the original sense of 'step out of oneself': time steps out of itself into past, present and future. While the 'phenomenal character' of the future is 'towards-oneself [Auf-sich-zu]' and that of the present is 'letting something come to meet one', that of having-beenness is 'back to [Zurück auf]'. As the future involves being 'ahead of oneself' and the present 'being alongside' things, so the past involves 'already being in' the world (BT, 317, 328f.).

How does the past live on in the present? Not simply in virtue of effects that past events have on our present state. Stones, trees and animals are affected by their past, but they have only a *Vergangenheit*, not a *Gewesenheit* that they can go 'back to'. Nor does it do so owing to historical research: recognizing a presently extant text or artefact as evidence of what has been presupposes a prior understanding of the past (XX, 290, etc.). Later, Heidegger associates historiology with the dead rather than the living past: *Historie* is the 'determining and explanation of the past [Vergangenen] from the viewpoint of the calculative preoccupations of the present' (LXV, 493; cf. NII, 49/niv, 16f.). Namier expressed a comparable thought: 'One would expect people to remember the past and imagine the future. But in fact, when discoursing or writing about history they imagine it in terms of their own experience, and when trying to gauge the future they cite supposed analogies from the past: till, by a double process of repetition, they imagine the past and remember the future' (Namier, 69f.).

Various words express our relationship to the past: 1. *behalten, (das) Behalten*, 'to retain; retention'. Husserl had argued that listening to a tune involves 'retaining' the notes we have already heard – not recalling, but a precondition of it. Heidegger uses *behalten* in a similar way (XXI, 413). 2. *vergessen, (das) Vergessen, (die) Vergessenheit*, 'to forget; forgetting; forgottenness, oblivion'. 3. *(sich) erinnern; (die) Erinnerung*, 'to recall, recollect; recollection'. 4. *wiederholen; (die) Wiederholung*, ' to repeat, retrieve, lit. fetch back; REPETITION, retrieval'. In BT these are related thus: AUTHENTIC having-beenness is repetition, that is, going back to the past, of one's own life and/or of one's 'tradition', and retrieving possibilities, one's 'very own ability-to-be'. In inauthentic having-beenness one's thrownness and very own ability-to-be are 'forgotten' in the concerns of the present. On the basis of this fundamental forgetting, one retains past things and events insofar as they serve one's present concerns. One can

155

also fail to retain, 'forget' them in a 'derived sense'. Remembering is made possible by forgetting, the fundamental 'forgetting' that contrasts with 'repetition', not with 'retention'. This involves two ideas: 1. Fundamental forgetting makes the past *past* rather than present, opening up the past as a field of recollectables. 2. Since Dasein has forgotten itself and is 'lost in the "superficiality" [Äusserlichkeit, lit. externality] of its concerns', it can *sich erinnern*, remember, but lit. 'get itself in(to)', the field opened up by forgetting (BT, 339).

Forgetting remains important after BT. It is 'the dominant mode of having-beenness [Gewesenseins], i.e. it arises from the illusion that what has been [das Gewesene] "is" no longer there and that Dasein, while it can in self-understanding go back to itself from its ability-to-be, just goes back to what is currently present, which has just closed the door behind it on having-beenness. But closing the door on it is itself always a way of realizing [Zeitigung] having-beenness, of bringing in its own way what has been into being' (XXVI, 267). He takes issue with Plato: 'Our acquaintance with being is based not on anamnesis [recollection] [. . .] but on a forgetting, forgetting that we have returned [from being thrown in the PROJECT]. [. . .] So all that remains is the return: the retention of beingness ([Platonic] idea), which is a forgetting of what happened in the EVENT' (LXV, 453). Heidegger owes much to Plato's *Phaedrus*; he interprets its account of us fallen souls, who have forgotten what we saw before our fall but slowly recollect it, in terms of our understanding, and forgetfulness, of being (cf. NI, 218ff./ni, 188ff.).

'Having-beenness arises in a certain way from the FUTURE' (BT, 326).

people *Volk* corresponds closely, but not exactly, to 'a/the people'. Originally the 'mass of the people', especially the army, it came to mean, with the rise of nationalism in the Renaissance, all the people sharing a common language, culture and history, and often united in a state. The romantics gave it a more cultural flavour with such coinages as *Volkslied*, 'folk-song', and *Volkstum*, 'folkdom, the special character of a people expressed in their life and culture'. From early on it also meant the 'masses', in contrast to the elite. The old adjective *völkisch* originally meant the same as the later *volkstümlich*, 'belonging to, in tune with, the people; popular'. It later came to mean 'national' and was used by the Nazis in this sense, but with the added flavours of 'popular' and 'racial'. *Volk*, with its suggestions of the racial 'folk', the 'nation', and the 'common people', suited the Nazi combination of authoritarian nationalism with a not wholly illusory democratic egalitarianism. Such usage displays the 'insensitivity to ambiguity' that Heidegger regards as a symptom of 'abandonment by being'; *Volk* signifies: 'the communal, the racial, the base and lower, the national, the permanent' (LXV, 117).

Volk occurs rarely in the BT period (cf. BT, 384, where it is the historical community). It became more frequent with Heidegger's growing interest in the origins of 'western history' and in Hölderlin and the Greeks (cf. XXXIX, 120ff. on the ' "fatherland" as the historical beyng of a people'). The Greeks were a *Volk* despite their division into many autonomous city-states. Was not the philosophy of the 'first beginning' the 'philosophy "of" ['des'] the *Greek* people? And the great end of western philosophy, "German idealism" and "Nietzsche", is it not the philosophy "of" the *German* people?' (LXV, 42). Philosophy is not, like dress and cookery, something done by an already fully formed people; it comes 'over' a people as much as 'from' them: 'The philosophy of a people is what makes it the people of a philosophy, grounds the people historically in its Da-sein and appoints it to watch over the truth of beyng'. A people is made a people by rare individuals: thinkers and poets. The philosophy of a people, such as the Germans, cannot be worked out and prescribed on the basis of their talents and capacities; philosophy has to pull itself up by its own bootstraps or 'spring forth [erspringen] its very own original spring [Ursprung]', which can only succeed if philosophy 'still belongs to its essential first beginning' (LXV, 43). In this respect the Germans differ from the Greeks, who had no prior beginning to consider. They differ too in other respects. What was once the property of the Greeks has now become the common European heritage: 'The thinking of Descartes, Leibniz's metaphysics, Hume's philosophy – each of these is European and therefore planetary. Nietzsche's metaphysics too is never at bottom a specifically German philosophy. It is European and planetary' (NII, 333/ niii, 251). Racial stereotypes have no place in Heidegger's thought: 'The pure nonsense of saying experimental research is nordic-germanic while rational inquiry is *alien*! In that case we must decide to count Newton and Leibniz as "jews" ' (LXV, 163). Politics too transcends any particular *Volk*: 'the final form of Marxism [. . .] has essentially nothing to do with judaism or indeed with russianism; if a still latent spiritualism lies dormant anywhere, it is in the Russian people; Bolshevism is originally western, a european possibility: the rise of the masses, industry, technology, the decay of Christianity; insofar as the reign of reason as the equalization of all is just the consequence of Christianity, which is at bottom of jewish origin [. . .] Bolshevism is indeed jewish; but then Christianity too is at bottom Bolshevist!' (LXV, 54).

Heidegger objects to racism: ' A short while ago we looked for the

157

psycho-analytical roots of poetry, now everything is dripping with folkdom and blood and soil, but it remains the same old story' (XXXIX, 254). 'Blood and race become the bearers of history' – history (*Geschichte*) has become ahistorical in the hands of historiology (*Historie*) (LXV, 493). Romantic attempts to renew 'culture', to root it in the 'people' and communicate it to everyone are a futile 're-action' against the pervasive explanatory and calculative spirit (LXV, 496). He also objects to the elevation of the 'people' to the transcendent position recently vacated by the Christian God (LXV, 24): 'the preservation of the people is never a possible goal, only the condition of having goals' (LXV, 99). To make the people a goal is 'supreme nihilism, organized eye-closing to the goal-lessness of man' (LXV, 139). Science cannot be justified by a 'folkish-political or any other anthropological purpose' (LXVm 142). Science is 'the same everywhere, and precisely through the various goals assigned to it, it becomes at bottom ever more uniform, i.e. more "international"' (LXV, 149). It can serve the interests of a particular people only if it loses its local peculiarities and becomes 'liberal', capable of serving any end and any people. In Germany, Russia and everywhere else the 'national' organization of science is 'american' (LXV, 149) – but little is gained by speaking of 'americanism'. 'Americanism is something European', stemming from European metaphysics (AWP, 103/153).

The *Volk* is an unsatisfactory answer to the question 'Who are we?' (LXV, 49f.). It is only when man has already become a SUBJECT that he needs to ask whether he is a freewheeling individual or a community, a *Volk*. Only man as a subject can either succumb to individualism or combat it on behalf of the community as the condition of all goals (AWP, 85/132f.). Thus to make the *Volk* an end, to dissolve one's 'I' in 'the life' of the *Volk*, solves nothing, if we do not reflect on 'being a self [Selbst-sein] and its essence' (LXV, 321). It is a '"folkish" extension of the "liberal" "I" -thought and of the economic idea of the maintenance of "life"' (LXV, 319). Heidegger was an honest elitist, with none of the Nazis' bogus egalitarianism and little of their authoritarianism: 'The essence of the people is its "voice". This *voice* precisely does not speak in the so-called immediate effusion of the common, natural, unspoiled and uncultured "chap". The witness thus appealed to is already very *spoiled* by education and has not for a long time moved in the original relations to beings. The *voice* of the people speaks rarely and only in the few, [. . .]' (LXV, 319). A people needs to be moulded by thinkers and poets: 'Dominance over the masses who have become free (i.e. rootless and self-centred) must be established and maintained by the fetters of "organiz-ation"'. But since this can only dam them up, not transform them, we need another sort of dominance: 'we must prepare for the future ones [die Zukünftigen], who create new positions in being itself, from which again a constancy happens [sich ereignet] in the conflict of earth and world' (LXV, 62. Cf. 97, 398).

phenomenology (Heidegger)   In the 1920s Heidegger held that all philosophy must be phenomenology: to regard phenomenology as a mere 'preliminary discipline' to some other sort of philosophy is like regarding physics as a preliminary to astrology or chemistry as a prelude to alchemy (XX, 108.f). He gives an account of the two constituents of 'phenomenology' (BT, 28ff; cf. XX, 110ff.):

1. A *Phänomen* or, in Greek, *phainomenon* (from the 'middle-voiced' *phainesthai*, 'to show itself') is 'what shows itself in itself'. It is distinct from 'semblance [Schein]' and 'appearance [Erscheinung, lit. 'shining forth']'. Tom's spots show themselves, are manifest, a phenomenon. The spots may be a semblance, a trick of the light or painted. Such semblance is a 'modification' of a prior phenomenon. Only what purports to show itself can be a semblance: they seem to be manifest, self-showing spots, but are really not. The spots, if genuine, are a symptom of measles. Measles 'announces' itself in the spots. The spots 'refer' to measles. Measles appears in the spots, which are an appearance of measles. Measles is an appearance, but not a phenomenon: measles does not show itself in the way that spots do. If anything, such as measles, appears, something else, such as spots, must show itself. Conversely, something may show itself without being the appearance of anything that does not show itself.
2. The Greek *logos* came to mean 'reason, judgement, concept, definition, ground, relation'. But its primary meaning is 'making manifest' and the root-verb, *legein*, 'to lay, arrange, gather, talk, etc.', is primarily 'to make manifest, reveal'. Hence *logos* means 'talk, discourse [Rede]', since talk reveals what is talked about. It also reveals something *as* something, a as b; it has the structure of 'synthesis', saying that a is b. Then it can be true – or false, presenting something as what it is not. Aristotle's word for 'statement, predication', *apophansis*, comes from *apophainein*, 'to show forth, display'. The prefix *apo*, 'from, etc.', indicates that talk lets what it is about be seen 'from' itself.

The meanings of *phainomenon* and *logos* thus converge. 'Phenomenology' means 'to let what shows itself [the phainomenon] be seen [-phainesthai] from [apo-] itself in the very way in which it shows itself from itself' (BT, 34). It does not specify what the phenomena are, just how we are to approach them. Phenomena must be 'demonstrated directly', not postulated on the basis of other phenomena or traditional doctrines.

Does phenomenology examine everything that shows itself, even spots and Tom himself? No, it considers not particular entities, but features of the being of entities, features that usually show themselves inconspicuously or 'unthematically', but can be got to show themselves thematically. Space and time show themselves, but usually unthematically. Phenomenology squeezes them into focus. Phenomenology is only needed because some matters, especially being itself, are hidden. Hidden not because we have not yet discovered them or have simply forgotten them, but because they are too close and familiar for us to notice or are buried under traditional concepts and doctrines.

Heidegger compared Husserl with Descartes (XVII, 254ff.). Both assume the supreme importance of certain knowledge of truth, of the theoretical truth found primarily in the mathematical and natural sciences that they want to ground. Both seek certainty within themselves, in consciousness. Unlike Descartes, Husserl does not wish to exclude any science or the everyday 'life-world' from his purview; he recognizes intentionality and develops phenomenology, invariably considering phenomena and science in relation to consciousness; he has no theological agenda. But Husserl – against the spirit of phenomenology – took over too much traditional baggage from Descartes and other philosophers: the *ego cogito* or consciousness, the ideal of certainty, an ideal of 'rigorous' science, at the expense of the life-world from which science begins, of 'inexact' sciences such as history, and of more probing, reflective and holistic 'non-scientific' philosophizing. Husserl's concept of intentionality is too theoretical. Love is based on a representation of someone as a physical entity to which significance and value are then ascribed. A table is first seen as an isolated *res extensa*, an extended thing, not as something for eating at, too far from the window, etc. (LXIII, 88–92). For Husserl, 'everything affecting me, as a "developed" ego, is apperceived as an "object", a substrate of predicates' (CM, 79). This account, permeated by traditional concepts, distorts my awareness of a table, let alone a light breeze or what I see from the corner of my eye. Intentionality makes everything too sharp and explicit, ignoring the background of which I am tacitly aware (XVII, 318). Husserl's cartesian account of entities conforms to his view of the subject. He focuses on the bare ego, introducing the body and being-in-the world as afterthoughts. Hence he describes such things as tables from the viewpoint of a visual spectator. The ego is, for

Husserl, existent 'for itself in continuous evidence' (CM, 66). In fact, I am often hardly aware of myself, but absorbed in a task; I am usually inauthentic, doing and thinking things because that is what *one* does and thinks.

We are not as perspicuous to ourselves as Husserl assumes. We misinterpret ourselves, both because we cannot see what is under our noses and because we succumb to tradition. One remedy is to examine our philosophical situation and the tradition informing it. Husserl surveyed the history of philosophy in search of anticipations of his own 'scientific philosophy'. He remained captive to the tradition he inadequately explored. Heidegger takes issue with tradition in order to free himself from it. He saw his phenomenology as hermeneutical – like extracting the meaning of a text as a whole, a text obscured by past interpretations of it. He often denigrates Husserl; 'For a whole semester pupils of Husserl have quarrelled over what a letter-box looks like. [. . .] If that's philosophy, then I'm for dialectic!' (LXIII, 110). He questions the basic concepts of Husserlian phenomenology: I, ego, consciousness, object. Yet his analysis of DASEIN, its being-in-the-world and temporality, is a recognizably phenomenological enterprise, commensurable with, and later influencing, Husserl's work. He tries to reveal the inconspicuous without making it conspicuous. Dasein itself must be able to discern the features ascribed to it by the philosopher. More doggedly than Husserl, Heidegger seeks motivations *within* everyday life for the philosophical attitude. He finds a version of *Epoche*. Angst strips the world of pre-assigned significance and prepares it for the philosopher. Later, when being as such (in contrast to the 'being of beings') replaces Dasein as his main interest, phenomenology is supplanted by the 'history of being' (NII, 415/ep, 14f.). 'Phenomenology' is one of those fashionable words that BT, a situation-bound transition to higher things, inevitably but misleadingly used (XLIX, 28).

phenomenology (Husserl) 'Phenomenology' comes from the Greek *phainomena* and *logos*, 'word, saying, reason, etc.'. The passive of *phainein*, 'to make appear, show', is *phainesthai*, 'to appear, come to light', in the sense both of 'to be manifest, obvious' and 'to seem'. *(Ta) phainomena*, the neuter plural of its present participle, is thus '(the) things that appear', 'that which is manifestly/seemingly the case'. For Husserl 'phenomenology' was the study of what appears to us, to our consciousness. He saw it as an antidote to the widespread 'psychologism' – the analysis of all our achievements, especially philosophy, logic and mathematics, in terms of human psychology – which he had condemned in LU. (In PRS he extended his critique to 'historicism' and 'naturalism'.) He first expounded phenomenology in *Ideas*, but it is agreeably summarized in CM. Like Descartes, he urges us to suspend the 'natural attitude', belief in the external world, in the sciences, mathematics, even logic, and focus on one's own ego. This suspension of belief is the *Epoche*, from the Greek *epochē*, 'restraint', a word used by Greek sceptics for 'suspension' of belief. There are two reasons for the *Epoche* and the ensuing 'transcendental reduction': 1. only the ego and its states can supply certain and secure 'foundations' for the sciences; 2. the ego and its states constitute a rich field for investigation in its own right – a field that Descartes discovered but quickly vacated: 'If Descartes had stopped at the end of his second Meditation, he would have arrived at phenomenology'. (Descartes abandoned the phenomenological attitude at the end of his second Meditation, in claiming to be a *res cogitans*, 'thinking thing', something not immediately given in experience.) The field has three constituents, besides the ego itself: 1. The ego's *cogitationes*, 'thoughts', including perceivings, imaginings, rememberings, feelings, etc. 2. The ego's 'intentional objects', chairs, tables, etc. not as real objects, whose chemical composition can be analysed, but as objects of our mental attitudes. 3. The relation between fleeting *cogitationes* and relatively stable intentional objects. How does the continuous flux of our inner life congeal into a stable world?

An 'intentional' object is something on which my mind is 'directed'. (The Latin *intendere* is 'to direct on, towards'.) It need not be a real object: I can dream about unicorns or Sherlock Holmes. A real object need be no one's intentional object: there may be things no one ever has or will think about. An intentional attitude, an attitude directed on an object, need not be intentional in the usual sense: I may love, or dream about, someone without intending to. An intentional object is rarely given all at once in perception. As I enter the room I expect a table to be there. Perception of it 'fulfils' my expectation, but what I immediately perceive is not the whole table but an aspect of it, shimmering in the light and perspectively modulated according to my viewpoint. My further expectations are fulfilled as I walk towards and round it: I continually see new aspects of the table that relate to each other systematically and continuously. I feel the table's resistance when I plant my elbows on it. In 'synthesizing' these sequentially unfolding aspects into a single object I 'retain' aspects I have already seen and 'protain' aspects I have yet to see. This is not just a description of how *Husserl* sees a *table*. It applies to any human's seeing any object of roughly that size: it gives the 'essence' of seeing an object. Usually Husserl describes seeing a table as he imagines or remembers it. (How else can he be sure that his experience is relevantly similar to that of someone who does not perform the epoche?) This is distinct from describing 'remembering (or imagining) seeing a table' – a 'transcendental structure' more complex than seeing a table. Phenomenology explores in this way, seeing, remembering, imagining, etc; artefacts, natural entities, numbers, cultural institutions; my own body and my experience of other people; the idea of a whole world containing regions and objects I have never seen.

The ego that performs these syntheses is constantly aware of itself as the same ego persisting through its manifold experiences. It forms habits: hearing a familiar tune is not like hearing it for the first time. Like anything else, it has an essence: by varying my experience in imagination I find the essential structure of any possible ego, and of its possible life: a life could not pass from adulthood, through infancy, to adolescence. The ego's intentional activities do not just disclose the world of objects, it constitutes it. Any distinction between what is real and what is not is made within my consciousness: 'Objects exist for me, and are for me what they are, only as objects of actual and possible consciousness' (CM, 65). ('Object' here is ambiguously both 'intentional' and 'real'.) Hence Husserl endorses 'transcendental idealism'. But not solipsism. I experience others as '*subjects of this world*, as experiencing it (this same world that I experience) and, in so doing, experiencing me too, even as I experience the world and others in it' (CM, 91). If other egos were not possible, the world would be purely natural, with no artefacts or cultural objects, and purely *my* world, lacking any objectivity. If by a further 'reduction' I imagine a world of this sort, I can ask how I could become aware of the existence of others. I first become aware of my body as an animate organism, and of the relation between my body and my psychical states. I then notice other organisms similar to myself and conjecture that they have perceptions similar to those I would have if I occupied their standpoint. We have different perspectives on a common world: 'By means of the alien constitutings constituted in my own self, there becomes constituted for me the common world for "all of us"' (CM, 87); 'the otherness of "someone else" becomes extended to the whole world, as its "objectivity", [. . .]' (147). From there we proceed to the idea of a community of egos sharing a culture and their daily life, and to the idea of humanity as such, including aliens outside my community. We can explore an enterprise distinct from Husserl's own: 'genetic psychology', the child's acquisition of the concept of an objective world, etc. All this is constituted in my intentional activity: 'everything existing for me must derive its existential sense exclusively from me myself, from my sphere of consciousness' (150).

Husserl has many faults: he makes the epoche and reductions – just ways of focusing on one's own consciousness – excessively mysterious. He neglects the role of language in the formation of our view of the world and in our experience of others. He implausibly suggests that in forming our view of the world we proceed from lower levels to higher: physical entities, then animate organisms, then people, and finally culture and language. (His reply that he is not doing 'genetic psychology' leaves it obscure what he is doing.) His arguments for idealism are fallacious. The intentional activities by which I become aware of the world no more constitute the world than the activity of reading a book amounts to writing it. But Heidegger learned from him and is one of his best expositors and critics (XVII, 42ff, 254ff; XX, 13–182; XXIV, 81ff.).

philosophy Husserl distinguished two types of philosophy: philosophy as world view (*Weltanschauung*), a general view of the world and of man's place in it, and scientific philosophy. Dilthey in TW and Jaspers in PW explored the world view and its varieties. Philosophical world views vary over time and one world view often cannot be rationally preferred to another. Scientific philosophy is not philosophy based on the sciences, but 'Philosophy as rigorous Science' (PRS). It steadily progresses over history; Husserl is its latest practitioner.

Heidegger rejects both alternatives: 'The distinction between "scientific philosophy" and "world view-philosophy" is the last gasp of the philosophical helplessness of the 19th century, in the course of which "science" attained a peculiar technological cultural significance and on the other hand the "world view" of the individual was, as a substitute for the firm basis that had disappeared, to continue to hold together, feebly enough, "values" and "ideals"' (LXV, 37). Early on, he speaks of philosophy as a "science", but, unlike the 'positive' sciences, it is a science of being, not of beings (XXII, 6ff; XXIV, 17). A world view too is concerned with beings and thus distinct from philosophy (XXIV, 15). Philosophy digs beneath sciences and world views to what underlies and makes them possible: DASEIN and being. It differs from science and world view in several respects: philosophy does not consider one region of beings, like botany, or one aspect of beings, like physics; it deals with beings as a whole. it considers not beings, but their being(ness) or being as such; even metaphysics, which from the mid-1930s Heidegger distinguishes from philosophy, considers what makes beings beings, their beingness, not just beings themselves. It reflects on its own concepts, which a science or world view does only at the cost of becoming philosophy. It engages and transforms the Dasein of the philosopher (XXIX, 422f; XXXI, 127). Since it involves a complete change of outlook, it offers no proofs: 'In philosophy propositions can never be proved, not because there are no *supreme* propositions from which others could be derived, but because here what is true is not "propositions" at all, nor is the true simply that which propositions talk about. All "proving" presupposes that someone who understands the proof remains the same and unaltered in the comprehension of the nexus of representations constituting the proof as he was when he representingly approached the matter. [. . .] In philosophical cognition by contrast there begins with the first step a transformation of the person who understands, not in the moral-"existential" sense, but in Da-sein. [. . .] Since in philosophical cognition everything always enters into dislocation [Verrückung, also 'derangement'] – human being in its standing in the truth, truth itself and thus the relation to beyng – and thus an immediate representation of something present-at-hand is never possible, philosophical thinking remains disconcerting' (LXV, 13f.). Philosophy cannot be tackled piecemeal, and there are no specialisms in philosophy: 'Every philosophical question questions into the whole' (XXXI, 14). The philosopher is always a 'beginner' (LXI, 13), yet historically situated: 'Since we are standing on the line, we cannot, from a position outside it, get to the first point on it' (LVIII, 4). For 'thoughtful thinking has a continuity of its *own*. It consists in the succession of ever more primordial beginnings, a way of thinking so remote from scientific thinking that we cannot even say it is just opposed to it' (NI, 618/niii, 125). The scientist 'always operates on the basis of what is already decided, that there is nature, history, art, [. . .] For the thinker there is nothing of the sort; he faces a decision, about what there is and what beings are' (NI, 477/niii, 6). Hence philosophy makes no progress (XXXI, 75; NI, 319/nii, 63). All great philosophers 'think the same. Yet this same is so essential and rich that no individual ever exhausts it' (NI, 46/ni, 36. Cf. XXVI, 198).

What is the point of philosophy? 'If anything is true it is this: philosophy is of no use in human Dasein. But one question still remains open: is the question "What use is that to me?" addressed to *me* or to – at best – an inquisitive animal?' The 'inner greatness of man lies not in the use he makes of things, but in the possibility of going beyond himself and taking a stand, [. . .] philosophy is just the letting-happen of this stand-taking' (XXVIII, 7). Philosophy is also responsible for great changes in history. The diesel engine could not have been invented, 'had not philosophy, at the historical moment when it entered the sphere of its un-essence, thought the categories of this nature and so first opened up the sphere for the quests and attempts of inventors'. Knowing this will not make better engines, but it enables us to ask 'what this machine-technology is within the history of man's relationship to being' (NII, 76/niv, 39f.; cf. 92/niv, 53).

Philosophy is rooted in our preconceptual understanding of being (XXXI, 44). But if it is useless, enabling us only to invent things for which we do not yet see a need, it is hard to see what motivates us to engage in explicit philosophy. Early on, Heidegger asks of Descartes and Husserl: 'What care [Sorge] motivates the development of consciousness as a theme [. . .]? [. . .] In itself it is an atrocity to describe love as consciousness-of-something' (XVII, 59). It is 'care for certainty' or for 'known knowledge' that drives them (XVII, 258), a CARE that Heidegger later sees as a descendant of the Christian's need to be certain of his salvation (NII, 142ff./niv, 97). In BT and more explicitly afterwards, philosophy is motivated and made possible by unsettling moods such as Angst and boredom, which reveal to us beings as a whole and the Nothing that underlies them. As being becomes more central to Heidegger's thought, the decision to do philosophy is no longer a choice made by individual Dasein. Being takes Nietzsche by the scruff of the neck and makes him do its bidding (NII, 290f./niii, 215). But Heidegger rejects Hegel's view, that philosophy, like the owl of Minerva, appears only when the main business of life is done. Philosophy provides the ground for the future (NII, 147/niv, 100f.). It will help prepare the other beginning and save us from being reduced to 'mechanized animals' by technology (LXV, 98, 275). But it is of no use to politicians. To expect philosophy to help the revolution is like wanting to fly on a joiner's bench (IM, 8/8). Genuine philosophy cannot be the 'philosophy of a people'. To demand a specifically German philosophy assimilates philosophy to dress and cooking (LXV, 42; cf. S, 108/90).

play and games   *Spiel* is close to 'play' in the sense of 'game, recreation', but it also once meant a 'dance, dancing movement'. *Spielen* means 'to play', but also meant 'to dance, move in a lively way'. The older meaning survives in *Spielraum*, 'room to move, leeway, elbow-room, free play'. To encounter entities DASEIN needs *Spielraum*, space to move; things that are too close, like the spectacles on one's nose, are 'further away than the picture on the wall opposite' (BT, 107). In BT Heidegger links *Spielraum*, literally 'play-space', with SPACE, but later he associates it with TIME-SPACE by coining *Zeit-Spiel-Raum*, literally 'time-play-space' (OWL, 214/106).

'A man of the world', Kant said, 'is a player [Mitspieler] in the great game [Spiel] of life' (A, Preface). This expression, like all linguistic usage, contains latent philosophy – after all 'philosophizing belongs to the essence of Dasein' (XXVII, 309). Hence if the 'historical being-with-one-another of men' has the diversity and variability of a game, this is because Dasein is essentially playful (XXVII, 310). This is why children play, in a way quite different from animals: 'Perhaps the child is only a child because it is in a metaphysical sense something that we adults no longer comprehend at all' (XXVII, 311). Play is prior to games: 'We do not play because there are games. On the contrary: there are games because we play'. Play has four main features: 1. It is not a 'mechanical sequence of events, but a free, i.e. always rule-governed happening'. 2. What matters in play is not what one actually does, but one's state, one's 'peculiar finding-oneself-therein [Sich-dabei-befinden]', that is, one's mood. Hence 3. The rules form in the course of play. They bind us with a special sort of freedom. Our play develops into a game, which may or may not become detached as a system of rules. Thus 4. A rule of a game is not a fixed norm that we adopt; it varies in the course of the play: 'Playing always creates for itself the space within which it can form and that also means transform itself' (XXVII, 312). Being-in-the-world is playing (TRANSCENDENCE) a game (the WORLD). A reformulation of the four points explains this: 1. 'Playing is a free forming [Bilden] that always has its own unanimity [Einstimmigkeit], insofar as it forms this unanimity for itself in the play'. 2. Play is not a detached structure, but involves binding or committing oneself to the play and the forming. 3. Play is not a 'comportment' to an 'object' or to anything else; 'the playing of the game and the game of the playing [das Spielen des Spiels und Spiel des Spielens]' are a single, insoluble happening. 4. 'Playing in this sense we call being-in-the-world, transcendence, [. . .] surmounting beings. Being-in-the-world has beforehand always already played beyond [überspielt] and around [umspielt] beings; in this playing it first of all forms the space (even in the literal sense) within which we come across beings' (XXVII, 316). World-formation is not an individual, but a joint enterprise, just as a game is 'not played out in a subject' (XXXVII, 313). Beings, human and non-human, are formed by transcendence, as, in our play, a beer-can becomes a football, trees become goal-posts and we become footballers. We take pleasure in the game, but not only that: 'in all pleasure – and not just in pleasure – , in every mood there lies a sort of play' (XXVII, 312).

Heidegger plays with words, or, as he prefers, 'plays along with the game of language' (XXIX, 414). He quotes Heraclitus: 'Lifetime [aiōn] is a child [pais] playing [paizōn], moving pieces on a board. The kingdom is a child's', and translates it: 'World-time – it is a child, playing, moving the pebbles to and fro on a board, of [such] a child is the mastery [over being]'. Hölderlin reworked this idea into the thought that, in Heidegger's words, history 'is the great game that the gods play with peoples and a people; for the great times of world-time are a game, [. . .]' If 'the earth is to enter fully into the real game, i.e. history and historical time', it must 'be cultivated for the gods, presented for the reign of the gods in the succession of the seasons and their festivals'. This happens 'in the "fore-play" ["Vor-Spiel"] of a ruder time'. Then the gods settle down for their game (XXXIX, 105).

poetry and Dichtung   German has two words:

1. *Poesie*, from the Greek *poiēsis*, 'making, fabrication, production, poetry, poem', which in turn comes from *poiein*, 'to make, to do'. Aristotle distinguishes *poiēsis*, 'making' – which essentially has an end-product, a *poiēma* – from *praxis*, 'action' – which does not (cf. BT, 68). That the Greeks gave this inherently general name to poetry in particular is 'evidence for the pre-eminence of this art within Greek art in general' (NI, 193/ni, 165). *Poesie* has a narrower meaning than *poiēsis*, applying especially to verse in contrast to prose.
2. *Dichtung*, from *dichten*, 'to invent, write, compose verses', which sounds Germanic but comes from the Latin *dictare*, 'to say repeatedly, dictate, compose'. This has a wider meaning than *Poesie* or 'poetry'. It applies to all creative writing, including novels, not only verse. The verb has the flavour of 'to dispose, order, shape'. Heidegger uses *dichten* and *Dichtung* in a narrow and a 'wide sense' (OWA, 61/198f.). In the wide sense, *dichten* means 'to invent, create, project', but it is distinct from 'untrammeled invention' (OWA, 60/197). 'From the inventive [dichtenden, creative, projective] essence of art, it happens that art in the midst of beings clears an open place in whose openness everything is other than before' (OWA, 59/197). Hence all art is in essence *Dichtung*, in the wide sense, not in the sense of *Poesie* (Cf. XXXIX, 25ff.).

Heidegger associates *dichten* with *erdichten*, 'to invent, fabricate, make up', and *ausdichten*, a word used by Nietzsche in a similar sense: The birch tree looks different in different seasons, weathers and perspectives, but I take it to be the same tree, not by elaborate comparisons of and inferences from its changing aspects, I have 'always already' taken it to be the same tree. Since the self-identical tree is not strictly given to me, the 'positing of something "alike" is thus an invention and fabrication [ein Erdichten and Ausdichten] [. . .] this inventive [dichtende] character is the essence of reason and thinking. So before we think [gedacht wird] in the usual sense, we must invent [gedichtet werden]' (NI, 583/niii, 95). Kant 'was the first to specifically notice and think through the inventive character of reason in his doctrine of the transcendental imagination [Einbildung-skraft]' (NI, 584/niii, 95f. Cf. K, 80ff./54ff.). Even our words for sense-impressions – 'red, green, sour, etc.' – depend on the fabrication of a likeness, sameness and constancy that are not given in the onpressing throng of sensations. 'The categories of reason are horizons of fabrication [Ausdichtung], a fabrication that first clears [einräumt] for what encoun-ters us that free place, in which it is set up and from which it can appear as a constant, as a standing object [als ein Beständiges, als Gegen*stand*]' (NI, 587/niii, 98). All thinking, *Denken*, is *dichtend*, 'inventive', but not all thinking is *dichterisch*, 'poetic', nor is it all *denkerisch*, 'thoughtful'. But great philosophy is *denkerisch-dichterisch*, both thoughtful and poetic (NI, 472/nii, 208. Cf. Anax, 303/19).

'Language itself is Dichtung in the essential sense' (OWA, 61/199). That is, language 'first brings the entity as an entity into the open' by naming it. It is 'projective saying [entwerfende Sagen]' and this is *Dich-tung*: 'the saying [Sage] of the world and the earth, [. . .] the saying of the unhiddenness of beings' (OWA, 61/198). Hence 'Poesie, Dichtung in the narrow sense, is the most original Dichtung in the essential [i.e. wide] sense. [. . .] Poesie happens in language because language safe-guards the original essence of Dichtung. Building [Bauen] and forming [Bilden] by contrast happen always already and always only in the open of the saying and naming' (OWA, 61/199). *Poesie*, art in the form of language, is prior to the other arts – architecture ('building') and painting and sculpture ('forming') – since they operate in the realm already opened up by language. Heidegger implies that creative language, language that names things for the first time, in contrast to language as a means of communicating what is already disclosed, is *Dichtung* in a narrow sense, i.e. poetry.

Heidegger liked Rilke, George, Trakl, Goethe, but his favourite was Hölderlin, to whom he assigns a crucial role in the recovery of being (LXV, 129). Like Heidegger, Hölderlin was torn between two loves: Greece and its gods, Germany and its God. He was a poet's poet, concerned about the nature of poetry and the poet's place in the cosmic order. In his first essay on him, Heidegger considers five of his sayings about poetry and interprets them in his own way (HEP, 33ff./293ff.):

1. *Dichten* 'is the most innocent of all occupations'. Poetry is play with language, inventing a realm of images to inhabit, with no decisions that incur guilt.
2. 'Language [Sprache], the most dangerous of all goods, is given to man [. . .] so that he can testify to what he is [. . .]'. Language opens up beings, and makes world and history possible. Man testifies to his central position by the worlds he successively creates and destroys throughout history. By opening up beings language exposes us to danger from them. Language is simplified to become our common possession, a message from the gods is diluted for mortal consumption: hence language puts us in danger of delusion.
3. 'Much men have learnt. Have called by their names many of those in heaven/Since we have been a conversation [Gespräch]/And able to hear from each other.' Language is essential to man, and language is essentially conversation, which involves both speaking and hearing. A single coherent conversation requires the identification of stable, objective beings that persist through the flux of time. When we name things, and name the gods, a world appears. Naming the gods is a response to their claim on us. Our response is a fateful act for which we take responsibility.
4. 'But what is lasting the poets found [stiften]'. Poets name, and thus invent, beings, bringing order and measure (i.e. being) to the measureless onrush of time and thus grounding human existence in the 'lasting'.
5. 'Full of acquirements, but poetically [dichtersich] man dwells upon this earth'. Poetry names beings and grounds human life. Poetry makes language possible. Poetry endangers the poet: 'Yet, fellow poets, us it behoves to stand/Bare-headed beneath God's thunderstorms,/To grasp the Father's ray, no less, with our own two hands/And wrapping in song the heavenly gift,/To offer it to the people'. The apparent innocence of poetry disguises the danger. The poet's free creativity has two constraints: the 'hints [Winke]' of the gods and the 'voice of the people', the legends that he has to interpret. The poet is a demi-god, between the gods and the people, standing in the Between where it is decided who man is and where he is to dwell.

Hölderlin does not give the eternal essence of poetry. He says what poetry must be in the 'impoverished time' between the departure of the old gods and the arrival of the new god. The attempt drove him mad. What he said of Oedipus applies to himself: 'King Oedipus has an eye too many perhaps.'

possibility, actuality and necessity   In BT 'possibility' is used in two ways:

1. Something is the 'condition for the possibility' of something else: e.g. 'The question about being aims at an apriori condition of the possibility of the sciences [...]' (BT, 11). Heidegger also speaks of 'inner' possibility, in contrast to 'outer', e.g. physical, possibility: 'To what extent does the inner possibility of such a thing as ground lie in transcendence?' (ER, 100). The Kantian question 'How is x possible?' has two applications: (a) Heidegger starts with an ordinary conception, e.g. truth as the correctness of an assertion or science as a system of propositions, and argues that truth or science in this sense is not possible unless we postulate a deeper conception of it, from which the ordinary conception is derived (BT, 153ff; XXVII, 238). (b) One respectably Heideggerian phenomenon makes possible another: e.g. temporality is the 'ontological condition of the possibility' of being-in-the-world (BT, 350). BT works back from a phenomenon to its condition. 'We do not ask what must be actual for something else to be actualized, but about what must be possible for something else to be possible' (XXVII, 87). Later, Heidegger is wary of the expression 'condition of possibility': he rejects (i) the Kantian and generally metaphysical view that being is the condition of the possibility of beings (LXV, 183, 289), an ancestor of the identification of being with 'value' (NII, 338/niv, 201), and (ii) the procedure of working back from beings to being, preferring to 'grasp the truth of beyng from its own essence' (LXV, 250).

2. 'Possibility' is the possibility open to DASEIN: 'Dasein is not something present-at-hand which possesses its ability to be something as an extra; it is primarily being-possible. Dasein is always what it can be, and in the way in which [wie] it is its possibility' (BT, 143). Hence Heidegger alters the traditional, Aristotelian order of priority among the 'modalities': 'Higher than actuality stands possibility' (BT, 38). 'Possibility' in this sense is quite different from 'empty logical possibility' and from the 'contingency of the present-at-hand, to which various things can "happen"' (BT, 143). It is close to 'ability-to-be': 'Dasein is the possibility of being-free for its very ability-to-be' (BT, 144). *(Das) Seinkönnen*, from *sein*, 'to be', and *können*, 'to be able', is 'ability [können] to be [sein]' or perhaps 'capacity/potentiality for being [Sein]'. It differs from 'possibility' in that as a nominalized infinitive it has no plural, unlike *Möglichkeit, -en*, 'possibility, -ies'.

171

That Dasein has various possibilities open to it is one of Heidegger's reasons for supposing that Dasein is aware of beings as a whole. Focusing on an isolated being may tell us that it is actual. But what is possible depends on a wider whole. I cannot know whether I can e.g. give a lecture unless I know that it has been publicized, a room is available, I am in a university, etc. (cf. XXIX, 528ff.). But the range of possibilities that Dasein conceives as open, and in terms of which it understands itself, is not fixed. I can lecture on the advertised topic in this way or that; I can lecture on the advertised topic or on a quite different topic; I can continue to lecture or give it up and become a farmer. Different ways of conceiving my possibilities invoke wholes of varying ranges: if I consider becoming a farmer, I take account of my past training, the price of land, etc. I may not consider my *own* possibilities, but select from the menu offered by the THEY. Then I focus on the present and immediate future, giving little thought to beings as a whole.

'Actuality' (*Wirklichkeit*) is of comparatively little interest in BT. It is equivalent to *Vorhandenheit*, PRESENCE-AT-HAND, or to *Realität*, and is associated with the present and with mere things (BT, 99, 373f; NI, 392f./ nii, 129f.). *Wirklich(keit)*, from *Werk*, 'work', and *wirken*, 'to work, effect, act', was thus originally 'active, efficacious; activity, efficacy'. The late Latin *actualis, actualitas* have the same original meaning. Heidegger connects both sets of words with Dasein's making or production (XXIV, 143, 147). But he takes *wirklich* to mean 'produced' (*hergestellt*) rather than 'productive', and *Wirklichkeit* to mean 'producedness' (*Hergestelltsein*) (XXIV, 159ff.). (The suffix -*lich* can be passive: *lieblich* is 'loveable, what one loves or can love [lieben]' rather than 'loving'.) This need not make the actual overly dependent on Dasein: the producer lets the product go its own way (XXIV, 160). Not everything is produced by Dasein (XXIV, 162ff.), but Dasein views being in terms of its own producing (156), so that medieval thinkers saw everything as God's creation (167f.). Later, Heidegger traces technology, for which everything is subordinate to man's unlimited productive activity, back to the priority of actuality in META-PHYSICS (LXV, 147, 246, 475).

'Necessity' is not important in BT but becomes so later. Heidegger has no more interest in logical necessity than in logical possibility. *Notwendig(keit)*, 'necessary; necessity', comes from 1. *Not*, 'need, distress, want', which also generates *nötig*, 'necessary', *nötigen*, 'to force, compel', and *Nötigung*, 'compulsion, coercion', and 2. *wenden*, 'to turn'. Hence *notwendig* originally meant 'turning need or distress' (NI, 435, 471/nii, 172, 207; XXXIX, 244). Hence: 'All necessity is rooted in a need' (LXV, 45). What need? 'This need is what drives man around among beings and first brings

him before beings as a whole and into the middle of beings and so brings
him to himself and thus always lets history begin or decline. [. . .] man's
THROWNNESS among beings' (LXV, 45). (In IM, 112f./123f., this is
illustrated by Sophocles's 'poetic projection of being-human', the choral
ode of *Antigone*, ll.332–375, beginning: 'There is much that is strange, but
nothing/that surpasses man in strangeness'.) This need is the source of
philosophy: 'The necessity of philosophy consists in the fact that, as
reflection, it must withstand the need and ground it, make it the ground
of the history of man, rather than remove it' (LXV, 45). The need is for
being (LXV, 328), the distress is the distress of abandonment by being,
and is 'to be transformed into the necessity of creation' (LXV, 18). 'Who
has an inkling of the necessity of thinking and questioning, of the
necessity that requires no crutches of the Why, no props of the Where-
fore?' (LXV, 19).

presence and the present German has several words connected with
'presence':

1. *Präsenz* is an elevated word, derived from the Latin *praesentia* via the
    French *presence*.
2. *Gegenwart*, lit. 'waiting [wart(en)] towards [gegen]', usually refers to
    the present time, but it can signify spatial presence ('in his presence').
    The adjective *gegenwärtig* also primarily means what is temporally
    'present, current, of today', but can apply to e.g. guests present at a
    party. The verb *(sich) vergegenwärtigen* means 'to envisage, imagine,
    recall, lit. make present to oneself'. Husserl coined *gegenwärtigen*,
    Gegenwärtigung ('to make present; making present'), which is similar
    not only to *vergegenwärtigen* but also to *gewärtigen*, 'to expect, await, be
    prepared for': '[Husserl's] thesis that all knowledge aims at "intuition"
    has a temporal sense: all knowing is making present. [. . .] Husserl
    uses the expression "making present" to characterize sense-percep-
    tion. [. . .] The intentional analysis of perception and intuition in
    general inevitably suggested this "temporal" account of the phenom-
    enon' (BT, 363 n.). Heidegger rejects Husserl's verificationism but
    still uses *gegenwärtigen* in the sense of 'letting what is present [Anwes-
    endes] come to meet us [begegnen] in a present [Gegenwart]' (XXI,
    192. Cf. BT, 326).
3. *Der Augenblick*, 'the moment (of vision), lit. eye-glance', is the authen-
    tic present, the moment of RESOLUTE decision in which Dasein

seizes the possibilities presented by its 'situation' (BT, 338; NI, 311/
nii, 56f.).

4. *(Das) Anwesen* is the nominalized infinitive of a now defunct verb,
   anwesen, 'to be there, in, at or involved in something'. The participle
   anwesend still means '(being) present at something'. In the fifteenth
   century *Anwesen* acquired its current sense of 'estate, homestead,
   residence, dwelling', and by the eighteenth century lost its earlier
   sense of 'presence'. (Plato's and Aristotle's word for 'being, substance,
   essence', *ousia*, meant, in ordinary Greek, 'what is one's own, one's
   substance, property' (XXIV, 153; IM, 46/50).) *Anwesen* in the sense of
   'presence' was replaced in the seventeenth century by *Anwesenheit*,
   'presence', usually but not invariably in a spatial sense ('in his
   presence'). Heidegger also revives the old use of *Anwesen*, mainly in
   the verbal sense of 'presencing, coming into presence' (NI, 160, 452,
   598/ni, 135; nii, 187; niii, 106f.), but also for 'presence' (NII, 394/
   niv, 247). The verbal sense is more explicit in his coinage, *Anwesung*
   (P, 223/262; LXV, 188, etc.).

5. The Greek *parousia*, 'a being present, presence, arrival', is com-
   pounded from *ousia* and *para*, 'beside, by, etc.'. *Pareinai* similarly
   means 'to be [einai] present [para]'. (The form *ousia* stems from the
   feminine present participle of *einai*, *ousa*.) Heidegger held that *ousia*
   meant 'presence [Anwesenheit]' (XXI, 71). Spengler had argued that
   the Greeks, unlike the Egyptians and modernity, had 'no memory, no
   organ of history' and lived in the 'pure Present': 'For Herodotus and
   Sophocles, as for Themistocles or a Roman consul, the past is subtil-
   ized instantly into an impression that is timeless and changeless, polar
   and not periodic in structure – in the last analysis, of such stuff as
   myths are made of – whereas for our world-sense and our inner eye
   the past is a definitely periodic and purposeful organism of centuries
   or millenia' (DW, 9). Spengler appeals to the Doric column, the
   'greatest symbol' of the pure Present, the poor chronology and
   record-keeping of the Greeks and their preference for cremation.
   Heidegger appeals to etymology: *ousia* means 'presence [Anwesen-
   heit]' owing to its association with *parousia* (BT, 25). Later, he
   contronts the difficulty that *pareinai*, -*ousia* is only one of several
   compounds of *einai*, *ousia*. Another is *apeinai*, *apousia*, 'to be absent;
   absence'. Why is presence special? There are, he replies, two types of
   parousia or *Anwesenheit*; one contrasts with *apousia*, *Abwesenheit*, the
   other is presupposed by it: 'The specifically meant, explicit apousia
   that is contrasted with parousia occurs only on the basis of original
   parousia' (XXXI, 61). He also appeals to Greek philosophers. He

174

wrongly infers from Plato's claim that beautiful things are beautiful owing to the presence of beauty in them (*Euthydemus*, 301a4; *Phaedo*, 100d) that Plato equates being with presence: that x is F owing to the presence of Fness does not entail that x's being (F) is x's presence.

Heidegger often speaks of *beständige* ('constant') *Anwesenheit* (XXXI, 60), and of *Beständigkeit*, 'constancy' (NI, 465/nii, 200, etc.). This comes from *stehen, Stand* ('to stand; standing(-position)'), and he often associates it with *Beständigung*, 'bringing something to a stand(still)' (NI, 655/niii, 156; NII, 286f./niii, 212). To converse or communicate we need to extract relatively stable, intersubjectively accessible entities from the flux of becoming. But this is possible only if we have an enduring framework in which such entities can appear, in particular words whose meanings do not change every time we use them: 'But the One and Same can only be manifest in the light of the lasting and constant [Ständigen]' (HEP, 39/ 302). Not everything is constant; but the fleeting and variable can be recognized only in the light of the constant.

Often Heidegger uses *Gegenwart, Anwesenheit* and *Präsenz* interchangeably, but often he differentiates them. *Anwesenheit* can refer to the type of presence that includes absence, but *Gegenwart* cannot. Thus BEING is identified with *Anwesenheit*, not usually with *Gegenwart*, which is more likely to be 'uncoveredness [Entdecktheit]' or TRUTH, while *Präsenz* covers both *Anwesenheit* and *Gegenwart* (XXI, 193f.). He distinguishes several senses of *Gegenwart* (XXI, 402f.): 1. 'now [jetzt], the current epoch, today'. This leads to the 'pure Now [Jetzt]' which dominates the philosophical understanding of time. 2. 'He did not want to speak in the Gegenwart of Tom'. Here *Gegenwart* is close to *Anwesenheit*, but distinct from 'PRESENCE-AT-HAND [*Vorhandensein*]'. 3. 'He did not dare to say it in my Gegenwart'. Here 'in my Gegenwart' means not presence-at-hand but: 'in my being towards him and his being towards me, in reciprocal making-present [Gegenwärtigen], in reciprocally having the same world together'. 4. 'In my Gegenwart' also means: 'in my Anwesenheit, in my Dasein-with [Mitdasein] in the same place and location', a sense close to 2. 3 is the basic sense of *Gegenwart* in terms of which we understand the others. *Anwesenheit* is a category, applicable to the present-at-hand; *Gegenwart* (in the 'actively transitive sense' of *Gegenwärtigen*) is an EXISTENTIAL, applicable only to Dasein; *gegenwärtig* too has an active sense: 'it primarily expresses just the being of Dasein towards its world' (XXI, 402).

Gegenwart is prior to the Now: 'Making-present is above all the condition that makes it possible for such a thing as "Now" – now this, now that – to be expressed. Knowledge of nature, e.g., is a making-present of a definite type, and making-present characterizes Dasein in its being-in-the-world. That is why this Dasein, when it addresses the world, nature – and that always means that it expresses itself, its very own being towards the world – can say "now this, now that"' (XXI, 401).

projection and the apriori The verb *entwerfen* comes from *werfen*, 'to throw'; it suggests 'throwing away, off[ent-]'. It originally meant 'to form a picture, design' in weaving by turning the shuttle to and fro. It then came to apply to literary and mental formation. It acquired the sense of 'provisional, preliminary drafting' under the influence of the French *projeter*, 'to plan, lit. throw before'. Today *entwerfen* means 'to sketch, design, draft, draw up, depict, outline'. Similarly, an *Entwurf* is a 'sketch, outline, design, blueprint, draft'. Heidegger revives the association with throwing. The words are thus aptly translated as 'project' and 'projection', from the Latin *proicere*, 'to throw forward'.

An *Entwurf* in Heidegger's sense is not a particular plan or project; it is what makes any plan or project possible (BT, 145; XXIX, 526). He gives various accounts of what is projected: a world (XXIX, 526); the being of beings or the 'constitution of their being' (XXIV, 29f; XXVII, 198ff.); fundamental scientific conceptions of being such as the mathematical view of nature (XXVII, 185ff.); DASEIN itself (BT, 145). He also speaks of the projection of something onto something else: the understanding projects the being of Dasein onto its 'For-the-sake-of' and onto the SIGNIFICANCE of its world (BT, 145); understanding, or Dasein itself, projects Dasein onto (its) possibilities or onto a possibility (BT, 145; XXIV, 392f.); beings are projected onto their being (XXIV, 29, 396); being is projected onto time (XXIV, 397, 437).

A project(ion) is 'free'. It is not determined by our prior knowledge or desires, since it is only in the light of a project that we can have any specific knowledge or desires. A project is not projected piecemeal, by gradual steps, but all at once, by a leap ahead (NI, 392/nii, 129; LXV, 352). There are three main types of project (e.g. XXVII, 185ff.):

1. Any Dasein must project a world and have a pre-ontological understanding of being, i.e. project being, including its own being. Such a projection occurs at no definite time: it is an 'original action [Urhandlung]' of Dasein. This projection enables Dasein to understand e.g. what a tool is or what another person is, independently of the particular tools and persons it encounters. It is comparable to one's

176

overall understanding of what a town is and one's general sense of direction.

2. A science involves a project(ion) of the constitution of the entities it deals with, e.g. Galileo's and Newton's projection of being as mathematical. Such a project is not grounded in experience of beings: the project decides in advance what counts as a being and as experience. Nor is it grounded in a previous project or in criticism of it: a new project is not commensurable with its predecessor, it alters our whole view of being and beings. This type of project does not supplant the project of type 1: a mathematical physicist still needs a pre-ontological understanding of tools, people, time, etc. A scientific project is analogous to a selective map of a town; it cannot dispense with one's overall pre-ontological understanding of beings any more than a map-user can do without a sense of direction.

3. A philosopher acquires a conceptual, ontological understanding of being, which involves an understanding of projects 1 and 2. The philosopher cannot simply painstakingly describe these projects without any specifically philosophical projection. The nature of being, of Dasein, etc. is 'covered up' (e.g. BT, 376), not open to unvarnished empirical inspection. Thus the philosopher must undertake an 'existential' projection or a 'phenomenological construction [Konstruktion]' of e.g. Dasein's historicality (BT, 375ff.). Again, the philosopher must project a being (e.g. Dasein) 'onto its being and its structures' (XXIV, 29f.). We understand something, x, by projecting it onto something else, y, the 'Upon-which [Woraufhin]' of the projection and the 'sense [Sinn]' of x (BT, 323ff.). There is thus a 'stratification' of projects. We understand beings by projecting them onto being (XXIV, 396). We understand being by projecting it onto time. The regress ends with time: time, owing to its 'ecstatic unity', is 'self-projection'; it need not be projected onto anything else to be understood (XXIX, 437). The philosopher's projections proceed in the reverse direction to the projection they conceptualize, Dasein's basic project (XXIV, 399). This accords with Aristotle's view: what is prior in itself is posterior for us. Time is prior to being and makes it possible, being is prior to beings and makes them possible. But owing to the obscurity of these relationships, we proceed from beings to being, and thence to time.

Later, Heidegger takes a more historical view of project 1, speaking of the 'original Greek projection' of being as the 'constancy of PRESENCE' (e.g. NII, 8/niii, 162). The Dasein-constituting project is seen as the

177

accomplishment of philosophers and/or poets rather than of everyday Dasein.

A project involves 'anticipation' [Vorgriff]' and the 'apriori'. What a tool is; other people; that there is a world: these are apriori within project 1, and thus for every Dasein. That things are exactly measurable: this is apriori for mathematical physics. That Dasein 'exists': this is apriori for Heidegger. 'Apriori' comes from the Latin for 'what comes before, earlier'; the apriori is 'the earlier' (XX, 99). The apriori is not true or 'correct', beyond the project which it helps to define: 'The apriori is the title for the essence of things. The apriori and its priority are interpreted in accordance with our conception of the thinghood of the thing and our understanding of the being of beings in general' (WT, 130/166). A project is more like a decision than a discovery (NI, 561f./niii, 75f.); it cannot be correct or incorrect: correctness, and criteria for it, only apply within the light shed by the project (LXV, 327). What the light of a project reveals are possibilities – for ontical knowledge, but also for other ontical dealings with beings, the beings understood and delimited by the project. Thus in projecting, Dasein always projects itself on its possibilities, though the range of possibilities varies depending on whether it is resolute or not (BT, 385). In doing this it understands itself in terms of the possibilities open to it. Dasein projects itself in its own project – one of the meanings of the claim that a project is THROWN. Dasein does not have a constant, project-independent understanding of itself: it first understands itself, or understands itself anew, after the projection (LXV, 357, 452).

R

reality of the external world *Realität, real,* come from the late Latin *realis,* which in turn comes from *res,* 'thing, etc.' (Its Germanic equivalent, *Wirklichkeit,* 'actuality', comes from *wirken,* 'to work, etc.' and thus has a more dynamic tone.) Hence to say that something is real or has *Realität* implies, for Heidegger, not just that it exists, but that it is a thing, PRESENT-AT-HAND rather than ready-to-hand or DASEIN-like (BT, 201, 209). In this sense *Realität* is only one mode of being among others – readiness-to-hand, existentiality, subsistence (*Bestehen*), which applies especially to abstract entities such as those of arithmetic and geometry (XXIV, 73) – and has no special priority (BT, 211). Heidegger explains the supposed priority of *Realität* from Dasein's FALLING and thus interpreting being in terms of intraworldly entities. The 'being of the directly ready-to-hand is passed over' in favour of the present-at-hand (BT, 201), since if we focus explicitly on a tool, it is 'withdrawn from the world [Entweltlichung, lit. 'deworlding']' and seen as present-at-hand (BT, 75).

Heidegger's main interest is not the term *Realität,* but the idea that the reality of the 'external world [Aussenwelt]' needs to be proved. Kant spoke of the need to prove, not the *Realität* of the *Aussenwelt,* but 'the Dasein of things outside us' (BT, 203). Kant used *Dasein* in the sense of 'reality, actuality', reserving *Realität* for the nature of something rather than its actual existence (XXIV, 45f.). Still, whether expressed in terms of *Realität* or in some other way, the problem of the reality of the external world involves four distinct questions:

1. Are there any 'consciousness-transcendent' entities at all?
2. Can this reality of the 'external world' be sufficiently proved?
3. How far can these beings, if they are real, be known in their being-in-itself (*An-sich-sein*)?
4. What does the sense (*Sinn*) of these beings, viz. reality, mean in general? (BT, 201).

Heidegger's answers are:

1. Yes, there are 'consciousness-transcendent' entities, but that is a misleading way of putting it. I am not a 'worldless subject' or consciousness. I am Dasein, and Dasein is essentially in the world. Being-in-the-world is prior to my relations with entities; it is not the aggregate of the entities I am conscious of. Nor is consciousness my primary relationship to entities. I wield the hammer without any special consciousness of it. Items I may need later are there, but inconspicuous. 'Consciousness' suggests a focused attention that is inappropriate to most of my dealings with things.

2. No, the reality of the external world cannot be proved, nor need it be. Since Dasein is in the world, and anyone who tries to prove its reality is Dasein, we are trying to prove what is already obvious to us. If we try to prove it, we must find premises that do not beg the question by assuming that we are already in the world. This leads to the above-mentioned distortion, whittling Dasein down to a worldless consciousness. The conclusion supposedly established by such proofs usually misrepresents the external world as a collection of present-at-hand physical things lying alongside our present-at-hand states of consciousness. What we need to do with Descartes's *cogito ergo sum* is not to use it to prove the reality of the world, but to invert it, to explore the *sum*, my being, first: it turns out to be being-in-the-world (BT, 211; XX, 210).

3. The notion of the 'in itself' needs to be interpreted before we can use it to characterize the reality of the world. If what things are 'in themselves' is contrasted with what they are for consciousness or for the subject, we have already found the 'in-itself', since 'consciousness' and the 'subject' have been replaced by being-in-the-world and Dasein. When one is absorbed in working with equipment, the equipment is 'inconspicuous' and thus 'in itself', whereas if we focus on it and view it as present-at-hand, it is no longer 'in itself' but drawn out of itself by our intervention. There is no reason to think that being-in-itself is especially connected with presence-at-hand (BT, 75f. Cf. XX, 299f.).

4. Like being in general, including being-in-itself, reality depends on our understanding of being: 'only as long as Dasein is, i.e. the ontical possibility of understanding of being, "is there" ['es gibt'] being' (BT, 212). Beings and real entities are independent of Dasein, but being and reality are not. Reality is subordinate to Dasein as CARE; its meaning is given above.

Heidegger considers and rejects the view that the reality of the external world consists in the lively or full-bodied perception of things (XX, 300f; XXIV, 62ff.). This neglects the world around us, the *Umwelt*, with its familiar, but inconspicuous significance. More satisfactory is the view that reality is resistance to our will and impulse, a view suggested by Dilthey and developed by Scheler (XX, 302ff; BT, 209ff. Cf. LXI, 148, 177). Among other merits this view does not restrict our dealings with things to knowledge and judgement, and it acknowledges the role of our bodily nature in our experience of the world. But the problem is this: I can only experience resistance to my will if I am *after something* before I encounter resistance. But if I am after something the world must already be disclosed to me, even if I do not know precisely what it contains. Resistance may tell me what is real and what is not, but it cannot tell me that there is a world.

Scheler responded to Heidegger (Scheler (1976), 185ff., esp. 254ff.): Resistance is essential to our experience of reality. Care would be impossible in Cockaigne, a land of milk and honey in which our desires are automatically satisfied: 'A world without evil could essentially never be given as real – even if it were real' (279). Heidegger's concept of world is a 'solipsism of Dasein [Daseinssolipsmus] [...] a pure inversion of the cartesian cogito ergo sum into a sum ergo cogito' (260). 'Being-with-one-another – that could still be so, even if everyone lived solus ipse in their and only their own world' (280). 'If world-being [Weltsein] founds real-being [Realsein] (thus surely causality too) and if Dasein (of the solus ipse) is being-in-the-world – how does Heidegger know at all that he and I are in the same world?' (266).

Such attacks provoked Heidegger's later explanation of BT, 212. When he wrote 'Only as long as Dasein is, [...] is there [es gibt, 'there is', but literally 'it gives'] being', he meant *es gibt* in the literal sense: 'it, viz. being, gives being', i.e. 'only as long as Dasein is, does being "give" itself' or 'hand itself over' to man (LH, 331ff./238ff.). Within the terms of BT, a better response to Scheler is: the 'common world' is the world of the THEY.

repetition, destruction and conversation Heidegger uses various terms for the appropriate attitude to the past. *Wiederholung*, 'repetition, retrieval', comes from *wiederholen*, which has two senses: 1.'to repeat, reiterate, say or do again [wieder]'; here the verb is inseparable, that is, it cannot appear as *holen . . . wieder*, with other words intervening between the two constituents. 2.'to retrieve, get back [e.g. a ball]'; here it is separable. When Heidegger speaks of 'the necessity of a(n explicit)

Wiederholung of the question about being' (BT, 2, 3), he means that we need to repeat it, ask it again. He also uses it in a sense closer to 2: 'By the Wiederholung of a basic problem we understand the disclosure of its original, so far hidden possibilities; by working these out we transform it and the substance of the problem is first preserved' (K, 204/139). His treatment of Kant exemplifies such repetition. He first considers Kant's 'grounding of metaphysics in its originality', presenting an interpretation that goes beyond Kant's words to his 'unsaid' thoughts: that reason and sensibility are rooted in transcendental imagination, that imagination is the source of time, and that Kant withdrew from this 'abyss' in the second edition of CPR (K, 126ff./87ff.). He then considers the 'grounding of metaphysics in a Wiederholung' and presents not an interpretation, but a summary of his own thought, drawing attention to its affinity to Kant's (K, 204ff./139ff.). Another case is this: for Plato, learning is recollecting knowledge acquired before birth. Leibniz 'repeated' this, rejecting pre-natal existence, but arguing that we are born with innate ideas or dispositions, like veins in the marble of our souls. Chomsky repeated Leibniz, arguing that we have a certain grammatical structure innate in us.

Not only philosophers, but all DASEIN, if it is authentically resolute, repeats 'a past possibility of existence'. It 'chooses a hero', such as Eleanor Roosevelt, and, without reproducing her thoughts and deeds exactly, 'returns [erwidert, = 1. reply (to), 2. reciprocate]' the possibility she presents. This is also a 'disavowal [Widerruf]' of the way in which the 'dead past' affects the present: by breathing new life into the past one loosens its dead grip on the present, and uses it purposefully to face the future (BT, 386). '*Repetition is explicit tradition or handing down [Überlieferung*], that is, the return to possibilities of Dasein that has been there' (BT, 385). Inauthentic Dasein does not repeat in this way; its hero is the THEY (BT, 371).

Repetition involves, BT implies, a *conversation* with a past 'hero'. Later, Heidegger speaks of a 'dialogue [Zwiegespräch] with philosophers, especially with Kant'. The point is not simply to acquaint ourselves with past opinions, but that philosophical problems 'have their authentic vitality only in this historical discussion [Auseinandersetzung], a history whose happening lies outside the sequence of events' (XXXI, 136f.). Later still, a 'dialogue' or 'conversation [Gespräch]' with the thinkers of the 'first beginning', the Greeks, is an essential preparation for the 'other beginning' (LXV, 6, 169, 187, 432). We also need to *repeat* the first beginning. But this cannot be exact repetition: 'the beginning can never be grasped as the *same*, since it is anticipatory [vorgreifend] and always outflanks (übergreift] what is begun by it differently and thus determines the Wieder-holung of itself' (LXV, 55. Cf. 57, 73, 185, 475, 504).

Dialogue is not wholly amicable: 'To ask *again* [*wieder*fragen] the question asked by Plato and Aristotle [. . .] means: *to ask more originally than they*. It is – in the history of everything essential – the privilege and also the responsibility of all descendants to become the murderers of their forebears and themselves be subject to the fate of a necessary murder! Only then do we attain the way of posing the question in which they existed with *effortless immediacy*, but which they were, for that very reason, unable to work out in its ultimate *transparency*' (XXXI, 37). Dialogue involves *Auseinandersetzung*, 'discussion', with some of the flavour of its Latin source: *discutere*, 'to smash to pieces'. This does not mean criticizing and refuting, but 'bringing the other party and above all oneself to what is original and ultimate. This is the essence of the matter and is automatically the common cause of both parties, so we do not need to make up afterwards. *Philosophical discussion is interpretation as destruction*' (XXXI, 292).

Heidegger avoids the usual word for 'destruction', *Zerstörung*, in favour of the Latinate *Destruktion*. *Destruktion* 'must be understood strictly as de-struere, "de-construct" ["Ab-bauen"], and not as devastation. But what is deconstructed? Answer: what covers up the sense of being, the structures piled on top of each other that make the sense of being unrecognizable' (XV, 337. Cf. XXIV, 31; NII, 415/ep, 14f.). We must 'loosen up the hardened tradition and dissolve the concealments it has engendered'. Hence '*guided by the question about being*' we '*destroy* the traditional content of ancient ontology down to the original experiences in which the first and henceforth guiding determinations of being were acquired'. *Destruktion* does not 'shake off the ontological tradition', it stakes out its 'positive possibilities' and confines it within its 'limits'. It is critical not of the past, but of the present and the prevalent approach to the history of ontology (BT, 22f. Cf. LXV, 221). *Destruktion* here sounds similar to *Wiederholung*. It subverts current and traditional accounts of, say, Aristotle and also unquestioned concepts that tacitly derive from a possibly misunderstood Aristotle. It does not destroy Aristotle; it reveals hitherto unnoticed possibilities in his thought and works back to the 'experiences' that inspired it. But Heidegger does not treat all philosophers in the same way. He often reads Kant (though not in BT) as a proto-Heideggerian. Hegel gets different treatment; he is in the cartesian mould: 'If there is anywhere where it is entirely absurd to look for the ideas of BT, it is in Hegel' (XXXII, 209). But none of the philosophers whom Heidegger 'destroys' is entirely barren of 'possibilities' for his own thought. Later, he says that in BT 'Destruktion, like "phenomenology" and all hermeneutical-transcendental questioning, is not yet conceived in terms of the history of being [seinsgeschichtlich]' (NII, 415/ep, 15).

Heidegger briefly considered the significance of the 'repeatability [Wiederholbarkeit] of the experiment' (LXV, 166). Kierkegaard wrote a work, *Repetition* (1843): 'Just as the Greeks taught that all knowing is a recollecting, so the new philosophy shall teach that the whole of life is a repetition'. Neither of these concepts influenced Heidegger's main concept of repetition.

representation and idea *Stellen* is 'to place [something], make it stand'. The preposition *vor* means 'before, in front of, etc.' Thus *vorstellen* is 'to bring, move forward; to put something in front of something else', hence 'to represent, mean, signify' and 'to introduce, present a person', etc. The reflexive *sich vorstellen* means 'to present, introduce oneself' – with an accusative *sich*, and 'to represent to oneself, imagine, conceive' – with a dative *sich*. *Vorstellung* is a 'performance, presentation, introduction' and 'idea, conception, imagination, etc.' *Vorstellung* also shares the ambiguity of many *ung*-words: it can mean the act of 'representing [Vorstellen]' or 'what is represented [Vorgestelltes]' (NII, 151/niv, 105).

Brentano recognized three classes of mental phenomena: 1. representing; 2. judgement; 3. interest, emotions, etc. To represent something is to be aware of it or have it in mind, without making any judgement about it, or evaluating it. All mental phenomena involve representation: 'This representing forms the foundation not just of judging, but of desiring and of every other mental act. Nothing can be judged, nothing can be desired either, nothing can be hoped for or feared, if it is not represented' (quoted from PES at XX, 27f. Cf. XXI, 95ff; BT, 139). Heidegger has several objections. It involves a theoretical bias that survived in Husserl, but was discarded by Scheler, following the lead of Augustine and Pascal (XX, 175fff BT, 139). Fear is not based on a prior *Vorstellung* or knowledge of a threat. I see a threat only because I fear it (XX, 396. Cf. NI, 68/ni, 56, on the will). Basic moods such as Angst and boredom are not *of* or *about* anything that might be represented. Descartes's and Kant's assumption that what is first given is a *Vorstellung* blinds them to the world around them, which is neither represented nor pieced together from representations (XXI, 337). Brentano's view suggests, though it does not strictly entail, that when I see, hear or think about something, what I primarily or directly hear, see or think about is a *Vorstellung*. I see a chair, not a *Vorstellung*; I remember a voyage, not a *Vorstellung* – the 'most primitive of facts [. . .] overlooked just for the sake of a theory' (XX, 45; cf. XXI, 100f.). *Vorstellen* occurs, but it is 'letting something be seen [Sehen-lassen von etwas]', not something that is itself seen, like a picture (XX, 45). Seeing a picture, and seeing something in a picture, are quite different from seeing things in the flesh. Seeing does not involve a mental picture: 'Nothing of that sort is to be found; in the simple sense of perception I see the house itself' (XX, 56; cf. XXI, 162ff., 361f. on the death-mask, 364ff. on paintings; BT, 217f; NI, 505f./niii, 29f.). Seeing is permeated by language and categories: 'We do not so much primarily and originally see objects and things; at first we speak about them; more precisely we do not express what we see, rather we see what one says about the matter' (XX, 75). Heidegger sees a close affinity between the representational theory of perception and the correspondence theory of truth: both involve 'representations in the soul copying beings outside' (XXI, 162; NI, 511, 534ff., 554/niii, 34, 53ff., 70).

Vorstellung goes with a view of the self as a subject: in Kant 'the I was forced back again to an *isolated* subject, which accompanies representations in an ontologically quite indefinite way' (BT, 321). Heidegger rejects this – in the BT period because it misrepresents our being-in-the world, later because it adequately represents our man-centred attitude to the world. He exploits other *stellen*-compounds and various senses of *vorstellen*, often writing *vor-stellen* to stress its origins. *Vor-stellen* might mean, if we stress *stellen* rather than *vor*, 'to make something stand (fast) in advance/ before us'. Thus it expresses Nietzsche's view that, in what we call 'truth', we bring chaotic becoming to a standstill, converting it into 'static constancy [vor-gestellte Beständige]' (NI, 635/niii, 139f.; cf. 576/niii, 89). *Vor-stellen* can also mean 'to bring before' a court. Then it suggests that man is a judge who decides what beingness is and what qualify as beings, who lays down the law and applies it to beings (NII, 295f./niii, 219). To be is then to-be-represented, *Vorgestelltheit*, to be presented before the bench. (Heidegger often links *vorstellen* with *zustellen*, 'to deliver, serve, especially a writ', NII, 433, 450/ep, 29f., 46.) This is Descartes's main achievement, not that he regarded the ego as a thing – as BT implied (BT, 211), but that he equated being with being-represented by a subject (NII, 163f./niv, 114ff.). It does not matter whether the subject is a pure ego or, as Nietzsche believes, embodied. What matters is that everything comes to man for judgement. (NII, 295ff./niii, 329ff.) The two central features of modernity are that man is the centre of beings as a whole, the subject to which they are all referred, and that 'the beingness of beings as a whole is conceived as the being-represented of the producible and explainable' (NII, 24/niii, 178). 'To produce' is *herstellen*, often linked with *vorstellen* to suggest the relationship of cartesianism and technology (LXV, 109, 478) – *Vorgestelltheit* has nothing to do with objects being produced by the soul or mind (NII, 433/ep, 30). Two features of *vorstellen* help to put man at the centre. First, *etwas vorstellen* means 'to represent something' in the sense of 'to count, stand for something, to cut a fine figure' (NII, 449/ep, 45; LXV, 306). Second, the reflexive *sich vorstellen* stresses the subject: 'Every human representing [Vor-stellen] is by an easily misinterpreted figure of speech a "self"-representing ['Sich'-vorstellen]' (NII, 153/niv, 106). This converges with Descartes's view that whenever I think about anything I also think that I think. In *Vorstellen* the representing and the representer are always co-represented as well. But this is wrong. I can imagine or look at a cathedral without representing myself, without making myself an object alongside the cathedral (NII, 153ff./niv, 106ff.).

Vorstellen gives a new sense to the equation of being with presence. For the Greeks being was 'presence' as *Anwesenheit*. Greek *Anwesenheit* concerns the 'presencing [Anwesen]' of beings into the realm of the unhidden. The closest Greek counterpart to *vorstellen*, *noein*, 'to think, etc.', was 'dwelling in the unhidden', receptive rather than intrusive, and concerned as much with the whole, unhiddenness as such, as with individual entities. *Vorstellen* is the autocratic interrogation of and jurisdiction over entities, whose presence is now *Präsenz* rather than *Anwesenheit*. (NII, 319f./niii, 239; 450/ep, 46). The decline began with Plato's equation of being with the *idea* (NII, 230/niv, 174; 410/ep, 10; AWP, 84/131; LXV, 135, 208ff., 478).

resoluteness, decision and the moment *Schliessen* means 'to close, shut, fasten, etc.' and also 'to infer' i.e. to join in thought to what precedes'. The prefix *ent-* indicates opposition or separation. Hence *entschliessen* originally meant 'to open, unlock'. But by the sixteenth century the reflexive *sich entschliessen* meant 'to decide, reach a decision', 'i.e. unlock one's mind, clarify, make definite one's thoughts' (DGS, 90). The perfect participle *entschlossen* was used for 'resolute' and *Entschluss* for 'decision, resolution'. *Erschliessen*, 'to disclose, open', and also 'to infer' (cf. BT, 75, 315), comes from *schliessen*; *er-*, 'out, forth', here has a similar force to *ent-*. But *erschliessen* means 'to disclose', not 'to decide'. Heidegger associates resoluteness with being opened up: 'Resoluteness [Entschlossenheit] is a distinctive mode of Dasein's disclosedness [Erschlossenheit]' (BT, 297). *Entschlossenheit* is 'the *specifically* undertaken self-opening of Dasein *for* the open' (G, 59/81). He also uses *beschliessen*, originally 'to close, shut, etc.', but now 'to include' and also 'to decide', i.e. to conclude one's thoughts on the matter (BT, 299, 300).

(Sich) entscheiden, 'to decide, settle', comes (like 'decide') from a word meaning 'to cut, split, separate', *scheiden*. *Ent-* fortifies the sense of 'separate'. Hence Heidegger connects *entscheiden* with *Entweder-Oder*, 'Either-Or' (LXV, 90, 101), and with separating and distinguishing (*Unterscheidung*): Das Geschiedene ist so entschieden geschieden, dass überhaupt kein gemeinsamer Bezirk der Unterscheidung obwalten kann, 'The terms thus parted are set apart by an incision so decisive that no common sphere can prevail at all in which to tell them apart with precision' (LXV, 177. Cf. NI, 476/niii, 5). Both *Entschlossenheit* and *Entschiedenheit*, 'decisiveness', are associated with the *Augenblick*, lit. 'the twinkling of an eye', hence 'moment (of vision)'. Kierkegaard used its Danish equivalent, *øjeblik*, especially in the *Concept of Dread* (1844), for the point of contact between time and eternity, the instant of decision between truth and illusion, in which the believer becomes contemporaneous with Christ (cf. BT, 338n.). In BT it is 'the *present* [*Gegenwart*] that is held in authentic temporality and is thus *authentic*. [. . .] It means Dasein's resolute rapture – but a rapture *held* in resoluteness – towards the possibilities and circumstances of concern to it that come to meet it in the situation' (BT, 338). The creative transformation, postulated by Nietzsche, of chaotic becoming into stable beings involves 'standing in the moment of decision [im Augenblick der Entscheidung], in which moment whatever precedes it and is given along with it is raised up into the projected task and so preserved' (NI, 466f./nii, 202f.). Resolute decision transforms, yet preserves the past. (Cf. Scheler's view that the point of repentance is that it alters the significance of a past deed.)

In BT resolute DASEIN is not simply absorbed in the present; it 'runs ahead' to its own death and 'repeats' or 'retrieves' the past. Thus the *Augenblick*, unlike the inauthentic present, is explicitly the intersection between the past and the future. The 'vulgar intellect' tends to misinterpret such concepts as 'running ahead to death [Vorlaufen in den Tod]' (BT, 305) and resoluteness (XXIX, 425ff.). It thinks in terms of PRESENT-AT-HAND clockable psychological or physical episodes. For it, running ahead to death consists in thinking often about one's death, resoluteness is making frequent resolutions or engaging in intense deliberations and forceful actions, and 'recollection', *Erinnerung*, amounts to 'a memory [Gedächtnis]' that 'preserves what was earlier present-at-hand as now no' longer present-at-hand'. This is wrong. One might think often and intensely about death, yet not conduct one's life in view of it, and one need not be obsessed with death to be unwilling, say, to postpone taking one's examinations for ten years. Frequent resolves, agonized deliberation and vigorous acts are no guarantee of resolute and coherent conduct, guided by a conception of what sort of person one is and how one's life should go. This requires a certain detachment from the immediate present. If one focuses exclusively on the present, one is unlikely to see any reason to vote in elections or to leave parties in good time. There are invariably more profitable ways of filling the time it takes to vote; it hardly ever makes a difference whether I leave the party now or stay another ten minutes. Since such concepts cannot be adequately specified in terms of present-at-hand episodes or states of affairs, Heidegger speaks of his own accounts of them as a 'formal indication [formale Anzeige]'. They do not convey explicitly what e.g. resoluteness is, any more than what it is to go for a walk is adequately conveyed by saying that it is placing one foot in front of the other in such a way that both feet are never off the ground. Heidegger can point us in the direction of resoluteness, but we can only find out what it is by becoming resolute.

After BT, *entscheiden*-words tend to supplant *entschliessen*-words. In BT what matters is Dasein's *Entschlossenheit*, not the particular decision it takes. As history and being become more central, Heidegger is less interested in the condition of the individual man or Dasein than in what gets decided about being and beings. He suitably (re)interprets BT: it is easy 'to misinterpret BT in this way, "existentielly"-"anthropologically", to see the connections between Entschlossenheit – truth – Dasein in terms of resolution [Entschliessung] in the moral sense, instead of the converse: in terms of the prevailing ground of Da-sein, conceiving truth as openness and Ent-schlossenheit as extemporizing and making space [die zeitigende Einräumung] for the time-play-room [Zeit-Spiel-Raumes] of beyng.' If we concentrate on the question about the sense of beyng, then 'what is here called de-cision [Ent-scheidung] moves to the innermost core of beyng's essence and then has nothing to do with what we call making a choice and suchlike, but means: the very divergence which separates and in separating first admits into play the eventuating [Er-eignung] of precisely this *Open* in the apartness, the open as the lighting for the self-concealing and still un-decided [Un-entschiedene], the belonging of man to beyng as the grounder of its truth and the assignment of beyng to the time of the last god' (LXV, 87f.). *Entscheidung* is now used in three ways: 1. The separation involved in the event of being, separation between EARTH, world, men and gods, and between beyng and beings (LXV, 479). 2. Momentous decisions about human life that determine whether a new beginning, a new event of being, will happen and what it will be like, such decisions as 'whether man will remain "subject" *or* grounds Da-sein [...]

188

whether art is an organization of experiences *or* the setting-into-work of truth', and so on (LXV, 90f. Cf. OWA, 66./204.). 3. Ordinary human decisions, whether individual or collective, about whether to marry, to go to war, etc. Decisions of type 1 are not human acts and are not concerned with an 'Either-Or' (LXV, 84ff.). They are beyng's own divisions into separate regions. They create a space or 'time-(play-) space', for decisions of type 3 (LXV, 187, 234, 405, 464). They cannot be human acts, since they create, or wholly transform, human beings. Decisions of type 2 are intermediate between 1 and 3. Like 3, they concern an Either-Or; like 1, they concern a 'beginning' (LXV, 90). Human acts and decisions of type 3 play a part in them, but they too are not ordinary human acts; the very nature of man depends on how the decision goes. In BT *Entschlossenheit* can be (mis)interpreted as pertaining to decisions of type 3. Later, it pertains more to decisions of type 2 and hence of type 1; it is the opening up less of man or Dasein than of being; it is ultimately the work of being itself (LXV, 101, 283, 397f.). It is less like leaving a party to write an essay than falling down on the road to Damascus.

S

saying   *Sagen* is close in sense to its relative 'to say'. It was originally related to *sehen*, 'to see', and meant 'to let see, to show'. It forms many compounds, in particular *aussagen*, 'to assert, state'. A derived noun, *Sage*, once meant 'something said, a saying, saw', then 'talk, report, story, rumour'; in the eighteenth century it came to mean 'legend, saga'. Heidegger often uses *Sage* in the sense of 'saying' (e.g. OWA, 61/198f.). It is, in his view, quite different from *Aussage*, 'assertion', as *sagen* is from *aussagen*. What is asserted is a proposition, and an assertion is spoken or written; what is said need not be spoken or written, nor propositional. We can 'say' beyng, but we cannot make assertions about it (LXV, 473). Saying is distinct from speaking: 'Someone can speak [sprechen], speak endlessly, without saying anything. Conversely, someone is silent, he does not speak and can say a lot in his not speaking.[...] "Saying" means: to show, to let appear, to let be seen and heard' (OWL, 252/122). German (like English: 'His silence speaks volumes') is not consistent in this respect. Heidegger purports to elicit from Kant 'what is put before our eyes as still unsaid [Ungesagtes] by what is said' (K, 201/137). Here the 'unsaid' is what is not expressly stated, the unspoken, not what is not shown to us.

Saying is a showing that is prior to speaking: 'The essential being of language [Sprache, from sprechen, 'to speak'] is saying [die Sage] as showing [die Zeige]' (OWL, 254/123). It is associated with the EVENT: 'The moving force in the showing of saying is owning [das Eignen]. It brings everything that is present and absent into its own [Eigenes], from where they show themselves for what they are and abide according to their kind.[...] The event [Ereignis] gathers the design [Aufriss] of saying and unfolds it into the structure of manifold showing' (OWL, 258f./127f.). Saying here is the original 'projective saying [entwerfende Sagen]', which lays down what can and what cannot be said in ordinary speech, supplies a people with concepts and thus opens up a world for them. Projective saying is *Dichtung*, 'POETRY' (OWA, 61/198). Thus *Sage* as 'legend, saga' is not far from Heidegger's mind. Elsewhere he quotes the ending of Hölderlin's 'Voice of the People', viz. the legends that orient a people in the world, but need to be interpreted by the poet: '[. . .] and no doubt such legends [die Sagen]/Are good, for they are a reminder/Of the Highest; yet there is also need/Of one to interpret the holy legends' (HEP, 46/312).

science *Wissenschaft* is applied more widely than 'science'. Any systematic study of a field is a *Wissenschaft*. History, theology, classical philology, art-history are all *Wissenschaften*, though they belong to the *Geisteswissenschaften*, the 'humane', 'social' or 'moral' sciences, in contrast to the *Naturwissenschaften*. Mathematical physics was, for Heidegger, the prime example of a science, though its type of 'rigour [Strenge]', viz. 'exactness [Exaktheit], is not appropriate to other sciences (LXV, 149).

Science is not the primary way in which we open up the world. Before science, the 'land is discovered [. . .] in tilling the fields, the sea in navigation' (XXVII, 162). Science presupposes a pre-scientific, pre-onto-logical understanding of being. A science is not primarily a set of propositions, nor the discovery of new facts. Facts and propositions presuppose a prior unhiddenness of beings. What happens in science is a change in the 'questions asked and the way of seeing – the facts change in consequence.' Psychological and sociological explanations of science are of little use: 'Sociology of that sort stands in the same relation to actual science and the philosophical understanding of it as the cat-burglar to the architect or [. . .] the honest craftsman (XXIX, 379). Science is not merely theoretical; it performs practical experiments and builds equipment. 'Contemplative Dasein is no science' (XXVII, 178). 'Science means: being in the unhiddenness of beings for the sake of unhiddenness' (XXVII, 179, Cf. PT, 48/6). All DASEIN is 'in the truth' and 'lets beings be [Seinlassen des Seienden]', but science values truth for its own sake and lets beings be in a special way. The implicit knowledge of resistance and pressure and their regularities we gain from our dealings with tools is expanded by science to explicit knowledge of the laws of pressure and counter-pressure as such, laws obtaining beyond the realm of our everyday practical activity and involvement. Science abstracts from our practical affairs. It sees the plough as a present-at-hand body, not as a tool. It involves 'merely looking [nur Hinsehen]' at things, a way of letting them be that is not easy to achieve. After all, mere inactivity, ceasing to work on things, need not reveal them as they are 'in themselves'; it may reveal them as requiring work to be done on them. Science does not essentially disclose new beings, just a new way of looking at old ones, of viewing being. This is the essence of Galileo's mathematical physics, not induction and not experiment, which presupposes a concept of nature as homogeneous and thus mathematical (XXVII, 179ff.). This view of nature is a 'projection [Entwurf] of the thinghood of things that as it were leaps over the things', an 'anticipatory intervention [Vorausgriff[in the essence of things', a 'groundplan [Grundriss]' (WT, 71/291f.). Hence, 'we cannot say that Galileo's doctrine of the free fall of bodies is true and Aristotle's doctrine that light bodies strive upwards is false; the Greek conception of the essence of body and place and their relationship rests on a different interpretation of beings and thus engenders a correspondingly different way of viewing and examining natural processes' – no more than we say Shakespeare's poetry is better than Aeschylus's (AWP, 71/117).

A science can undergo a 'crisis [Krisis]': the 'real "movement" of sciences takes place when their basic concepts undergo a more or less radical revision which is not transparent to them. The level that a science has reached is determined by how far it is *capable* of a crisis in its basic concepts' (BT, 9. Cf. XX, 3ff; XXVII, 26ff.). Relativity and quantum theory are examples of a crisis, but crises also occur in mathematics, biology and theology (BT, 9f; XXXI, 142). Science 'is not an original happening of truth; it always develops an already open realm of truth, [. . .] insofar as a science goes beyond correctness to a truth, and that means to the essential unveiling of beings as such, it is philosophy' (OWA, 50/187). Science in crisis becomes philosophy. But even science in crisis does not found a world in the way that art can; it operates within an established prescientific understanding of beings.

Philosophy is not a science. It deals with 'the whole', while a science deals with a specific field, which is demarcated and grounded not by science as such but by metaphysics (XXVII, 13ff., 22; NI, 477, 520ff./niii, 6, 42ff.). A science cannot comprehend itself, its own limits and concepts, unless it becomes philosophy (XXVII, 38; NI, 372/nii, 112). It is thus absurd to suggest that science could replace philosophy or, as Husserl did, that philosophy should become 'scientific'. But philosophy and science are not like two separate buildings. Philosophy, metaphysical reflection on the field of a science, is implicit in science itself (NI, 373/nii, 112f.), though the transition from science to philosophy involves a 'leap', not the steady development by which everydayness passes into science (NI, 522f./niii, 43).

Heidegger became hostile to contemporary science as his attention turned to technology and the political regimentation of science: 'One need not want the return of the stagecoach to see the inner brutalization and degradation of taste wrought by the technology science makes possible' (XXVII, 161). The philosopher examines the sciences not for their own sake, but because they are involved in the 'abandonment by being' (LXV, 141ff.). Modern science is quite distinct from medieval 'doctrine' or ancient 'knowledge'. It is not knowledge in the sense of grounding and preserving essential truth, but correctness and MACHINATION. The scientifically knowable is always given beforehand in a truth, inaccessible to science, about its region of beings. Specialization is essential to science, unlike art or philosophy; this stems from beingness as representedness. A science explains the unknown in terms of the known, but only in a certain 'respect [Hinsicht]': a painting e.g. may be explained in respect of its physico-chemical composition, the physiological and psychological conditions of its production, its historical genesis, or its artistic qualities. A science gets rigour from sticking strictly to its region and the respect in which it considers it. Its rigour consists in its method and other features that get 'results [Ergebnisse]'. Its explanations are causal, of the 'if . . . then' type in the form of 'when . . . then'. This is required by machination. Even history [*Historie*] operates causally, making life and experience open to calculation and manipulation. But life cannot be explained in this way. Science aims not at genuine knowledge, but at information and utilizable results attained by a certain method. It needs to justify itself by its service to the nation. It can be turned to different ends, serving bolshevism and American capitalism as readily as Nazism; it is 'international'. As science achieves more and more results, it acknowledges no crisis, no essential change in its mode of vision; this is excluded ever more definitively as it proceeds uniformly to its end. All science relies on experience, but not all science is experimental. *Historie* uses sources; it never gets to history (*Geschichte*), as its variant *Prähistorie* strikingly shows. As science becomes more technological and manipulative, the difference between the natural and the humane sciences decreases. Natural science becomes a part of machine-technology and -enterprise, the humanities become a journalism of gigantic range, interpreting current experience and making it public for everyman as quickly and attractively as possible. Universities become purely organizational institutes, ever more realistic and relevant, with some cultural adornment for propaganda purposes. Science will make gigantic progress, in the exploitation of the earth, in human resource management, hindered by no romantic recollection of the past. Science is heading for its own dissolution along with all beings. Its hidden goal is complete boredom, the yawning abandonment of beings by being. But science always presents itself as beginning: 'Only the blind and fools will speak today of the "end" of science' (LXV, 157).

193

sight and circumspection   Sight is a persistent motif in Heidegger. 'To see' is *sehen*. The derived noun, *Sicht*, 'sight', once meant seeing as well as what is seen, but is now restricted to what is seen and means 'view, visibility'. But in compounds *Sicht* retains the sense of 'seeing' or 'looking': *Umsicht*, lit. 'looking around', means 'circumspection, prudence', *Vorsicht*, lit. 'looking ahead', is 'circumspection, caution', and *Rücksicht*, lit. 'looking back', is 'respect, consideration'. Corresponding adjectives often end in *-ig: umsichtig, vorsichtig*, 'circumspect, etc.' *Sicht* supplies *sichtbar*, 'visible', but not *sichtig*. But Heidegger extracts *Sicht* from its compounds and restores its active sense. He coins *sichtig*, 'sighted(ly)' (BT, 149). *Sicht* is a fundamental trait of DASEIN, appearing in various forms: 'The sight that goes existentially with the disclosedness [Erschlossenheit] of the There [Da] is what Dasein *is*, with equal originality in each of the basic ways of its being described above: as circumspection [Umsicht] of concern, as respect [Rücksicht] of solicitude, as sight [Sicht] directed on being as such, for the sake of which Dasein always is as it is' (BT, 146). *Sicht* 'corresponds to lightedness [Gelichtetheit]', to the 'disclosedness of the There'. 'Seeing' does not mean 'perceiving with one's bodily eyes' nor the 'pure non-sensory apprehension of something present-at-hand'. What matters for the 'existential meaning of sight' is that seeing 'lets the beings accessible to it come to meet us unconcealedly in themselves' (BT, 147). It is difficult to see something without seeing it *as* something, '*as* table, door, carriage, bridge': 'The seeing of this sight is always already understanding-interpretative. [. . .] The plain seeing of the things closest to us in our having to do with ... [im Zutunhaben mit ...] carries the interpretation-structure so originally in itself that an as it were *as-free* [*als-freies*] grasping of something requires a certain readjustment' (BT, 149).

The most important of BT's *Sicht*-compounds is *Umsicht*: 'The look that merely gazes [hinsehende Blick] "theoretically" at things can do without an understanding of READINESS-TO-HAND. But using, manipulating and dealing [Umgang] are not blind, they have their own kind of sight, and this guides the manipulation and gives it its specific reliability [Sicherheit]. Dealing with gear subjects itself to the assignment-manifold of the "in-order-to" ['Um-zu']. The sight of such self-adaptation is *circumspection*' (BT, 69). Heidegger usually takes the constituent parts of words at their face value or, in this case, values. As a preposition *um* means '(a)round', but as a conjunction, followed by *zu* and an infinitive, 'in order to'. *Umsicht* is looking 'around' to see what one needs, etc. 'in order to' get something done.

Philosophy has always been 'oriented primarily by "seeing" as a mode of access to beings *and to being*' (BT, 147. Cf. 358). Later, Heidegger attributes this mainly to Plato. Plato argued that if we are to identify particular things as e.g. similar, we must first be acquainted with, get in sight, similarity, i.e. an *idea* (NII, 217/niv, 162). Since *idea* comes from the Greek *idein*, 'to see', the interpretation of being as *idea* suggests that beings are grasped by seeing. Even the word 'theoretical' comes from Greek see-words: *thea*, 'view, spectacle', and *horan*, 'to see'. Why did the Greeks, since Plato at least, conceive knowledge as a sort of seeing? Not because they were 'optically disposed and "eye-people" ['Augen-menschen']', but because they interpreted being as 'presence [Anwesen-heit] and constancy [Beständigkeit]'. Sight is very appropriate for explaining our grasp of the 'present and constant'. For 'in seeing we stand in an emphatic sense "face to face" with what is grasped, assuming that an interpretation of beings does not already underlie our seeing. The Greeks did not explain our relationship to beings by seeing because they were "eye-people"; they were, if you like, "eye-people" because they experienced the being of beings as presence and constancy' (NII, 223f./ niv, 167. Cf. P, 222ff./261ff. Cf. XIX, 394ff. on *Sehen-lassen*, 'letting [us] see'). Heidegger regularly translates Plato's *idea* and *eidos*, 'form', by *Aussehen*, 'look, appearance, aspect'. But he sometimes backtracks, insist-ing that *Aussehen* is not a visual aspect and has little connection with literal seeing: 'As the Greeks thought of it, the "aspect" ['Aussehen'] of an entity, e.g. of a house, hence houseness [das Haushafte], is that in which this entity comes into view, i.e. to presence, i.e. to being' (NII, 218/niv, 162). His interpretation of the Greeks thus depends on more than an etymologizing mistranslation.

signs and hints A *Zeichen* is a '"clear sign" of any kind, the meaning of which is understood or established'. It is distinct from *Anzeichen* (cf. BT, 78), 'a "symptom", an "intimation" of something to come which may or may not be recognized and interpreted aright' (DGS, 314). It comes from *zeihen*, originally 'to show, indicate, reveal', but now 'to accuse [someone of something]' and used only poetically. *Zeigen*, 'to show, point, indicate, etc.', also comes from *zeihen*. Hence Heidegger associates *Zeichen* with *zeigen*: signs show or 'sign(al)' (BT, 77). He begins with a quasi-Husserlian analysis of the concept of a sign (XX, 276ff; BT, 77ff. Cf. DS, 295ff.). Every 'referral' is a 'relation' but not every relation is a referral: a hammer 'refers/is referred' to hammering and also to nails and wood, but the moon and the earth, though related, do not refer to each other in these ways. Every sign is a 'referral' or 'assignment' (*Verweisung*), but not every referral is a sign: a hammer 'refers/is referred' to hammering and nails but is not usually a sign of/for them. A sign is a special piece of equipment, signalling-equipment, *Zeigzeug*, and its 'referral' or 'assignment' is signalling as the hammer's is hammering: it is serviceable for, its In-order-to is, signalling.

Little is gained by regarding a referral and a sign as types of relation, *Beziehung* – a word Heidegger usually reserves for a PRESENT-AT-HAND relation between present-at-hand things, such as a subject and its object. Though this 'formal determination' is more general than 'referral' or 'sign', it has its 'ontological origin in a referral': like all terms appropriate for the present-at-hand, including those of formal logic, it is rooted in the ready-to-hand and our talk about it. More important than a definition of 'sign' by its genus and specific difference is an account of the relationship of a sign to other equipment and the world to which it belongs. This account falls under three headings (BT, 82): 1. A sign is a tool with the assignment of signalling. Like any other tool, it is not primarily or without effort seen as a mere 'thing [Ding]'. A car indicator, even if we do not know what it is for, is seen as an unfamiliar sign, at the very least as a functional part of the whole car. A knot in a handkerchief, whose point is forgotten, is still seen as a sign of unknown significance, or at least as deliberately produced for a purpose. This is true even of a natural sign, such as the south wind that forecasts rain. Meteorologists may be aware of the south wind as a distinct phenomenon, independently of its signalling rain. But the farmer is not aware of the south wind as such, in contrast to other winds, until he takes it as a sign of something. Signalling discloses the entity that serves as a sign. 2. A sign belongs to a context of equipment which does not consist exclusively of signs. A 'No Smoking' sign, next to a US flag, on the moon's surface presupposes the possibility of tobacco and means of lighting it. A signpost in an otherwise unadulterated wilderness assumes that there is somewhere worth going that is thereby brought within the sphere of the ready-to-hand. If there were nothing except signs and people signalled to, there would be nothing to be signalled. A sign, moreover, is essentially striking, it stands out from its inconspicuous surroundings. We notice the knot in the hankie, the flashing indicator, the south wind, because we do not notice everything all the time. Hence 'referral itself, if it is to be the ontological foundation of signs, cannot be conceived as sign' (BT, 83). 3. In the sign 'the world around us always becomes expressly accessible for circumspection' (BT, 82). I mistrust the flashing indicator if I just stare at it or look in the direction it indicates. It does not just point to itself or to a road off to the right. It lights up my whole environment in a certain way and re-orients me to it. If the sign signals a right-turn, it gives me not just information, but directions about what I may or must do. If I am following the car, I must keep to its left to avoid it; if I am a pedestrian I can cross the road, since the car is not coming my way. Hence a 'sign is something ontically ready-to-hand which is not just this particular equipment, but functions as something that indicates the ontological structure of readiness-to-hand, referral-totality and worldhood' (BT, 82).

A *Wink* is a signal given with one's hand or an object, not just with one's eyelid. It comes from *winken*, originally 'to shake, wave, etc.', now 'to signal with one's hand, etc.' Hölderlin wrote: '[. . .] and hints [Winke] have been/From olden times the language of the gods' ('Rousseau', ll.39f.). The poet receives these hints and passes them on in his own hinting words to his people. Heidegger finds a parallel in Heraclitus: 'The lord whose oracle is at Delphi neither says nor hides but hints [sēmainei]' (XXXIX, 127). A *Wink* differs from a *Zeichen*. Hinting differs from pointing to something, drawing attention to it. *Der Winkende*, 'someone waving', does not just draw attention to himself, letting us know where he is. 'Waving [Winken] good-bye is holding on to the nearness as the distance grows, while waving on arrival is revealing the still prevailing distance in the gladdening nearness. But the gods hint simply, since they *are*' (XXXIX, 32). Poetry, *Dichtung*, is not an 'expression of emotional experiences' or a description of anything 'actual'. It soars above the actual in imagination and presents the actual to us, if at all, only after poetic transformation. 'When the hint of the gods is as it were built into the foundations of a people by the poet, [. . .], beyng is founded in the historical existence [Dasein] of the people, [. . .]. Poetry – expression of emotional experiences? How far off is all that! Poetry – enduring the hints of the gods – founding of beyng' (XXXIX, 33. Cf. LXV, 400, 408, 410).

silence Silence is important for Heidegger from his early lectures: 'Taking a *premature* impassioned stand for or against reveals only a deficiency of genuine passion, [. . .], of resoluteness of understanding, which is all the more surely there the less it erupts, but keeps silent [schweigt] and can wait. Since we can no longer bide our time and lie in wait for life (in the genuine sense, not in the manner of detective-psychology and soul-snooping), but cannot wait in our noisy zeal to get the matter sorted out, we fall prey to surrogates of intellectual showmanship or an illusory, because blinkered and fleeting objectivity' (LXI, 71). Later, he incorporates silence into his account of TALK (XX, 368f; BT, 161, 164f.). Only someone who can talk can be silent. If one never says anything, one cannot be silent. Nor if one has nothing to say. For silence stems from 'reticence'. 'To be silent' is *schweigen*, with *das Schweigen* for 'silence'. *Verschweigen* is 'to keep silent about something, to conceal it'; its perfect particle, *verschwiegen*, means 'kept silent, secret', and also 'discreet, reticent'; it generates *Verschwiegenheit*, 'reticence, discretion'.

Silence does not invariably conceal: 'Silence is one of talk's ways of being and as such it is a definite way of expressing oneself about something to others' (XX, 368). Heidegger later expresses this by coining *erschweigen*, 'to be silent forth [er-], to express by silence'. Talkative people often say less than the reticent. Silence thus plays a crucial role in conversation: 'From such reticence stems the genuine ability to hear and, in this ability to hear, genuine being-with-one-another is constituted'. Silence too can 'in being-with-one-another call and bring back Dasein to its very own being', rescuing it from absorption in everydayness (XX, 369). Hence silence is involved in the silent call of CONSCIENCE and in the 'reticent RESOLUTENESS that exacts anxiety of itself' (BT, 322. Cf. 296f.).

Later, Heidegger says that language originates in silence (NI, 471/nii, 208; LXV, 408, 510; OWL, 252/122). The sounds of language are secondary. They supervened on a primary vision of the world and the entities within it. Language arose not from the significant grunts of primitive conversationalists, but from the solitary, resolute poet communing silently with the gods. Hence silence 'cor-responds [entspricht] to the soundless chiming of the stillness of eventful-showing saying [ereignend-zeigenden Sage]' (OWL, 262/131). Silence is the appropriate way of thinking about being and about the grounding of its 'truth', the event (cf. LXV, 36, etc.). Heidegger's love of silence coheres with several features of his thought: his concern that we should 'let beings be'; his conviction that great thinkers do not express everything that they mean and thus need to be interpreted 'forcibly'; and his aversion to public talk about Nazism and his involvement with it.

space and spatiality *Raum* is 'space', and also 'room', but usually a spacious or roomy room, not a small room. *Raum* generates adjectives, especially *räumlich*, 'spatial', and the abstract noun *Räumlichkeit*, 'spatiality'. It also generates verbs, especially *räumen*, 'to clear, shift, etc.' (LXV, 192, 261, but not BT) and *einräumen*, 'to clear a place, make room, concede; to put in the proper place, put away, arrange'. Heidegger's understanding of spatiality is influenced by these and other verbs. DASEIN is spatial in a way that no other extended thing is. It clears a space around it to give itself 'leeway' or elbowroom: 'In existing it has always already made room [eingeräumt] for its own elbowroom [Spielraum, lit. room to play, to move]'. Other things occupy or 'take up' (*einnehmen*) space, but 'Dasein – in the literal sense – takes [nimmt] space in [ein]' (BT, 368).

Heidegger uses several words for 'place': 1. *Ort* is used for the positions of things in space as conceived by mathematical physics (BT, 91 on Descartes's of *res extensae*) and also metaphorically, e.g. the place or 'locus' of truth (BT, 226). 2. *Platz* is used for the *proper* 'place' of/for something: 'The Platz is the specific "there" and "over here" to which a piece of equipment belongs' (BT. 102). 3. *Stelle*, 'spot, position', is used, like *Ort*, for the position of something in geometrically conceived space. 4. The more elevated *Stätte*, 'site', hardly occurs in BT but it is important later as the 'site' of a decisive event in the history of being (cf. BT, 388: *Kultstätte*, 'site of a cult'). The Greek '*polis* is the site of history [Geschichtsstätte], the There *in* which, *from* which and *for* which history happens' (IM, 117/ 128).

Larger than a place is a 'region', *Gegend*, the general 'whereabouts' of something rather than its exact position. We need regions, since we often know the whereabouts of something, when we do not know or cannot specify its exact location. What counts as a region is determined by our practical needs, not by geography; some things belong in one region, the kitchen, others in the garden. Regions are often specified in terms of Dasein's orientation: up above – down below, at the front – round the back, and so on. A region involves a direction (*gegen*, 'towards, etc.'), and also proximity to something of a known location in that direction (BT, 103). We orient ourselves by regions on various scales, from the sunny and shady sides of the house to the directions marked by sunrise, midday, sunset and midnight: churches and graves are 'layed out by the rising and the setting of the sun, the regions of life and death, [. . .]' (BT, 103. Cf. XX, 315).

An important feature of Dasein's spatiality is *Ent-fernung* (BT, 105ff; XX, 308ff.). This comes from *fern*, 'far', and *Ferne*, 'distance, remoteness'. These generated *fernen*, 'to make/be distant', which has now been replaced by *(sich) entfernen*, 'to remove (oneself), depart, etc.' with a perfect participle *entfernt*, 'distant, remote, etc.' The verbal noun *Entfernung* commonly means 'distance; removal'. But Heidegger deviates from standard usage in several respects: 1. *Entfernung* pertains to the distance of things from Dasein, not the distance between things, *Abstand*. 2. Distances from Dasein are, unlike an *Abstand*, estimated not in quantitative but everyday terms: 'to go over yonder is "a good walk", "a stone's throw", "as long as it takes to smoke a pipe"' (BT, 105). 3. It is used 'in an active and transitive meaning', i.e. it means the activity by which we *entfernen* something (BT, 105). 4. *Entfernung* and *entfernen* have a sense almost the opposite of their standard meaning: Since *fern* means 'far, remote' and *ent-* can be privative (cf. *decken*, 'to cover'; *entdecken*, 'to discover, uncover'), *Entfernung* can mean 'removing the distance, bringing near, deseverance, de-distancing': 'Entfernen means making farness [Ferne], i.e. the remoteness [Entferntheit] of something, vanish, bringing it near. [...] In Dasein there lies an essential tendency to nearness' (BT, 105). Why use for this, the usual word for 'farness, making far', rather than 'bringing near [Näherung]'? For two reasons: (a) saying how far something is, e.g. 'two pipefuls away', is also to bring it near, within the orbit of Dasein's concerns. (b) Things that are in quantitative terms or 'objectively' very near (spectacles on one's nose, the street one is walking on) are too close to be conspicuous, are 'further away' than things less close (the book, an approaching friend) (BT, 107). Dasein has to remove (*entfernen*) things to a distance, beyond the boundary of its elbowroom, to get them near (*entfernen*) enough to deal with. Only 'relief', taking our distance, from the beings that 'besiege' or 'beleaguer' us, enables us to engage with them as beings (LXV, 482). Having cleared a space around itself, a space that it can never cross or escape, Dasein can occupy a place within that space.

Another feature of Dasein's spatiality is 'orientation' (XX, 308, 319ff: *Orientation*) or 'directionality; directedness' (XX, 308; BT, 104, 108ff: *Ausrichtung, Ausgerichtetheit*). *Ausrichtung* is associated with 'directions' (*Richtung(en)*), especially 'left-right-straight ahead', which, like our ability to point at things, are based on our general ability to orient ourselves ((XX, 319; BT, 108). Right and left depend on our bodies. Things that move with our bodies, gloves and shoes, are right- or left-oriented, while things that we move with our bodies, hammers, are not (XX, 320f; BT, 108f.). (This is not invariably true. Finger-rings are not right-/left-oriented; golf-clubs are.) But orientation depends not on the 'mere feeling of the difference between my two sides' (as Kant in OT), but also on being-in-the-world: if I enter a familiar but dark room, whose contents have in my absence been completely reversed along the left-right axis, I will detect no difference unless I locate a familiar object and compare its present position with the one I remember. My present disorientation presupposes a prior orientation in a world of interrelated equipment (XX, 321; BT, 109f.). (Why need the room be dark?) Unlike us, a bee does not find its way home by orientation: 'Strictly there is only orientation where space is opened up as such and thus the possibility is given of distinguishing regions and determinable places in the regions' (XXIX, 354).

Later, Heidegger unifies space with time in TIME-SPACE. On left-right reversal, see H. G. Wells, 'The Plattner Story'.

spirit   *Geist,* a relative of 'ghost', means 'spirit, mind'. It is an important word in Hegel (cf. BT, 435f; XXXII; HCE, 183ff./144ff.), who uses it not only for the individual 'mind' or 'subjective spirit', but also for social and political structures, 'objective spirit', and for art, religion and philosophy, 'absolute spirit'. In a traditional doctrine of which Heidegger disapproves, a human being consists of a spiritual, intellectual element, *Geist*; an animating principle or 'soul', *Seele*; and *Leib,* the 'body' (BT, 48, etc.). Heidegger prefers other terms: for the individual human being, 'Dasein', and for such Hegelian concepts as the *Weltgeist* ('world-spirit'), 'being'.

Heidegger avoids *Geist* not only because it serves Hegel's purposes better than his own, but because the word, and Geist itself, have degenerated since Hegel's time (IM, 34ff./37ff.) The degeneration has four phases: 1. *Geist* is interpreted as 'intelligence', proficiency in dealing with things already available. 2. Intelligence then becomes a tool for various purposes. It can serve the regulation of production (Marxism), the ordering and explanation of everything we come across (positivism), or the 'organizational direction of the vital resources and race [Lebensmasse und Rasse] of a people' (Nazism?). 3. The 'spiritual [geistige] world' – poetry, art, statesmanship, religion – is subjected to '*conscious* cultivation and planning'. It becomes *Kultur* and is split into distinct realms, each with its own values and each to be pursued for its own sake. 4. Spirit, both as functional intelligence and as *Kultur,* are put on public display to show that we do not disapprove of culture or favour barbarism.

If spirit is simply intelligence, Heidegger argues, there is no reason to value it above the virtues of the other constituents of a person, vigour of body and character of soul. But spirit is not one constituent among others. It is the ground of our other virtues, of bodily vigour, military prowess and resourceful understanding. He quotes his 1933 'Rectoral Address': 'Spirit is not empty astuteness, nor the disengaged play of wit, nor the boundless pursuit of intellectual analysis, nor even [Hegelian] world-reason. Spirit is attuned [gestimmte], knowing [wissende] resoluteness for the essence of being' (IM, 37f./41). Spirit in this sense is of decisive importance for the salvation of the world, but in other works he generally uses other words for it rather than *Geist.*

Later, Heidegger explores the meanings of *Geist,* and its relationship to *Seele,* in the poetry of Hölderlin and Trakl. Often it recalls the *Geist* of the 'Rectoral Address': 'The spirit is the knowing will of the origin' (EHP, 90). Trakl 'understands spirit not primarily as pneuma [Greek: *pneuma* = 'breath, spirit'], not "spiritually" [spirituell], but as a flame that inflames, startles, horrifies [entsetzt, lit. 'unsettles'], disconcerts. [. . .] Trakl views "spirit" in terms of the essence [Wesen] named in the original meaning of the word "Geist"; for the root *gheis* means: being incensed, horrified, beside oneself [ausser sich, lit. 'outside oneself']' (OWL, 60/179). Heidegger's language is intended to remind us of *Ek-sistenz* and *Ekstase*, 'standing forth' into being.

subject and object   German has two words for 'object', *Objekt* and *Gegenstand*, but only one for 'subject', *Subjekt*. *Objekt* comes from the Latin *obiectum*, literally what is thrown or placed against (*ob*); *Gegenstand* is Germanic and means literally what stands against (*gegen*). The words differ little in meaning or in Heidegger's use of them. *Objekt* is more naturally paired with *Subjekt*, especially in the expression 'subject-object-relation'. To a German the literal sense of *Gegenstand* is more obvious than that of *Objekt*, and Heidegger often writes *Gegen-stand* (e.g. NII, 153/niv, 107; 461f./ep, 58), though he punningly speaks of beings as '"throwing themselves against" pure discovery' and thus becoming 'objects [Objekt]' (BT, 363). His frequent use of *begegnen*, 'to encounter', in such phrases as 'the beings that encounter [us] within the world' (BT, 44), where we would normally say: 'the beings we encounter [. . .]', depends on its derivation from *gegen*: beings come up against, en-counter, confront us, as they stand over against us (LXV, 269). 'Object' and its German equivalents are ambiguous, meaning: 1. a real object, 2. an intentional object, an object of a subject or of a intentional attitude such as knowledge, love or curiosity. A real object (e.g. an undiscovered island) need not be the object of any subjective attitude, and an intentional object (e.g. the unicorn I dream about) need not be a real object. If every object is an object for a subject, then *Objekt* and *Gegenstand* are used in sense 2, and not every being is an object, since e.g. natural processes occur without being objects for a subject (XXIV, 222f.). Later he distinguishes the two words: 'Every Objekt is a Gegenstand, but not every Gegenstand (e.g. the thing in itself) is a possible Objekt' (PT, 73/26). 'The category "Gegenstand" was alien to the Greeks. In its place stood pragma ['a thing done, deed, thing, etc.'], that with which one has to do and deal – what is present for concernful dealings with things' (XVII, 14. Cf. BT, 68). (This is wrong: Aristotle uses *antikeimenon*, *-a*, lit. 'what lie(s) opposite', as the exact equivalent of *Gegenstand* and *Objekt*, of e.g. sight or intellect.)

Subjekt comes from the Latin *subiectum*, literally 'what is thrown under'. Originally it differed little in meaning from *Substanz*, *substantia*, lit. 'what stands under' (e.g. NII, 430/ep, 27). *Subjekt* is ambiguous, meaning: 1. the underlying substratum or subject of predication, inquiry, etc., 2. the human subject. Sense 1 was introduced by the Greek *hupokeimenon* ('what lies under'), but the 'Greeks know nothing at all about man as an I-subject' (NI, 505/niii, 29). Heidegger asks how a word that originally applied to everything came to be used especially for the human being. He concludes that with the new freedom following the decline of traditional Christianity man becomes the centre round which everything else revolves and thus the subject, what underlies, par excellence (NII, 141ff./niv, 96ff.). The human subject may be a disembodied I, whose certainty determines what there is (NII, 431ff./ep, 28ff.). But it need not be: Nietzsche's subject is embodied and governed by desire and passion more than by thought, but still cartesian in that it is the arbiter of being and value (NII, 187/niv, 133).

As often, Heidegger begins by treating as a misguided philosophical theory what he later regards as a central feature of fallen modernity. His early objections to the subject-object model are: 1. It ignores the WORLD that is a precondition of our encounters with objects or beings as such: ' "World" is something in which one can live (one cannot live in an object)' (LX, 11). 2. It implies that the subject and the object have the same mode of being, are both PRESENT-AT-HAND or things. 3. It 'thematizes' entities, makes them conspicuous, neglecting what we see out of the corner of our eye, what we are vaguely, unobtrusively aware of (BT, 363). 4. It suggests that our primary mode of access to things is cognition or theoretical knowledge. 5. It implies that the subject is separated from the object by a gulf or barrier (like a snail in its shell, XX, 223f.), and its access to the object mediated by a REPRESENTATION. 6. It suggests that a person is primarily an I or ego, detached from the body, the world and the THEY, and that one is aware of oneself by reflection on the I. In fact DASEIN is primarily aware of itself in what it deals with (BT, 119; XXIV, 227).

Later, Heidegger argues as follows: modern man is not simply mistakenly regarded as a/the subject. He is a subject, and to that extent he is not Dasein (NII, 25f./niii, 179f; LXV, 90, etc.). This 'subjectivity' is descended from Descartes's quest for an 'absolute and unshakeable foundation' (NII, 429ff./ep, 26ff.), but it has gone beyond cartesian confines. The subject is no longer an individualized I, it is embodied man, even collective man. It is no longer restrained by a barrier; its dominance of producible and manipulable objects is unrestrained (NII, 25f./niii, 179f; 171/niv, 121; AWP, 85f./133). Objects are still represented, but this means not that man has a mental picture of them but that it is man who decides whether and what they are. Everything is an object for this subject: there are no unexplored areas or aspects of the world beyond man's theoretical and practical reach. Subjectivity, and the 'objectivization'

(*Objektivierung, Vergegenständlichung*) it involves, may go so far that 'subjects' disappear in favour of a comprehensive utilizability (NII, 26/niii, 180), and humanity becomes a 'human resource' (*Menschenmaterial*), to be managed and exploited like any other material (NII, 387/niv, 241f.).

The subject-object model gives rise to the contrast between subjectivism (idealism) and objectivism (realism) (XX, 305f; NII, 297f./niii, 221). Both alternatives are mistaken, since 1. the subject-object model is misguided, and 2. subject and object are correlative: a subject has an object that stands on its own two feet, and an object is always an object for a subject. The distinction between the objective and the subjective is relative and shifting (LIX, 99). Thus whenever Heidegger raises the question whether e.g. time, world or being is subjective, he replies that 1. it cannot be, since Dasein is not a subject, and 2. if it is subjective, it is also objective, indeed 'more objective than any possible object' (BT, 366), or 'earlier than any subjectivity and objectivity' (BT, 419). His hostility to the contrast survives BT (NII, 195/niv, 141f; LXV, 456). He coins the word 'subjectity', *Subjektität* (HCE, 122/34) or *Subjectität* (NII, 451ff./ep, 46ff.), as an alternative to 'subjectivity' (*Subjektivität*), with its misleading suggestion of subjectivism (in contrast to objectivism) and its apparent restriction of the subject to the mental and the I.

system and (en)joining Like Kierkegaard and Nietzsche, Heidegger was wary of philosophical 'systems' of the type associated with Hegel: 'The time of "systems" is past. The time of the construction of the essential form of beings from the truth of beyng has not yet come' (LXV, 5. Cf. 41). System depends on the model of mathematics and the quest for certainty: '"System" is only possible in the wake of the dominance of (in the wide sense) mathematical thinking.[...] A thinking that stands outside this realm and the corresponding definition of truth as certainty is thus essentially lacking in system, un-systematic; but not thereby arbitrary and confused' (LXV, 65). The Greeks had no system: 'A "system" in the sense of a structure projected and executed as a unity and embracing all essential questions and matters uniformly is nowhere to be found [in Plato]. [...] The most varied questions are posed from different starting-points and on different levels [...] Everything is gathered together in the guiding question of philosophy: what beings are' (NI, 221/ni, 190. Cf. S, 32f./26f; AWP, 93f./141f.).

However, while 'system-building and the false form of system must be rejected again and again', this is because 'system in the true sense is a, or rather the, task of philosophy' (S, 32/27). 'Every philosophy is systematic, but not every philosophy is a system' (S. 35/29). Concepts and questions are not to be stowed away in pigeon-holes, but they are systematically connected to each other, and each has its appropriate place: 'The "systematic place" of a problem is the substantial interconnections that mark out the direction and range of our questioning' (XXXI, 201). These interconnections depend on DASEIN: 'the original and unique connection of concepts is already established by Dasein itself' (XXIX, 432). Later, they depend on being: 'And so far as the joint-character [Fugencharakter] belongs to the essence of beyng in general [. . .], the orientation to joint [Fuge] and enjoining [Fügung], to system, lies in all philosophy as questioning about beyng' (S, 35/29. Cf. 78f./65). In the mid-1930s Heidegger prefers the Germanic *Fuge* to the Greek-derived *System* (XV, 298f.). (*Fuge* in the sense of 'fugue', by contrast, comes from the Latin *fuga*, 'flight'. But this sense cannot invariably be excluded from Heidegger's uses of *Fuge*.) The basic meaning of *fügen* is 'to join, fit together'. It acquired other senses: 'to ordain, decree [esp. of fate or chance]', and, in the reflexive form *sich fügen*, 'to adapt oneself to, obey, bow to, accept [e.g. fate]'. It forms compounds: *(sich) einfügen*, 'to fit, insert, into; to fit in, adapt (oneself)'; *verfügen (über)*, 'to decree; to have in one's charge, at one's disposal'. It generated: *Fuge*, 'fitting together, joint, seam', which is alo used metaphorically, as in 'the world is out of joint'; *Fug*, 'what fits, the fitting', which now survives only in *mit Fug und Recht*, 'with complete justification'; *Fügung*, 'joining, construction, dispensation [of fate, providence]'; *Befugnis, befugt*, 'warrant, authority', 'authorized'; *füglich*, "convenient(ly), fitting(ly); and *fügsam*, 'obedient'. *Unfug*, 'unfitting doings', now means 'mischief, nuisance', but Heidegger restores its link with *Fug(e)* by writing *Un-fug*, 'what does not fit'. In the 1930s he became increasingly fond of *Gefüge*, 'conjunction, structure, order', which supplants the Latinate *Struktur* used in BT (LXV, 4; NII, 240/niv, 182).

Since *Fug*-words are often both descriptive and evaluative in sense they serve Heidegger's attempt to downgrade ethics in philosophy. Plato's *Replublic*, for example, is often supposed to be about politics and justice, a practical rather than a theoretical work. This, Heidegger argues, is mistaken. *Dikē* and *dikaiosunē* do not, as is commonly supposed, mean 'justice'. *Dikē* is a metaphysical, not a moral or legal concept: 'it names being with regard to the essential en-joining or in-junction [Fügung, = 1. 'joining', 2. 'ordaining'] of all beings', the 'en-joining laws [Fügungsgesetzen] of the being of beings' (NI, 194/ni, 165f.). This lies deeper than any distinction between the theoretical and the practical or political: the theoretical and the practical, and 'the distinction between them, can only be comprehended from the essence of being at the time, i.e. metaphysically. [. . .] The practical does not change on the basis of the theoretical, nor the theoretical on the basis of the practical; they always change together on the basis of the fundamental metaphysical position' (NI, 178/ ni, 152). *Dikē* is thus 'the fitting [Fug] and the unfitting [Unfug] with regard to being' (NI, 197/ni, 168). *Dikē* in Sophocles's *Antigone* is also *Fug*, in several senses: 'We understand Fug here first in the sense of joint [Fuge] and structure [Gefüge]; then Fug as injunction [Fügung], as the directive that the overpowering gives to its realm; finally Fug as the enjoining structure [das fügende Gefüge] which exacts adaptation [Einfügung] and obedience [Sichfügen].[. . .] Being, phusis [roughly 'nature'], as power, is original gatheredness: logos; it is enjoining order [fügender Fug]: dikē' (IM, 122f./134f.).

Later, Heidegger examines a fragment of Anaximander: 'out of those things whence is the generation for existing things, into these again does their destruction take place, according to what must needs be; for they make amends [dikēn] and give reparation to one another for their offense [adikias], according to the ordinance of time' (Kahn, 166. Cf. 199: 'Anaximander's conception of the world is [. . .] the prototype of the Greek view of nature as a cosmos, a harmonious realm within which the waxing and waning of the elemental powers march in step with the astronomical cycles'). Heidegger again introduces *Fug*: 'Dikē, thought in terms of being as presence [Anwesen], is the joining-enjoining order [fügend-fügende Fug]. Adikia, the out-of-joint [Un-fuge], is dis-order [Unfug]' (Anax, 329/43. Cf. LI, 118).

Heidegger sometimes describes his own thought as a *Fuge*: 'Philosophy is a joint [Fuge] in beings; it is the disposal [Verfügung] over the truth of beyng that submits [sich . . . fügende] to beyng' (LXV, 45). He offers a 'joint' of primordial thinking (LXV, 81). Thinking effects certain *Fügungen*, 'joinings', not with the 'exactitude' of a mathematical system, but with the 'rigour' appropriate to philosophy: 'the freedom of the joining of its joints' (LXV, 65). Such themes as thinking, history, language, and Da-sein are like 'blocks in a quarry, in which the original stone is broken' (LXV, 421). We need to fit them together, to see if they make a bridge, to reconstruct the inherent fitting or articulation of being itself (LXV, 81, 436).

T

talk and language   Heidegger's thought on language passes through three phases:

1. In early works he follows Husserl's LU: language expresses a sense and meaning that is essentially extralinguistic, independent of any particular language, of the psychological states of speakers and hearers, and of the contexts in which sentences are uttered: 'The two structures, sentence and sense, word and meaning, however peculiar and close their connection may be, belong to different realms of reality. The linguistic elements are *sensorily* perceptible (visually, acoustically, by motor activity); they belong in the world of what really exists, they endure over time, arise and pass away. Sense and meaning by contrast elude all sensory perception, are subject as such to no changes. They are timelessly identically the same. Amidst all diversity of sound-formation in individual languages the identity of the realm of sense persists unaffected in its validity, however various the word- and sentence-forms in which its content is "grasped" and conveyed to understanding' (DS, 292f.). Everything other than meaning belongs under the heading 'psychology' or 'factual reality', and is rigorously excluded from consideration in accordance with Husserl's attack on 'psychologism', the attempt to base logic on human psychology.
2. By the time of BT Heidegger has shed the 'banal Platonism' stemming from Husserl's 'theoretical attitude', the sharp distinction between 'factuality [Tatsächlichkeit]' and 'validity [Gültigkeit]' (XVII, 94. Cf. XXI, 62ff; BT, 155f.). Grammar is to be liberated from 'logic' (BT, 165f.). Language is no longer the expression of a timeless web of meaning, but rooted in human activity. This does not reinstate psychologism: human beings are now DASEIN, being-in-the-world, not receptacles of psychological events. Thus the '*existential-ontological foundation of language is talk*' (BT, 160. Cf. XXI, 134). *Rede*, originally 'account, reason, etc.', corresponding closely to the Latin *ratio*, now

207

means 'talk, (a) speech, words, conversation, discourse, etc.'. It gave rise to *reden*, 'to talk, etc.' *Sprache*, 'speech, language, etc.', is associated with *sprechen*, 'to say, speak, etc.'. Later, *Rede* is displaced by *sagen*, 'to say, saying', *Sage*, 'saying, legend', and *nennen*, *Nennung*, 'to name, naming', but these words are not very significant in BT. *Rede* is informal talk in a particular context. It need not involve a grammatically complete sentence. It need not be an assertion, even an incomplete assertion. 'Fire!' is a kind of *Rede* (XXI, 21); so is a request, though under Aristotle's influence Heidegger insists that a request does not reveal something 'in the sense of letting it be seen by pointing it out' (BT, 32). 'Hearing is constitutive for talking' (BT, 163). On Heidegger's early view, the 'doctrine of meaning' excludes problems about 'the difficulty and ease of understanding meanings' (DS, 338); what matters is the meaning expressed, not whether anyone understands or even hears. But talk requires a hearer; a listener is also talking. Hence, talk involves silence too (BT, 161). We are not really talking when we both talk at once. Silence can be as pregnant as words. *Rede* is distinct from *Gerede*, 'chatter, idle talk, gossip'. *Gerede* is talk that is uprooted from the particular situation and experience of particular Dasein, and conveys the general, or the THEY's, interpretation of things: 'The case is so, because one says it' (BT, 168); 'The They prescribes the state one is in, it determines what and how one "sees"' (BT, 170). My belief that everyone dies, for example, is based not on my personal experience, but on what they all say.

Language is not primary in BT. Prior to language, logically if not temporally, is our understanding of the world and its significance, and our interpretations of particular entities. 'Talk is the articulation of intelligibility' (161). 'But significance itself, with which Dasein is always already familiar, harbours the ontological condition of the possibility that Dasein that understands can, as it interprets, disclose such a thing as "meanings", which in turn found the possible being of word and language' (BT, 87).

3. 'Untrue', protests Heidegger later. 'Language is not superimposed; it *is* the original essence of truth as There' (BT, 442 *ad* 87). The change in view, or at least in emphasis, coheres with a change in Heidegger's conception of world. World is I. a familiar realm of interwoven significance, II. beings as a whole, which constitute a world even if Angst strips away their customary significance. In world I language can grow out of prelinguistic significance. In world II it cannot: there is no prelinguistic significance. World II is required, among other reasons, if we ask: How is World I first established? It can only be

done by forming words, basic words, such as *phusis* (roughly Greek for 'nature') that open up a certain view of beings as a whole (world II), and other words that lay the foundations for a form of life (world I). Words gather or assemble phenomena into stable, persisting intersubjective entities; they create an open space of entities for us to talk about and deal with, and thus create speakers and hearers: 'But with the question about the essence of language the question about beings as a whole is already posed, if indeed language is not a collection of words for denoting individual familiar things, but *the original resonance of the truth of a world*' (NI, 364/nii, 104f. Cf. XXIX, 442, 447; S, 152/126; NI, 564, 578f., 583f., 586f./niii, 78, 91, 95f., 97f.). In the style of Hölderlin: 'When the gods call the earth and in the call a world echoes and thus the call resounds as Da-sein of man, then language is as historical, history-grounding word' (LXV, 510). Now 'language is the house of being' (LH, 311/217).

Language suffers from technology: 'metalinguistics is the metaphysics of the thoroughgoing mechanization of all languages exclusively into the operative instrument of interplanetary information. Metalanguage and sputnik, metalinguistics and missile-technology are the same' (OWL, 160/58). Its salvation is poetry (XXXIX, 61ff.). 'Language is the original poetry [Urdichtung] in which a people poetizes [dichtet] being' (IM, 131/144).

technology, machination and enframing   *Technik*, 'technology, engineering, technique', comes from the Greek *techne*, 'art, handicarft; an art or regular way of making or doing something [in contrast to *episteme*, 'science']; skill, cunning; a work of art'. *Techne* is related to *tiktein*; 'to beget, bear [offspring, fruit]; to produce'. Heidegger denies all this. *Techne*, he claims, contrasts with *phusis*, beings as a whole emerging on their own. *Techne* is not 'making', or the art of making, but the *Wissen*, 'knowing', that guides our dealings with *phusis* (NI, 96f./ni, 80f.). The *technites*, the possessor of *techne*, primarily knows how to reveal beings, not how to make them (OWA, 47f./184f.). This interpretation of *techne* survives in his view of *Technik*. Technology is not primarily a way of making or doing things, but a way of revealing things that precedes the making: 'That there is such a thing as e.g. a diesel engine has its decisive, ultimate ground in the fact that the categories of a "nature" utilizable by machine technology were once specifically thought and thought through by philosophers' (NII, 76/niv, 39). Heidegger uses the Germanic *Machenschaft* as a

209

near-synonym of *Technik*. It comes from *machen*, 'to make, build, do, etc.', and once meant 'type, quality' but now ordinarily means, especially in the plural, 'machinations, intrigues, wheelings and dealings'. Heidegger retrieves its link with making and interprets it as 'makership, machination, productivity', the tendency to value only what we have made and what we can make into something. It is conveniently similar, albeit etymologically unrelated, to *Macht*, 'power', and *Maschine*, 'machine' (NII, 21/niii, 174f; LXV, 392, etc.).

The 'essence of *Technik* is by no means anything technological' (QT, 9/4). It is *Ge-stell*. *Gestell* originally meant a 'position; something put together', then a 'framework, especially of a mill', and now a 'stand, frame, rack', e.g. a hat-stand (cf. NI, 202/ni, 174). It comes from *Stall*, once 'place, position', but now a 'stable, cowshed, etc.'. The prefix *ge-* originally meant 'together, with' and was later used to form collective nouns: *Gebirge*, 'mountains, mountain range', from *Berg*, 'mountain'; *Gemüt*, 'mind, etc.', '(the seat of) all one's thoughts and feelings', from *Mut*, 'courage, mood, etc.' (cf. QT, 23/19f.). It also expresses the result of an action: *Geschenk*, 'gift', from *schenken*, 'to give'. Thus *ge-* forms the perfect participle of most verbs, indicating the completed action or event: *gestellt*, 'placed', from *stellen*, 'to place', etc.

Heidegger interprets *Gestell* as a collective noun formed from *ge-* and *stellen*, with a new meaning indicated by writing *Ge-stell*. He uses it to express the way in which the conflictual 'rift' between earth and world is placed and composed in the *Gestalt* ('form, figure' – also from *stellen*) of a work of art, such as a temple (OWA, 52/189). Later, *Ge-stell* comes close to the *Gestalt* of the worker, which 'mobilizes standing resources [Bestand] as a whole without distinction' (Jünger (1932), 160. Cf. QB, 58ff.), a concept introduced by Jünger to convey the 'total mobilization' of the technocrat devoted to purposeless production, transport and management. *Ge-stell*, 'enframing', now 'means what assembles that placing [Stellens] which places [stellt], i.e. commandeers [herausfordert, 'challenges, provokes'], man to unconceal [entbergen] the actual in the manner of placing an order for it [Bestellens] as standing resources [Bestand]' (QT, 24.20). *Stellen* means 'to make [something] stand', but it has many other senses, e.g. 'to provide, contribute' something to a common stock. It gives rise to *bestellen*, 'to order [e.g. materials], reserve, appoint, etc.' The association of *stellen* with 'to stand; stand(ing)' (*stehen*; *Stand*) suggests a link between *bestellen* and *Bestand*, 'continuance; stock, (standing) reserve, resource' (QT, 20ff./17f.). Earlier, Heidegger associated *Technik* with *Vergegenständlichung*, 'making things Gegenstände, objects' (NII, 387/niv, 241f; cf. 25f./niii, 179f.). Now he distinguishes between *Bestand* and

Gegenstand: a plane at rest may be a *Gegenstand*, but on the runway it is *Bestand*, owing its 'standing' to the use we make of it (QT, 20f./17).

These words alone do not suffice to distinguish technology from pretechnological production. *Bestellen*, e.g. also means 'to till' the fields, a respectably pretechnological occupation (QT, 18/14f.). How does a power-station supplied by a dam on the Rhine differ from a potter's wheel or a windmill? The potter reveals pots by 'bringing them forth', the windmill reveals wind energy, but neither 'commandeers [herausfordert]' nature's energies or stores them for future use (QT, 18/14). When we do this, we regard the whole of nature as *Bestand*, as a stockpile of resources; we view the fields as coal-mines and as the site of mineral wealth. Man too is seen as *Bestand*, as exploitable manpower or human resources (QT, 30/26f; NII, 387/niv, 241). The instrumental view of *Technik* – that it is a way of fulfilling our purposes, differing from pretechnological handicraft only in its greater efficiency – is 'correct', but not 'true'; it is alright as far as it goes but it does not get to the bottom of things (QT, 11/5). *Technik* reveals the earth, man himself, and now even the moon and planets, as *Bestand*. It is not just something done by us, but a phase of our destiny (QT, 28f./24f; LXV, 126, 131). Like every way of revealing, it takes us over, moulding as much as fulfiling our purposes; for 'there is no such thing as a man who is simply man just of his own accord' (QT, 36/31). *Technik* engulfs and diminishes the world, thus threatening to turn man from a being in the world into a 'mechanized animal' (NII, 165, 395/niv, 116f., 248; LXV, 98, 442, 495).

Why did *Technik*, industrial technology, arise in the late eighteenth century? It was not just an application of the mathematical natural science of the seventeenth century. Science itself involves the 'commandeering gathering into ordering unconcealing', but we did not notice it until *Technik* made it obvious (QT, 25/22). Science and *Technik* have a common source in a way of understanding or disclosing things, the man-centred metaphysic initiated by Descartes (NII, 24/niii, 178; 129ff./niv, 86ff.). But this too can be traced back to Christianity's creator God and the conception of everything as *ens creatum* (LXV, 107, 111, 126f., 130ff., 348f.) and further still to Plato's association of *technē* with ideas (NI, 494/niii, 20; LXV, 135, 336).

How should we respond to technology? Not by a flight into mysticism, superstition and irrationalism; these are an essential adjunct of technological rationalism (NI, 531, NII, 28/niii, 50, 182). We should reflect on beings in such a way as to 'ground the lighting, so that it does not become the void in which everything presents itself as uniformly "intelligible" and controllable' (LXV, 349; cf. 391). We can in particular reflect on the

211

essence of *Technik*, 'the remedy that grows where the danger is' (Hölderlin), for this is related to *Technik*, yet not itself technological and will lead us to think about art (QT, 39/34f.). We inevitably use machines that tend to uproot us from our native habitat. But we should cultivate 'detachment', not letting *Technik* take us over (G, 23ff./54ff.).

the They, the One   *Mann*, 'man', originally applied, like the Latin *homo*, to men and women, but is now usually restricted to males. It gave rise to the indefinite third-person pronoun, *man*, which applies to humans of both sexes. (The French *on*, '(some)one', similarly developed from *homo*.) At first it meant 'some man', then 'any man whatever'. Today it is used both with a singular and with a plural force, and can be translated as 'one, you, we, somebody, someone, they, people' or by an impersonal expression: '*One* does not do that, that's not done'; '*Someone* told me, I was told'; '*They/people* used to burn witches'.

Heidegger often turns a pronoun into a noun by adding a neuter definite article and capitalizing the initial letter: *das Nichts*, 'the Nothing'; *das Was*, 'the What'; *das Wer*, 'the Who'; etc. One of his more felicitous coinages of this type is *das Man*, 'the They, the One'. It antedates BT: 'So far as Dasein is an entity that I am and is also determined as being-with-one-another, for the most part and on average it is not I myself who am my Dasein, but the others; I am with the others and the others too are with the others. In everydayness no one is himself. What he is and how he is, is nobody: no one and yet all together with one another.[. . .] This Nobody by whom we ourselves are lived in everydayness is the "One". One says, one hears, one is for it, one sees to it. The possibilities of my Dasein lie in the stubborn grip of this They, and the "I am" is possible in virtue of this levelling' (CT, 8f. Cf. LXIII, 17, etc.).

Heidegger begins his account of *das Man* with the notion of *Abständigkeit*, 'distantiality': DASEIN constantly measures itself against others, trying to keep up with them, catch them up or outdo them. We always have an eye on what others are doing and how they are doing it. Hence what we do and how we do it is mostly determined by others – not definite others, but nameless others: 'We take pleasure and enjoy ourselves as they [man] take pleasure; we read, see, and judge art and literature as they see and judge' (BT, 126f.). Distantiality is based on our real concern, *Durchschnittlichkeit*, 'averageness'. We usually want not to do much better or much worse than others, but to hover around the average. (Cf. Namier, 219: 'In the pace of a narrative or of a journey, as in human stature, the normal supplies a point beyond, or short of which, every unit becomes increasingly remarkable'.) Averageness entails *Einebnung*, 'levelling', the levelling off of distinctions. We cannot be average if what is averagely expected is beyond the reach of most of us.

Distantiality, averageness and levelling constitute *Öffentlichkeit*, 'publicness'. Publicness 'controls every way in which the world and Dasein get interpreted' (BT, 127). It ensures that we have a shared world: 'the world is always already given primarily as the common [gemeinsame] world. We do not start out as individual subjects, each with its own particular world, who then have to put their different worlds together by a sort of agreement and arrange for a common world. That is how the philosophers represent matters when they ask about the constitution of the intersubjective world. We say: the first thing that is given is this common world of the One, i.e. the world in which Dasein submerges itself, in such a way that it has not yet come to itself and can constantly be in this world without having to come to itself' (XX, 339). The They takes away Dasein's choice and its responsibility for what it does and believes. It is not I who decide what a hammer is for or to wear clothes in public. Nor does anyone in particular decide all this. No one does. It is just what one, the One, thinks and does.

The phenomenon of the One shows that Dasein is not an I or ego in Descartes's sense. If it is a 'self' it is not its own self, but the *Man-selbst*, the 'They-self' (BT, 129). It can become its own authentic self, and *das Man* provides the resources for it to do so. We must be careful here, since *das Man* can make us think we are authentic individuals when we are really still under its sway: 'we shrink back from the "great mass" as *they* [*man*] shrink back' (BT, 127). Dasein is a peculiarly fluid entity. Mostly it is submerged in the One, in the network, but it can extricate itself to become an individual I or self. It is neither subject nor world: 'The being of Dasein is the being of the "Between" subject and world' (XX, 347). When we ask 'Who [Wer]' Dasein is, rather than 'What [Was]' it is, we are asking about its current or its usual mode of being, not about its 'What' or intrinsic nature: Dasein is too protean to have a What. 'The One' is an answer to the question who it is. Even when it is absorbed in the One, Dasein's being is *je meines*, 'always mine', it has its own being to be (XX, 206, 336, 347; BT, 41). This means not that even when it is the One, Dasein still retains a vestigial ability to make *some* choices (such as which shirt to wear this evening), but that it always retains the choice of opting out of the One; it can choose to choose.

The One is neither a good nor a bad thing. We owe it to our common world and our shared time or ' "They"-time ['Man'-Zeit]" (CT, 17). But the 'intrusiveness and explicitness of its dominion is historically variable'

(BT, 129), and Heidegger's jaundiced account of it suggests that they have gone too far in modern times. He drops the expression after BT, because (i) what was not intended as a 'casual contribution to sociology' (LH, 315/221) was adopted by sociologists (cf. Mannheim, 196ff.); (ii) his interest turns from individual Dasein to historic cultures; and (iii) the authenticity of Dasein comes to depend more on its relation to being than on its relation to others (XLIX, 66f.). The One is sometimes replaced by the 'normal man [Normalmensch]', the 'eternal average', who 'makes his contentments the standard of what is to count as joy [. . .] his feeble timorousness the standard of what can count as terror and fear [. . .] his replete stolidity the standard of what can count as security or insecurity' (XXIX, 32).

thing *Ding*, 'thing', is distinct from *Sache*, 'thing, (subject-)matter, affair'. *Sache*, like the Latin *res*, originally denoted a legal case or a matter of concern, while *Ding* was the 'court' or 'assembly' before which a case was discussed (D, 166ff./174f.). *Sache* occurs in Husserl's slogan 'To the things [Sachen] themselves!', prescribing an unblinkered view of things, free of traditional prejudices and assumptions. Heidegger endorsed this aim: it is one source of his constant concern about our 'access [Zugang]' to things (e.g. BT, 6). But Husserl neglected his own prescription, accepting traditional concepts such as 'consciousness' without adequate inspection (XX, 147). *Sache* is non-committal about the nature of the 'thing' in question. *Ding*, in BT, implies something PRESENT-AT-HAND, an object of neutral contemplation, in contrast to ready-at-hand equipment and to DASEIN. It is especially associated with Descartes's view that the self is a *res cogitans*, a 'thinking thing' (BT, 67f., 98). In the 1930s Heidegger develops a more complex view of the *Ding*. He distinguishes three senses of the word: 1. the 'present-at-hand' (and also the ready-to-hand in his BT usage): stone, a bit of wood, pliers, clock, etc; 2. a wider sense that includes stone, etc., but also events: 'plans, resolutions, thoughts, temperaments, deeds, the historical'; 3. the widest sense which includes 1 and 2, but also anything that is 'a something not nothing [. . .] the number 5, luck, courage' (WT, 5/6). He examines various accounts of the *Ding*: the physicist's account of a sunset and a table; a thing as the occupant of a certain spatio-temporal position; Leibniz's view that a thing is a 'particular this [je dieses]' independently of its spatio-temporal location (WT, 8ff./11ff.); a thing as the unity of a manifold of perceptible qualities; and as a form superimposed on matter (OWA, 14ff./150ff; NI, 564/niii, 77f.). The most 'natural' view is that a thing is a 'bearer of properties'. It also fits the correspondence theory of truth. An assertion involves a subject and a predicate, corresponding to a bearer and its property: 'the structure of the thing coheres with the structure of the assertion' (WT, 48/64. Cf. OWA, 12ff./148ff.). 'The "natural" is always historical', however (WT, 30/ 39). The 'natural' view is an old prejudice originated by Plato and Aristotle. But we would need to 'bring into play the whole of Greek existence, their gods, their art, their state, their knowledge, in order to experience what it means to uncover the like of a thing'. For the answer to the question 'What is a thing?' is not a proposition, but 'the beginning of a change of our former attitude to things, a change of questioning and assessment, of seeing and deciding, in short: of Da-sein in the midst of beings' (WT, 38/50).

Later, Heidegger exploits the original meaning of *Ding* or the Old High German *thing*, the 'assembly' of the people, and the derived verb *dingen*, 'to thing', now used rarely for 'to hire, engage', but once 'to discuss before the assembly'. He takes *dingen* to mean 'to assemble, gather', and takes a thing to be something that 'assembles' the 'fourfold', EARTH, sky, gods and mortals: 'The jug is a thing not in the Roman sense of res, nor in the sense of an ens as the medievals represented it, nor in the modern sense of a represented object. The jug is thing insofar as it things. [. . .] By thinging, it detains a while [verweilt] earth and sky, the divinities and the mortals; by detaining, the thing brings the four close to each other in their distances' (D, 170/177). As in WT, the question 'What is a thing?' brings the whole world into play.

thinking and questioning *Denken* is 'to think'. Heidegger exploits its affinity to *Dank, danken*, 'thanks', 'to thank', which once meant 'to think, remember' (WCT, 149/244). *Denken* forms several compounds: *Andenken*, 'remembrance', but as *An-denken*, 'thinking of [an]' (NII, 402/ep, 4); *erdenken*, 'to think out, up, forth' (LXV, 428). 'Thoughtful(ly)' is *denkerisch*, a word that Heidegger contrasts with merely 'thinking [denkend, denkmässig]' (LXV, 95, 235), and often links with *dichterisch*, 'poetic(ally), inventive(ly)' (NI, 329/nii, 73). He often uses *sich besinnen, Besinnung*, 'to reflect (on); reflection', for philosophical thinking, especially since, unlike the sciences, it essentially reflects on its own standpoint (XXIX, 415; LXV, 44; G, 13f./46f.). *Besinnung* is often distinguished from *Reflexion*, which Heidegger (like Hegel) associates with the reflection or 'bending back' of light, and thus with Dasein's turning back from things to itself (XXIX, 226). *Reflexion* was a concept favoured by Husserl. Heidegger assimilates it to Descartes's *cogito*, which is essentially self-reflexive, *cogito me cogitare*, 'I think that I think' (XVII, 284. Cf. 261, 175 on Aquinas).

Thinking forms a hierarchy. At the bottom is *das rechnende Denken*, 'calculating thinking', or *das Rechnen*, 'reckoning, calculation', from *rechnen*, 'to reckon, etc.', a word that, together with compounds such as *berechnen*, 'to calculate', usually conveys Heidegger's disapproval: 'Everydayness takes Dasein as a ready-to-hand matter of concern, that is, something managed and reckoned up [verrechnet]. "Life" is a "business", whether or not it covers its costs' (BT, 289). 'Thinking in the sense of calculating [Berechnens] [. . .] roams to and fro only *within* a fixed horizon, within its boundary, although it does not see it' (NI, 639/niii, 143). The scientist's thinking is not invariably as blinkered as the shopkeeper's but neither of them transcends their horizon to reflect on it and on their own thinking (NI, 372/nii, 111f.).

At the top of the hierarchy is genuine philosophical thinking. In the BT period thinking involves asking questions. A question (*Frage*) is distinct from a *Problem*. A problem (such as the freewill problem) is an objectified timeless entity, extracted by such philosophers as Windelband and Hartmann from the works of Plato, Kant, etc. A question is a concrete, situated event. Questions, unlike problems, are not restricted to a traditional menu. '*There is a history of problems only on the basis of an explicit philosophical standpoint.* By contrast, a *genuinely* standpoint-free inquiry knows only "matters" ['Sachen'] as possible sources and motives of questioning and of the development of the respects in which they are to be questioned' (XVII, 78). Answers to questions are not cut-and-dried propositions: 'an answer [Antwort] is an answer just when it knows how to disappear in the right way' (XVII, 76). An answer propels us into more questions: *Philosophie ist Philosophieren*, 'philosophy is philosophizing', not a body of truths (XXVII, 15, 25). The questioner develops as the questioning proceeds: 'what philosophy deals with reveals itself only in and from a transformation of human Dasein' (XXIX, 423, Cf. NI, 383/nii, 120f.: thinking and the thought are not separable like a vehicle and our destination).

In the 1930s philosophical thinking is more steadfastly focused on the question about being: we should not answer the question 'What are beings?' but 'unfold' it into the question about being (NI, 457f./niii, 5). Thinking comes closer to poetry: 'All philosophical thinking, and precisely the most rigorous and prosaic, is intrinsically poetic [dichterisch] and yet never poetry as an art-form [Dichtkunst]. [. . .] great philosophy is thoughtful-poetic' (NI, 329/nii, 73). Thinking is 'building; or 'constructive' (*bauend*), 'removing' (*ausscheidend*), and 'eliminating' (*beseitigend*) or 'destructive' (*vernichtend*) (NI, 640ff./niii, 143ff; NII, 322f./niii, 242; LXV,

58). It clears the ground to build to hitherto unknown heights. With the decline of religious authority philosophers such as Descartes sought a reliable method for discovering truths (NII, 133f./niv, 89f.). No such method is to be sought or found: 'the way of this thinking out [Erdenkens] of beyng has not already been firmly marked on a map. The terrain first *arises through the way*, and at each point on the way is unfamiliar and not to be worked out by calculation [errechnen]' (LXV, 86).

Thinking is traditionally paired with being (IM, 88ff./98ff.). BT broke this connection, linking being with time instead (LXV, 183). The connection begins with Parmenides: *to gar auto noein estin te kai einai*. Heidegger accepts the traditional view of its uncertain syntax: 'For thinking [noein] and being [einai] are the same [to auto]', but he varies the translation of *noein* and *einai* in accordance with his current view of thinking and being as interpreted by early Greeks. Early on, he took Parmenides to be a precursor of Husserl: real being is disclosed (but not idealistically *constituted*) by theoretical apprehension (LXIII, 91f.). Later, he interprets *noein* differently. It is *Vernehmen*, combining its senses of 'to hear, perceive' and 'to examine, interrogate': a receptive bringing-to-a-stand of what appears, rather like the reception soldiers give to the enemy advance (IM, 105/116. Cf. NI, 528/niii, 45f.). Parmenides means not that being and thinking in this sense are identical but that they belong together (IM, 111/122). Later still, *noein* is interpreted as *In-die-Acht-nehmen*, 'taking into one's care', and being as *Anwesen des Anwesenden*, 'presence of what presences'; again these 'belong together' (WCT, 147f./241f.). 'Western-european thinking' is 'at bottom a series of variations on this one theme' (WCT, 148/242. Cf. BT, 171). Kant's account of beings in terms of our possible experience of them stems from Parmenides, only Kant regards beings as 'objects [Gegenstände]' (WCT, 149/243). *Noein* deteriorated under the influence of Plato's interpretation of being as *idea*. It became *dialegesthai*, 'to argue, etc.', thus converging with the parallel decline of Heraclitus's *logos* into 'assertion [Assage]' (LXV, 457; cf. 197). Now it has become the REPRESENTATION of 'objects': the liberation of man involved in the 'unfolding of being as subjectivity' that accompanied the decline of religious authority is 'the way in which the transformation of the representing [Vorstellens] of Vernehmen as receiving (noein) to Vernehmen as a judicial hearing (per-ceptio ['perception', stressing its origin in *capere*, 'to seize, capture']) comes about' (NII, 319f./niii, 239; cf. 450/ep, 46: *noein* involves dwelling [*Verweilen*] in the unhidden). Heidegger thus becomes less fond of questioning as the role once assigned to Dasein is allotted to being itself or to related suprapersonal things such as language. When we ask about the essence of language we must listen to what it says to us: 'the authentic attitude of thinking cannot be questioning; it must be hearing the voice [Zusage] of that which all questioning must first consult when it inquires about the essence' (OWL, 176/72). Heidegger's dictum: 'For questioning is the piety of thinking' (QT, 40/35) is to be taken in this spirit. *Frömmigkeit* is not exactly 'piety', but has its older sense of 'obedience', obedience, that is, to 'what thinking has to think' (OWL, 175/72).

thrownness and facticity *Werfen* originally meant 'to spin, turn, wind', hence 'to fling by turning one's arm', and now 'to throw, cast'. It also means 'to give birth (to)', esp. of animals. Derivatives of *werfen* are *Wurf,* a 'throw' of a ball or a die (*Würfel*), and *entwerfen,* 'to PROJECT'; also *vorwerfen,* 'to reproach; throw down', and *Vorwurf,* a 'reproach', to which Heidegger restores their original sense, 'to throw before, throwing before' one(self) e.g. possibilities (BT, 145) or a world (XXIV, 239). The perfect participle of *werfen* is *geworfen,* 'thrown'. From this Heidegger forms a noun, *Geworfenheit,* 'thrownness'.

Along with EXISTENCE and FALLING, thrownness is a central feature of DASEIN. Dasein is thrown into its There (*Da*) (BT, 135). The relation between existence and thrownness is captured by Schiller, writing to Goethe on 23 August 1794: 'Now that you have been born a German, now that your Grecian spirit has been thrown [geworfen] into this northern world, you had but two alternatives, either to become a northern artist, or [. . .] to produce your Greece as it were from within, by an intellectual process' (quoted in Trevelyan, 193). Every Dasein is thrown, not only misfits: 'Brought up in the very centre of London life, he had early entered into the spirit of the stirring times on which his young life was cast' (Seebohm, 13f.).

'Thrownness' is closely connected to 'facticity', a word that precedes it both in BT and in earlier lectures (cf. LXIII: *Ontology (Hermeneutic of Facticity)*). Stones and trees are PRESENT-AT-HAND within the WORLD. That is a fact (*Tatsache*), and we speak of their *Tatsächlichkeit,* 'factuality'. Dasein is also at hand in the world, but not only or primarily in the way that stones and trees are; they are 'worldless', Dasein is not. Heidegger uses for Dasein's factuality the latinate *Faktizität*; this 'implies that an entity "within the world" has being-in-the-world in such a way that it can understand itself as bound up in its "destiny" with the being of those entities which it encounters within its own world' (BT, 56). 'Thrownness' too refers to the sheer 'That it is' of Dasein, and indicates the 'facticity of [Dasein's] handing over [Überantwortung]' (BT, 135).

Dasein is handed over to its 'That it is and has to be' (BT, 135). For thrownness is not a fact that is over and done with, like details of one's ancestry which one can discover by research. It is a constant accompaniment of Dasein's existence, poignantly revealed in certain MOODS. It involves several features: 1. Since Dasein is simply thrown, and does not throw itself, thrownness, the fact that Dasein is, is not in Dasein's own control: 'In its existence it never gets back behind its thrownness, so that it could first release this 'that it is and has to be' from its very own selfhood and lead it into the There' (BT, 284; cf. 228: 'Has Dasein itself ever decided freely whether it wants to come into "Dasein" [i.e. existence] or not, [. . .]?'). 2. Dasein is a being 'in the midst of beings as a whole' (e.g. WM, 109/99). It is thrown 'into the midst [in das Inmitten]' of beings (LXV, 327). It is FINITE (XXV, 85). 3. Dasein does not come to rest after it has been thrown. It 'remains in the throw [im Wurf] and is sucked into the turbulence of the INAUTHENTICITY of the THEY' (BT, 179. Cf. K, 235/161 on thrownness and falling). 4. Thrownness also leads to projection: 'And as thrown, Dasein is thrown into a certain mode of being: projecting' (BT, 145). Since Dasein 'is its possibilities' and projects itself on them (BT, 181), Dasein 'is a being-possible handed over to itself, thrown possibility through and through' (BT, 144). Projecting is closely associated with existence. Thus Dasein's thrownness pervades its other two central features.

Projecting is a type of throwing, but it differs from Dasein's thrownness in that it is performed by Dasein itself. Dasein's project(ion) is, however, often said to be 'thrown'. This has three different senses: (a) Projection itself is a sort of throwing. (b) Projection starts out from Dasein's prior thrownness, rebounds from the position to which Dasein is thrown: 'Every project – and thus all "creative" human action – is thrown, i.e. determined by Dasein's dependence on what there already is as a whole, a dependence that is not in control of itself' (K, 235/161). That is, Dasein cannot project whatever it likes; it is limited by its position among beings. (c) The projector, or thrower, of the project is thrown in the projection (LXV, 231, 452ff.). That is, in projecting a world, 'man casts himself loose [loswirft] from "beings", [and] first becomes man' (LXV, 452); only in such projection does man become aware of himself as such as well as of other entities. This involvement of the projecter in the projection is distinct from Dasein's thrownness; it is a response to thrownness, a way of 'taking it over' without 'getting behind' it (cf. BT, 325).

Heidegger's stress on thrownness differentiates him from Kant and Husserl: '[. . .] the thrower of the project experiences himself as thrown, [. . .] Opening up by the project is an opening up only if it happens as experience of thrownness and thus of belonging to beyng. That is the essential difference from every merely *transcendental* mode of cognition with respect to the conditions of possibility' (LXV, 239). The transcendental ego postulated by idealism has no location among beings prior to the location it assigns to itself in the world that it projects. Heidegger's man, or Dasein, is thrown among beings from the start. Thus 'as the ek-sisting counterthrow [Gegenwurf] of being, man is more than the [merely biological] rational animal and correspondingly less than the [idealistically conceived] man, who comprehends himself in terms of subjectivity' (LH, 338/245).

time, temporality and timeliness *Zeit* means 'time'. The adjective *zeitlich*, 'pertaining to time, temporal', also has the sense of 'transitory'. Heidegger also uses *Zeitlichkeit*, 'temporality'. 'Timely' and 'timeliness' have the sense of '(being) on time, in (good) time, at the right time', which is absent from *zeitlich(keit)* both in ordinary and in Heideggerian usage. But 'timely; timeliness' are apt renditions, since 1. their standard senses diverge no more from *zeitlich(keit)* in *Heidegger's* sense than does *zeitlich(keit)* in the standard sense; 2. he uses words with a better claim to be translated as 'temporal(ity)': the neutral *zeithaft*, 'pertaining to time' (BT, 327), and especially the Latinate *temporal* and *Temporalität*, in contrast to *zeitlich(keit)*. Only DASEIN is *zeitlich* in Heidegger's sense; other entities, traditionally viewed as *zeitlich*, are *innerzeitig*, 'within time'. *Innerzeitigkeit*, 'within-time-ness', is to *Zeitlichkeit* what 'being within the world' is to 'being-in-the-WORLD'. *Temporal(ität)*, by contrast, applies to being, not to Dasein or to any other entity (BT, 19).

Zeitig, 'happening at the right time', hence 'early', gave rise to *zeitigen*, 'to let/make ripen, bring to maturity, bring about, produce'. Its affiliation with *Zeit* is lost in standard German, but Heidegger revives it, using *(sich) zeitigen* in the sense of 'produce (itself) in time, extemporize, temporalize (itself)'. It retains the flavour of 'producing'; hence it is not 'to time', and Heidegger does not coin a verb *zeiten*. It applies, in this specifically Heideggerian sense, to timeliness ('Timeliness extemporizes, it extemporizes possible modes of itself' (BT, 328)); to aspects of timeliness ('the horizon of a present extemporizes itself' (BT, 365)); and to Dasein: 'In so far as Dasein extemporizes itself, a world *is* too' (BT, 365). Two ideas underly such locutions: 1. Things differ in their being or nature; to avoid homogenizing them in the traditional way, we should apply different words to them: 'Time does not have the mode of being of anything else; time extemporizes' (XXI, 410). 2. In particular, some 'things' are not entities, objects or stuffs: Dasein, though an entity, is a peculiarly active entity, more like fire than a stone. Time(liness) is not an entity, a container or a stuff, it is more like an activity: 'Timeliness "is" not an entity at all. It *is* not; it *extemporizes* itself' (BT, 328).

Timeliness is *ekstatisch*, 'ecstatic, lit. stepping outside (itself)'. Its extemporizing consists in expansion into three *Ekstasen*, 'ecstases': FUTURE, PRESENT, and PAST. 'Ecstasy' is essential to it: 'It is not first an entity, which only later steps outside itself; its essence is to extemporize in the unity of the ecstases' (BT, 329). Heidegger also uses *entrücken, Entrückung*: 'to carry away, transport, enrapture; transport, carrying away, being carried away, rapture'. *Entrückung* is the Germanic equivalent of the Greek *ekstasis*, meaning 'shaking, rocking', and then 'moving', 'away [ent-]', and also a heightened emotional state. (Stefan George's poem, *Entrückung*, may have recommended the word to Heidegger.) Often *Entrückung* and *Ekstase* are used synonymously: The term *Augenblick*, the 'moment of vision', 'must be understood in the active sense as ecstasis. It means the resolute rapture [Entrückung] with which Dasein is carried away to whatever possibilities and circumstances of possible concern to it come to meet it in the situation [. . .]' (BT, 338). But elsewhere they differ: 'Ecstases are not simply raptures that carry one away somewhere or other [Entrückungen zu . . .]. The ecstasis has a "Whither" to which one gets carried away [ein 'Wohin' der Entrückung]' (BT, 365).

Temporality with its ecstases is intimately involved with Dasein's activity. The 'Whither' or 'horizonal schema' of the past (*Gewesenheit*) is the sheer fact that one is THROWN and has to make something of oneself; that of the future is 'For-the sake-of itself', Dasein's aim or purpose; that of the present is the 'in-order-to', the means by which it realizes its aim (BT, 365). Whether Dasein is authentically resolute, or the contrary, in conducting its affairs determines whether its temporality is authentic or inauthentic, original or derivative. The nadir of inauthentic temporality is 'time as a sequence of nows' or instants, time conceived apart from Dasein's activities and purposes, time as conceived by Aristotle and Hegel (BT, 420ff.).

Time and space are not co-ordinate. Time is prior to space. Dasein's timeliness makes possible its spatiality (BT, 367ff; K, 200/136f.). Time as timeliness is responsible for Dasein's individuality: 'Time is always the time in which "it is time", in which there is "still time", "no more time". As long as we do not see that time is only timely, that it satisfies its essence when it individualizes each man to himself, timeliness as the essence of time remains hidden from us' (XXXI, 129). Dasein understands being in virtue of its timeliness and in terms of time. Hence the analysis of Dasein and its timeliness is a prelude to a philosophical understanding of being in terms of time intended to occupy the missing Division III of Part I of BT (BT, 17): 'Being is, both in the common understanding of being and in the explicit philosophical problem of being, understood in the light of time'. If asked what a table is, we say that it is a utensil. If asked what a triangle is we say that it is a shape. If asked what being is, we find that there is no more general concept available. Traditionally, philosophers have understood being in terms of thinking and the LOGOS (LXV, 183). This led to the conception of being as presence, since e.g. what I think is present to me (LXV, 200). Not just thinking, but other contrasts with being – becoming, appearance, ought – lead back to the idea of being as constant presence (IM, 154/169). But this idea can only be understood in the light of time (IM, 157/171f; XXXI, 109). We need to explore time to understand not only how Dasein opens up a world of beings, including itself, but also what philosophers have said, or left unsaid, about being.

In the period of BT, 'soul, spirit, subject *of man* are the site of time' (XXXI, 121). Later, as man recedes from the centre of Heidegger's thought, time becomes more important than timeliness. Time is unifed with space in TIME-SPACE.

time-space   Time and space are not for Heidegger co-ordinate. Dasein's spatiality is based on or 'embraced' by temporality, though this 'connection is different from the priority of time over space' that he found in Kant (BT, 367; cf. K, 199f./136): 'Only on the basis of ecstatic-horizonal temporality is it possible for Dasein to break into space' (BT, 369). Nevertheless, after BT Heidegger envisages a unified 'time-space'. This is not the 'space-time [Raum-Zeit]' of physics, but *Zeit-Raum*, a word coined from *Zeitraum*, the usual word for a 'period/ interval/space of time'. He also coins *Zeit-Spiel-Raum*, lit. 'time-play-space', on the basis of *Zeitraum* and *Spielraum*, lit. 'play-room/space', hence 'elbowroom, leeway'.

Time and space are very different. Space can be conceived as the order and framework of things PRESENT-AT-HAND together, and is thus represented in a making-present (*Gegenwärtigung*), in a definite temporality. The representation of space is a temporalization (*Zeitigung*). But that does not entitle us to reduce space to time. Each has its own essence, and not only in the different number of their 'dimensions' as ordinarily conceived. But if we explore the essence of each, we see that their essence is an original, unified time-space: 'But already thinking time through in this way [in its 'ecstatics'] brings it, in its relatedness to the There of Da-sein,

222

into essential relation with Da-sein's spatiality and hence with space' (LXV, 189; cf. 377; OWL, 213f./106) We can proceed in two opposite directions: 1. from time-space to time and space, 2. from time and space to time-space (LXV, 386, 388). The idea of a *Zeitraum* is of limited use, since it is purely temporal: it represents time in the traditional way as 'spacious, roomy [geräumig]', and is not identical with the non-'spatial' openness of time with its 'transports [Entrückungen]' as described in BT. Time-space is not the space-time of physics, nor is it the idea that every historical occurrence occurs somewhere and at some time, and is thus spatio-temporally determined. These are superficial couplings of space and time, whereas time-space is their unitary origin, their 'common root' (LXV, 377f.).

Heidegger gives no very explicit account of the second way, from space and time to time-space. 'The opposite way [from space and time to time-space] is most reliably taken if we bring to light in an interpretation the spatiality and temporality of the thing, the tool, the work, the MACHI-NATION and all beings as sheltering [Bergung] of truth' (LXV, 388). He notices that words primarily associated with time – *Zeitigung*, 'ripening, letting arise', *Anwesenheit*, 'presence' – are not exclusively temporal, and words associated with space – *Spielraum*, *Räumung*, 'clearing, making space, room', *Einräumung*, 'arranging, conceding, making room' – are not exclusively spatial. The elbowroom I need to do things is both spatial and temporal. The room that I make for an appointment is temporal rather than spatial. The pipe I smoke on the walk measures the time I take as well as the distance I cover. Considered properly time and space reveal a deep affinity: 'Time as time that carries away and opens up is thus at the same time intrinsically room-making [einräumend], it creates "space". Space is not of the same essence as time, but belongs to time, as time belongs to space. But space too must here be conceived originally as clearing space [Räumung] [. . .]' (LXV, 192). The constancy and PRES-ENCE, in terms of which the Greeks saw being, are 'temporo-spatial [zeiträumlich]': constancy [Beständigkeit] is 'endurance of the rapture [Entrückung] into past and future [i.e. temporal], [. . .] Presence [Anwesenheit] is the present [Gegenwart] in the sense of collectedness of endurance according to its retreat from the raptures [i.e. temporal], [. . .] Constancy is, conceived spatially, the filling out and filling up of the space that is itself not specifically conceived, thus a making-room [Einräumung, i.e. not here emptying space to let something in, but making space *space* by filling it up]. Presence is making-room in the sense of giving-space [Raumgebens] for the beings put back into it and so stable [ständige]. The unity, the intercrossing, of Zeitigung and Einräumung [. . .] constitute the essence of beingness' (LXV, 192; cf. 260f.). The early Greeks, that is, did not extricate time and space; they conceived them together as opening up a stable realm for their activities: the There, the 'time-space-elbowroom, in which beings can come into being [seiend] again, i.e. become the custodian of beyng' (LXV, 243). Time-space is not a neutral medium that exists independently of human affairs: 'The Between [between men and gods] [...] first grounds the time-space for the relation [between men and gods] [...]' (LXV, 312). The big bang in which being ex-plodes into EARTH, world, men and gods, also creates the time-space in which the fragments are related to each other (LXV, 311, 485). Thus time-space is not simply a field for routine activity. It is 'the site of the moment [Augenblicksstätte] for the grounding of the truth of beyng' (LXV, 323; cf.384). The moment is the moment of decision, the momentous decision in which a new civilization is established. This was the first beginning. But philosophy must, in the transition to the other beginning, perform 'the projection, i.e. the grounding opening up, of the time-space-elbowroom of the truth of beyng' (LXV, 5).

We must also proceed from time-space in the direction of space *and* time. Space and time have now become empty, quantitative or mathematical frameworks for computing the positions of things and events (LXV, 136, 372f., 375f., 387). Time (Aristotle, Kant) and space (Kant) are held to be in the ego or subject, when in their original unity in time-space they grounded 'the There, through which selfhood and everything true in beings is first grounded' (LXV, 376). In saying how this happened, we must distinguish four aspects of the problem (LXV, 386f.): 1. The emergence of a distinction in Greek thought between *topos*, 'place', and *chronos*, 'time', within the undifferentiated interpretation of beings as *phusis*, approximately 'nature', and on the basis of *alētheia*, 'unhiddenness' (cf. LXV, 374). 2. The unfolding of space and time from 'time-space as the underground [Abgrund] of the ground within the thinking of the other beginning'. 3. The 'empowerment of time-space as essencing [Wesung] of truth within the future grounding of Dasein through the sheltering of the truth of the event in the beings that are thereby transformed'. 4. The solution of problems, such as the 'actuality' and the 'infinity' of space and time, and their relationship to 'things', which cannot be answered, unless time and space are conceived in terms of time-space.

A unified time-space is implicit in BT. The later account is more historical: the unitary view is attributed to the early Greeks and is involved in their 'first beginning', rather than in later routine activities. It needs to be revived for the 'other beginning' to come: computational space and time may do for our daily routine, but not for momentous, history-founding beginnings.

tradition BT uses two words for 'tradition'. *Tradition* comes from the Latin *traditio*, 'surrender, handing down', from *tradere*, 'to hand over, etc.' *Überlieferung* comes from *überliefern*, 'to hand down', and from *liefern*, 'to supply, deliver', which looks Germanic, but stems from the Latin *liber(are)*, 'free; to set free', via the French *livrer*. The converse of *überliefern* is *überkommen*, 'to come over/down'; what is handed down has come down to us. Thus Heidegger has three words for 'traditional': *traditionell, überliefert* ('handed down'), and *überkommen* ('having come down'). He also uses *Erbe* and *Erbschaft*, 'heritage' (BT, 383ff.).

Überlieferung differs little in meaning from *Tradition*, but it is more flexible and lends itself to punning associations with other *über*-verbs, though *Tradition* can participate in this, since Heidegger knew that *tradere* was originally *transdare*, to give [dare] over [trans]: 'When tradition [Tradition] has become master, it firstly and mostly makes what it "hands over" ['übergibt'] so inaccessible that it rather covers it up. It delivers up [überantwortet] what has come down to us [das Überkommene] to self-evidence and bars our access to the original "sources" from which the categories and concepts handed down to us [überlieferte] were drawn in a partly genuine manner' (BT, 21). Often, though not invariably, *Überlieferung* is more favourable than *Tradition*. *Tradition* is more likely to obscure and is associated with *Destruktion* (BT, 22); *Überlieferung* is more likely to provide possibilities and is associated with REPETITION (BT, 385). *Das Überlieferte*, 'what is handed down to us', is one of the meanings of *geschichtlich*, 'historical' (BT, 379). Heidegger tends to reserve *traditionell* for philosophical doctrines he dislikes: the traditional concept of time' (BT, 18, etc.), the 'traditional concept of truth' (BT, 214ff.), and 'traditional ontology' (BT, 22, etc.). But the good and bad sides of tradition cannot easily be disentangled: 'Liberation from tradition [Tradition] is appropriating, ever anew, the resources we recognize in it' (XXIX, 511).

transcendence *Transzendenz, transzendent,* and *transzendieren* ('to transcend') come from the Latin *transcendere*, 'to climb (scendere) over, across (trans)'. Heidegger also uses its Germanic counterparts, *übersteigen*, 'to climb over, surmount, exceed, transcend', and *überschreiten*, 'to cross, exceed'.

The Latin *transcendens* and *transcendentalis* were applied by medieval philosophers to being, truth, unity and goodness, for the reason that these terms apply to entities in all the categories, the highest genera, and do not themselves demarcate a genus (BT, 3, 14, 38). To suppose that there is a genus of beings, as there is a genus of animals, would be like supposing that there is a genus of healthy things, where 'healthy things' includes what possesses health (e.g. healthy men), what manifests health (e.g. healthy cheeks) and what produces health (e.g. healthy food). Like 'being', 'healthy' is too equivocal to demarcate a genus, but it does not qualify as a *transcendens*, since, unlike being, it does not apply to everything. (Aquinas held that everything is true or knowable, unitary and good, to the extent that it is created by God.) Heidegger agrees that being is heterogeneous: we cannot give a single, unequivocal account of what it is to be.

Kant distinguished between the 'transcendent', a concept or entity that surpasses our experience (e.g. God), and the 'transcendental', what pertains to the possibility of our experiential knowledge, both in the sense of our 'pre-ontological understanding of being', and in the sense of the explicit, conceptual interpretation of it such as Kant provides (XXVII, 207f.). But Kant does not explain what 'transcendence' is. Heidegger does: It is DASEIN's transcendence or surmounting (*Überstieg*) of beings to beings as a whole or WORLD (XXVI, 203ff; XXVII, 207ff; ER, 34ff.).

Heidegger thus distinguishes four senses of 'transcendence' (LXV, 216f):

1. ONTICAL transcendence: another being has transcended beings; in Christianity, God the creator has transcended created beings. This is a confused notion, especially when God is said to be 'transcendence' or even 'being'.
2. The ONTOLOGICAL transcendence that lies in the *koinon* ('common' in Greek) as such, beingness as the general (genera – categories – 'above' and 'before' beings, apriori). This is the approach of Aristotle and his medieval followers, who examined being(ness) as a *transcendens*, but left unclear the DIFFERENCE between being and beings.
3. 'Fundamental-ontological' transcendence (cf. BT, 350–67, esp. 364–6): this reverts to the original sense of 'transcendence', surmounting (*Übersteigung*), and is conceived as a distinctive feature of Dasein (or rather, 'Da-sein'), indicating that it 'always already stands in the Open of beings'. Dasein's transcendence involves UNDERSTANDING of being (cf. XXVI, 280; XXVII, 217). So ontological transcendence (2 above), with its understanding of being, combines with fundamental-ontological transcendence. But understanding is

now conceived, in a non-medieval fashion, as 'THROWN PROJECT'. So transcendence means: 'standing in the truth of beyng', which does not imply explicit knowledge of beyng. This transcendence secures man's freedom.

4. 'Epistemological' or cartesian transcendence: a subject surmounts the barrier or gulf between itself and its object, between its inner space and the external world. No such transcendence occurs, Heidegger insists. In virtue of transcendence in sense 3, Dasein is open to intraworldly objects, separated from them by no gulf or barrier; it transcends to world, not to objects (cf. XXVI, 211f.).

Having defended 3, his BT use of 'transcendence', against confusion with possible rivals, Heidegger nevertheless criticizes his earlier use of the term. For two main reasons: (1) To speak of Dasein's transcendence might be taken to imply that *before* it transcends Dasein starts out, as a world-less 'I' or subject, from a range of world-less, untranscended beings (LXV, 217f., 322). (2) If Dasein's transcendence is made more explicit and conceptual, as a philosophical or metaphysical transition from beings in particular to beings as a whole and from there to beyng, it is an attempt to reach beyng by way of beings, to read its nature off from the nature of beings. But this cannot be done. Beyng is unique and incomparable, not to be reached by gradual steps from beings, but only by a direct leap into it. 'So we must not surmount beings (transcendence), but leap over this distinction [between being and beings] and thus transcendence, and question primordially from the viewpoint of beyng and truth' (LXV, 250f.)

Heidegger rejects the *word* 'transcendence' rather than the concept. he still speaks of man casting himself loose (*Sichloswerfen, Loswurf*) from beings (LXV, 454) and of 'relief' (*Entsetzung*, which also has the flavour of *Entsetzen*, 'terror') by beyng from the beings that besiege or beleaguer us (LXV, 481f). Nothing in the BT account of transcendence suggested that it was a gradual or inferential process from as yet untranscending Dasein and untranscended beings; beings are only regarded *as* beings in virtue of being transcended, and Dasein would not be Dasein (or a subject) if it did not transcend (XXVI, 211). Heidegger does not consistently regard philosophy as involving an unmediated leap into the new paradigm: in explaining TIME-SPACE to his contemporaries, he agrees to start from space and time as traditionally conceived (LXV, 372). But he feels that beyng will be contaminated if we approach it by way of beings. (Duns Scotus similarly felt that to argue, like Aquinas, for God's existence from the existence and motion of finite entities diminishes our concept of God.)

Heidegger rejects *ontical* transcendence, but is constantly intrigued by it. He wonders how the idea of being as the 'all-powerful' arose from our fundamental-ontological transcendence and our understanding of being (XXVI, 211n.3). He suggests that setting up the 'PEOPLE' as the purpose of history is only apparently unChristian; it sets up a transcendent idea or value in the same way as Christianity postulates a transcendent God. The various competing 'world-views', whether Christian or anti-Christian, have this in common: they presuppose man as a being whose nature is already fixed and known as the basis for their transcendence. By contrast, fundamental ontological transcendence, and the 'leap' involved in Heidegger's later philosophy, determine what man is to be (LXV, 24f.).

Later, Heidegger coins the term 'rescendence' (*Reszendenz*) for the reversal of transcendence that occurs in man-centred technology (QB, 56).

truth as agreement   The German for 'true, truth' are *wahr, Wahrheit*. Like its relative, the Latin *verus*, and the English 'true', *wahr* originally meant 'trustworthy, reliable, dependable'. Hence it now has two main senses: 1. 'true, real, genuine', in contrast to 'apparent, sham, fake, flawed, etc.': true love, gold, friends, etc; 2. 'true, factually correct, etc.': a true account, statement, story, theory, etc. (cf. ET, 175ff./115ff.). The *Shorter Oxford English Dictionary* defines 'truth' in sense 2 as: 'conformity with facts, agreement with reality', and thus embodies the correspondence theory of truth. This theory is usually supposed to have been originated by Aristotle, but Heidegger disputes this interpretation (XXI, 128ff; BT, 214ff.). He locates its origins in Plato and its full flowering in the scholastic definition of truth as *adaequatio rei/rerum et intellectus*, 'conformity of thing(s) and intellect' (Albertus Magnus, *Summa Theologiae*, 1, 25, 2; Aquinas, *de Veritate*, 1, 1).

Heidegger attacks this view of truth, or at least it primacy, from several directions:

1.   What agrees with reality must be seen as a PRESENT-AT-HAND entity, an assertion or proposition distinct from the reality it is about. When I talk I do not normally focus on the words I utter or hear. My mind is on what the talk is about. I often know what was said without noticing or remembering the precise words uttered. Silence can convey a message more effectively than words. There are no eternal

propositions distinct from what is said on particular occasions, nor do words have fixed meanings or connotations, distinct from the entities they apply to and our beliefs about these entities (XXIV, 280f.). Here there is nothing, distinct from what the talk is about, to agree with it. What is said in the talk is, more or less, just what the talk is about. (Heidegger sometimes comes close to an identity theory of truth, though he would – rightly – reject this label.) The agreement theory of truth, like the representative theory of perception, highlights a mental, logical or purely sensory entity intervening between ourselves and reality – a meaning, proposition, sensation, representation – when even if there are such entities we do not usually notice or attend to them (BT, 214ff; LXV, 327ff.). I can nevertheless focus on a sentence or assertion, such as 'The cat is on the mat', and ask whether it agrees with reality. Then I treat the words as present-at-hand. If the sentence does agree with reality, then it is true, or rather 'correct [richtig]'.

2. A chunk of reality with which a given sentence or assertion agrees must also be seen as present-at-hand, severed from its connections with other entities within the world. When I assert 'The hammer is heavy', the workshop, nails, wood, and carpenter – everything that makes a hammer the tool that it is – are out of sight. Out of sight too are any reasons why one should care whether the assertion is true or not. If truth is valuable, and 'truth' amounts to 'true propositions', why not memorize the London telephone directory? Nevertheless, we can, and do, 'de-world [entweltlichen]' chunks of reality, and then the assertions that bear the equally present-at-hand relation of agreement with them are 'correct'.

3. Assertions, or utterances in general, whether or not we interpret their truth as agreement with reality, are not the primary locus of truth: 'Proposition [Satz] is not the place of truth; truth is the place of the proposition' (XXI, 135). Truth is not primarily a property of assertions or judgements; it is what enables us, unlike stones, plants and animals, to make any assertions or judgements at all. Before a proposition can be uttered or understood, the world around us and entities within it must be disclosed in a way that cannot be equated with a set of discrete beliefs or expressed in a set of discrete propositions. In search of the cat, I enter the room and I am aware of the room as a whole. Then I see the cat on the mat, and say 'It's on the mat'. My seeing the cat on the mat amounts to a judgement or belief, and its being on the mat can be expressed in a proposition. But my overall awareness of the room cannot. I am aware of the room as a whole,

229

not in all its details. Some details I am hazily aware of, I could not put them into words. I am aware of the general shape of the room, of the 'involvement totality', of the interconnections between areas and items, not of discrete chunks. Explicit assertion presupposes all this. The same goes for a scientific theory. It is not primarily a set of propositions. It is primarily a new way of looking at things, or certain things, and this, in turn, presupposes the familiar old way of looking at things that enables scientists to eat their meals and find their way to, and around, the laboratory. Truth does not require us to memorize the telephone directory. It involves having something to say, wanting to phone people, knowing how to do it and where to find their number, in short, knowing our way around in the space in which particular truths matter to us and can be unearthed. Correspondence theorists of truth typically deal not with the truths that we discover in the context in which we discover them, but with the sort of truth that gets 'passed along in "further retelling"' (BT, 155), 'The cat is on the mat' and 'Snow is white'.

Heidegger's account of truth as 'unhiddenness' has several consequences. Truth is no longer something we can or need to be *certain* of in a cartesian or Husserlian manner. What we can be certain of is propositions, I am certain *that* such and such is so. The quest for truth is not a quest for certainty about what we already know or believe, but a quest for the disclosure of hitherto unknown realms. 'Truth' no longer contrasts with '*falsity*'. Propositions can be true or false, correct or incorrect. But false propositions presuppose an open realm of truth as much as true ones. Falsity, e.g. mistaking a bush for a roe in the twilight, has three conditions (XXI, 187f.): 1. The world is already disclosed to me and I can discover things within it: *something* is approaching. 2. I do not just gape at things, I interpret them *as* something. 3. I know enough about my surroundings to know that a roe is something that can appear in a forest; I would not mistake a bush for the Shah of Iran or the cube root of 69. Error is a localized distortion within a realm of truth. If 'truth' contrasts with anything, it is with 'untruth [Unwahrheit]'.

A correspondence theorist might object that Heidegger conflates (i) conditions of asserting a proposition, (ii) conditions of the truth of a proposition, and (iii) conditions of a proposition's being known, and wonder whether he is entitled to identify (i) and/or (iii) with truth proper. But in view of the complex and variegated usage of the words 'true, truth' and the skill with which he dissects the ambiguities and confusions of Lotze's *Geltungslogik,* 'logic of validity' (XXI, 62ff; BT, 155f.), it is not obvious that Heidegger would lose the argument.

turn 'The verbs *wenden, kehren, drehen* translate "turn" in its literal sense of bringing into another position, to which is sometimes added that of facing another direction. [...] *Kehren* generally means "to make face the opposite direction", but sometimes denotes merely a partial turn. [...] It can also imply speed, force, or hostility. It also has the meaning of "to sweep [with a broom]" (DGS, 359f.). *Kehrt!* is 'About turn!' It forms several compounds: *umkehren,* 'to turn back, retrace one's steps', and *sich umkehren,* 'to turn round on the spot'; *einkehren,* 'to stop off[e.g. at an inn]'; *bekehren,* 'to convert [e.g. to a faith]'; *verkehren,* 'to turn into, invert, reverse, etc'. *Kehre,* a (sharp) 'turn, bend', was formed from the verb. This too forms compounds: *Abkehr,* 'turning away'; *Ankehr,* 'turning towards'; *Wiederkehr,* 'return', as in Nietzsche's 'eternal return/recurrence of the same' (NI, 25/ni, 17, etc.). Heidegger often uses *wenden* and *Wende,* '(to) turn, change' as near-synonyms of *kehre(n).*

In BT Dasein's existence involves various 'turns'. A mood 'discloses not by looking at thrownness but as turning towards and turning away' (BT, 135). In falling 'Dasein turns away from itself' (BT, 185). Authentic historicality 'understands history as the "return" of the possible, and knows that the possibility returns only if existence is open for it, fatefully and in a moment of vision, in resolute repetition' (BT, 391f.). Man errs: he is 'turned towards [zugewendet] the immediate accessibility of beings' and 'turned away [weggewendet] from the mystery'. This 'turning towards and away [Zu- und Weg-wenden] follows a peculiar turn [Wende] in the to and fro in Dasein' (ET, 193f./132f.).

Later, Heidegger uses *Kehre,* and sometimes *wenden*-words, for a sharp turn in our thought about being, truth, etc., and also for a turn in being itself. Plato's story of the cave initiated a 'turning [Wendung] in the determination of the essence of truth' (P, 201/251). In the missing third section of the first part of BT, to be entitled 'Time and Being', 'there is a complete reversal [kehrt sich das Ganze um].' The section 'was withheld, since thinking failed in the adequate saying of the turn [Kehre] [...]'. ET 'gives a certain insight into the thinking of the turn from "Being and Time" to "Time and Being". This turn is not an alteration of the standpoint of BT; in the turn the attempted thinking first reaches the location of the dimension from which BT is experienced, experienced in the basic experience of being's oblivion' (LH, 325/231f. Cf. XXVI, 196, 201). 'The turn', *die Kehre,* is often used to denote a sharp turn in

Heidegger's own thinking that is supposed to have occurred between BT and LH. There are certainly large differences, of style and content, between BT and his post-war writings. Heidegger often speaks of BT as a work of 'transition [Übergang]' from metaphysics to the 'basic question' about being (LXV, 84, 223, 229, 234, etc.). But the change is gradual, not a *Kehre*. And what Heidegger himself calls a *Kehre* in his thought involves, as he says, no change of 'standpoint'. He says the same of Kant: 'Kant's philosophy is full of "U-turns" ['Umkippungen']. But one cannot understand these by the fatal method of common sense, which takes anything of this sort as a change of standpoint, i.e. compares two different results. A genuine U-turn, sustained by objective necessity, is on the contrary always the sign of inner continuity and can thus be comprehended only by grasping the nexus of problems which embraces the change as a whole. Thus we must, in every case of two opposing assertions, take the trouble to understand the problem. Then we see that there is no question of a change of standpoint' (XXXI, 267f.).

A *Kehre* or U-turn usually involves a reversal of two terms. 'Being and time' turns into 'time and being'. The answer to the question about the essence of truth is: 'the essence of truth is the truth of essence' (ET, 198/137). The reversal changes the meanings of 'essence' and 'truth'. *Wesen* first means 'ESSENCE' in the traditional sense, but in its second occurrence is understood 'verbally' and approximates to 'beyng as the prevailing distinction of being and beings'. *Wahrheit* begins as 'truth' in the sense of 'correctness' but becomes 'truth' in the sense of 'lighting sheltering'. Thus the 'answer to the question about the essence of truth is the saying of a turn [die Sage einer Kehre] within the history of beyng. Since lighting sheltering belongs to beyng, it appears primordially in the light of concealing withdrawal' (ET, 198f.137f. Cf. LXV, 288, 415). The turn in beyng's history is not only the original lighting of being by the Greeks, but a paradox internal to being itself that makes this possible: 'In the turn [Kehre] of the event the essencing of truth is also the truth of essencing. And this very tergiversation [Widerwendigkeit] belongs to beyng as such' (LXV, 258; cf. 189). Heidegger tries to explain the EVENT in terms of the turns, reversals, circles and reciprocal relations, that he initially found in our thought: 'The event has its innermost happening and its widest range in the turn. The turn essencing in the event is the hidden ground of all other subordinate turns, cycles and circles – obscure in origin, unquestioned, readily taken as "ultimate" in their own right (cf. e.g. the turn in the structure of the guiding-question, the circle in under-standing). What is this original turn in the event? Only the assault [Anfall] of beyng as eventualizing of the There brings Da-*sein* to itself and so to the realization (sheltering) of insistently grounded truth in beings, which find their site in the lighted concealing of the There. [. . .] If *through* the event Da-sein as open centre of truth-grounding selfhood is first thrown to *itself* and becomes the self, Dasein must in turn [wiederum] belong to the event as hidden possibility of the grounding essencing of beyng' (LXV, 407). This recalls another 'turn [Kehre]; the thrower of the PROJECT is a thrown thrower, but first in and through the throw' (LXV, 259), and also the 'reciprocal [kehrig]' grounding of Da-sein and event, the 'reciprocal [kehrigen]' relation of Dasein and being (LXV, 261, 316). The reciprocal interplay of the turn and its initiation of a new epoch in the history of being is close to Hegel's dialectic, but Heidegger insistently disclaims any affinity to 'dialectic' (ET, 198/137).

Later, Heidegger speaks of a *Kehre* of the oblivion of being, consummated by technology, into the 'safeguarding of the essence of being' or the 'truth of being' (T, 40/41; 42/43f.). It will be unmediated and 'abrupt [jah]'. It cannot be predicted by extrapolation from the present, since that sort of 'hunt for the future' operates within the attitude of 'technological-calculative representing' and 'what is merely technological can never get into the essence of technology' (T, 45f./48), the 'turning [kehrige] danger' that needs to come to light for the turn to happen (T, 40/41).

U

understanding and being 'To understand', *verstehen*, comes from *stehen*, 'to stand' in the intransitive sense, though it was originally used transitively too. After BT, Heidegger sometimes writes *ver-stehen*, stressing that to understand something is to stand, or to make it stand, in the open (LXV, 259, 286, 303). Unlike *verstehen*, *Verstand*, '(the faculty of) understanding, intellect, common sense', is, for Heidegger, a term of disapproval. It is often qualified as the 'common' or 'vulgar' *Verstand*, and is, as in Hegel, associated with cut-and-dried distinctions and traditional logic (XXIX, 264, 427ff; WM, 107/97). By contrast, *Verständnis*, '(the act or state of) understanding', is favoured. *Verständlich*, 'intelligible', and *Verständlichkeit*, 'intelligibility' are also favourable in BT, though later everyday 'intelligibility' is disparaged (LXV, 328, 435). *Verständigkeit*, 'common sense', and *verständig*, 'commonsensical', are unfavourable: Heidegger agreed with Hegel, that the world of philosophy is, in relation to common sense, an 'inverted world' (XXIV, 19). However, *Verständigung*, from *(sich) verständigen*, 'coming, to come, to an understanding', is viewed with approval, especially in the fundamental sense of agreement in identifying the common subject of our discourse: 'Since misunderstanding [Missverständnis] and lack of understanding [Unverständnis] are only variants of coming to an understanding [Verständigung], the approach to each other of the same men in their sameness and selfhood must everywhere first be grounded by coming to an understanding' (NI, 578f./niii, 91).

Verstehen implies a 'clear grasp of a thing as a whole, but no necessary reference to any preceding process of thought' (DGS, 291). Hence *verstehen* is distinct from *begreifen*, 'to comprehend (conceptually)': one can understand being without comprehending it, but one cannot comprehend it without understanding it (XXIV, 18, 117; XXXI, 43). Understanding is 'not a particular type of knowing, distinct from other types such as explaining [Erklären] and comprehending, nor is it knowing at all in the sense of grasping something thematically. [...] All explaining as an understanding disclosure of what we do not understand is

234

rooted in Dasein's primary understanding' (BT, 336). Dilthey and Weber held that while the natural sciences 'explain', the social sciences and humanities 'understand'. This does not go deep enough: explanation and understanding in this sense both presuppose a more fundamental understanding that enables us to find our way around in the world (LVI, 207). *Verstehen* has a practical flavour: *verstehen* followed by an infinitive means 'to understand, know, how to do something', and *sich verstehen auf* means 'to understand, know, how to do, deal with, something'. 'Sometimes in ontical talk we use the phrase "understanding something" in the sense of "being able to manage [vorstehen] something", "being up to it", "being competent in something". What we are competent in in understanding as an existential is nothing definite [kein Was, lit. 'no What'], but being as existing' (BT, 143). DASEIN understands the world and its own possibilities: 'Understanding projects the being of Dasein on its For-the-sake-of just as originally as on significance as the worldliness of its particular world. [. . .] As long as it is, Dasein understands itself – it always has and always will – in terms of possibilities' (BT, 145).

As a being whose own being is at issue, Dasein essentially has *Seinsverständnis*, an 'understanding of being' (BT, 12), not only of its own being. As Heidegger said in a later note: 'But being here not only as being of man (existence). [. . .] Being-in-the-world includes *in itself* the relation of existence to being as a whole: understanding of being' (BT, 440 *ad* 12). Before it understands anything else Dasein understands being. This involves an understanding of the verb 'to be' and its basic uses: 'am', 'is', 'was', etc. It also involves a tacit understanding – despite our tendency to blur such distinctions (XXXI, 44, 124, 236) – of the basic modes of being, of the difference between a person, equipment and PRESENT-AT-HAND things. Such understanding is not primarily linguistic: 'It is not first in talking and speaking about beings, in explicit "is"-saying, that we operate in the understanding of the "is"; we already do so in all our silent conduct towards beings. [. . .] also in our conduct towards ourselves, who are beings, and towards others of our kind, with whom we are, we understand such a thing as being. [. . .] Yes, we can only use "is" and "was" and suchlike words, and express what we mean in them, because we already understand being of beings before any expression and any sentences' (XXXI, 41).

Understanding, like interpretation, involves the 'As-structure'. To understand what a hammer is is to take it or see it as a hammer, as a tool for hammering. Similarly understanding the being of beings involves taking them *as* beings. We cannot be aware of beings as such if we do not transcend beings to the WORLD or to beings as a whole, since I cannot be aware of an entity as such unless I am aware of alternative POSSI-BILITIES, and these depend on a wider whole (XXIX, 528ff.). Nor can I properly exist unless by transcending beings I can choose to conduct myself to this being or to that. Thus understanding of being is not just a set of categories accumulated like a coin-collection; it develops together with the formation of the world, with transcendence (XXVII, 314; LXV, 217).

In BT being depends on our understanding it: 'Beings *are*, independently of experience, acquaintance and grasping, by which they are disclosed, discovered and determined. But being "is" only in the understanding [im Verstehen] of the beings whose being involves such a thing as understanding of being [Seinsverständnis]. Being can therefore be uncomprehended, but it is always to some extent understood' (BT, 183). Later, Heidegger rejects the 'crudest of misinterpretations', that 'through the understanding of being beyng (meaning by this "beings" to boot) becomes "dependent" on the subject and it all amounts to an "idealism", [. . .]' (LXV, 259). It stems from taking 'understanding as a sort of ascertaining cognition of the inner "experiences [Erlebnisse] of a "subject" and the understander correspondingly as an I-subject', whereas understanding is a 'projection [. . .] an opening up, hurling oneself out to, and planting oneself in, the open space in which the understander first comes to himself as a self' (LXV, 259).' "Beyng" is not a product [Gemächte] of the subject; Da-sein overcomes all subjectivity and springs from the essencing [Wesung] of beyng' (LXV, 303). However, understanding of being has in BT a 'transitionally ambiguous character', corresponding to BT's 'characterization of man ("human Dasein", the Dasein *in* man)'. On the one hand, it is 'as it were metaphysically retrospective, [. . .] the ground, albeit ungrounded, of the transcendental and in general of the Re-Presenting [Vor-Stellens] of beingness (right back to the [Greek] *idea*)'. On the other, it is '(since understanding is conceived as pro-ject [Ent-wurf] and also as thrown) the indication of the grounding of the essence of truth (manifestness; lighting of the There; Da-sein)'. 'But understanding of being is everywhere the opposite [. . .]' of making beyng dependent on human opinion [Meinen]. When we are dealing with the pulverization of the subject, how on earth can being still be made "subjective"?' (LXV, 455f.)

Neither in BT nor later is being subject-dependent or 'subjective'. BT implies that being is dependent on humans or Dasein. Later, there "is" beyng in the absence of Da-sein (which 'springs from the essencing of beyng') and human understanding, but beyng is then absent, it 'remains away'.

unhiddenness, disclosure and lighting Truth is for Heidegger 'unhiddenness [Unverborgenheit]' or 'unconcealment [Entborgenheit]'. All unhiddenness depends on man and unhiddenness is essential to him: 'Man is not transferred as Da-sein into an open realm as a pair of shoes is placed before the door of a room; as Da-sein man *is* the wandering abandonment into the open, whose openness and lighting is the world' (XLIX, 43). But not everything is unhidden in the same way; he uses several words for different types of unhiddenness (XXVII, 203ff.). *Unverborgen(heit)* comes from *verbergen*, 'to hide, conceal', especially things about one's person or one's inner life. *Verbergen* comes from *bergen*, 'to bring to safety', and retains the flavour of protecting something. It also applies to things hidden naturally, e.g. the sun by clouds. *Unverborgenheit* is a generic term: beings of any type, and being itself, may be *unverborgen*, or conversely undergo *Verbergung*, 'concealing', or *Verborgenheit*, 'concealment, hiddenness'. If what is *unverborgen* is being, then Heidegger speaks of its *Enthülltheit*, 'uncoveredness, unveiledness', from *enthüllen*, 'to remove the covering, reveal what is hidden', and *hüllen*, 'to cover'. The uncoveredness of being is 'ontological' truth, or if it is informal and nonconceptual, 'pre-ontological' truth. If beings are *unverborgen*, then this is their *Offenbarkeit*, 'manifestness', from *offenbar*, 'manifest, revealed', which is in normal usage applied to fairly lofty things. This is 'ontical' truth. But not all beings are manifest in the same way. The manifestness of the PRESENT-AT- and READY-TO-HAND is *Entdecktheit*, 'discoveredness, uncoveredness', from *entdecken*, 'to discover, uncover' what is hidden, and *decken*, which, together compounds such as *verdecken*, means 'to cover' in various ways. The manifestness of DASEIN, by contrast, is *Erschlossenheit*, 'disclosedness', from *erschliessen*, 'to open up, explore [e.g. a continent]', and *schliessen*, 'to close, shut, etc.'. The world – not a being, but intimately connected with Dasein – is also *erschlossen*: 'the Entdecktheit of intraworldly beings is *grounded* in the Erschlossenheit of the world. But Erschlossenheit is the basic mode of Dasein, according to which it *is* its There' (BT, 220). Heidegger does not always use these terms in exactly these ways. In XX, *Entdecktheit* is generic, equivalent to the later *Unverborgenheit*; Dasein is there *entdeckt*, though the world is *erschlossen*, as in BT (XX, 348ff.). In XXIV *Enthüllen* is generic (XXIV, 307). But the importance of unhiddenness, and the idea that items of different types are unhidden in different ways or senses, is constant: 'Just because truth is essentially unconcealment [Entborgenheit[of beings, the particular mode of unconcealment (truth) is governed and determined by the mode of the being, i.e. by its being' (XXXI, 93).

Dasein is always unhidden, as long as it is Dasein, and so are, even if only pre-ontologically, being and the world. Beings within the world can be hidden or unhidden, though usually some of them are unhidden. Heidegger uses various terms for the unhiddenness of the world, besides *Erschlossenheit*. He speaks of Dasein's *Weltoffenheit*, 'openness to the world' (BT, 137), and later *Offenheit, das Offene*, 'openness, the open', are often used for the world, or segment of the world, that Dasein 'opens up [eröffnet]' (LXV, 304). Similar to the open is 'the There' (*das Da*). Dasein is like an unextinguishable candle or light bulb, one entity among others that nevertheless illuminates itself, other entities, and a lighted area that is not itself an entity but constantly accompanies Dasein: Dasein '*is* in the way of being its There. It is "illuminated" ['erleuchtet'], meaning: lightened [gelichtet] in itself *as* being-in-the-world, not by another entity but in *being* itself the lightening [Lichtung]' (BT, 133). To deal with man in terms of his psychology and physiology is like concentrating on the candle while ignoring the light it sheds – the very light that enables us to see the candle: 'we are not here [in our account of feeling, etc.] concerned with psychology, not even with a psychology underpinned by physiology and biology, but with the basic modes on which human Dasein is based, with the manner in which man withstands the "There", the openness and hiddenness [Verborgenheit] of beings in which he stands' (NI, 55/ni, 45).

Lichtung and *lichten* stem from *Licht*, 'light', but have since lost this link and mean, in standard usage, a 'clearing, glade' in a forest and 'to clear' an area. Heidegger restores their association with light, so that they mean 'light(en)ing; to light(en)'. His use of the terms is influenced by Plato's story of prisoners in a cave who, at first aware only of shadows cast by a fire in the cave, climb out of the cave and eventually see the sun, the source of all truth and being (*Republic*, 514a1ff.). He considered this story in several lecture courses (XXII, 102ff., 250ff; XXIV, 402ff., 465ff; XXXIV, 21ff.). Sometimes he regards it as an early version of his own thought. Often he describes his own procedure in similar terms, as striving towards the light that illuminates his path: 'the problem stands in the clarity [Helle] of the natural everyday understanding of being, but the light itself is not lightened [. . .] But the *source of this clarity*, its *light*, is *time*' (XXXI, 93, 109. Cf. QB, 92, 98ff.). That he later charges Plato with the decline of truth as unhiddenness into truth as agreement (P, 203ff./251ff.) does not diminish the influence on him of Plato's imagery.

In BT Dasein is the source of truth. Dasein is what is primarily true: 'What is primarily "true" – that is, uncovering [entdeckend] – is Dasein. Truth in the secondary sense means not to-be-uncovering [. . .] but to be uncovered' (BT, 220). Later, truth is not primarily the truth of man or

Dasein, but the truth of being. (If man is a light bulb, being is electricity.) Truth is the 'lighting concealing [lichtende Verbergung] of being as such' (LXV, 61). When BT spoke of the 'sense [Sinn]' of being, it meant, he now says, the 'truth of being' (LXV, 43). This phrase is obscure: 'The question about the truth "of" beyng reveals itself as the question about the beyng "of" truth. (The genitive here is sui generis and can never be captured by the current "grammatical" genitives.)' (LXV, 428). Being is lightened and concealed. Being lightens and conceals, both itself and entities. All lighting and concealing is ultimately the work of being itself, even man is the vehicle, or the *Wahrer*, 'preserver', of its revelation (LXV, 16). It conceals as well as lightens, since it never reveals everything at once – there always remain hidden things and aspects: men could no more live if they knew everything than if they knew nothing. Even when being abandons beings, this too is a 'lighting of being': being is conspicuous by its absence (NII, 28/niii, 181). The essence of truth is historical: 'The history of truth, of lighting up and transformation and grounding of truth's essence, has only rare and widely separated moments. For long periods this essence seems solidified (cf. the long history of truth as correctness: [. . .]), since only the truths determined by it are sought and cultivated. [. . .] Do we stand at the end of such a long period of hardening of the essence of truth and then on the brink of a new moment in its clandestine history?' (LXV, 342). 'Truth is the great despiser of all "truths", for truths immediately forget truth, which assuredly kindles into complexity the simplicity of the unique as the ever essential' (LXV, 331). A civilization is constituted by a certain revelation of being, the truth of being, which also involves a certain conception of truth. Heidegger is more concerned with our large-scale ways of viewing things and with changes in them than in particular truths.

V

values and validity (*Der*) *Wert* is 'value'; *wert* means 'worth [e.g. something, nothing], useful'; *werten* is 'to rate, assess, value'. *Gelten* was once 'to pay [e.g. taxes, tribute], to do [e.g. penance], to consecrate, dedicate', but is now 'to be valid, in force, effective [of tickets, laws, currency, etc.]'. The present participle *geltend* means 'valid, etc.', as does the adjective *gültig*. *Geltung* too once meant 'payment of what one owes' in a religious or social context, but is now 'validity'. *Wert* and *Geltung* were given philosophical prominence by Lotze, who argued that as scientific propositions and theories are based on and validated by 'facts', so our practical convictions are based on and validated by 'values'. Brentano, Scheler, Hartmann, and such neo-Kantians as Windelband and Rickert developed the idea of an ethic of values, in opposition to Kant's ethic of duty. Not all values are ethical: the basic values are 'the true, the good and the beautiful' (XXI, 83). 'Value-philosophy' embraces our theoretical as well as our practical and aesthetic interests, since truth itself is a value (XVII, 125; XX, 42; XXI, 82). A value implies an 'ought', a *Sollen*: if generosity is a value then we ought to be generous. But a value does not automatically generate an unconditional obligation to promote it, since different values often conflict. If they are to guide our actions, values need to be ranked. Hartmann distinguished an 'empirical' hierarchy of values, the values acknowledged by a given individual, group or society and the order in which they place them, from the 'ideal' hierarchy, the order that values intrinsically have apart from what particular people think about them. Nietzsche's *Umwertung aller Werte*, 'revaluation of all values', concerns 'empirical' rather than 'ideal' values: the old values – objectivity, sympathy, truth, etc. – are devalued, have lost our allegiance; the old values are unmasked and shown to be disguises of will to power; they are replaced by new, non-moral values – health, beauty, etc.

Physical and psychological things and events 'are' or 'exist', but values, laws, truths, and ideas *gelten*, 'are valid', independently of what anyone does or thinks about them. More exactly, Lotze distinguished four forms

240

of 'actuality', *Wirklichkeit*: the being, *Sein*, of things; the happening, *Geschehen*, of events; the subsistence, *Bestehen*, of relations; the validity, *Geltung/Gelten*, of propositions (XXI, 69, 73). Truth, as a value, is 'valid', *gilt*. A particular truth is valid, both because it is an ideal, not a physical or psychological entity, and because it embodies truth: *Gelten* refers both to the being of a true (or a false) proposition and to its being true (XXI, 74). The 'magic word Geltung is', Heidegger concludes, 'a tangle of confusions, helplessness and dogmatism' (XXI, 79). It has at least three senses: 1. The 'being' of an 'ideal' entity such as a sense or a proposition, in contrast to the psychological act of judging or its physical embodiment in sounds, writing, etc. 2. The proposition's 'validity of' its intended object, its objectivity or truth; *Geltung* in this sense is equivalent to *objective Gültigkeit*. 3. Its 'validity for' all rational judgers, its *Verbindlichkeit*, 'binding-ness, obligatoriness', or its *Allgemeingültigkeit*, 'universal validity' (BT, 156, Cf. XXI, 80ff.).

Heidegger rejected the concept of *Geltung* for several reasons besides its undoubted confusion. The idea of a realm of *Geltung* in contrast to being, or of a realm of 'ideal' being in contrast to 'real' being (XXI, 50), needs to be investigated in view of our general concept of being, and probably needs to be rejected. The ideal entity looks like an intermediary between ourselves and real entities that is not to be found in our phenomenological reflection on our judgings (XX, 42); it has a special appeal to those who believe that the 'subject does not "really" "get out" to the object' (BT, 156. Cf. XXI, 81). The 'logic of Geltung' presupposes that the primary vehicles of truth are propositions, neglecting ALETHEIA, truth as unhiddenness (XVII, 200; XXI, 78f. Cf. BT, 156 on 'sense', *Sinn*).

In the BT period Heidegger objects to the notion of *Wert* for three main reasons:

1. Value-philosophy regards truth as a 'value' alongside other values. This makes sense only if truth is confined to propositions, primarily theoretical propositions. If truth is unhiddenness, our overall being-in-the-world, we cannot choose to pursue truth or to sacrifice it to other values. Unless we are 'in the truth' we cannot choose anything at all (BT, 227f.).

2. The neo-Kantians and Hartmann agreed with Descartes that the primary entities, and the entities with which we are primarily acquainted, are natural things, describable in such value-neutral terms as 'extension'. Values are superimposed on these things so that they become 'value-laden things', such as tools and works of art (BT, 63f. Cf. XX, 247ff; OWA, 20ff./146ff.). Heidegger objects: we are not first

241

aware of a tool as a mere thing, on which we then impose a value; a tool is quite different from a natural thing, not a thing with some additional properties; a world does not arise from the piecemeal assignment of value to each intraworldly entity, since we can only encounter entities if we are already in-the-world, but from the overall 'significance' of their 'totality of involvements' (BT, 68, 99f., 150).

3. Heidegger is averse to evaluation and especially to 'value ethics'. The word 'falling [Verfallen]' implies 'no negative evaluation [Bewertung]' (BT, 175. Cf. 222); the analysis of it and of such phenomena as 'chatter' is not a 'moralising critique of everyday Dasein' (BT, 167). BT's account of Dasein is not purely 'theoretical'; it is also 'practical' or rather it operates at a deeper level than the usual distinction between theory and practice. Hence it does not need to be supplemented by a practical philosophy or an ethic (BT, 316). BT is concerned with the ONTOLOGICAL and the EXISTENTIAL, not with the ontical and the existentiell. Thus it considers how Dasein necessarily is, and what it can be, its possibilities. Whether Dasein should be resolute or not, let alone what it should do when it is resolute, are ontical and existentiell matters, about which *Fundamentalontologie* has nothing to say. Heidegger defends a version of Kant's formalism against a 'material value ethic': 'A material table of values, however rich its articulation and range, remains a pure phantom, with no obligating lawfulness, unless pure willing as the authentic reality in all ethical action really wills itself. [...] The morality of action consists not in my actualizing a so-called value, but in the fact that I actually will, i.e. decide, will in decisiveness, i.e. take responsibility on myself and in accepting responsibility become existent' (XXXI, 279f.). An ethic of everyday decency is implicit in average everydayness. At crucial moments Dasein wills decisively, beyond, perhaps against, the requirements of everyday decency. Neither everyday ethics nor philosophy can tell us whether or when to will decisively, or what to will: 'To will what? Now everyone who really wills knows this, for everyone who *really wills wills nothing else than the ought of his being-there* [*das Sollen seines Da-seins*]' (XXXI, 289).

Later, Heidegger associates 'values' with the 'reckoning' of technology and machination (NII, 28/niii, 182, Cf. AWP, 94/142: 'No one dies for mere values'). Nietzsche regarded even being as a value (NII, 35/niv, 6). But the rot started with Plato, whose 'Idea of the Good', once associated with *das Umwillen*, Dasein's 'for the sake of' itself (XXVI, 237), is now the ancestor of 'values' (NII, 222ff./niv, 165ff; LXV, 210, 480).

W

words *Wort* is 'word', but often 'words, (a) sayng'. It has two plurals: *Wörter* are detached words, *Worte* are words in a context (e.g. Anax, 297/14). Heidegger's view of words, as of language, goes through three phases:

1. Words are intrinsically meaningless: 'In words as such there is no connection, no order; they are simply conglomerates, which stand next to each other as something senseless and meaningless with no discernible relationship' (DS, 291); 'words and word-complexes as such indicate nothing' (DS, 299). Words are given a meaning by their use in sentences to express judgements.
2. Words grow out of prelinguistic significance: 'Intelligibility's totality of meaning *comes to words*. Words accrue to meanings [Bedeutungen]. But word-things [Wörterdinge] are not supplied with meanings' (BT, 161). Though 'language can be split up into present-at-hand word-things' (BT, 161), there are no pre-existing meaningless 'word-things', as DS implied: an unknown language is heard as '*incomprehensible* words' (BT, 164), seen not as 'chaos' but as 'a visible inscription that we cannot read' (NI, 563/niii, 77f.). Grammar is as important, and for Heidegger's purposes as defective, as words: 'it is one thing to give a narrative report about an *entity*, it is another to grasp beings in their *being*. For the latter task we lack not only most of the words, but above all the "grammar"' (BT, 39). Nevertheless, words are of intrinsic importance, apart from their use in assertions to express judgements. This is suggested by his insistence that Greek words, such as *zōon logon echon*, cannot be translated without loss into Latin, *animal rationale* (BT, 165), and also by his tendency to link words from the same stem: *fragen*, 'to ask', *anfragen*, 'to ask, inquire (of someone)', *befragen*, 'to question, interrogate (someone about something)', *erfragen*, 'to ask about, ascertain (something)' (BT, 5); *hören*, 'to hear', *hörig*, 'enslaved, in thrall', *zugehörig*, 'belonging' (BT, 163). A word, or word-family, is

more important than a clear-cut concept. A word such as *katēgoria*, 'address, accusation, category', or *alētheia*, 'unhiddenness, truth', is a 'primordial word [Urwort]', whose 'original content has got lost and needs to be restored to it' (XXVII, 79. Cf. NII, 74/niv, 37f.). But Heidegger not only links words, he also distinguishes between words: 'question' and 'problem' (XVII, 73ff.), 'hoping [Hoffen]' and 'hope [Hoffnung]' (BT, 345), and so on. Ambiguities reveal rather than obfuscate. 'The Dasein in man *forms* [*bildet*] the world' means: (a) it produces it, (b) it pictures it, (c) it constitutes, circumscribes it. 'If we speak of world-forming in this threefold sense, is that playing [Spiel] with language? Certainly – more exactly it is playing along with the play of language. This play of language is not playful; it springs from a lawfulness that precedes all "logic" and makes deeper demands of us than does following the rules of definition-formation. [. . .] we must dare to play this game, to [. . .] escape the spell of everyday talk and its concepts' (XXIX, 414. Cf. QB, 105). This baffles the 'vulgar intellect', which takes the question about the essence of the world in the same way as a question about today's prices on the stock exchange.

3. As Heidegger's thought becomes more historical, he notes that certain 'basic' words – 'art', 'beauty', 'truth', 'being', 'knowledge', 'history', 'freedom', *Bildung* ('education, culture'), 'nature' – have obscure or 'concealed' meanings, denote things essential to DASEIN, but, within limits, vary in meaning. *Bildung* as used by Goethe and Hegel differs in meaning from *Bildung* as used in the 1890s, since the 'world embodied in the saying is different' (NI, 169f./ni, 144). The meanings even of non-basic words, such as 'house', vary with the things they apply to; the houses of 1890 differed from those of 1820. But our fundamental view of the world, indeed our world, depends on the meaning of a basic word – of all basic words, since a change in any one affects all the others. 'Basic words [Die Grundworte] are historical' (NI, 169/ni, 144). Not only do their meanings change over history; Dasein has to decide what it will mean by them and its decision determines the course of history. (Later, Heidegger gives a different list of *Grundworte*: form, dominance, representation, power, will, value, security: QB, 67.)

Heidegger is interested not only in relatively recent, small-scale historical changes, but also in the 'first beginning' of western history and in being itself. These three interests converge. 'Being' is the most basic of words: 'every word as word is a word "of" being ['des' Seins], and not only when the talk is "about" and "of" ['vom'] being, but a word "of" being in the sense that being expresses itself in every word and in that way conceals its essence' (NII, 252/niv, 193). But the 'truth of beyng' cannot be said in our increasingly worn out ordinary language. All language is language of beings. We cannot invent a new language for beyng. 'All saying must let the ability to hear arise too.' So we must use 'the finest natural language as language of beyng. This transformation of language penetrates realms still closed to us, since we do not know the truth of beyng. So we tell of the "renunciation of pursuit", of the "lighting of concealing", of "e-vent" ('Er-eignis'], of "Da-sein", not winkling truths out of words, but opening up the truth of beyng in such transformed saying' (LXV, 78. Cf. 3). Heidegger uses etymology to revive worn out words and retrieve the original words of the first beginning. He prefers Greek, German and Sanskrit, 'philosophical' languages, 'not permeated by philosophical terminology but philosophizing as language and language-forming' (XXXI, 50. Cf. NII, 73/niv, 37; LI, 16; XXVII, 309). He values their tendency to combine words to form new words and to use old words for philosophical purposes, rather than borrow them from other languages, and thus to preserve their ancient roots. We learn things from words that are not evident to or consciously intended by the speaker: 'language is no work of man: Language speaks' (PT, 72/25).

Heidegger is intrigued by the closing stanza of George's 'The Word': 'So I renounced and sadly see: / Where word breaks off no thing may be' (OWL, 163ff./60ff., 220ff./140ff.). We can understand something in a way even if we have as yet no word for it (XXXI, 52). But 'the word conditions [be-dingt, lit. 'be-things'] the thing into a thing' (OWL, 232/151). Words are more crucial than assertions, words that 'gather' or 'assemble' things. Words fit together, but not in ordinary grammatical ways: 'The freeing of language from grammar into a more original essence-structure is reserved for thinking and poetic creating' (LH, 312/218). Thus he prefers *Sagen*, 'saying', to *Aussagen*, 'asserting, lit. saying out': 'The saying of primordial thinking stands outside the distinction between concept and cipher' (LXV, 281). Naming is crucial. He connects the *Name*, and the Greek *onoma*, 'name', with *gnōsis*, 'knowledge': 'The name makes known. [. . .] Naming is a saying, i.e. showing, that opens up for us how, and as what, something is to be experienced and retained in its presence [Anwesenheit]' (EHP, 188).

world and beings as a whole   There are three possible approaches to the question 'What is world?' (XXIX, 261ff.):

245

1. In ER and elsewhere (e.g. XXVII, 239ff.) Heidegger approaches it by way of a 'history of the concept of world', which involves the philosophical history of not only the German *Welt*, but also of the Greek *kosmos* and the Latin *mundus* in a journey extending from the presocratic Greeks, by way of St Paul, Augustine and Aquinas, down to Kant, and beyond to the degenerate nineteenth-century uses of *Weltanschauung*, 'world-view'. The conclusion of this survey is that there are three notions of world: (a) BEINGs as a whole (*das Seiende im Ganzen*); (b) the community of men; and, most satisfactorily, (c) men in relation to beings as a whole.
2. BT approaches the question by an interpretation of man's or DASEIN's everyday operations in its familiar environing world.
3. XXIX approaches it by a comparison of man, who is 'world-forming' (*weltbildend*), with 'worldless' (*weltlos*) stones and especially 'world-impoverished' (*weltarm*) animals, which are affected by beings, but cannot relate to beings *as* such or to beings as a whole.

Dasein, a properly functioning human being, is, BT argues, essentially in the world, and conversely, a world – in contrast to a collection of entities – essentially has Dasein in it. 'Being-in-the-world' (*In-der-Welt-sein*) is almost equivalent to 'Dasein'. Only Dasein is in the world, and the adjective 'worldly' (*weltlich*), with the abstract noun 'worldliness, worldhood' (*Weltlichkeit*), can be applied only to Dasein, and to features of Dasein, such as the world itself. Non-human entities are said to be 'within the world' (*innerhalb der Welt*, e.g. BT, 13), 'within-the-world' (*innerweltlich*), or 'belonging to the world' (*weltzugehörig*), but never 'worldly' or 'in the world'. But when 'world' occurs in scare-quotes ('*Welt*', "world"), it is usually intended in the non-Heideggerian sense of '(all) things within the world'. In early lectures Heidegger speaks of three co-ordinate subworlds: the *Umwelt* ('environment, the world around us'), the *Mitwelt* ('with-world, the people about one') and the *Selbstwelt* ('self-world, selfdom', a precursor of the later *Dasein*) (LVIII, 31; LXI, 63; LXIII, 102; LIX, 84). But he soon rejects the terms *Mitwelt* and *Selbstwelt* in favour of *Mitsein* (BEING-WITH) and *Dasein*, since 'others [. . .] do not and never have the type of being of the world' (XX, 333). The *Umwelt*, one's immediate surroundings – workplace, neighbourhood, etc. – within the larger *Welt*, survives in BT. *Mitwelt* plays a subdued role, marking the fact that one shares the world with others (e.g. BT, 118: 'The world of Dasein is a with-world'). *Selbstwelt* disappears.

BT involves two divergent views of (being-in-)the-world:

246

1. The world is introduced by way of the familiar *Umwelt*, and being-in-the-world retains the flavour of familiarity, of knowing one's way around in the world (BT, 80). Things are knit together to form a unified world by significance: the tools we use refer to other tools, and together they form a workplace, which in turn refers to the wider world beyond the workplace. The craftsman's hammer refers to his nails, to wood and leather, and the bench on which he works; beyond the workplace are his customers, the cows that supply the leather, the forest that supplies the wood, and so on in indefinitely expanding circles of decreasing familiarity.
2. In certain MOODS, notably anxiety, everyday things lose their significance: 'Everyday familiarity collapses. Dasein has been individualized, but individualized as being-in-the-world. Being-in enters into the existential "mode" of the "not-at-home"' (BT, 189). Dasein is no longer 'at home' in the world, but it has not ceased to be in it; it could not do so without ceasing to be Dasein.

Shortly after BT, Heidegger distances himself from world in sense 1; he does so, characteristically, by complaining that he has been misunderstood: 'The existential analysis of everydayness does not intend to describe how we deal with a knife and fork' (K, 235/160) or to 'show that the essence of man consists in handling a spoon and fork, and travelling by train' (XXIX, 263). The *Umwelt*, so central to BT and so neglected by earlier philosophers, is now regarded as merely a preliminary way of introducing the world as beings as a whole and Dasein's relation to it (ER, 80 n.55). The familiar world in sense 1 need not amount to 'beings as a whole'. (BT refers only once to *das Seiende im Ganzen* (248), in a derogatory sense.) The question whether it includes Alpha Centauri, or where its boundary lies, does not arise. When anxiety deprives things of significance, the world becomes decentred, and includes the remote as well as the nearby – beings (as such) as a whole. This is the world that interests the metaphysician and, for a time at least, Heidegger himself. He quotes Periander of Corinth: *meleta to pan*, 'Take care of the whole' (NI, 475/niii, 5; XV, 263/162).

ER complains that BT's account of world excludes nature (ER, 82f.). In the mid-1930s Heidegger remedies this by contrasting world with the EARTH that grounds it and is in conflict with it (OWA, 35ff./171ff; NI, 170/ni, 145; LXV, 7). World is no longer equivalent to beings as a whole, though world is required for there to be beings as a whole: there might be beings without world, but not beings *as a whole*. Heidegger does not simply revert to world in BT's sense 1. World is now more explicitly historical than BT: 'Worlds ordain themselves [sich fügen] and decline, earths open up and suffer destruction' (LXV, 476). Worlds and earths (roughly, civilizations and their natural locations) come and go. Later still, *Welt* regains its status as a title for beings as a whole, embracing earth, heaven, men and gods (D, 172/180).

The world, and beings as a whole, is not a being, nor simply a collection of beings. Hence Heidegger is loath to say that it *is*, or to apply the verb 'to be' to it. He sometimes says that the world 'whirls' (*waltet*, lit. 'prevails, etc.') and/or 'worlds' (*weltet*) (ER, 102; XXIX, 530. Cf. LVI, 73 where *es weltet*, 'it worlds', is used to convey our experience of equipment in the *Umwelt*, in contrast to a mere 'something', *Etwas.*). As in the case of TIME, SPACE and the NOTHING, Heidegger appropriates, or coins, a verb made to measure for the noun, if a phenomenon cannot be adequately conveyed in standard usage.

world-view and world-picture *Weltanschauung* is formed from *Welt*, 'world', and *Anschauung*, 'view, etc.', and means 'view of, outlook on, the world'. *Weltbild* is a 'picture [Bild] of the world'. They are not interchangeable. A *Weltbild* is usually associated with science or a science ('the mechanistic world-picture', 'the physicist's world-picture', etc.), while a *Weltanschauung* can be prescientific or scientific. A *Weltbild* is usually a theoretical view of the external world, while a *Weltanschauung* is essentially a 'view of life', a view of our position in the world and how we should act (cf. AWP, 86/133f.). Adherents of the same *Weltbild* may hold different world-views, and enter into conflict, employing the weapons supplied by their common *Weltbild* (AWP, 87/134f.). A *Weltbild* is only one constituent of a *Weltanschauung*. 'According to [Dilthey's] characterization we thus have three features in the structure of the Weltanschauung: life-experience, Weltbild, and, arising from the relation of these, an ideal of life' (XXVII, 236).

Heidegger is interested in the *Weltanschauung*, because it is related to 'world', and it contrasts with science and with philosophy. He asks: Does Dasein's being-in-the-world essentially involve a *Weltanschauung*? How is *Weltanschauung* related to Dasein's transcendence? How is it related to philosophy? (ER, 80 n.54. Cf. XXVII, 229ff., 344.). Philosophy and *Weltanschauung* 'are so incomparable that no possible picture is available to illustrate their difference. Any picture would still bring them too close together' (LXV, 39). The 'Weltanschauung narrows and constricts real experience. [. . .] Philosophy opens up experience, and for that reason cannot directly ground history. Weltanschauung is always an end, mostly a long drawn-out and unconscious end. Philosophy is always a beginning and requires its own overcoming' (LXV, 37). A *Weltanschauung* is often arbitrary and peremptory. It may be 'personal', expressing one's own particular life-experience and opinions, or 'total', extinguishing all personal opinions. A total *Weltanschauung* cannot understand itself, for this would put it in question. Hence its initial creativity is soon diverted 'into the gigantomania of machination' (LXV, 40). Philosophy too makes a claim to 'totality', if it is 'knowledge [Wissen] of beings as such as a whole'. But this applies to metaphysics, especially in its Christian guise as German idealism, not to the continually developing and self-surmounting philosophy of the 'other beginning' (LXV, 41. Cf. 435f.).

The modern *Weltbild* involves several constituents: mathematical science; machine technology; the reduction of art to an object of 'experience [Erlebens]'; the conception of human activity as 'culture' and as the realization of 'values', the concern of a 'cultural policy'; a godlessness that co-exists with the 'modernization' of the Christian 'Weltanschauung' and with intense 'religious experience' (AWP, 69f./115f.). Underlying all this, even natural science, is the very idea of a *Weltbild*. At first sight it means a 'picture of the world', where the picture is not co-extensive with the world. But if we read it in the light of such expressions as 'being in the picture', 'putting oneself in the picture', 'getting the picture' – which, like their German equivalents, imply a complete mastery of what the picture is a picture of – we see that 'world-picture essentially means not a picture of the world, but the world conceived as picture. Beings as a whole are now taken in such a way that they are in being first and only insofar as they are presented [gestellt] by man the representer and producer [vorstellend-herstellenden Mensch]. The emergence of the Weltbild involves an essential decision about beings as a whole. The being of beings is sought and found in the representedness of beings' (AWP, 82f./129f.). *Weltbild* is distinctively modern. There is no medieval *Weltbild*: men are assigned their place by God in his created order. There is no Greek *Weltbild*: man is at the beck and call of being. There is no ancient or medieval 'system', an essential requirement for the reduction of the world to a picture (AWP, 93f./ 141ff.). Ancient and medieval man was not a 'subject': 'The world's becoming a picture is one and the same process as man's becoming a subjectum among beings' (AWP, 85/132). Hence humanism arises at the same time as the *Weltbild*, a 'philosophical interpretation of man that explains and assesses beings as a whole in terms of man and with a view to man' (AWP, 86/133).

Since man is 'in the picture', is the central focus of the world as picture, *Weltanschauung*, which concerns man's position in the world, goes together with *Weltbild*: 'As soon as the world becomes a picture, the position of man is conceived as Weltanschauung' (AWP, 86/133f.). *Stellung*, 'position', comes from *stellen*, 'to position, set up, stand' – which also forms *vorstellen*, 'to REPRESENT'. It can mean a military 'position', a physical 'posture' in relation to one's surroundings, or one's 'position, attitude' towards a person, question, etc. Man's present 'position in the midst of beings' not only differs from that of ancient and medieval man: 'Now for the first time is there anything like a position of man at all' (AWP, 84/132). For just as modern man decides about the contents of the world as picture and their arrangement, so he decides what his own position in it is to be; he positions himself, takes up a position, in a way that no previous type of man has done. Our age is 'new' or 'modern' not only because it differs from previous ages, but because 'to be new belongs to the world that has become a picture' (AWP, 85/132). The whole picture and our position in it is within our control, so we can start from scratch and remake everything anew.

There remains, however, an 'invisible shadow that is cast over all things, when man has become the subjectum and the world a picture'. To manage the world as picture we need to think in terms of quantity and measurement, the 'calculable'. 'Each historical age [. . .] has its own particular concept of greatness'; and our concept of it is purely quantitative, the 'gigantic' – not only gigantic monuments, but the traversal of vast distances at immense velocities, etc. The difference between one concept of greatness and another is not, however, a quantitative, but a qualitative difference. Hence the 'gigantic of planning and calculating [Berechnung] [. . .] veers round into a quality of its own' and then it becomes incalculable. (AWP, 88/135. Cf. LXV, 441ff.). Just as the essence of technology is not itself technological, so the essence of calculation and the calculable is not accessible to calculation. We should not retreat into tradition and reject the *Weltbild*, but think it through in an uncalculating way.

Further reading

Ott, Hugo [1993], *Martin Heidegger: A Political Life*, London, Harper Collins – focuses on Heidegger's political involvement.

Petzet, H.-W. [1993], *Encounters and Dialogues with Martin Heidegger, 1929–1979*, Chicago, University of Chicago Press – a genial and sympathetic portrait written by a friend.

Safranski, Rüdiger [1998], *Martin Heidegger: Between Good and Evil*, Cambridge, MA, Harvard University Press – the fullest biography of Heidegger available.

Zimmerman, Michael [1990], *Heidegger's Confrontation with Modernity*, Bloomington, Indiana University Press – describes the intellectual and cultural background to Heidegger's thought.

There are several helpful commentaries on *Being and Time*:

Dreyfus, Hubert [1991], *Being-in-the-World: A Commentary on Heidegger's Being and Time, Division I*, Cambridge, MA, MIT Press – has become a classic.

Schmitt, Richard [1969], *Heidegger on Being Human*, New York, Random House – detects similarities between Heidegger and Wittgenstein.

The lectures from which Dreyfus's book stems have influenced much later work on Heidegger, including:

Guignon, Charles [1983], *Heidegger and the Problem of Knowledge*, Indianapolis, Hackett.

Inwood, Michael [1997], *Heidegger*, Oxford, Oxford University Press – focuses heavily on *Being and Time*, but it also gives an account of Heidegger's thought on art and poetry.

Mulhall, Stephen [1993], *Heidegger and Being and Time*, London, Routledge – gives useful guidance.

Especially valuable are those works that explore the roots of *Being and Time* in Heidegger's earlier lectures. These are well represented in a collection of essays edited by:

Kisiel, Theodore and van Buren, John [1994], *Reading Heidegger from the Start*, Albany, State University of New York Press.

There are several short books dealing with Heidegger's thought as a whole. The best of these is perhaps:

Pöggeler, Otto [1987], *Martin Heidegger's Path of Thinking*, Atlantic Highlands, NJ, Humanities Press.

Others include:

Cooper, David [1996], *Thinkers of Our Time: Heidegger*, London, Claridge.
Olafson, Frederick [1987], *Heidegger and the Philosophy of Mind*, New Haven, Yale University Press – an excellent book on this particular theme.
Steiner, George [1992], *Heidegger*, 2nd edition, London, Fontana.

Two recent collections of articles cover Heidegger's whole intellectual career:

Dreyfus, Hubert and Hall, Harrison, eds [1992], *Heidegger: A Critical Reader*, Oxford, Blackwell
Guignon, Charles, ed. [1993], *The Cambridge Companion to Heidegger*, Cambridge, Cambridge University Press.

Relatively few works deal with Heidegger's relationship to philosophers of the past. Two that deserve special mention are both by John D. Caputo. They are of great value for the exploration of the sources of Heidegger's thought, and especially his vocabulary, in his predecessors.

Caputo, John D. [1978] *The Mystical Element in Heidegger's Thought*, Athens, Ohio, Ohio University Press.
—— [1982], *Heidegger and Aquinas: An Essay on Overcoming Metaphysics*, New York, Fordham University Press.

General index

Buddhism 123
building 169, 216f.

calculation 68. 73f., 92, 100, 117, 137, 140, 155, 158, 193, 216f., 233, 250
call 37ff., 51, 79, 198, 209
Calvinism 67
capitalism 44, 67, 193
captivation 134
CARE 2f., 18, 23f., 33, 35ff., 39, 44, 54, 65, 151f., 166, 180f., 194, 217
Carnap, Rudolf (1891–1970) 22, 144
cartesianism see Descartes
Cassirer, Ernst (1874–1945) 70, 109f., 111
categories 22, 61, 109, 120, 124, 133f., 141, 166, 169, 175, 185, 226, 236
catholic/protestant 82, 113
causality 61, 67f., 75f., 81, 82ff., 92, 133, 150, 181, 193
cave 14, 231, 238 see also Plato
certainty 44f., 127, 138, 160, 166, 203, 204, 230
change 133f., 215
chaos 99f., 120, 143, 185, 187
CHATTER 6, 65f., 112f., 208, 242
children 43, 167f.
choice 18, 62, 95, 96, 117, 166, 213, 236
Chomsky, Noam (1928–) 182
Christ, Christianity 7, 40, 61, 65, 76, 80ff., 100f., 142f., 157f., 166, 187, 203, 211, 226, 228, 249
churches 199
Cicero, Marcus Tullius (106–43 BC) 100
CIRCULARITY 87ff., 232f.
CIRCUMSPECTION 36, 106, 136, 194f., 196
Clauberg, Johannes (1622–1665) 147
clearing 4, 238
Cockaigne 181
cognition see KNOWLEDGE
commonsense 152, 232, 234

community 163, 246
comparison 92
COMPORTMENT 133ff., 167
composure 60 see also releasement
compound words 9, 103
comradeship 45
concealment 13ff., 54, 74, 88, 97, 143, 183, 232f., 245
concept 7, 28, 80ff., 83, 107, 109, 147, 151, 177, 205, 226f., 234, 244f., 246
CONCERN 23, 35ff., 65f., 134, 152, 194
concrete logic 93
condition of possibility 171, 175f., 208, 220
conduct 121, 235f. see also COMPORTMENT
conflict 50f., 146, 159, 248
CONSCIENCE 37ff., 63, 198
consciousness 60, 62, 111, 121, 130, 160f., 161ff., 166, 179f., 214
constancy 99f., 103, 159, 169, 175, 177, 185, 195, 223
contemplation 132, 191, 214
contradiction 120
CONTRIBUTIONS TO PHILOSOPHY (OF THE EVENT) 39ff.
CONVERSATION 170, 175, 191ff. see also dialogue
Copernicus, Nicolas (1473–1543) 67
correctness 10, 13f., 54, 125, 137, 140, 171, 178, 192f., 211, 229f., 239
correspondence theory of truth 185, 215, 228ff. see also AGREEMENT
Couturat, Louis (1868–1914) 22
creation 144, 172, 211, 226, 249
crisis 192f.
culture 163, 201, 244, 249
curiosity 65f., 79

DASEIN, Da-sein 3f., 9f., 13, 16f., 18, 20, 22ff., 29f., 31ff., 33f., 35ff., 38f., 42ff., 44ff., 52, 56f., 57f., 59, 60ff., 63, 65ff., 68, 69f., 72f., 75, 77f., 82,

83f., 87ff., 90f., 93f., 97f., 99, 107,
110, 111, 112f., 118f., 121, 124f.,
126, 128, 131ff., 133f., 138, 143, 145,
147ff., 151f., 154, 157, 161, 164f.,
167, 171f., 175f., 176ff., 179ff., 182,
187f., 191, 194, 198, 198ff., 201,
203f., 204f., 207f., 212ff., 214f., 216,
218ff., 220f., 222, 226f., 231ff., 235f.,
237ff., 242, 245, 246f.
Damascus, road to   189
danger   170, 212, 233
Darwin, Charles (1809–1882)   42
DEATH   33, 44ff., 56, 66, 67f., 69,
77ff., 93, 113f., 146, 151, 187, 199
death of God   81f., 139, 142
death-mask   45, 185
DECISION   20, 53, 61, 66, 113, 137,
141, 143, 165, 170, 173f., 178, 186ff.,
224, 242, 244, 249f.
deconstruction   183
deficient mode   33, 36, 129
definition   53, 244
degeneration   201
Delphi   197
demise   44
derangement   165
Descartes, René (1596–1650)   2, 6, 14,
28, 30, 31, 61, 76, 104f., 112f., 125,
127, 138, 140, 143, 147, 157, 160,
162, 166, 180f., 183, 184ff., 199, 203,
211, 213, 214, 215f., 217, 227, 230,
241
deseverance *see* distance
DESTINY   67ff., 96, 211, 218
DESTRUCTION   88f., 94, 95, 181ff.,
216f., 225
detachment *see* releasement
detective-psychology   197
dialectic   161, 233
dialogue   114, 182f.
DICHTUNG   168ff.
diesel engine   165f., 209
DIFFERENCE, ONTOLOGICAL   27,
46ff., 127, 148, 150, 226, 232

Dilthey, Wilhelm (1834–1911)   28, 29,
62, 87ff., 105f., 118f., 123f., 164, 181,
235, 248
directionality   200
DISCLOSURE, disclosedness   65, 186,
194, 211, 229, 237ff.
discourse *see* TALK
distance   4f., 33, 138f., 197, 199f.
distantiality   212f.
distress. *See* need
Dostoievsky, Fyodor (1821–1881)   141
dots (Heidegger's use of)   xvi
Duns Scotus, Johannes (ca.1265–1308)
227f.
duty   240
DYING   44ff., 242

ears   87
EARTH   18, 34, 39, 40, 50f., 71, 94,
132, 136f., 143, 146, 148, 159, 169,
188, 193, 209,210f., 215, 224, 247f.
Eckhart, Johannes (Meister) (ca.1260–
ca.1327)   83, 117f.
ecstasis, ecstatic   44, 60f., 83, 91, 99,
155, 177, 202, 221, 222
Eddington, Sir Arthur Stanley
(1882–1944)   59
egalitarianism   156ff.
ego   37, 61, 103ff., 121ff., 160f., 162f.,
185, 213, 220, 224 *see also* I
Egypt   174
Either-Or   187ff.
elbowroom   14, 75, 144, 166, 169,
198ff., 222ff.
emotion   15ff., 98, 184, 197
empiricism   64
encountering   202
end   44, 71, 193, 248f.
ENFRAMING   69, 100, 209ff.
ENJOINING   204ff.
entities   220f. *see* beings
environment   106 *see also* world
around us

EPISTEMOLOGY 14f., 48, 108f.,
110ff., 119, 126, 138, 148, 227
epoch 69, 96f., 233
epoche 96f., 119, 133, 161, 162ff.
equipment 18, 36, 113, 116f., 128ff.,
180, 191, 196, 199f., 214, 248 *see also*
tools
equipmental totality 129
equiprimordiality 152
Erasmus, Desiderius (ca.1469–1536)
100
errancy 54
ESSENCE 7, 10, 13, 26, 43, 48f., 52ff.,
60, 68, 97, 127f., 134, 137, 140, 143,
150, 162f., 178, 201, 211, 217f., 222,
232f., 239, 250
essencing 4, 70, 73, 137, 232f.
essential words 6f.
essentially contested concept 53
eternal recurrence 48, 127, 140f.,
142, 231
eternity, eternal truths 61, 70, 81,
110, 142, 187, 228f.
ethics 10, 38, 109f., 119, 205, 240ff.
etymology 5, 15, 195, 201f., 245
Europe, european 157f.
EVENT 37, 40, 51, 53, 54ff., 84, 123,
152, 156, 188, 190, 198, 199, 224,
232f., 241, 245
EVER 57f., 154f., 213
EVERYDAYNESS 2, 20, 24, 31, 36, 46,
59f., 73, 97, 105, 151, 160f., 192,
198, 199, 121f., 242, 244, 246f.
evil 181
EXISTENCE 14f., 37, 39, 43, 60ff.,
65f., 83, 88f., 91, 95, 101f., 110, 111,
113, 128, 134, 147, 202, 218ff., 235
exactitude/rigour 63f., 160, 164, 191,
206
existence/essence 26f., 60f., 102, 140
existential/existentiell 14f., 39, 61f.,
80, 88, 141, 147, 177, 188, 194, 242
existentials, existentialia 22, 36, 61f.,
175

expecting 78f., 118, 162
EXPERIENCE 6, 19, 37, 60, 62ff.,
104f., 113, 119, 137,145, 162f., 177,
183, 189, 193, 197, 208, 215, 217,
226, 236, 248f.
experiment 63f., 112, 184, 191ff.
explanation 105f., 158, 185, 193, 201,
234f.
extemporizing 220
EXTERNAL WORLD 99, 162, 179ff.,
227
eye-people 195

FACTICITY 37, 58, 65f., 87, 119, 144,
218ff.
facts, factuality 191f., 207, 218
faith 61, 80, 109, 240
FALLING 13, 17, 23f., 36f., 39, 43,
65ff., 113, 133, 144, 179, 218f., 231,
242
falsity 14, 159, 192, 230
familiarity 208, 246f.
FATE 67ff., 96, 205, 231
FEAR 15ff., 184, 214
feeling 15ff., 19, 63, 131f.
Feick, Hildegard 148
Fichte, Johann Gottlieb (1762–1814)
108, 141
film 117, 125
FINITUDE 51, 64, 68, 69ff., 78, 98,
108f., 120, 127, 145, 152, 219
Fink, Eugen (1905–1975) 46, 149
fissuring 46, 51
flight, fleeing 131f.
for the sake of (which, itself, etc.) 3,
37, 43f. 77, 124, 176, 221, 235, 242
fore-having, -sight, -grasp 88, 107, 151
FORGETFULNESS OF BEING 9,
72ff.
forgetting 9, 48, 72ff., 155f.
form (Platonic) 112, 195
form and matter 95, 133, 214
formal indication 80, 188
formalism (ethical) 242

semblance 159
sending 68f.
sensations 169
SENSE 8, 72, 123ff., 140, 142, 177,
179f., 207, 241 *see also* MEANING
sense-organs 69
senselessness 140, 142
sensibility 108, 110, 182
sentence 20, 123, 229f., 243
separation 186ff.
Seuse, Heinrich (ca.1295–1366) 117
sex 33, 43, 121
Shakespeare, William (1564–1616)
192
sheltering 232f.
shepherd of being 140
showing 87, 159f., 190, 195, 245
SIGHT 3, 15, 36, 111, 194f.
SIGN 123, 195ff.
signalling 195f.
SIGNIFICANCE 17, 38, 43, 106, 113,
118, 123ff., 133, 160f., 176, 181, 208,
242, 243, 247
SILENCE 22, 39, 79, 190, 197f., 208,
228
similarity *see* likeness
Simmel, Georg (1858–1918) 80, 90
sin 38, 80f.
situation 131, 151, 161, 165, 174, 187
sky 51
Smith, Adam (1723–1790) 120
social sciences 99, 136 *see also*
humane sciences
sociology 107, 191, 214
Socrates (ca.470–399 BC) 2, 87
soldiers 45, 217
SOLICITUDE 35ff., 152, 194
solipsism 43, 163, 181
something 144, 214, 248
Sophocles (ca.496–406 BC) 98, 123,
173, 174
soul 43, 83, 104, 108, 113, 121f., 122,
201
soul-snooping 197

sounds 125
SPACE, SPATIALITY 33, 52, 98, 113,
117, 128, 138f., 160, 166f., 198ff.,
209, 221, 222ff., 227, 248
specialization 192f.
speech 106, 114, 190, 235
speed 73f., 112, 250
Spengler, Oswald (1880–1936) 67,
71, 90, 174
Spinoza, Baruch (1632–1677) 145
SPIRIT 7, 43, 96, 104, 110, 113, 117,
121f., 136, 157, 201f.
spring *see* leap
standing 175, 210f., 217, 234
STATE ONE IS IN 65, 130ff., 167
stoicism 117, 145
struggle for survival 42, 120
Suarez, Francisco (1548–1617) 61
SUBJECT 31, 33, 44, 61, 62, 64, 96,
101, 104, 111, 121, 127, 131, 158,
160, 163, 167, 179, 185, 188, 202ff.,
213, 215, 224, 227, 236, 249
subject-object relation 14, 33, 52, 118,
196, 202ff., 227, 241
subjectity 204
subjectivism 204, 236
subjectivity 15, 125, 203f., 217, 220,
236
substance 4, 56, 103ff., 127, 133
sufficient reason 83
suicide 60, 103
sun 199
superman 140, 142f.
symbolic forms 109
synthesis 159, 162f.
SYSTEM 40, 61, 140, 204ff., 249

TALK 20, 65, 86f., 112f., 121, 152,
159, 197f., 207ff., 228f.
TECHNOLOGY 6, 7f., 50f., 63, 68f.,
73f., 76, 79, 82, 84, 92, 94, 98, 100,
112, 117f., 127, 130, 137f., 139, 140,
143f., 148, 157, 164, 166, 172, 186,
192f., 209ff., 228, 233, 242, 249f.

265

Index of foreign words
and expressions

All words are German, unless they are marked as Greek (Gr.), Latin (L.), French (F.), Italian (I.) or Danish. A hyphen enclosed in brackets within a word indicates that Heidegger sometimes introduces a hyphen into a word that usually has no hyphen. Thus *Ab(-)bauen* means that while normal German usage is *Abbauen*, Heidegger sometimes writes *Ab-bauen*. In the case of German nouns I have usually added the definite article – *der* (masculine), *die* (feminine), *das* (neuter) or *die* (plural) – in brackets after the word.

a- (Gr.)   13
abbauen, Ab(-)bauen (das), Abbau
    (der)   88, 183
abfallen, abgefallen   65
Abgrund (der), ab(-)gründig   82ff.,
    224
Abkehr (die)   231
ableben, Ableben (das)   44
ableiten, abgeleitet   151
absagen, Ab(-)sage (die)   84
Abstand (der), Abstandlose (das)
    138f., 199
Abständigkeit (die)   212
abwesend   52
Abwesenheit (die)   173
actualis, actualitas (L.)   60,
    172
actus essendi (L.)   49, 82

adaequatio (rei/rerum et intellectus)
    (L.)   13f., 228
adikia (Gr.)   206
Affekt (der)   15
agere (L.)   60
Ahnung (die)   17
aiōn (Gr.)   167
aisthēsis (Gr.)   18
Akt (der)   124
alētheia, alēthes, alētheuein (Gr.)
    13ff., 97, 125, 137, 224, 244
all   59
Allgemeingültigkeit (die)   241
Alltag (der), alltäglich, Alltäglichkeit
    (die)   59
als, Als (das)   21, 105ff., 124, 149
als-frei(es)   194
Als-struktur (die)   107
amor fati (L.)   68
an   65
An-sich-sein (das)   179
anamnēsis (Gr.)   156
An(-)denken (das)   215
aneignen   54
anēr (Gr.)   121
Anfall (der)   232
anfangen, Anfang (der), anfänglich
    56, 71, 151f.
anfragen   243
angehen   132
Angst (die)   15ff., 134
ängsten, sich ängstenden   45
animal metaphysicum (L.)   128

269

erdichten   168f.

ereignen, sich ereignen, Er(-)eignis (das), Er(-)eignung (die)   34, 40, 51, 53, 54ff., 95, 159, 188, 190, 198, 245

er(-)fahren, Erfahrung (die)   62ff.

Erfahrungswissenschaft (die)   62

erfragen   243

Ergebnis (das)   193

ergo (L.)   104

Ergriffenheit (die)   98

ergründen   82, 150

erinnern, sich erinnern, Erinnerung (die)   155f., 187

erkennen, Erkennen (das), Erkenntnis (die)   34, 103, 111f.

Erkenntnistheorie (die)   110ff., 126

erklären, Erklärung (die)   105, 234

Erklüftung (die)   51

erleben, Erleben (das), Erlebnis (das) 19, 55, 62ff., 115, 119, 236, 249

Erlebnisaufsatz (der)   62

erleuchten   238

eröffnen   125, 238

errechnen   217

Erscheinung (die)   159

erschliessen, erschlossen, Erschliessung (die), Erschlossenheit (die)   125, 186, 194, 237

Erschrecken (das)   17

erschweigen   198

erspringen   150, 157

erwarten   78

erwidern   182

esse (L.)   47, 49, 82

essen   3

essentia (L.)   52, 60, 96, 102

Essenz (die)   52

etwas als etwas sehen lassen   116

etwas, Etwas (das)   144, 248

Exaktheit (die)   191

ex(s)istentia (L.)   52, 60f., 96, 102

existanai (Gr.)   155

Existenz (die), Ex-sistenz (die), Ek-sistenz (die)   4, 42, 60ff., 83, 101f., 111, 202

existenzial/existenziell   61f., 147

Existenzialien (plural: die)   61

Existenzphilosophie (die)   61

existieren   60ff., 80

exsistere (L.)   60

fahren   62

faktisch, faktisches Leben (das), Faktizität (die)   119, 218

fallen, Fall (der)   65

fangen   151

fern, Ferne (die), fernen   4f., 138f., 199f.

finden   131

folgen, Folgenlassen (das)   134

formale Anzeige (die)   80, 188

forschen, Forschung (die)   111

fragen, Frage (die), Fragesatz (der) 20, 216, 243

fragwürdig, Fragwürdigkeit (die)   115

Freiheit zum Tode (die)   45

fressen   3

Frömmigkeit (die)   218

Fug (der), mit Fug und Recht   205f.

fuga (L.)   205

Fuge (die)   40, 205f.

fügen, sich fügen, Fügung (die), Fügungsgesetzen (plural: die)   40, 205f., 248

Fugencharakter (der)   205

füglich   205

fügsam   205

Fundamentalontologie (die)   148, 242

fürchten, sich fürchten   16

Fürsorge (die)   35ff.

Fürsprache (die)   114

Fürstentum (das)   24

ganz, Ganze (das), im Ganzen, das Seiende im Ganzen, Ganzheit (die) 82, 98, 149f., 231, 246f.

Ganzseinkönnen   151

Grundfrage (die) 48
Grundgeschehen (das) 56
grundlegen, Grundlegung (die) 83
grundlos 82
Grundriss (der) 50, 192
Grundsatz (der) 20, 83
Grundstimmung 83, 132f.
Grundwort (das) 76, 244
Grundzüge (plural: die) 50
gültig, Gültigkeit (die) 207

haben 154
halten 134
Haus (das), zu Hause sein, zuhause
   sein, Zuhause (das), das Haushafte
   97f., 195
Hauswesen (das) 53
Heim (das) 97
Heimat (die) 97, 117
Heimatlosigkeit (die) 98
heimisch 97
Heimkehr (die) 98
heimlich 97
Heimweh (das) 98
Helle (die) 238
herausfordern 210f.
Herkunft (die) 151
hermēneus, hermēneia, hermēneuein
   (Gr.) 87
Hermeneutik (die) 87ff.
hermeneutisch 88
herstellen, hergestellt, Hergestelltsein
   (das) 172, 185f., 249
hinhören 86
hinsehen 191, 194
Hinsicht (die) 193
histanai, histasthai (Gr.) 111
historein (Gr.) 90f.
Historie (die) 68f., 88, 90ff., 93, 139,
   155, 158, 193
historisch 90ff., 93, 101, 110
Hoffen (das), Hoffnung (die) 244
holen 181
homo (L.) 121, 212

homoiōsis (Gr.) 14
horan (Gr.) 195
horchen 86
hören 86f., 243
hörig, Hörigkeit (die) 86, 243
horizein, ho horizōn (kuklos) (Gr.)
   98
Horizont (der) 98ff.
horos (Gr.) 98
hüllen 237
humanista (L./I.) 100
huparchein (Gr.) 60
huparxis (Gr.) 60
hupokeimenon (Gr.) 202f.

ich, das Ich 103
Ichding (das), Ichheit (die),
   Ichsubstanz (die) 103
ichhaft 122
idea (Gr.) 14f., 111, 186, 195, 217,
   236
Idee (die) 91, 108
idein (Gr.) 14, 195
immer 57
immer noch 57, 154
immer schon 57, 76, 154
in 5, 98
in- (L.) 13, 27
In-der-Welt-sein (das) 5, 246
In-die-Acht-nehmen (das) 217
In-Sein (das) 5, 28
Indifferenz (die) 24, 83
inmitten, in das Inmitten 219
innerweltlich, innerhalb der Welt 246
innerzeitig, Innerzeitigkeit (die) 220
innestehen, Innestehen (das) 61
inständig, Inständigkeit (die) 46, 61
intendere (L.) 162
interpretieren, Interpretation (die)
   105ff.
intuitus derivativus/originarius (L.)
   69
ist 27, 149, 154

ur- 151
Urdichtung (die) 209
Ur-geschichte (die) 152
Urgrund (der) 83
Urhandlung (die) 176
Ursache (die) 83
Ursprung (der), ursprünglich,
  Ursprünglichkeit (die) 150ff., 157
urteilen, Urteil (das) 20
Urwort (das) 244

ver- 65
verbergen, verborgen, Verbergung
  (die), Verborgenheit (die) 13ff.,
  72, 237ff.
verbindlich, Verbindliche (das),
  Verbindlichkeit (die) 74, 241
verdecken 237
verdinglichen 130
verfallen, Verfallen (das), Verfall (der)
  65ff., 242
verfügen (über), Verfügung (die)
  205f.
Vergegenständlichung (die) 204, 210
vergegenwärtigen, sich
  vergegenwärtigen 173
vergehen, vergangen, Vergangenheit
  (die) 77f., 91, 93, 154ff.
vergessen, Vergessenheit (die) 72ff.,
  155
verhalten, sich verhalten (zu
  Seiendem), Verhalten (das) 3,
  120, 121, 134f.
Verhaltenheit (die) 17, 117
Verhältnis (das) 134f.
verkehren 231
verlassen, Verlassenheit (die) 72ff.,
  116
vernehmen 217
vernichten(d), Vernichtung (die)
  144f., 216
verrechnen 216
Verrückung (die) 165
Versammlung (die) 150

verschweigen, verschwiegen,
  Verschwiegenheit (die) 198
ver(-)setzen, Sichversetzen (das) 33,
  131
Verstand (der) 234
verständig, Verständigkeit (die) 234
verständigen, sich verständigen,
  Verständigung (die) 234
verständlich, Verständlichkeit (die)
  234
Verständnis (das) 234
ver(-)stehen, sich verstehen auf, 80, 87,
  106, 111, 234ff.
verstellen, verstellt, Verstelltheit (die)
  14
verus (L.) 228
Verweigerung (die) 72
verweilen 57f., 132, 137, 215, 217
verweisen, Verweisung (die) 124, 129,
  195
verwesen, Verwesung (die) 52
Verweser (der) 52
verwinden, Verwindung (die) 128
vir (L.) 121
Volk (das) 156ff.
völkisch 156
Volkslied (das) 156
Volkstum (das), volkstümlich 156
vollenden, Vollendung (die) 71
vor(-) 55, 98, 184f.
Vorausgriff (der) 192
vorbei, das Vorbei 154
Vorblick (der) 40
Vorenthalt (der) 72
vorfinden, Sich-vorfinden 55
vorgängig 55
vorgehen, Vorgang (der) 55f., 134
vorgreifen, Vorgriff (der) 34, 63, 107,
  178, 182
Vorhabe (die) 88, 107
vorhanden, Vorhandensein (das),
  Vorhandenheit (die) 55, 91, 117,
  128ff., 136, 172, 175
vorkommen, Vorkommnis (das) 55f.

vorlaufen, Vorlaufen (das)   45f., 77f.,
   187
Vorliegenlassen (das)   150
vorontologisch   147
Vorsicht (die), vorsichtig   107, 194
Vorspiel (das), Vor-Spiel (das)   168
vorstehen   111, 235
vor(-)stellen,sich vorstellen, etwas
   vorstellen, Vorgestelltes (das),
   Vorgestelltheit (die), Vor(-)stellung
   (die), Vor-Stellen (das)   6, 8, 100,
   184ff., 217, 236, 249f.
Vor-struktur (die)   89, 107
vorweg, sich vorweg   3, 55, 77f.
vorwerfen, Vorwurf (der)   218
vor-wesende Wesen (das)   54

wahr, Wahrheit (die)   8, 18, 228, 232
wahren, Wahrer (der)   18, 239
währen   53
Wahrheit des Seins (die)   8
walten, das aufgehend-verweilende
   Walten   4, 53, 137, 248
warten   78, 118, 173
was, das Was, Was-sein (das), kein Was
   26, 128, 149, 212f., 235
weg, Weg (das), Weg (der), Weg(-)sein
   (das)   24f., 133
weg(-)wenden   231
weil   57
Weile (die)   57f.
weilen   57
Weise des Setzens (die)   20
Weise zu sein (die)   27
weit, weiter, Weite (die)   57, 138
Welt (die), 'Welt' (die)   65, 118, 129,
   145, 246ff., 248
Weltanschauung (die)   164, 246,
   248ff.
weltarm, weltbildend, weltlos   246
Weltbild (das)   248ff.
welten, Weltenlassen (das), es weltet
   118, 145, 248
Weltgeist (der)   201

Weltgeschichte (die)   93
weltlich, Weltlichkeit (die)   246
Weltoffenheit (die)   238
Weltsein (das)   181
weltzugehörig   246
wenden, Wende (die), Wendung (die)
   129, 172, 231
wer, das Wer   212f.
werfen, Wurf (der)   176, 218f.
Werk (das), ins Werk setzen   18, 172
wert, Wert (der), werten, Bewertung
   (die)   111, 142, 240, 242
Wesen (das), sein Wesen treiben   8,
   10, 52ff., 138, 201, 232
wesen   4, 10, 34, 52ff., 71, 82
wesenhaft   52
Wesensbestimmung (die)   52
Wesenserhellung (die)   53
Wesensverfassung (die)   52
wesentlich   52
Wesung (die)   53, 224, 236
Widerruf (der)   182
Widerwendigkeit (die)   232
wie einem ist und wird   131
wie, Wie-sein (das)   27, 59, 128, 171
wieder   181
wiederfragen   183
wiederholen, holen . . . wieder,
   Wieder(-)holung (die),
   Wiederholbarkeit (die)   155, 181ff.
Wiederkehr (die)   231
wiederum   232
Wille zum Tode (der)   45
winken, Wink (der)   71, 170, 197
wirken   60, 172, 179
wirklich, Wirklichkeit (die)   60, 172,
   179, 241
wissen, Wissen (das), wissbar   37,
   111f., 143, 201, 209, 249
Wissenschaft (die)   191
wobei, ein Wobei   124
wohin, ein Wohin   221
womit, ein Womit   124
woraufhin, das Woraufhin   125, 177